高等院校应用型规划教材

国际结算、支付与单证——理论与实务（中英双语教程）

International Settlements, Payments and Documents—Theories and Practice

主　编　陈红兵　聂钟鸣

主　审　林赛·威斯特罗姆　罗莎·琼斯

天津大学出版社
TIANJIN UNIVERSITY PRESS

图书在版编目(CIP)数据

国际结算、支付与单证：理论与实务：中英双语教程 = International Settlements, Payments and Documents—Theories and Practice / 陈红兵，聂钟鸣主编. — 天津：天津大学出版社，2017.5（2021.8 重印）
高等院校应用型规划教材
ISBN 978-7-5618-5848-6

Ⅰ. ①国… Ⅱ. ①陈… ②聂… Ⅲ. ①国际结算－双语教学－高等学校－教材－汉、英②国际贸易－支付方式－高等学校－教材－汉、英③国际贸易－业务核算－原始凭证－高等学校－教材－汉、英 Ⅳ. ①F830.73

中国版本图书馆 CIP 数据核字(2017)第 130675 号

出版发行　天津大学出版社
地　　址　天津市卫津路 92 号天津大学内(邮编:300072)
电　　话　发行部:022-27403647
网　　址　publish. tju. edu. cn
印　　刷　天津泰宇印务有限公司
经　　销　全国各地新华书店
开　　本　185mm × 260mm
印　　张　21.75
字　　数　624 千
版　　次　2017 年 5 月第 1 版
印　　次　2021 年 8 月第 2 次
定　　价　49.00 元

编 委 会

主　编　陈红兵　聂钟鸣

副主编　夏　芬　詹才琴

主　审　林赛·威斯特罗姆　罗莎·琼斯

前 言

迈入新世纪的第二个10年，中国国内生产总值位居世界第二，达到568 845.21亿元；进出口总额为41 603.10亿元。伴随着经济全球化，国际竞争越来越激烈，国际贸易越来越频繁，因而国际贸易中的结算与支付也变得愈加重要。

国际结算、支付业务是国际贸易活动的重要组成部分，能否安全收汇与企业的信誉有直接关系，选择合理的支付方式能够控制整个合同与交易的风险，高昂的违约成本会迫使交易双方履行合同。结算实务必须遵循国际惯例，这就要求学习者和从业者要十分熟悉国际结算与国际贸易实务的相关惯例，以指导自身的国际贸易实践活动。本书在附录中收录了几乎所有与之有关的惯例，方便读者理解国际结算与单证业务的操作。另外，由于交易是跨越国界的，专业语言沟通十分重要。本书以双语对照编写结算与支付业务的内容，有助于相关业务人员学习运用专业语言处理这些业务。在本教程的编写中，我们突破传统，将国际结算与单证结合起来，主要是因为信用证支付业务的量越来越大，而且在所有支付中，该支付方式是难度最大的。

此中英对照双语教材具有以下几个特点。

1. 教材第1~7章介绍了国际贸易结算与支付的主要方式、结算工具、单据的理论知识。为了做到通俗易懂又便于实务操作，每一章都用中文详细介绍了理论知识，又用英文做了简练的说明。英文内容并不是机械地针对中文的翻译，也不是对中文内容的单调重复，而是自成体系，并有所侧重。

2. 教材第8~10章详细介绍了国际支付业务实务、国际结算单据实务以及信用证下制单与审单。实务内容板块就是为了解决学生与从业者在学习理论知识后，面对实际业务毫无头绪、不能上手的难题。

3. 教材附录还收录了国际结算的相关规则与惯例。不仅教师可以在教学中选择性地讲授一部分重要内容，而且学生还可以在课后复习时参考，另外，也便于从业者在工作中查阅。

4. 教材适用于国际贸易，国际金融，商务英语专业本、专科以及商科其他相关专业本、专科高年级的必修课或选修课。全书共10章，可分64个学时讲授，一学期或两学期完成。教师也可根据自身需要选择其中的一些章节进行讲授。另外，国际贸易业务人员与银行工作人员也可以在工作中查阅参考本教材。

本书由陈红兵、聂钟鸣担任主编，夏芬、詹才琴担任副主编。全书由陈红兵和聂钟鸣负责统稿，美籍专家 Lindsey J. Widstrom 与 Rosa M. Jones 校审。在编写过程中，我们参阅了大量的相关著作、报刊文章与网络信息，对文章、样本和资料的所有者，在此深表感谢。本书在出版过程中得到了天津大学出版社余婷编辑的大力支持，亦表示深深的谢意。

由于时间、条件、水平的限制，书中或有不足之处，敬请读者批评指正。

编者
2014 年于武昌

目 录

第 1 章

国际结算概述

1.1 国际结算的含义

国际结算(International Settlement)是指通过银行办理两国间的货币收付以清偿国际债权债务的业务活动。一般来说,国家间的债权债务关系的清偿除了国际结算(跨国的货币收付)以外,还有易货、黄金清偿等,但当今世界后两种清偿方式较少用到。国际资金收付的原因之一是由于跨国商品交换产生的货币收付,可归结为货物贸易或有形贸易产生的收付;另一个是由于跨国商品交换引起的货币收付以外的原因,主要是国际资本流动、国际技术转让、侨汇、捐赠、国际旅游、运输服务、保险、银行服务等,可归结为技术及服务贸易(无形贸易)和单方面转移。因此,国际结算可根据引起国际货币收付的原因不同而分为国际贸易结算和国际非贸易结算。由于后者手续简单,前者涵盖了后者,因此本书重点介绍国际贸易结算方式。

国际结算的内容主要包括结算工具、结算方式和结算单证。结算工具即票据,包括汇票、本票和支票;结算方式包括汇款、托收、信用证、银行保函、福费廷、国际保理等,其中前三种是主要的结算方式,也是本书的重点;结算单证即结算业务中使用到的单证,其中信用证下制单要求"单证一致、单单一致",这关乎出口商能否顺利从银行收到货款,本书也将其列为重点。

国际结算内容结构如图 1.1 所示。

- 国际结算
  - 国际贸易结算
    - 结算工具(汇票、本票、支票等)
    - 结算方式(汇款、托收、信用证、国际保理、福费廷等)
    - 结算单证(发票、提单、保险单、装箱单、产地证等)
  - 国际非贸易结算

图 1.1 国际结算内容结构图

1.2 国际结算系统

国际贸易的"物权单据化(Document of Titles)"及"象征性交货(Symbolic Delivery)"使得银行能够更深地介入国际买卖双方的支付活动中,带来了国际结算方式的发展。另外,电信网络系统的发展也促进了国际结算的发展。目前,国际上银行处理国际结算业务的电子数据交换系统主要有 SWIFT 系统和 CHIPS 系统。

SWIFT(Society for Worldwide Interbank Financial Telecommunication)系统是当今最普遍使用的国际银行业务服务电信网络系统。它于1971年创建于比利时首都布鲁塞尔,总部设在布鲁塞尔,在荷兰和美国设有两个运行中心,在各个会员国设有地区处理站,连接数千用户,每天处理数百万笔汇款、银行资金拨付、托收、跟单信用证等银行间国际电信业务。SWIFT系统提供标准化电信格式及代码,其全球计算机通信网络每天24小时连续运行,能够自动存储银行发送的信息,自动对信息进行加押与核押,为会员的国际结算业务提供安全、快捷、标准化和自动化的信息服务。由于该系统安全,运行成本更低,目前世界上绝大部分银行均加入了该系统,成为会员银行,使用该协会提供的通信系统办理国际业务。我国的中国银行最早于1983年加入该协会,成为会员银行。迄今,我国银行国际结算业务均使用该系统。

CHIPS(Clearing House Interbank Payment System)创建于1970年,总部设在纽约,是当今最重要的国际美元支付系统。加入该系统的银行必须向纽约清算所申请成为CHIPS会员。每个会员拥有一个美国银行协会颁发的号码ABA No.(American Bankers Association Number),作为参加CHIPS清算的代码。每个CHIPS会员银行所属客户在该行开立账户,由纽约清算所颁发统一确认号码UID No.(Universal Identification Number),作为收款人的代码。通过CHIPS支付和收款的双方必须都是CHIPS会员银行,才能通过CHIPS直接清算。据不完全统计,CHIPS每天处理10万笔同业间美元收付业务,总金额在9 000亿美元左右,占世界银行同业间美元收付的95%。

CHAPS(Clearing House Automated Payment System)是英国伦敦银行自动收付系统的简称,该系统不仅是英国伦敦同城的清算交换中心,也是世界英镑的清算中心。它创建于1984年,由12家清算银行组成,非清算银行进行英镑的支付需要借助这12家清算银行来完成。

1.3 国际结算的主要规则与惯例

国际结算的规则与惯例是为了避免全世界不同当事人对业务的不同理解而产生分歧与误解,是不断反复总结的结果,具有世界通用性的特点。由于规则与惯例都具有法律上的强制性,因此,作为外贸从业人员,应该掌握这些规则与惯例,从而避免因误解产生错误,更好地保护自己的利益。

与国际结算相关的规则与惯例有:

International Rules for the Interpretation of Trade Terms: INCOTERMS 2000 or 2010;

United Nations Convention on Contracts for the International Sale of Goods;

Uniform Customs for Collection, ICC Publication No. 522;

Uniform Rules and Practice for Documentary Credits, ICC Publication No. 600;

1988 International Standby Practices(ISP98);

International Standard Banking Practice for the Examination of Documents under Documentary Credits Subject to UCP 600。

以上国际结算的主要规则与惯例的原文将呈现在附录中,以供大家学习参考使用。

思考题

1. 国际贸易结算包括哪些内容？
2. 什么是 SWIFT 金融系统？

Chapter 1

Introduction to International Settlement

1.1 International settlement

Settlement of securities is a business process whereby securities or interests in securities are delivered, usually against (in simultaneous exchange for) payment of money, to fulfill contractual obligations, such as those arising under securities trades.

International payments and settlements refer to the money transfer via banks to settle accounts, debts and claims among different countries. They are originated from both international trade transactions such as the sales of tangible goods and intangible service transactions and international non-trade transactions such as international lending and investments.

Structure of international settlement is as follow(figure 1.1).

- International Settlement
  - Settlement of International Trade
    - Instruments: bill of exchange; promissory note; check etc.
    - Methods: remittance; collection; letter of credit; factoring; forfeiting etc.
    - Documents: invoice; bill of lading; insurance policy etc.
  - Settlement of International Non-Trade

Figure 1.1 Structure of international settlement

1.2 International settlement system

The Society for Worldwide Interbank Financial Telecommunication (SWIFT) provides a network that enables financial institutions worldwide to send and receive information about financial transactions in a secure, standardized and reliable environment. SWIFT also sells software and services to financial institutions, many of them are for use on SWIFT network, and ISO 9362. Business Identifier Codes (BICs) are popularly known as "SWIFT codes".

The majority of international interbank messages use SWIFT network. As of September 2010,

SWIFT linked more than 9,000 financial institutions in 209 countries and territories, who were exchanging an average of over 15 million messages per day (compared to an average of 2.4 million daily messages in 1995). SWIFT transports financial messages in a highly secure way but does not hold accounts for its members and does not perform any form of clearing or settlement.

SWIFT does not facilitate funds transfer; rather, it sends payment orders, which must be settled by correspondent accounts that the institutions have with each other. Each financial institution, to exchange banking transactions, must have a banking relationship by either being a bank or affiliating itself with one (or more) so as to enjoy those particular business features.

The SWIFT secure messaging network is run from two redundant data centers, one in the United States and one in the Netherlands. These centers share information in near real-time. In case of a failure in one of the data centers, the other is able to handle the traffic of the complete network.

SWIFT opened a third data center in Switzerland, which started operating in 2009. Since then, data from European SWIFT members will no longer be mirrored to the U.S. data center. The distributed architecture will partition messaging into two messaging zones: European and Trans-Atlantic. European zone messages are stored in the Netherlands and in a part of the Switzerland operating center; Trans-Atlantic zone messages are stored in the United States and in a part of the Switzerland operating center that is segregated from the European zone messages. Countries outside of Europe were by default allocated to the Trans-Atlantic zone but could choose to have their messages stored in the European zone.

Clearing House Interbank Payment System (CHIPS) is the main privately held clearing house for large-value transactions in the United States, settling well over $1 trillion a day in around 250,000 interbank payments. Together with the Fedwire Funds Service (which is operated by the Federal Reserve Banks), CHIPS forms the primary U.S. network for large-value domestic and international USD payments (where it has a market share of around 96%). CHIPS transfers are governed by Article 4A of Uniform Commercial Code.

CHIPS is owned by financial institutions. According to the Federal Financial Institutions Examination Council (FFIEC), an interagency office of the United States government, "any banking organization with a regulated U.S. presence may become an owner and participate in the network". CHIPS participants may be commercial banks, Edge Act corporations or investment companies. Until 1998, to be a CHIPS participant, a financial institution was required to maintain a branch or an agency in New York City. A non-participant wishing to make international payments using CHIPS was required to employ one of the CHIPS participants to act as its correspondent or agent.

Only the largest banks dealing in U.S. dollars participate in CHIPS; about 70% of them are non-U.S. banks. Smaller banks have not found it cost effectively to participate in CHIPS, but many have accounts at CHIPS-participating banks to send and receive payments.

Clearing House Automated Payment System (CHAPS) is a British company established in London in 1984, which offers same-day sterling fund transfers.

A CHAPS transfer is initiated by the sender to move money to the recipient's account (at another banking institution) where the funds need to be available (cleared) the same working day. Unlike a bank giro credit, no pre-printed slip specifying the recipient's details is required. Unlike checks, the funds transfer is performed in real-time removing the issue of float or the potential for payments to be purposefully stopped by the sender, or returned due to insufficient funds, even after they appear to have arrived in the destination account.

CHAPS is used by 19 Direct Participants including the Bank of England and over 4,500 Indirect Participants. In its first year of operation, average daily transactions numbered 7,000 with an annual value of 5 billion pounds sterling. In 2004, twenty years later, average daily transactions numbered 130,000 with an annual value of 300 billion pounds sterling. In 2010 there were 32 million CHAPS transactions totaling over £ 61 trillion, down from £ 73 trillion in 2008.

As well as making transfers originated by banks themselves, CHAPS is frequently used by businesses for high-value payments to suppliers, by mortgage lenders issuing advances, and by solicitors and conveyancers on behalf of individuals buying houses.

1.3 Terms and conditions

International Rules for Interpretation of Trade Terms: INCOTERMS 2000 or 2010;

United Nations Convention for International Sale of Goods;

Uniform Rules for Collection, ICC Publication No. 522;

Uniform Rules and Practice for Documentary Credits, ICC Publication No. 600;

The International Standby Practices—ISP 98 1998;

International Standard Banking Practice for the Examination of Documents under Documentary Credits Subject to UCP 600.

第 2 章

国际结算票据

2.1 票据概述

2.1.1 票据的含义及特点

票据(Instrument)是国际结算的信用工具,具有流通和支付的功能。广义的票据包括商业票据和金融票据:商务活动中使用的凭证都可以称为商业票据,例如发票、提单、保险单、装箱单等;金融票据是国际结算业务中使用到的票据,主要指的是汇票、本票、支票这三种代表货币的支付凭证,也称为狭义的票据。

票据之所以能够代表货币成为一种支付凭证,主要是因为它具有以下特点。

1. 流通性(Negotiability)

票据是可以转让流通的信用工具。票据经过交付或背书可以合法转让,无须通知债务人,而且受让人背书后还可以再转让。票据背书的次数越多,其付款担保性越高。由于票据具有流通作用,大大减少了现金的使用,减少了流通费用,方便了债权的自由转让,丰富了流通手段。

2. 无因性(Non-Causive Nature)

票据当事人之间的权利义务通过票据文义来确定,票据行为以签字交付为标志,无须调查出票、转让原因或原因是否正当。也就是说,票据本身的权利与票据的基础关系是无关联的。所谓票据的基础关系指的是出票人与付款人之间的权利义务关系和出票人与收款人、背书人与被背书人之间的对价关系。票据法认为,票据一经成立,只要是善意取得票据的当事人都可以行使票据的权利,而票据的债务人不可以拒绝履行义务。票据的无因性保障了票据得以广泛流通。

3. 要式性(Requisite in Form)

票据是一种要式凭证,即票据必须符合法定的形式要求。票据上面的记载内容必要项目必须齐全,各个项目都要符合相关规定,否则就不能产生票据的效力。各国法律对票据所必须具备的形式做了具体规定,出票人必须依据规定出票,否则票据不具有法律效力,为无效票据。另外,处理票据的行为也必须符合要求,这样才能保证票据的顺利流通。

4. 设权性 (Right to Be Paid)

票据做成后经过交付,即创设了对于给付一定金额的请求权,并由此派生出一系列的相关权利。这些权利分为两种:付款请求权和追索权。票据的权利人依法可以享有这两种权利,直至票据所代表的债权债务关系完全了结,票据退出流通。

5. 文义性(Subject to Written Clauses)

票据所表示的权利义务关系及其效力以票据票面上文字记载的内容为依据。票据上的文字记载一般能清楚显示相关当事人及其相应的票据责任或权利,债权人不可以票据上未记载的事项向债务人申请主张,债务人也不能用票据上未记载的事项对抗债权人,这样才能保证票据流通和票据权利的实现。

6. 提示性(Presenting for Payment)

票据的债权人在请求票据的债务人履行票据义务时,必须向付款人提示票据,才能请求付给票款。如果权利人不提示票据,付款人就没有付款的义务。为了促使持票人尽早行使票据权利,保护票据的权利人和债务人的合法权利,各国票据法都规定了票据的提示期限,超过期限,付款人的责任即被解除。

7. 返还性(Return Ability)

票据的债务人付清票款,持票人应当将票据返还给付款人。如果付款人是主债务人,此时票据关系消灭,收款人应当在票面注明"收讫"字样并签字;如果付款人是次债务人,其可在付款后持该票据向其前手追索。

2.1.2 票据的作用

由于票据的上述特点,因此票据在商务活动中具有如下作用。

1. 结算作用

国际贸易结算基本以非现金结算方式进行,但办理非现金结算必须使用一定的支付工具。票据就是用来结清国际贸易买卖双方债权债务关系的一种主要的支付工具。

2. 信用作用

票据的信用作用体现在两个方面。一是票据一经签发并交付,即成为取得一定金额款项的权利凭证。本身无价值的票据之所以能被接受并流通,是基于持票人对票据所包含的商业信用具有信心,即相信债务人具有较高的商业信用并能够履行其付款的义务。二是通过票据付款期限的限定,使得支付款项的时间相对更加灵活,资金的给付可获得延迟,相当于付款人获得了授信。

3. 流通作用

票据是可转让的流通的信用工具。票据经过背书可以转让,受让人背书后还可以再转让。而且票据背书次数越多,意味着担保付款的人越多,其流通性当然更强。正是票据的可转让流通,使得债权可以自由转让,起到了抵销债权债务的功能,极大节省了现金的流通,促进了结算的安全与便利。

4. 融资作用

票据不仅可以用来支付,而且通过将远期付款票据向金融机构寻求贴现,实时获得现金来周转,从而实现资金融通。此外,票据的融资作用使得许多大型企业通过发行无交易背景的商业票据来获得资金。这种票据被称为融通票据,其主要的作用是融资的信用工具,而非国际结算支付工具。

2.1.3 票据的当事人

票据的基本当事人有三个:出票人、付款人和收款人。票据在流转过程中又会产生相关的当事人:背书人、被背书人、持票人、承兑人、保证人等。

1. 出票人(Drawer)

出票人是开立票据并交付票据的人。票据一经签发并交付,出票人必须对票据的收款人及正当持票人承担最终付款或承兑的保证责任。在票据没有被付款或承兑前,出票人是票据的主债务人;票据被承兑以后,出票人是次债务人,而承兑人成为主债务人。

2. 付款人(Drawee 或 Payer)

付款人是接受票据,根据出票人的命令支付票款的人。如果付款人不接受出票人的命令付款或承兑,则收款人或持票人无法强迫付款人付款或承兑票据。但是,如果付款人已经对远期票据做了承兑,则付款人是票据的主债务人,必须承担到期付款的责任。无论何种情况下收款人或持票人遭到拒付或拒绝承兑,收款人或持票人都可要求其前手或出票人履行付款或承兑义务及支付相应的费用、利息损失。

3. 收款人(Payee)

收款人是票据记载的获取票款的人,是票据的债权人,享有付款请求权和追索权。即收款人有权提示票据要求获得承兑或者付款,如果遭到拒绝,可向出票人追索票款。票据到期前,收款人也可以背书将票据权利转让,转让后收款人成为背书人。背书人对受让人承担与出票人相同的保证责任。

4. 背书人(Endorser)

背书人是在票据背面签字,表示将票据权利转让他人的收款人或持票人。一切合法持有票据的人均可以成为背书人,受让票据的人成为被背书人。票据可以多次连续背书而转让,对于某个背书人来说,在他之前的背书人都是前手(Prior Parties),在他之后的背书人和持票人都是后手(Subsequent Parties)。

5. 被背书人(Endorsee)

被背书人是接受背书的人,他是票据的债权人。在票据到期前,被背书人作为持票人或收款人可以继续背书转让票据权利;或者作为最后的被背书人,享有要求付款人和前手背书人直至出票人支付票款的权利。

6. 持票人(Holder)

持有票据的人即为持票人,是票据的唯一债权人,享有付款请求权、追索权和票据转让权。根据取得票据的不同情况,持票人可以分为三类。

1)一般持票人

任何持有票据的人,只要取得的票据要项齐备,票据没有过期,就是一般持票人。

2)付对价持票人

一般持票人本人或其前手在取得票据时支付过对价,便是付对价持票人。所谓付对价是指取得票据时支付了一定的代价,代价可以为有价值的商品、服务或货币资金。

3)正当持票人

正当持票人指的是经过转让而获得票据的人,其必须满足以下条件:票据表面完整、合格且没有过期;持票人对票据是否曾被退票不知情;持票人善意地支付对价而获得票据;接受转让时没有发现前手的票据有任何缺陷。

7. 承兑人(Acceptor)

经持票人提示票据,远期票据的付款人在票据正面签字,明确自己到期付款的责任,该付款人即为承兑人。票据承兑后,承兑人成为第一付款人。承兑人必须保证到期付款,不可以出票人不存在、出票人签字为伪造或其他理由拒绝付款。如果远期票据遭到付款人拒绝承兑,其他第三人出于某种原因对该票据承兑,该当事人被称为参加承兑人。参加承兑人也不得寻找借口到期拒绝付款。

8. 保证人(Guarantor)

为保证票据责任的履行,非票据债务人应有关票据责任人的要求,以自己的名义在票据上签字担保即成为票据保证人。保证人与被保证人责任相同。如果票据到期遭到拒付,保证人将受到持票人追索;保证人履行付款义务后,可以向被保证人及其前手追偿。

2.1.4 票据行为

1. 出票(Issuance)

出票包含两个动作:一是写成要项完备的票据并签字,二是将票据交给收款人。

2. 背书(Endorsement)

背书包含两个动作:一是收款人或持票人在票据背面签字或记载有关事项,二是将票据交给被背书人或受让人。持票人应该以连续不断的背书证明其权利正当,因此银行处理票据时应该检查票据背书是否连续不间断。票据背书的连续性判断见表2.1。

表2.1 票据背书的连续性判断

	第一	第二	第三	第四	第五	…
被背书人	Pay to B	Pay to C	Pay to D	Pay to E	Pay to F	…
背书人	For A	For B	For C	For D	For E	…

根据背书时记载的内容不同,背书可以分为以下几种。

1)空白背书

背书人仅在票据背面记载自己的名字,不记载被背书人(受让人)的名字,即为空白背书。空白背书后,票据交付即可转让权利。信用证业务中,作为物权凭证的海运提单一般都要求做空白背书,这样物权可以转让给开证银行,降低开证银行在相符交单下对受益人(出口商)付款后,进口商拒绝付款赎单的损失。类似地,信用证业务中的海运保险单也要求做空白背书,这样保险的权利可以转让给进口商,如果货物运输中途遇险导致货损,进口商可以在目的港持保险单向保险公司索赔。

空白背书的形式如下：

For A Co. , London

Signature

2）记名背书

记名背书又称特别背书、完全背书，它是记载了背书人和被背书人双方名字的背书，是最正规的一种背书方式，保证了票据背书的连续性使后手有条件成为正当持票人。记名背书的受让人可继续背书转让权利。

记名背书的形式如下：

Pay to the order of B Co.

For A Co. , London

Signature

3）限制性背书

背书人在背书中添加限制票据进一步流通的文句，即为限制背书。做出限制性背书的背书人对被背书人的后手不再承担保证责任，即限制性背书后的票据不可以再转让。

限制性背书的形式如下：

Pay to B Co. only, not transferable

For A Co. , London

Signature

4）托收背书

收款人或持票人的背书仅仅表示授权被背书人代为收取票款，而票据所有权仍属于背书人，即为托收背书。通常，银行是托收背书的被背书人，充当收款的代理。托收背书后的票据仍可以再背书转让。在托收业务中，汇票通过背书可保证托收行、代收行作为汇票的正当持票人向付款人提示付款或承兑。

托收背书的形式如下：

Pay to B Bank for collection

For A Co. , London

Signature

5）附条件背书

背书人在背书中附加条件，即为附条件背书。通常背书条件不具有法律效力，付款人不必理会该条件。附条件背书后仍然可以再背书转让。

附条件背书的形式如下：

Pay to B Co. after the date of shipment

For A Co. , London

Signature

3. 提示(Presentation)

提示是持票人将票据提交给付款人，要求按票面指示获得付款或承兑的行为。对于远期票据要求先提示承兑，到期后提示付款；对于即期票据，只提示付款。无论是提示承兑还是提示付款，持票人的行为须符合以下规定才能取得票据权利。

1）在规定时限内或合理时间内提示

一般各国票据法对提示付款或承兑规定了相应的期限。一般情况下，持票人未能在规定时限内进行提示，将使持票人丧失对其前手的追索权。

2）在规定的地点提示

提示的地点应该是汇票上的付款地点或付款人、承兑人的营业地址、居住地址。如汇票上的付款人有多人，应该向所有的付款人提示。

4. 承兑（Acceptance）

承兑是指远期票据的付款人接受出票人的命令，承诺在票据到期日支付票据金额的行为。承兑的作用有两个：一是明确付款人的付款责任，二是便于付款人做好付款准备。承兑后，承兑人成为票据的主债务人，假如到期承兑人拒付，持票人可以直接依据票据法起诉承兑人。这也是承兑汇票能够在合同之外对出口商多加一层保护的原因。“承兑”字样和签章应该做于票据正面。特别的，当票据规定“见票后若干天付款”时，承兑人必须注明承兑日（即见票日），从而可以确定付款日期。承兑记载的事项如下：

（1）“Accepted（承兑）”字样；

（2）付款人签章；

（3）付款日期；

（4）承兑日期。

5. 参加承兑（Acceptance for Honour）

参加承兑是指票据遭到拒绝承兑而退票时，非票据债务人在获得持票人的同意后，要求承兑已经遭到拒绝承兑的票据的行为。参加承兑者被称为参加承兑人，被担保到期付款的票据债务人被称为被参加承兑人。持票人同意第三者参加承兑后，即不得于汇票到期日以前向出票人和各前手行使追索权。因此，参加承兑行为使得追索行为被推迟，从而维护了出票人和背书人的信誉。参加承兑记载的事项如下：

（1）“参加承兑”字样；

（2）被参加承兑人名称；

（3）参加承兑日期；

（4）参加承兑人签字。

6. 保证（Guarantee or Aval）

保证是非票据债务人对于出票、背书、承兑、付款等所发生的债务予以偿付担保的票据行为。保证人所负的汇票上责任与被保证人相同。附带保证的票据可靠程度更高，流通性更强。保证记载的事项如下：

(1)“保证”字样；

(2)保证人名称、住址；

(3)被保证人名称；

(4)保证日期；

(5)保证人签字。

7. 拒付（Dishonour）

拒付是指持票人向付款人提示承兑或提示付款时遭到对方拒绝的行为，拒付也称为退票。持票人遇到以下情况，也可视为遭到拒付：

(1)付款人死亡、失踪、没有付款能力或宣告破产；

(2)付款人避而不见；

(3)付款人是虚构的。

遭到拒付的持票人为避免损失应当尽快行使追索权。

8. 追索(Recourse)

追索是持票人遭到拒付后,向其前手(背书人、出票人)及其他票据债务人(保证人)行使付款请求权的行为。行使追索权须满足以下条件。

(1)必须在法定期限内提示票据。没有提示票据,持票人不得行使追索权。

(2)必须在法定期限内将拒付事实通知前手。

持票人在做出拒付通知时,可以先向其直接前手发出拒付通知,再经直接前手依次通知到其他前手,也可以自己同时向各个票据责任人发出通知。发出拒付通知同样需要遵循法定时效,这样才能保证持票人的票据权利。

有关拒付通知发出的时效,英美法系与大陆法系有不同的规定。英美法系规定:遭到拒付后,持票人要将拒付事实通知直接背书人,拒付通知必须在合理的时间内发出,当事人在同一地区的,拒付通知必须在拒付后的当日做出;当事人居住在不同地区的,拒付通知应在拒付后的第二天发出。大陆法系规定:持票人遭到拒付后应在4个营业日内做出拒付通知,如果没有及时做出,并不丧失追索权。

(3)必须在规定时限内做成拒绝证书(票据上注明“免于做成拒绝证书”或“免除拒付通知”的除外)。

拒绝证书的制作:持票人遭到拒付后,将票据交给当地的法定公证机构(公证人)或其他有权出具证书的机构(如法院、银行等),公证人将再次持票据向付款人提示承兑或提示付款,如果仍然遭到拒绝,公证人按照规定格式做成拒绝证书。拒绝证书是一种证明遭到拒付(或退票)的法律文书,内容是做成拒绝证书的原因、向付款人所提出的要求和他的回答。在拒绝证书的背后应附有汇票的副本,然后由公证人签名并按规定贴上印花。如果票据付款地无法定公证人,拒绝证书可以由当地有资历的居民出具,但需要两个证人在场。做成拒绝证书的做法目前已为世界公认,没有拒绝证书将使所有的票据当事人解除被追索的责任。

持票人有权追索的金额有:①票面金额;②提示付款日(即期票据)或到期付款日(远期票据)到清偿日之间的利息;③做成拒绝证书及发出拒付通知的相关费用。行使追索权可以按照票据背书人的前后次序,也可以直接向出票人或任何背书人追索。

9. 付款(Payment)

付款是票据流通过程的终结。对于即期票据,付款人于提示付款时付款;对于远期票据,付款人于提示承兑时先承兑,后于到期日付款。付款后,票据上的一切债权债务关系即告终结,持票人取得票款时要求在票据背面签名并注明“收讫”字样,然后将票据交给付款人。

2.2 汇票(Bill of Exchange)

2.2.1 汇票的含义及特点

根据我国票据法,汇票的含义是出票人签发的,委托付款人在见票时或者在指定日期无条件支付确定的金额给收款人或持票人的票据。

根据《英国票据法》,汇票的含义是一人向另一人签发的,要求即期或者定期或者在将来某个可以确定的时间，向某人或者其指定人或来人支付一定金额的无条件支付命令(A bill of exchange is an unconditional order in writing, addressed by one person to another, signed by the person giving it, requiring the person to whom it is addressed to pay on demand or at a fixed or determinable future time a sum certain in money to or to the order of a specified person, or to bearer)。

根据上述的定义，汇票具有四个特点：

(1)汇票作为票据的一种，具有票据的特点；

(2)汇票是无条件的支付命令；

(3)汇票有即期汇票和远期汇票两种；

(4)汇票的基本当事人有三个：出票人(Drawer)、付款人(Drawee/Payer)、收款人(Payee)。

2.2.2 汇票的内容

汇票的内容指的是汇票上记载的事项(图2.1)。汇票的绝对必要记载事项如下。

BILL OF EXCHANGE①

凭 信用证编号

Drawn under SAKURA BANK,LTD.,TOKYO L/C NO. 090-3001573

日期

Dated Aug.4th,2012 Payable with interest @…..%….. 按…..息….付款

号码 汇票金额 上海

NO.………… Exchange for USD74,157.00 ③ Shanghai Aug.25,2012… ⑥…

见票…………日后（本汇票之正本未付）付交

⑦At *** sight of this SECOND of Exchange (First of Exchange being unpaid)

Pay to the order of BANK OF CHINA ⑤收款人 …………②

金额

The sum of SAY US DOLLARS SEVENTY FOUR THOUSAND ONE HUANDRED AND FIFITY SEVEN ③

此致：

To: CHEMICAL BANK ④

NEW YORK ,NY

SHANGHAI GARMENT CORPORATION

NO.567 MAOTAI RD.,SHANGHAI CHINA

× × × ⑧

(SIGNATURE)

图2.1 汇票

1."汇票"的字样(图2.1①)

汇票上一般都标有"汇票(Bill of Exchange, Exchange, Draft)"的字样，主要是为了与本票

和支票相区别。我国票据法和《日内瓦统一票据法》都将票据的种类名称规定为票据的必要项目。

2. 无条件支付命令(图2.1②)

根据汇票的含义,汇票是一种要求对方付款的命令,并且付款是不附带任何条件的。否则,汇票是无效的。作为命令的语句不可以是疑问句或否定句,应该是祈使句。例如"pay to A Co. or order the sum of ten thousand US dollars"。

3. 确定的金额(图2.1③)

汇票以给付一定金额的货币为目的,因此要求:①币种是确定的,信用证下的汇票货币应该与信用证保持一致,不可以以其他货币表示;②票面的金额是确定的,不可为大约的数额,而且大小写应该保持一致;③当汇票没有要求付款人支付利息时,利息相关栏目可以为空,如果要求对方支付利息,应该在汇票上明确适用的利息和计息期限,以便于确定最终的支付金额。

4. 付款人名称(图2.1④)

汇票都应当写明付款人,通常还注明其地址。一般来说,付款人的营业场所、住所或经常居住地即被视为付款地点。

5. 收款人名称(图2.1⑤)

汇票的收款人俗称"抬头",票据法规定其不可或缺。汇票抬头通常有两种写法:一种是限制性抬头,另一种是指示性抬头。还有一种来人抬头,由于遗失后风险较大,我国票据法和《日内瓦统一票据法》都不允许来人抬头。

1)限制性抬头

汇票指明并限定仅付给某个当事人,不得转让。例如,"Pay to A Co., Ltd., Only","Pay to Mr. A, not transferable"。

2)指示性抬头

汇票指明由某个当事人或其指定的人收款。这种汇票必须背书转让才能保证持票人的票据权利。实务中一般使用指示性抬头比较多。例如,"Pay to A Co., Ltd. or order","Pay to the order of A Company"。

6. 出票日期和地点(图2.1⑥)

各国票据法均将出票日期作为汇票的必要项目,否则汇票无效。出票日期的重要性在于如下几点。

1)决定票据的有效期

决定汇票的提示期限是否已经超过。按照《日内瓦统一票据法》的规定,即期汇票从出票日期起算一年内有效。我国票据法规定即期汇票的有效期为两年。

2)决定远期汇票的到期日

对于根据出票日期确定到期日的远期汇票,计算到期日必须要知道出票日期。

3)决定出票人的行为能力

列明出票日期,可以确定出票人在签发汇票时有无行为能力。若出票时出票人已经宣告破产或清算,就丧失了行为能力,该汇票是无效的。

4)决定利息的起算日

若汇票为出票后定期付款并计息的汇票,出票日为起息日,到期付款日为到期日。

一般来说,出票人的营业场所、住所或经常居住地为出票地点。由于各国采用出票地法律或行为地法律,因此,出票地点决定了汇票适用的法律。

7. 付款日期(图2.1⑦)

汇票的付款日期一般有两种。

1)即期付款

即期汇票的票面有"at sight pay..","on demand pay to the order of..."字样,要求付款人在持票人提示付款时付款。

2)远期付款

远期汇票要求付款人在将来某个特定时间付款,票面上有可以确定的期限,要求付款人在持票人第一次提示时承兑,于到期日持票人第二次提示时付款。远期汇票的付款期限一般有以下表示方法。

(1)出票后定期付款。这种汇票要求持票人向付款人提示承兑从而确定付款责任,由于出票日期为必要记载事项,因此可以计算出付款日期。

例1:At 60 days after date,如果汇票的出票日为7月10日,则7月11日—31日,合计21天;8月1日—31日,合计31天;9月1日—8日,合计8天。7月11日—9月8日,共计60天,付款日为9月8日。

(2)见票后定期付款。这种汇票要求持票人向付款人提示承兑从而确定见票日期(即承兑日,也是付款日期的起算日),然后计算汇票的到期付款日。

例1:At 60 days after sight,如果汇票的见票日(承兑日)为4月5日,则4月6日—30日,合计25天;5月1日—31日,合计31天;6月1日—4日,合计4天。4月6日—6月4日,共计60天,付款日为6月4日。

例2:At one month after sight,如果汇票日见票日(承兑日)为2月25日,则到期日为3月25日。

例3:At one and half a month after sight,如果汇票日见票日(承兑日)为2月25日,则按照one month +half a month(15天)计算,即3月25日+15天,到期付款日为4月9日。

(3)定日付款。付款人也需要在规定期限内向付款人提示承兑,从而确定付款人的付款责任。

例1:On 21st,July 17, 2013,pay to...

8. 出票人签章(图2.1⑧)

签章是票据法规定的必要记载事项,出票人签章确定了其向收款人及其后手承诺并保证汇票能够获得承兑或付款,签章行为也确定了汇票承兑前出票人的主债务人地位。如果汇票没有签章或者签章是伪造的,则该汇票无效。常见的签章式样如下。

例1:John Smith

For × × Co.,Ltd.

例2:John Smith
　　For and on behalf of ××Company

例3:John Smith
　　(General Manager)

2.2.3 汇票的种类

(1)根据出票人的不同,汇票可以分为银行汇票(Banker's Bill)和商业汇票(Commercial Bill)。银行汇票指出票人是银行的汇票,而商业汇票是出票人是公司或个人的汇票。由于银行的信用高于公司和个人,因此银行汇票较之商业汇票更容易流通转让。银行汇票签发后,交汇款人,由汇款人交国外收款人向付款行取款。商业汇票较多使用于托收和信用证支付方式下,一般都附有货运单据(主要是具有物权凭证的海运提单或仓单)。

(2)根据付款时间的不同,汇票分为即期汇票(Sight Draft)和远期汇票(Time Draft)。即期汇票是见票即付的汇票,远期汇票是在将来某一天或某个确定的日期付款的汇票。

(3)根据是否随附货运单据,汇票可分为光票(Clean Bill)和跟单汇票(Documentary Bill)。光票汇票不附带货运单据,其流通完全依靠当事人的信用。银行汇票多为光票。跟单汇票是附带货运单据(主要是代表物权凭证的提单)的汇票。跟单汇票收款除了有当事人的商业信用以外,还有物权凭证的制约。在托收和信用证支付方式下的汇票多为跟单汇票,进口商取得物权凭证的前提是付款赎单。商业汇票一般都是跟单汇票。

2.3 本票(Promissory Note)

2.3.1 本票的含义和特点

根据我国《票据法》,本票的含义是出票人签发的,承诺自己在见票时无条件支付确定的金额给收款人或持票人的票据。我国只有银行本票而无商业本票。

根据《英国票据法》,本票的含义是一个人向另一个人签发的,保证即期或定期或在某个可以确定的将来时间,对某人或其指定人或来人支付一定金额的无条件书面承诺。(A promissory note is an unconditional promise in writing made by one person to another, signed by the maker, engaging to pay, on demand or at a fixed or determinable future time, a sum certain in money to, or to the order of, a specified person or to bearer.)

根据上述定义,本票具有如下特点。

(1)本票只有两个基本当事人:出票人和收款人,本票的出票人就是付款人。

(2)本票是无条件付款的书面承诺,也就是出票人保证自己履行付款的责任。

(3)本票的主债务人始终是出票人,无论是即期还是远期本票,出票人都作为主债务人承担第一性的付款责任。

(4)远期本票的出票人就是付款人,因此持票人无须提示承兑。但是,如果是见票后定期付款的远期本票则需要持票人向出票人提示,以确定到期日,此为见票。

2.3.2 本票的内容

本票的内容是本票票面记载的事项(图 2.2),本票记载的必要事项如下。

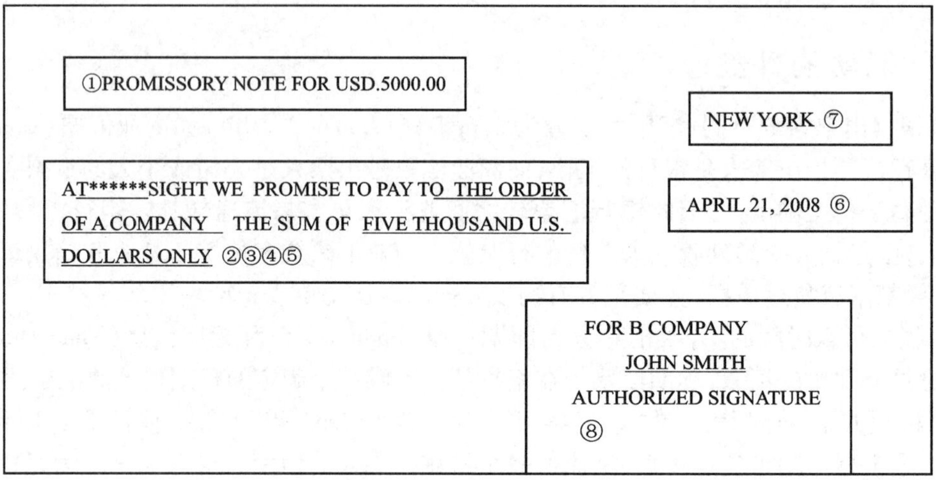
①PROMISSORY NOTE FOR USD.5000.00

NEW YORK ⑦

APRIL 21, 2008 ⑥

AT******SIGHT WE PROMISE TO PAY TO THE ORDER OF A COMPANY THE SUM OF FIVE THOUSAND U.S. DOLLARS ONLY ②③④⑤

FOR B COMPANY
JOHN SMITH
AUTHORIZED SIGNATURE
⑧

图 2.2 本票

(1)“本票(PROMISSORY NOTE)”的字样(图 2.2①)。
(2)无条件支付承诺(PROMISE TO PAY)(图 2.2②)。
(3)确定的金额(THE SUM OF FIVE THOUSAND U.S. DOLLARS ONLY)(图 2.2③)。
(4)收款人名称(THE ORDER OF A COMPANY)(图 2.2④)。
(5)付款期限(AT SIGHT;本票未写明付款期限的即为即期付款本票)(图 2.2⑤)。
(6)出票日期与地点(NEW YORK;APRIL 21,2008)(图 2.2⑥)。
(7)付款地点(本票未写明付款地点的,出票地即为付款地点)(图 2.2⑦)。
(8)出票人签章(图 2.2⑧)。

2.3.3 本票的种类

根据出票人的不同,本票可分为如下两种。

1. 商业本票

商业本票的出票人是企业或个人,商业本票可以为即期或远期的。由于企业或个人信用的原因不能按时付款,商业本票的使用范围逐渐缩小。在我国,票据法规定只有银行才能签发本票,而企业和个人是不可以签发本票的。

2. 银行本票

银行本票的出票人是银行,一般在票面注明“Cashier's Order”。由于银行发行的见票即付、不列明收款人或指定人的固定面额本票实际上相当于货币,因此,为加强金融监管,避免此类本票流通市场扰乱国家的纸币发行,各国均规定银行本票必须是记名的。

在国际贸易中,利用出口信贷融资进口大型设备时,进口商可开出类似的远期付款本票,经进口商银行背书保证,到期由出票人偿还本息。

2.3.4　本票与汇票的区别

本票与汇票存在以下不同。

(1)本票只有两个基本当事人:出票人(也是付款人)和收款人。汇票有三个基本当事人:出票人、付款人和收款人。

(2)本票是出票人无条件的付款承诺。而汇票是出票人要求付款人无条件付款的命令,一般在出票人和付款人之间存在债权债务关系。

(3)本票的出票人始终是主债务人,承担第一性的付款责任。而对于远期汇票,在承兑前,出票人是主债务人,在承兑后,承兑人成为主债务人,承担第一性的付款责任。

(4)远期本票无须提示承兑,因为出票人就是付款人。而远期汇票需要先行提示承兑,后到期提示付款。见票后定期付款的本票需要由持票人向出票人提示,以确定付款到期日。

(5)本票只能开出一张,而不是一套。但汇票一般是一式两份,当汇票承兑人或付款人对其中一张承兑或付款时,另一张则失效。

2.4　支票(Cheque)

2.4.1　支票的含义和特点

根据我国《票据法》,支票的含义是出票人签发的,委托办理支票存款业务的银行或者其他金融机构在见票时无条件支付确定的金额给收款人或者持票人的票据。

根据《英国票据法》,支票的含义是以银行为付款人的即期汇票。具体来说,支票是银行存户对银行签发的,授权银行对某人或其指定人或来人即期支付一定金额的无条件支付命令。(A cheque is a bill of exchange drawn on a banker payable on demand.)

根据上述含义,支票的特点是:银行或金融机构对出票人签发的支票无条件支付的前提是出票人应该在签发支票前,在银行办理支票存款账户。支票存款账户的开立条件是:①申请人向办理支票存款业务的银行申请开立支票存款账户必须使用其本名;②申请人应当向存款账户存入一定的资金;③申请人应当预留其本人的签名式样与印鉴。

各国票据法均禁止签发空头支票。空头支票是出票人签发的金额超过其存款账户余额的支票。根据票据法的规定,签发存款不足的空头支票要承担相应的法律责任。

2.4.2　支票的内容

支票的内容为支票票面的记载事项(图 2.3),支票的必要记载事项如下。

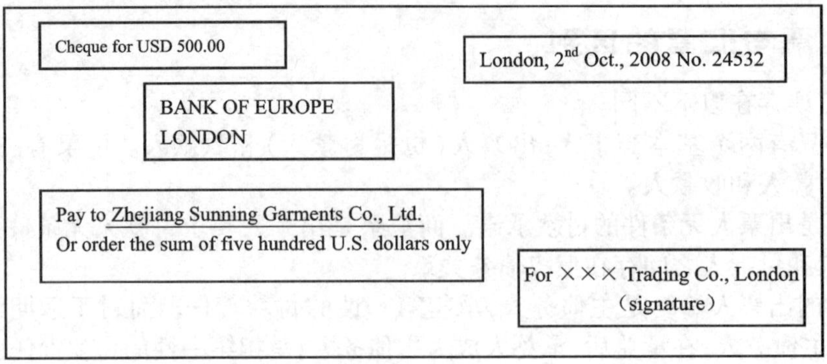

图 2.3　支票

(1)支票的字样。

(2)无条件支付命令。

(3)付款银行名称。

(4)出票人签字。

(5)出票日期与地点(未写明出票地点的,出票人所在地为出票地点)。

(6)付款地点(未写明的,付款行所在地为付款地点)。

(7)一定的金额。

(8)收款人或其指定的人。

支票与汇票的差别不大,除了汇票有关承兑的内容对支票不适用以外,其他规定基本都适用。

2.4.3　支票的种类

1. 记名支票(Check to Order)

记名支票须在收款人一栏写明收款人的名称,如“Pay to A or Pay to the order of A”。取款时须由收款人签名方能支取。

2. 不记名支票(Check to Bearer)

不记名支票亦称空白支票,即支票上不写明收款人的名称,只写“Pay Bearer”(付来人)。取款时持票人无须在支票背面签名即可支取,此类支票凭交付转让。

3. 一般支票(Uncrossed Check)

一般支票又称开放支票(Open Check),即非划线支票。支票的左上角如无两道斜的平行线就是一般支票。它可以通过银行转账,也可由持票人自行提取现金。只要提示的票据合格,支票的付款银行就得立即付款。为防止支票遗失,被人冒领取款,可以在左上角画两道平行的斜线,使之成为划线支票。

4. 划线支票(Crossed Check)

划线支票是在支票正面的左上角画两道平行线的支票。划线支票只能用于银行转账,不能提取现金。根据线内是否注明收款银行名称,划线支票又分为一般划线支票和特别划线支票。

1）一般划线支票（General Crossed Check）

一般划线支票是由出票人、收款人或代收银行在支票正面画两道平行线，但是不注明收款银行的划线支票。

2）特别划线支票（Special Crossed Check）

特别划线支票是在平行线内写明具体收款银行的划线支票，因此只能由该银行收账而不能委托其他银行收账。使用划线支票的目的是保证安全，避免因支票遗失或失窃而遭受损失。

5. 保付支票（Certified Check）

为了避免出票人开出空头支票，收款人或持票人可要求银行对支票保付，即付款银行在支票上加盖"保付"戳记并签字，以表明其在支票提示付款时一定照办。支票一经保付，付款银行就承担了付款责任，成为主债务人，而出票人、背书人都可免于追索，经保付后的支票信誉好，流通性更强。美国、日本等国的票据法有支票保付的规定，《英国票据法》《日内瓦统一票据法》都没有支票保付的内容，我国票据法也没有这种规定。

6. 银行支票（Banker's Check）

银行支票是由银行签发，并由银行付款的支票，即银行即期汇票（Banker's Demand Draft）。银行代顾客办理票汇汇款时，可以开立银行支票。

2.4.4　支票与汇票、本票的区别

（1）支票没有远期的，都是即期支票，因此也没有远期汇票的行为，例如承兑、参加承兑等。本票和汇票都有即期和远期的，但前者无须承兑，因为出票人就是付款人。

（2）支票的付款人是银行，而汇票与本票的付款人可以是银行，也可以是企业。在我国，由于只有银行本票，因此付款人是银行。

（3）支票有划线和保付的规定，以防止假冒和便利流通，但汇票、本票没有这种规定。

（4）支票签发时，出票人和付款人之间必须先有资金关系，即出票人在签发支票前已在付款银行的支票存款账户有足额存款；而汇票的出票人和付款人之间不必有资金关系；本票是出票人的无条件付款承诺，自己承诺付款，无所谓资金关系。

（5）支票的基本当事人有三个：出票人、付款人和收款人，与汇票相同。而本票的当事人只有两个：出票人和收款人。

（6）支票的签发与本票一样，只有一张，没有副本；而汇票的签发是一式两份，付一不付二。

以上三种支付工具的区别见表2.2。

表2.2　三种支付工具的区别

	汇票	本票	支票
基本当事人	出票人、付款人、收款人	出票人、收款人	出票人、付款人、收款人
性质	无条件支付命令	无条件支付承诺	无条件支付命令

续表

	汇票	本票	支票
有无承兑行为	有	无	无
期限	即期、远期	即期、远期	即期
付款人	银行、公司	银行、公司	银行
出票人与付款人之间的关系	未必先有资金关系	—	必须先有资金关系
主债务人	承兑前是出票人,承兑后是承兑人	出票人	出票人
张数	A Full Set	SOLA	SOLA

2.4.5 支票的有效期

支票是即期的支付工具,因此有效期较短。在支票的有效期内应该提示付款,否则支票会失效。根据我国《票据法》的规定,支票的持票人应当在出票日后的10日内提示付款,如果到期日为节假日则顺延至下个工作日。《日内瓦统一票据法》规定出票与付款在同一国家的是自出票日起算8天;出票与付款不在同一国家但在同一洲的是20天;不同国家又不同洲的是70天。

思考题

1. 票据的基本当事人有哪些?
2. 持票人行使追索权有哪些条件?
3. 汇票、本票和支票的异同点有哪些?
4. 什么叫空白背书?

Chapter 2

Negotiable Instruments

2.1 Introduction to negotiable instruments

A negotiable instrument is a document guaranteeing the payment of a specific amount of money, either on demand, or at a set time with the payer named on the negotiable instrument. More specifically, it is a document contemplated by a contract, which warrants the payment of money without condition which may be paid on demand or at a future date.

Examples of negotiable instruments include promissory notes, bills of exchange, bank notes and cheques.

Because money is promised to be paid, the instrument itself can be used by the holder in due course as a store of value. The instrument can be transferred to a third party and it is the holder of the instrument who will ultimately get paid by the payer on the instrument. Transfers can happen at less than the face value of the instrument and this is known as discounting, this may happen for example if there is doubt about the payer's ability to pay.

Due to the nature of the negotiable instrument as store of value, most countries passed laws specifically related to negotiable instruments.

2.1.1 Types of negotiable instruments

There are different kinds of negotiable instruments. Some of them are widely used.

1. Draft

Draft is an unconditional order to pay by which the party creating the draft (the drawer) orders another party (the drawee), typically a bank, to pay money to a third party (the payee)—e. g., a check.

2. Check

Check is a draft ordering a drawee bank and payable on demand.

3. Time draft

Time draft is a draft payable at a certain time.

4. Sight draft

Sight draft is a draft payable on presentment.

5. Trade acceptance

Trade acceptance is a draft that is drawn by a seller of goods ordering the buyer to pay a specified sum of money to the seller, usually at a specified future time. The buyer accepts the draft by signing and returning it to the seller.

6. Promissory note

Promissory note is a written promise made by one person (the maker) to pay a fixed sum of money to another person (the payee) on demand or at a specified future time.

7. Certificate of deposit

Certificate of deposit is a note by which a bank or similar financial institution acknowledges the receipt of money from a party and promises to repay the money, plus interest, to the party on a certain date.

2.1.2 Parties to negotiable instruments

The parties to a negotiable instrument (bill of exchange, promissory note and cheque) are discussed in detail.

1. Parties to a bill of exchange

1) The drawer

The person who draws a bill of exchange is called the drawer.

2) The drawee

The party on whom such bill of exchange is drawn and who is directed to pay is called the drawee.

3) The acceptor

The person who accepts the bill is known as the acceptor. Normally the drawee is the acceptor. But a stranger can also accept a bill on behalf of the drawee.

4) The payee

The person to whom the amount of the bill is payable is called the payee.

5) The endorser

When the holder transfers or endorses the instrument to any other person the holder becomes the endorser.

6) The endorsee

The person to whom the bill is endorsed is called the endorsee.

7) The holder

Holder of bill of exchange means any person who is legally entitled to the possession of it and to receive or recover the amount due thereon from the parties. He is either the payee or the endorsee.

The finder of a lost bill payable to bearer or a person in wrongful possession of such instrument is not a holder.

8) Drawee in case of need

The drawer of a bill or even an endorser may write in the instrument the name of a person directing the holder to resort to the person in case of need. Such a person is called a drawee in case of need. He is merely in the position of a drawee who has not accepted the bill. The bill cannot be presented to him for acceptance but only for payment.

If a drawee in case of need is mentioned in the bill, such a bill is not dishonored until it has been dishonored by such a drawee in case of need. The effect of this provision is to make the presentment to the drawee in case of need obligatory on the part of the holder.

9) Acceptor for honour

Any person may voluntarily become a party to a bill as an acceptor by accepting it for the honour of the drawer or of any person. When the original drawee refuses to accept or refuses to furnish better security when demanded by a notary, any person may step in to safeguard the honour of the drawer or any endorser and bind himself by an acceptance. The effect of such acceptance is that the bill is treated as alive and is not considered to be dishonoured till it is dishonoured by the acceptor for honour.

2. Parties to a promissory note

1) The maker

He is the person who promises to pay the amount stated in the promissory note.

2) The payee

The person named in the promissory note to whom the money is payable.

3) The holder

He may be either the payee or someone else to whom the promissory note has been endorsed.

4) The endorser

When the holder transfers or endorses the instrument to any other person the holder becomes the endorser.

5) The endorsee

The person to whom the bill is endorsed is called the endorsee.

3. Parties to a cheque

1) The drawer

He is the person who draws the cheque.

2) The drawee

The banker on whom the cheque is drawn.

3) The payee

The person to whom the amount of the bill is payable is called the payee.

4) The holder

Holder of bill of exchange means any person who is legally entitled to the possession of it and to receive or recover the amount due thereon from the parties. He is either the payee or the endorsee. The finder of a lost bill payable to bearer or a person in wrongful possession of such instrument is not a holder.

5) The endorser

When the holder transfers or endorses the instrument to any other person the holder becomes the endorser.

6) The endorsee

The person to whom the bill is endorsed is called the endorsee.

2.1.3 Particularities to negotiable instruments

First of all, a negotiable instrument is a written instrument, signed by the maker or drawer of the instrument, that contains an unconditional promise or order to pay, an exact sum of money (with or without interest in a specified amount or at a specified rate), on demand or at an exact future time and to a specific person, or to order, or to its bearer.

1. Negotiability: signatures

For an instrument to be negotiable, it must be signed by the maker/drawer. A signature may be any symbol made by the maker or drawer with the present intention to be a signature.

2. Negotiability: unconditionality

1) Promise or order

A negotiable instrument must contain an express order or promise to pay. A mere acknowledgment of a debt is not sufficient without evidence of an affirmative undertaking on the part of the debtor to repay the debt.

The exception to this rule is a certificate of deposit.

2) Unconditionality of promise or order

A promise or order is conditional (and, therefore, not negotiable) if it states: an express condition to payment, or that the promise or order is subject to or governed by another writing, or that the rights or obligations with respect to the promise or order are stated in another writing.

3. Negotiability: a fixed amount

The third requirement of negotiability is that negotiable instruments must state a fixed amount of money. Fixed amount means an amount that can be determined from the face of the instrument. This requirement applies only to the principal amount of money. The instrument can reference an outside source to determine the rate of interest. Payable in money means the medium of exchange authorized or adopted by the United States or foreign government as part of its currency.

4. Negotiability: time for payment

1) Payment on demand

An instrument is payable on demand, "at sight", or "upon presentment" if it is subject to payment immediately upon being presented to the drawee. If no time for payment is specified, a negotiable instrument is presumed to be payable on demand.

2) Payment at a definite time

An instrument is payable at a definite time if it states that it is payable on a specified date, within a definite period of time, or on a date or at a time readily ascertainable at the time the promise or order is made.

Such instruments are frequently referred to as time instruments.

3) Acceleration clause

A clause that permits a payee or other holder of a time instrument to demand payment of the entire amount or balance due, with interest, if a certain event occurs, such as default in the payment of an installment when due.

4) Extension clause

A clause in a time instrument that permits the date of maturity to be extended.

5. Negotiability: payment to whom

1) Order instrument

A negotiable instrument that is payable "to the order of" an identified person or "to" an identifiable person "or order".

2) Bearer instrument

A negotiable instrument that is payable "to bearer" or to "cash", rather than to an identifiable payee.

3) Bearer

The person possessing a bearer instrument.

Any instrument payable to the following is a bearer instrument:

(1) "Payable to the order of bearer";

(2) "Payable to Jane Smith or bearer";

(3) "Payable to bearer";

(4) "Pay cash";

(5) "Pay to the order of cash".

2.1.4 Factors not affecting negotiability

Certain ambiguities or omissions, resolvable by applicable U. C. C. provisions and/or rules, will not make an instrument non-negotiable.

For example:

The fact that an instrument is undated does not affect its negotiability, unless the date of the instrument is necessary to understand the payment term; postdating or antedating an instrument does not affect its negotiability; interlineation and other written or typewritten alterations does not affect negotiability; as with other contract terms, handwritten terms "trump" typewritten terms, and typewritten terms "trump" printed terms.

Words "trump" figures, unless the words are ambiguous in and of themselves; and if the instrument fails to specify the applicable interest rate, the judgment rate of interest (defined by state statute) becomes the interest rate on the instrument.

2.1.5 Transfer of instruments

1) Assignment

Under general contract principles, a negotiable instrument may be transferred to an assignee, who then holds the instrument with all the rights of the assignor.

2) Negotiation

Transfer of an instrument in such a form that the transferee becomes a holder, who has at least the same rights in the instrument as the transferor, and may have more rights than the transferor.

3) Negotiating order instruments

An order instrument may be negotiated by delivery with any necessary endorsements.

4) Negotiating bearer instruments

Unlike an order instrument, a bearer instrument need not be endorsed to transfer the payee's rights to the transferee. All that is required is delivered to the new bearer.

2.1.6 Endorsements

1) Endorsement

A signature, with or without additional words or statements (e.g., "for deposit only", "payable to Jane Smith", "payable from acct. # 000001", etc.), is made by the endorser in order to transfer his or her rights to the endorsee.

2) Blank endorsement

An endorsement that specifies no particular endorsee and can consist of a mere signature.

3) Special endorsement

An endorsement that indicates the specific person to whom the endorser intends to make the instrument payable—i.e., the endorsee.

4) Qualified endorsement

An endorsement which disclaims any contract liability on the instrument (e.g., "without recourse").

5) Restrictive endorsement

Any endorsement on a negotiable instrument that requires the endorsee to comply with certain instructions regarding the funds involved.

6) Endorsement for deposit or collection

"For deposit only".

2.2 Bill of exchange

2.2.1 What a bill of exchange is

A written, unconditional order by one party (the drawer) to another (the drawee) to pay a certain sum, either immediately (a sight bill) or on a fixed date (a term bill), for payment of goods and/or services received. The drawee accepts the bill by signing it, thus converting it into a post-dated check and a binding contract.

A bill of exchange is also called a draft but, while all drafts are negotiable instruments, only "to order" bills of exchange can be negotiated.

According to the 1930 *Convention Providing A Uniform Law for Bills of Exchange and Promissory Notes* held in Geneva (also called *Geneva Convention*) a bill of exchange contains:

(1) The term bill of exchange inserted in the body of the instrument and expressed in the language employed in drawing up the instrument;

(2) An unconditional order to pay a determinate sum of money;

(3) The name of the person who is to pay (drawee);

(4) A statement of the time of payment;

(5) A statement of the place where payment is to be made;

(6) The name of the person to whom or to whose order payment is to be made;

(7) A statement of the date and of the place where the bill is issued;

(8) The signature of the person who issues the bill (drawer).

A bill of exchange is the most lsmmonly used form of payment in local and international trade, and has a long history—as long as that of writing.

2.2.2 How a bill of exchange functions

An example will fully grasp the transactions relating to bill of exchange.

Suppose A sells goods with the value of $500 to B. The most ready means of closing the transaction will be cash payment by B to A. But payment of this nature is not many in actual practice. The greatest volume of business is done on credit. That being the case A will have to wait for some time to receive payment from B. A, merchant can hardly afford to be out of funds for long. Moreover, to sell goods on credit is rather a risky job. Therefore as soon as A sells goods to B, he will draw a bill for $500 on B and forward the same to him together with the goods with instructions to B to accept the bill and return the same to A. Upon receipt of the bill, B would write on the face of the bill "accepted" and put his signature below. It means that B approves the bill and also binds himself to pay the amount thereof when due. The bill is thus complete and comes back to A to remain in his possession till maturity or can be endorsed or discounted by him. On the due date the holder of the bill presents it before the acceptor and receives payment of the bill from the acceptor.

Thus the bill of exchange is the instrument; rather the mechanism which finances the major portion of all commercial transactions these days and it helps both the debtor and the creditor alike.

2.2.3 Features to bill of exchange

1. Tenor and usance

Tenor is the period of time after which a bill becomes payable. Thus, where a bill is payable after 90 days from the date of drawing or acceptance, the tenor of the bill is 90 days. Bill may be made payable:

(1) On demand—the bill so drawn is payable as soon as its payment is demanded by the holder of the bill;

(2) At sight—a bill of exchange so drawn becomes payable immediately it is brought to the notice of the drawee;

(3) After date—when a bill is drawn "after date" its due date is calculated from the date of the bill;

(4) After sight—when a bill is drawn "after sight" its due date is calculated from the date on which it is sighted or seen by the drawee i. e. , from the date of acceptance by the drawee;

(5) Usance—it is the usual time of payment of a bill of exchange as fixed by custom.

2. Days of grace

In calculating the due date of payment it is customary in business circle to allow three additional days to the drawee or acceptor to meet the bill. The extra days are called "days of grace" or "grace days". Thus a bill dated 15th March, for three months becomes payable on 18th June and this is the due date.

3. Holder

Holder of a bill is a person who is entitled in his own right to the possession thereof and to claim the amount due thereon.

4. Holder in due course

When a person takes a bill, complete and regular on the face of it and before its due date, in good faith and for valuable consideration he is called the holder in due course.

5. Acceptance

When a drawee signs his name across the face of along with the word "accepted" the bill is said to be accepted and this act of the drawee is called acceptance of a bill. Before this is done, the drawee cannot be made liable for the bill.

Mainly there are two kinds of a accptances.

General acceptance—when a bill is accepted with some qualifications to the order of the drawer it is called qualified acceptance.

Specific acceptance, which mainly has two different types. These are following types.

1) Time

When the acceptor agrees to pay the bill on some day other than the date required by the drawer, it is called qualified acceptance as to time.

2) Place

When a bill is payable at a particular place and there only, it is called local qualified acceptance.

2.3 Promissory note

Promissory note is a written, signed, unconditional promise to pay a certain amount of money on demand at a specified time. A written promise to pay money that is often used as a means to borrow funds or take out a loan.

It is a written promise by a person to pay a specific amount of money to another usually to include a specified amount of interest on the unpaid principal amount (what he/she owes).

The specified time of payment may be written as: ① whenever there is a demand, ② on a specific date, ③ in installments with or without the interest included in each installment, ④ installments with a final larger amount (balloon payment). A promissory note may contain other terms such as the right of the payee to order payment be made to another person, penalties for late payments, a provision for attorney's fees and costs if there is a legal action to collect, the right to collect payment in full if the note is secured by real property and the property is sold ("duc on salc" clause), and whether the note is secured by a mortgage or deed of trust or a financing statement (a filed security agreement for personal collateral). The promissory note is usually held by the party to whom the money is owcd. Thcrc arc lcgal limitations to the amount of interest which may be charged. Charging a rate in excess of the legal limit is called "usury", and this excess is legally uncollectible. When the amount due on the note, including interest and penalties (if any) is paid, the note must be cancelled and surrendered to the person(s) who signed it. A promissory note need only be signed and does not require an acknowledgement before a notary public to be valid.

2.4 Cheque

A cheque is a document that orders a payment of money from a bank account. The person writing the cheque, the drawer, has a transaction banking account (often called a current, cheque, chequing or checking account) where their money is held. The drawer writes various details including the monetary amount, date, and a payee on the cheque, and signs it, ordering their bank, known as the drawee, to pay that person or company the amount of money stated.

Cheques are a type of bill of exchange and were developed as a way to make payments without the need to carry large amounts of money. While paper money evolved from promissory notes, another form of negotiable instrument, similar to cheques in that they were originally a written order to pay the given amount to whoever had it in their possession (the "bearer").

Technically, a cheque is a negotiable instrument instructing a financial institution to pay a specific amount of a specific currency from a specified transactional account held in the drawer's name with that institution. Both the drawer and payee may be natural persons or legal entities. Specifically, cheques are order instruments, and are not in general payable simply to the bearer (as bearer instruments are) but must be paid to the payee. In some countries, such as the US, the payee may endorse the cheque, allowing them to specify a third party to whom it should be paid.

2.5 Differences between bill of exchange, promissory note and cheque

2.5.1 Differences between bill of exchange and promissory note

1. Parties

There are three parties to a bill of exchange, namely, the drawer, the drawee and the payee; while in a promissory note there are only two parties—maker and payee.

2. Nature of payment

In a bill of exchange, there is an unconditional order to pay, while in a promissory note there is an unconditional promise to pay.

3. Acceptance

A bill of exchange requires an acceptance of the drawee before it is presented for payment, while a promissory note does not require any acceptance since it is signed by the person who is liable to pay.

4. Liability

The liability of the maker of a promissory note is primary and absolute, while the liability of the drawer of a bill of exchange is secondary and conditional. It is only when the drawee fails to pay that the drawer would be liable as a surety.

5. Notice of dishonour

In case of dishonour of a bill of exchange either due to non-payment or non-acceptance, notice must be given to all persons liable to pay. But in the case of a promissory note, notice of dishonour to the maker is not necessary.

6. Maker's position

The drawer of a bill of exchange stands in immediate relationship with the acceptor and not the payee. While in the case of a promissory note, the maker stands in immediate relationship with the payee.

7. Nature of acceptance

A promissory note can never be conditional, while a bill of exchange can be accepted conditionally.

8. Copies

A bill of exchange can be drawn in sets, but a promissory note cannot be drawn in sets.

9. Payable to bearer

A promissory note cannot be made payable to a bearer, while a bill of exchange can be so drawn provided it is not payable to bearer on demand.

10. Payable to maker

In a promissory note, the maker cannot pay to himself. While in the case of a bill of exchange, the drawer and the payee may be one person.

11. Protest

Foreign bills must be protested for dishonour when such protest is required by the law of the place where they are drawn. But no such protest is required in the case of a promissory note.

The differences can also be concluded as table 2.1.

Table 2.1 The differences between bill of exchange and promissory note

Bill of Exchange	Promissory Note
It is an order to pay	It is a promise to pay
There are three parties, the drawer, the drawee, and the payee	There are only two parties, the drawer, and the payee
It must be accepted	There is no necessity of acceptance
The drawer is not primarily liable	The maker is primarily liable
Foreign bills are specially drawn in sets	It is never drawn in sets
A foreign bill must be protested upon dishonour	Protesting is not necessary after dishonour

2.5.2 Differences between bill of exchange and cheque

The differences between bill of exchange and cheque are concluded as table 2.2.

Table 2.2 The differences between bill of exchange and cheque

Bill of Exchange	Cheque
It may be drawn on any party or individual	It is drawn on a banker
Foreign bills are drawn in sets	It is seldom drawn in sets
It must be accepted by the drawee before he can be made liable to pay the bill	It does not require acceptance by the drawee
Three days of grace are always allowed to the drawee	Days of grace are not allowed to a banker
Stamp duty has to be paid on bill of exchange	No stamp duty is payable on checks
It may be drawn in any paper and need not necessarily be printed	It is usually drawn on the printed form

第 3 章

国际汇款

3.1 汇款的含义与当事人

3.1.1 汇款(Remittance)

汇款又称汇付,是付款人通过银行,使用各种结算工具将货款支付给收款人的一种结算方式。

国际货物买卖如采用汇款方式支付货款,通常由买方按照约定的时间和条件通过银行将货款汇交给卖方。由于汇付的资金流向与支付工具的传递方向一致,因此汇付也叫顺汇(Favorable Remittance)。在汇付方式下,卖方能否按时收回约定的货款或者买方能否如愿收到合同项下的货物,完全取决于对方的信用。因此,汇付的性质是商业信用。

汇款结算方式一般主要涉及四个当事人:汇款人(Remitter)、收款人或受益人(Payee/Beneficiary)、汇出行(Remitting Bank)、汇入行或解付行(Paying Bank)。其中汇出行汇出的汇款被称为汇出汇款(Outward Remittance),汇入行汇入的汇款被称为汇入汇款(Inward Remittance)。

3.1.2 汇款人(Remitter)

汇款人即付款人,指的是国际贸易中的进口商,向银行交付货款并委托银行将该款项交付出口商的人。汇款人在委托汇出行办理汇款业务时,首先需要填写汇款申请书(Application for Remittance),汇款申请书是汇款人与银行之间的一种契约。汇款申请书一式两联,一联为汇款申请书,一联为汇款回执。在申请书中汇款人应标明收款人的名称、地址、账户,开户行名称、地址、账户,汇款人的姓名、地址、汇款金额及币种、汇款附言等。其次,要交纳与汇款金额一致的款项与手续费。如果用人民币汇外币,除了要按当天的汇率交纳等值的人民币以外,还要提交国家外汇管理局批准使用外汇的证明。如果以其他银行的支票汇款,要待汇出银行通过交换等途径收妥款项之后才能办理汇出手续。

3.1.3 收款人或受益人(Payee/Beneficiary)

收款人是国际贸易中的出口商,是接受汇款人汇出款项的人。当收款人通过汇入行取得解付的款项后,意味着该笔汇款结算业务结束。

3.1.4 汇出行(Remitting Bank)

汇出行是受汇款人的委托对外汇出款项的银行,通常是汇款人(进口商)所在地的银行。汇出行的汇款业务基于汇款人填写的汇款申请书,它是汇款人与汇出行之间业务的法律依据。汇出行的汇款业务必须完全按照汇款申请书行事,汇出行缮制支付授权书(Payment Order,P. O.)以汇款申请书为根据,内容及汇款方式须与其一致,否则将承担违约及侵权损害赔偿的责任。另外,汇出行应当正确地选择汇款的路线,中转的环节越少产生的费用越低,对客户越有利。当然,特殊情况下以资金的安全为第一,效率为第二。

3.1.5 汇入行(Paying Bank)

汇入行也称解付行,是接受汇出行委托将款项支付给收款人的银行。汇入行通常是汇出行在收款人(出口商)所在地的分行或有代理协议的代理行,通常与出口商在同一个城市。汇入行的解付汇入款必须严格按照汇出行的 P. O. 办理。如果因擅自行事没有按照 P. O. 的内容解付而引起的任何后果均由汇入行负责。

3.2 汇款的种类

根据汇款业务使用的结算工具和汇兑方式不同,汇款分为三种:电汇、信汇和票汇。

3.2.1 电汇(T/T)

1. 含义

电汇(Telegraphic Transfer,T/T)是汇出行应汇款人的申请,通过发送加押电报、电传或SWIFT 形式通知其国外的分行或代理行,指示其解付一定金额给收款人的一种汇款方式。随着网上银行业务的开发,通过网上银行服务实现资金在国际的转移、汇兑。

2. 特点

(1)汇款最快捷。在银行,电汇的优先级别最高,一般当天处理,汇出行当天发出委托付款指示,汇入行当天或第二天能收到,汇入行马上通知收款人,整个业务流程只需要 2~3 天的时间。

(2)汇款安全可靠。由于是银行间的直接通信,差错率较低,遗失可能性很小,也更加安全准确。因此,电汇使用越来越多。

(3)电汇费用较高。由于电汇使用的是现代化的通信工具——电报、电传,电报按字收费,电传按时计价,直接成本相对较高。而且由于汇出行占压汇款资金的时间实际极短,甚至根本不占压,因此收费比较高。

3. 业务流程(图 3.1)

(1)汇款人填写汇款申请书,交款项、汇费,并在申请书上说明使用电汇方式。

(2)汇出行审核后,汇款人取得电汇回执。

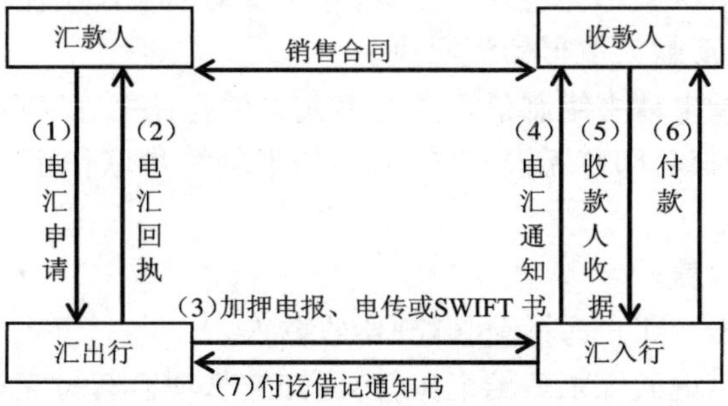

图 3.1　电汇业务流程

(3)汇出行发出加押电报、电传或 SWIFT 给汇入行,委托汇入行解付款项给收款人。

(4)汇入行收到核对密押后,缮制电汇通知书,通知收款人收款。

(5)收款人收到通知书后在收据联上盖章,提示汇入行。

(6)汇入行借记汇出行账户,并解付款项给收款人。

(7)汇入行将付讫借记通知书寄给汇出行,通知它款项已解付完毕。

3.2.2　信汇(M/T)

1. 含义

信汇(Mail Transfer, M/T)是汇出行应汇款人的申请,用航空邮寄信函的方式指示国外代理行支付一定金额的款项给收款人的汇款方式。

2. 特点

(1)收费低廉。用信函方式发出付款指示给国外的代理行,所发生的直接成本比较低,而且付款指示抵达国外代理行的邮寄时间较长,给了汇出行占压资金的时间,因此,银行收取的手续费较低。

(2)时间较长。信汇的优先级别较低,银行在办理信汇时不会像电汇那么迅速。而且以信函邮寄支付的指令必然比通过电传或 SWIFT 系统传送支付的指令要慢很多。

(3)安全性低。信函的传递要经历多次中转,传递过程中可能会导致积压或者丢失,这些都会影响汇款的顺利进行。目前信汇方式较少使用。

3. 业务流程(图 3.2)

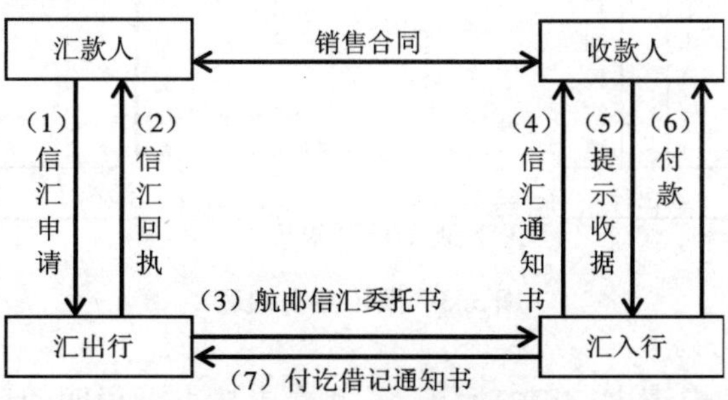

图 3.2　信汇业务流程

(1)汇款人填写汇款申请书,交款项、汇费,并在申请书上说明使用信汇方式。

(2)汇出行审核后,汇款人取得信汇回执。

(3)汇出行根据汇款申请书缮制信汇委托书或支付委托书,邮寄给汇入行。

(4)汇入行收到后,核对印鉴无误,将信汇委托书的第二联信汇通知书及第三、四联收据正副本一并通知收款人。

(5)收款人凭收据取款。

(6)汇入行借记汇出行账户,并解付款项给收款人。

(7)汇入行将付讫借记通知书寄给汇出行,通知它款项已解付完毕。

3.2.3 票汇(D/D)

1. 含义

票汇(Demand Draft,D/D)是汇出行应汇款人的申请,代汇款人开立以其分行或代理行为解付行的银行即期汇票(Banker's Demand Draft),支付一定金额给收款人的一种汇款方式。

这种支付方式下,银行用即期汇票作为汇款工具。具体做法是:汇出行应汇款人的要求,在其把汇款交给银行后开立一张银行汇票交给汇款人,由汇款人将汇票带到国外亲自取款或将汇票邮寄给国外的收款人,由收款人自己前去银行取款,或将汇票背书转让。

2. 特点

(1)取款灵活。电汇、信汇的收款人只能从汇入行一家取款;而采用票汇,汇票的持票人可以将汇票卖给任何一家汇出行的代理行,只要该行有汇出行的印鉴,能核对汇票签字的真伪,确认签字无误后,就会买入汇票。

(2)收款人方便。汇款人自行携带或寄出,随收款人方便,在有效期内可以随时取款。

(3)银行手续费用较低。汇入行不负通知债权人取款之责,不必花时间、人力去通知收款人,节省了手续。

3. 业务流程(图3.3)

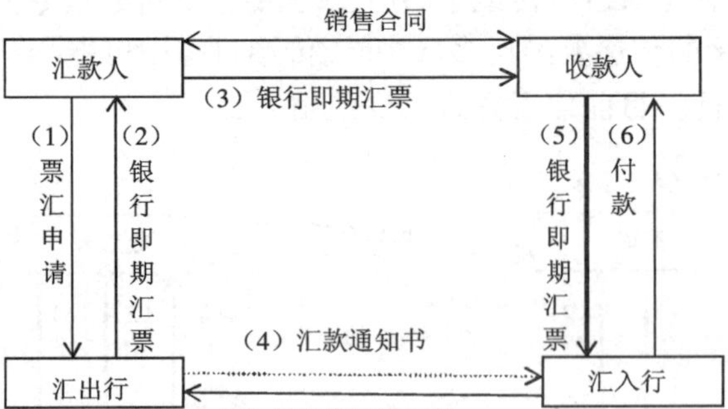

图3.3 票汇业务流程

(1)汇款人填写汇款申请书,交款项、汇费,并在申请书上说明使用票汇方式。

(2)汇出行作为出票行,开立银行即期汇票交给汇款人。

(3)汇款人将汇票寄收款人。

(4)汇出行将汇款通知书,又称票根,即汇票一式五联中的第二联寄汇入行。汇入行将此联与收款人提交的汇票正本核对。近年来,银行为了简化手续,汇出行已不再寄汇款通知书了,汇票从一式五联改为一式四联,取消了汇款通知书联。

(5)收款人提示银行即期汇票要求付款。

(6)汇入行借记汇出行账户,并解付款项给收款人。

(7)汇入行将付讫借记通知书寄给汇出行,通知它款项已解付完毕。

3.3 三种汇款方式的比较

电汇、信汇、票汇三种汇款方式比较如下。

3.3.1 使用支付工具的比较

电汇使用电报、电传或SWIFT方式,用密押证实;信汇使用信汇委托书或支付委托书,用印鉴或签字证实;票汇使用银行即期汇票,用印鉴或签字证实。

3.3.2 汇款人成本费用的比较

电汇因使用现代化通信设施且银行不能占用客户资金,所以成本费用较高;信汇、票汇的费用较电汇低。

3.3.3 安全方面的比较

电汇因银行间直接通信,能短时间迅速到达对方,减少了中间环节,安全性较高;信汇必须通过银行和邮政系统来完成,信汇委托书有可能在邮寄途中遗失或延误,影响款项的及时性;票汇虽有灵活的优点,但有丢失或毁损的风险,背书转让会带来一连串的债权债务关系,容易陷入汇票纠纷,汇票遗失以后,挂失或止付的手续比较麻烦。因此信汇、票汇的安全性不及电汇。

3.3.4 汇款速度的比较

电汇因使用现代化手段且优先级较高,一般均当天处理,交款迅速,是最快捷的汇款方式。尽管其费用较高,但可用缩短资金在途时间的利息来抵补。在目前的实务中,电汇在整个汇款业务笔数中有比例增大的趋势;信汇方式由于资金在途时间长,手续多,日显落后,在实务中已基本不用;票汇的速度不及电汇,但因其具有灵活简便的特点,使用量仅次于电汇。

三种汇款方式的比较见表3.1。

表 3.1　三种汇款方式的比较

	T/T	M/T	D/D
支付工具	电报、电传或 SWIFT	信汇委托书或支付委托书	银行即期汇票
成本费用	高	低	最低
安全性	比较安全	有可能在邮寄中遗失或延误	有丢失或毁损的风险，背书转让易陷于纠纷，挂失手续麻烦
汇款速度	最快	慢	最慢

3.4　汇款的偿付

汇款的偿付（Reimbursement of Remittance）也叫“头寸的调拨”，即汇出行委托汇入行付款给收款人，应及时将汇款金额向汇入行拨交头寸或偿付汇款。按照拨款和解付的先后来分，有两种偿付方式，一种是汇出行发出汇款指示（Payment Order，P. O.）后先拨付头寸给汇入行，另一种是汇入行解付货款给收款人后再向汇出行索偿。根据汇出行与汇入行账户的开设情况，头寸的拨付方式有以下几种。

3.4.1　汇出行在汇入行开有账户，汇出行授权借记（图 3.4）

如果汇出行在汇入行开有账户，汇出行发出付款指令后授权汇入行借记其账户金额，汇入行在付款后应向汇出行发送借记报单。通常支付委托书上的指示为“Please debit our a/c with you”或者“In cover, we authorized you to debit the sum to our a/c with you”（请借记我行在你行的账户）。

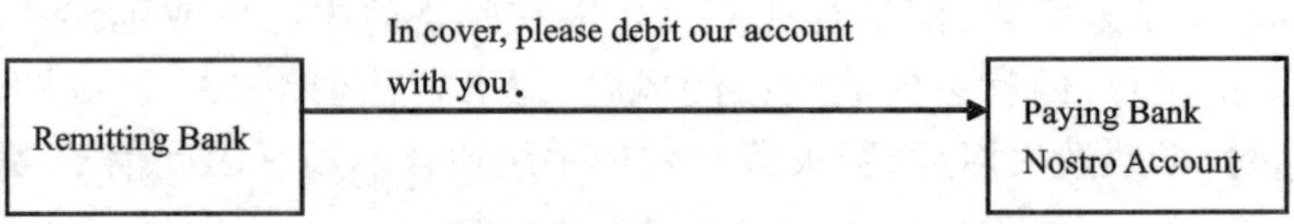

图 3.4　汇出行在汇入行开有账户，汇出行授权借记

3.4.2　汇入行在汇出行开有账户，汇出行主动贷记（图 3.5）

如果汇入行在汇出行开有账户，汇出行发出付款指令后，应主动将相应的头寸贷记该账户，并向汇入行发送贷记报单。通常在支付委托书上注明“In cover, we have credited the sum to your a/c with us”（已贷记你行在我行的账户）。

3.4.3　汇出行与汇入行没有账户关系（图 3.6）

汇出行与汇入行有共同的账户行，即双方在同一家银行开有账户，可以通过该银行进行转账。汇出行一方面向汇入行发出付款指令，另一方面向共同的账户行发出银行转账通知，要求其先借记汇出行的账户，然后再贷记汇入行的账户，将头寸拨付给汇入行在该行的账户。

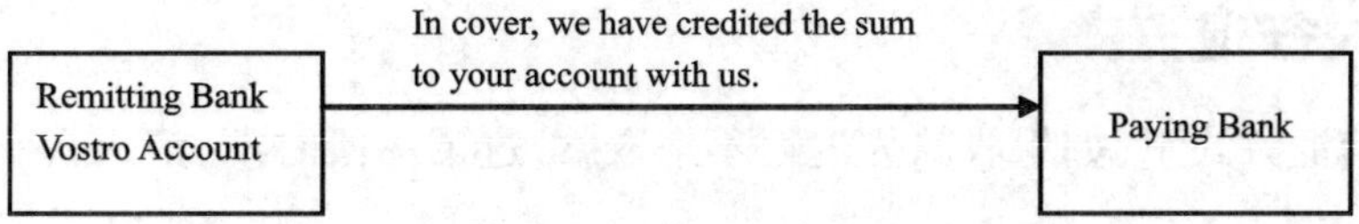

图3.5 汇入行在汇出行开有账户,汇出行主动贷记

汇入行在收到汇出行的电汇指令及共同账户的贷记报单后,即可付款给收款人。

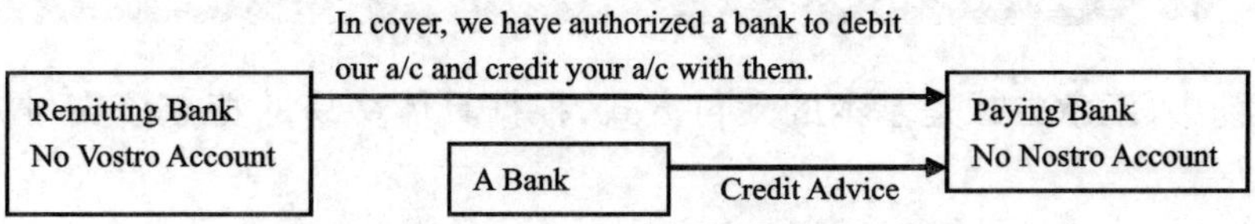

图3.6 汇出行与汇入行没有账户关系

3.5 汇款的退汇

退汇(Return of Remittance)也叫撤销支付,指在解付以前撤销汇款。退汇可能由收款人提出,也可能由汇款人提出。如果是汇款人提出的,当汇款尚未解付时,汇出行和汇入行应同意汇款人的退汇请求;如果汇款已经解付,则不能接受退汇的请求。

3.5.1 收款人退汇

收款人退汇比较方便,在电汇、信汇时,只要他拒收汇款,将退汇要求通知汇入行即可。汇入行将汇款委托书退回汇出行,然后由汇出行通知汇款人前来办理退汇,取回汇款。在票汇时,收款人退汇只需要将汇票寄给汇款人,然后汇款人到汇出行办理退汇手续即可。

3.5.2 汇款人退汇

汇款人退汇必须在汇入行解付以前,手续相对烦琐。退汇的办理程序如下。

(1)向汇出行递交退汇申请书。以书面形式向汇出行提出退汇申请,说明退汇理由。如果是票汇方式下的退汇,汇票已经寄给收款人或估计汇票已经在市场上流通,则汇款人就要直接找收款人交涉,将汇票背书后交回汇出行。

(2)汇出行审查退汇申请。如必要还可要求汇款人提供担保书,保证承担汇出行因退汇而可能受到的一切损失。在汇票遗失的情况下,通常必须提供担保书。

(3)汇出行发出退汇通知,告知汇入行停止支付款项,并退回已拨付的头寸。

(4)汇入行退汇。如果汇款未解付,汇入行应寄回汇款凭证及退汇通知,并退回汇款头寸。如果汇款已解付无法退回,则寄回收款人取款的凭条。

(5)汇出行收到头寸后,将款退还给汇款人,并注销有关汇票。

3.5.3 汇入行退汇

在电汇和信汇方式下，如果收款人迟迟不来取款，过了一段时期，汇入行有权主动通知汇出行注销，办理退汇。

3.6 汇款方式在国际贸易中的应用

在国际贸易中，汇款方式是基本的支付方式，根据具体交易的特点该支付方式可以分为如下几种。

3.6.1 预付货款(Payment in Advance)

预付货款又称先结后出，实务中一般通过电汇完成汇款，也称为“前 T/T”，是进口商对出口商出口交易的一种融资行为。进口商在出口商将货物或货运单据交付以前将货款全部或部分付给出口商，出口商收到货款后，再根据约定发运货物。

预付货款对出口商最有利，一方面出口商没有任何风险，另一方面出口商获得了进口商的融资，提高了资金使用效率。相反，预付货款对进口商非常不利，资金被占用且贸易风险极大，付款后要承担不能按时、按质、按量收到合同约定的货物，甚至因对方欺诈导致钱货两空的风险。

因为预付货款的上述特点，一般在国际贸易中在下述情形下考虑使用该支付方式。

(1)对于买方急需的紧俏商品，进口商为达成交易，以此为竞争性贸易条件吸引对方或被迫接受这种支付方式。

(2)出口商与进口商同属一个跨国公司，内部交易不存在风险问题。或出口商信誉极佳，是长期合作的伙伴，可以考虑预付货款。

(3)进口商信誉不佳，或出口商对进口商的资信不了解，为避免交易风险，须预付货款。

(4)生产成套设备、大型机械、飞机、船舶等，或出口商为进口商定制生产产品时，出口商一般在生产前要求进口商预付一定比例的货款作为生产订金，等货物生产完毕发运前支付全额货款或者分期支付货款。

(5)在某些运输方式下，由于出口商发运货物后将失去对货物物权的控制，因此需要预付货款。

由于预付货款对进口商风险太大，预防风险的一种措施就是充分了解对方的资信，另外可以要求出口商提供银行保函，如因各种原因出口商不能履约，银行返还预付货款。

3.6.2 货到付款(Payment after Arrival of the Goods)

货到付款在实务中一般通过电汇完成汇款，也称为“后 T/T”，与预付货款相反，它是出口商先发货，进口商收到货以后再安排支付货款给出口商的一种支付方式。这种支付方式有时也被称为延期付款(Deferred Payment)或赊销(Open Account，O/A)。

货到付款对进口商非常有利，可以说是出口商对进口商的一种交易融资，而且进口商不承担任何风险。如果货物不符合合同要求,进口商可要求退货、换货或者折价。相反,出口商由于已经交货,失去了对物权的控制,有钱货两空的风险。而且,一旦货物质量有瑕疵,容易被对方要挟降价。

考虑到该支付方式的上述特点,货到付款在国际贸易中一般应用于下列的情形。

1. 售定合同

这是规定出口商先发货,再由进口商按合同规定的货物售价和付款时间进行汇款的一种结算方式,又叫"先出后结"。该方式通常用于鲜活商品或快速消费品的买卖中,一般进出口商有多年的合作基础,相互信赖。

2. 寄售合同

这是规定出口商将货物发往国外,委托国外商人按照议定的条件在当地市场代为销售,等货物销售后,国外进口商将扣除佣金和相关费用的货款汇给出口商的交易方式。这种交易方式适用于国内滞销商品或有缺陷商品的促销;新产品在国外试销,为了打开国外市场;参加国外交易会或博览会后产品的处理等。由于出口商承担了完全的风险,因此要求进口商是负责任、有资信的企业。

3.6.3 见提单后付款(Payment after Receipt of the Fax of B/L)

见提单后付款在实务中一般通过电汇完成汇款,与货到付款有些类似,都是后T/T的一种。但其与货到付款不同的是,货物可能实际未到,进口商在见到出口商发货后取得的船公司提单传真件后即安排付款。

这种支付方式对进口商而言,见到提单意味着出口商发货了,避免了预付货款的风险——出口商收到钱不发货;对出口商而言,比货到付款要较早收到款项,加速了资金周转。当然,总的来说还是出口商承担的风险更大,而且即便见到提单,进口商可能还是会拖延付款,实际效果与货到付款一样。

3.6.4 交单付现(Cash Against Documents,缩写为C. A. D.)

交单付现又叫凭单付汇,指进口商通过银行将款项汇给出口商所在地银行(汇入行),并指示该行凭出口商提交的货运单据即可付款给出口商的一种结算方式。

相对前三种付款方式,交单付现对买卖双方来说风险更加均衡。出口商的货款以物权凭证的提单做交换取得,进口商的货物以向银行付汇换取提单取得。所以,交单付现是一种有条件的付汇方式,不同于前面三种无条件的付款方式。

3.7 汇款结算方式的特点

汇款方式是以银行为中间媒介来结算进出口双方的债权债务关系。在汇款方式中,进口商委托银行汇款,银行在接受汇款申请及收到进口商的款项后,通过其与国外代理行或分行的来往账户划拨资金来完成汇款业务。在整个业务中,银行扮演一个中介的角色,并不承担买卖双方的任何交易风险,仅仅需要按照汇款申请书代为付款即可,所以汇款是一种商业信用的结算方式。

汇款作为结算方式可以单独使用,也可以与其他结算方式结合使用。在国际贸易中使用汇款的结算方式,要考虑到其下述特点。

3.7.1 风险大

预付货款和货到付款都属于商业信用。无论是预付货款还是货到付款,总是一方承担极大的风险而另一方承担极小的风险,风险对买卖双方极不均衡。因此,承担风险较大的一方能否达到自己的商业目的完全依赖于对方的信用。因此,该支付方式适用于较熟悉和信誉较好的合作伙伴之间的交易或支付小额资金。

3.7.2 资金负担不平衡

预付货款的买方和货到付款的卖方在交易中均承担了最大的风险,而且这种支付方式相当于为交易向对方提供了融资,加重了自身的资金负担。

3.7.3 手续简便,费用低廉

汇款方式相对于其他的支付方式手续简便,银行收费较低。因此在交易双方相互信任的情形下,或者跨国公司内部的不同子公司之间,汇款是比较常见的支付方式。从全球的角度看,百分之七十的贸易结算都是采用汇款方式。

思考题

1. 汇付的当事人有哪些?采用汇付的支付方式要考虑哪些因素?
2. 电汇、信汇和票汇的工作流程是怎样的?
3. 汇付有哪些特点?

Chapter 3

International Remittance

3.1 International remittance

International remittance happens when a client (remitter) asks his bank to send a sum of money to the beneficiary abroad by one of the transfer methods at this option. The beneficiary can be paid at the designated bank, which is either the remitting bank's overseas branch or its correspondent.

3.2 Parties of international remittance

1. The remitter

The remitter is also the payer and the importer who asks his bank to transfer a sum of money to a beneficiary.

2. Remitting bank

Normally, it is the bank that located in the country the remitter. The bank transfers money to its correspondent or its branch in another country.

3. The beneficiary

The beneficiary is the payee, who is addressed to receive the remittance.

4. Paying bank

Paying bank is the bank entrusted by the remitting bank to pay a certain amount of money to the beneficiary named in the remittance advice.

3.3 Methods of international remittance

3.3.1 Remittance by cable/telex/SWIFT

Telegraphic transfer or telex transfer, often abbreviated to TT, is a historic term used to refer to an electronic means of transferring funds overseas. A transfer charge is collected while sending money.

Historically "T/T" meant a cable message from one bank to another in order to effect the transfer of money. Prior to the existence of electronic payment networks this was often directly between banks via telex message.

Originally, this process made use of the telegraph as a means of transferring money between a point of origin and a point of termination. Today, the process of transferring money between two parties no longer involves the telegraph, but the use of the term remains common in several countries.

Sometimes referred to as a telex transfer or simply TT, the telegraphic transfer has long been a means of communication between banking institutions. In days gone by, the telegraphic transfer could be used to send money from an account in one bank to an account at another bank located anywhere else in the world. Generally, there were charges associated with the performance of a transfer, with both the sender and the recipient paying a small fee for the transaction.

Well into the 20th century, persons could also make use of a telegraphic transfer to move entire balances of funds from one bank to another. For example, a person living in New York City may take a job located in Los Angeles. Rather than with drawing funds from existing bank accounts and physically transporting the funds across the country, the individual would establish new accounts in Los Angeles and then authorize the two banks involved to transfer all the funds into the new accounts. At that point, the accounts at the New York bank would be closed.

Most international transfers are executed through the Society for Worldwide Interbank Financial Telecommunication (SWIFT). It provides a network that enables financial institutions worldwide to send and receive information about financial transactions in a secure, standardized and reliable environment and it is a co-operative society founded in 1974 by seven international banks, which operate a global network to facilitate the transfer of financial messages. Using these messages, banks can exchange data for the transfer of funds between financial institutions. SWIFT's headquarters are in La Hulpe, on the outskirts of Brussels, Belgium. The society also acts as a United Nations-sanctioned international standards body for the creation and maintenance of financial-messaging standards. See SWIFT Standards.

Each financial institution is assigned an ISO 9362 code, also called a Bank Identifier Code (BIC) or SWIFT Code. These codes are generally eight characters long. For example: Deutsche Bank is an international bank with its head office in Frankfurt, Germany, the SWIFT Code for which is DEUTDEFF:

DEUT identifies Deutsche Bank,

DE is the country code for Germany,

FF is the code for Frankfurt.

Using an extended code of 11 digits (if the receiving bank has assigned extended codes to branches or to processing areas) allows the payment to be directed to a specific office. For example: DEUTDEFF500 would direct the payment to an office of Deutsche Bank in Bad Homburg. SWIFT deviate slightly from the standard though by using position nine for a Logical Terminal ID, making their extended codes 12 digits long.

3.3.2 Remittance by demand draft

Remittance by banker's demand draft (check) refers to a remitter instructs the remitting bank to draw a demand draft on its affiliate /correspondent/branch bank, ordering the drawee bank to make payment at sight to the payee or beneficiary upon presentation.

A demand draft is a cheque that contains an order of one branch of a bank (drawer branch) directing another branch of the same bank (drawee branch) to pay on demand a certain sum of money to a specified beneficiary (payee). It is an account payee instrument, meaning it can only be credited to the account of the payee and cannot be encashed over the counter by the payee.

A demand draft is a much safer and certain method of payment than cheques, since in the case of cheques, an individual is the drawer and hence the cheque can be dishonoured by the drawee bank due to insufficiency of funds in the drawer's account. But since in the case of a DD, the drawer is a bank, payment is certain and it cannot be dishonoured.

Universities require payment of application fee to be done through a secure means, like a DD. In this case, the student would apply to his bank to get a DD issued favoring Delhi University. Suppose the student resides in Mumbai. Suppose he holds an account in a particular branch of SBI in Mumbai. In this case, this particular SBI branch in Mumbai would be the drawer branch, a SBI branch located in Delhi (typically the service branch) would be the drawee branch and Delhi University would be the payee.

Since it is a cheque issued by a bank (that is, the drawer is a bank) it does not carry the signature of the customer, unlike the case of ordinary cheques which carry the signature of the customer (who is the drawer). Instead, a DD carries signatures of one or two bank officials, depending on the DD amount. Usually the DD will carry the name/code of the drawee branch and of the issuing (the drawer) branch both. The placement of this varies from bank to bank.

Pay orders, also called local DDs or bankers' cheques, are cheques where the drawer and the drawee branch is the same. These are used for local payments (that is, payments within a city).

An applicant for a demand draft is required to fill in a DD request slip, mentioning the amount, payee's name, issuing branch, location the draft should be payable at, his name, signature and account number etc. In most cases, the purchaser of the draft is an account holder with the bank, hence he can authorize the bank to debit (that is, take out funds from) his account either through a cheque or a debit mandate. The cheque should be drawn in favor of "Yourself for the issue of DD favoring XYZ", where XYZ refers to the payee of the DD.

The bank levies charges for the DD, in the form of a commission. Hence the customer has to pay an amount equal to (DD amount + commission + service tax).

DDs can also be issued against the payment of cash by the purchaser, but in this case, the total amount (inclusive of commission and taxes) should not exceed Rs. 49,999.

Since DD is a kind of cheque, the principle of cheque clearing also applies to DD. In the example mentioned above, if the payee, Delhi University does not hold an account with SBI, but with another bank, say PNB, it would deposit the cheque in its PNB branch and the PNB officials would lodge the DD in outward clearing. (The DD would be sent to the local Clearing House.)

第 4 章 托收

4.1 托收的含义与当事人

托收(Collection)是委托收款的简称,是出口商在货物装运后,开具以进口商为付款人的汇票(一般都随附商业单据,如发票、提单等),委托出口地银行通过它在国外的分行或代理行(进口国银行)向出口商收取货款的一种结算方式。

根据《托收统一规则》(*Uniform Rules for Collection*),托收的含义是银行根据所收到的指示处理金融单据或商业单据,以便取得付款或承兑,凭付款交单或承兑交单,或按照其他条款和条件交单的一种结算方式。其目的是:①取得付款或承兑;②凭付款或承兑交付单据;③按其他条件和条款交单。这里,金融单据指汇票、本票、支票或其他取得付款的类似凭证;商业单据指发票、运输单据、物权单据或其他类似单据,一切不属于金融单据的都可归于商业单据。

托收业务的基本当事人有四个:委托人、托收行、代收行和付款人,有时根据业务需要也会有其他当事人:提示行和需要时的代理。

4.1.1 委托人(Principal)

委托人也称出票人,是填写托收申请书,委托银行办理托收业务的人,通常是出口商。在实务中,出口商按照合同规定按时发货,将取得的货运单据连同开具的汇票交给银行,委托银行通过其国外代理行或分行向进口商索取货款。

4.1.2 托收行(Remitting Bank)

托收行也称出口商的银行,是接受出口商的委托办理托收业务的银行。托收行与委托人之间是委托代理关系,有义务按照托收申请书的要求行事。托收行有权审核托收申请并决定是否接受委托申请,一旦接受,只能按照申请书的要求办理托收业务。因此,托收行给代收行的业务指令也应该以托收申请书为基础,不能超越申请书的范围自由行事。作为业务的代办机构,托收行没有任何义务审核单据,也没有保证收到款项的义务。

4.1.3 代收行(Collecting Bank)

代收行也称进口商的银行,是接受托收行的委托向进口商收款的进口地银行,一般是托收行在国外的分行或代理行。代收行应遵从托收行的指令行事,审核随附单据的数量、名称是否与托收指示相符;按指示要求处理单据并尽快向进口商提示汇票,要求其付款或承兑;付款人付款或承兑后应毫无延误地通知托收行。

4.1.4 付款人(Payer 或 Drawee)

付款人也是汇票的受票人,通常是支付货款的进口商。代收行依据托收行的指示向付款人提示汇票要求其在即期汇票下见票付款或在远期汇票下先行承兑,后到期付款。付款人应当按照合同要求承担付款赎单的责任和义务,但付款人与托收行无任何关系,若其拒付,代收行也不能强迫其付款或承兑。

4.1.5 提示行(Presenting Bank)

提示行是向付款人提示汇票和单据并要求其付款的银行,通常由代收行兼任。如果代收行与付款人之间没有直接往来或不在同一个城市,就会安排提示行代为向付款人提示付款或承兑。

4.1.6 需要时的代理(Principal's Representative in Case of Need)

需要时的代理是委托人在付款人所在地的指定代理人,负责在付款人拒绝付款赎单时,代委托人办理货物存仓、保险、转售或运回等事宜,以最大程度地减少委托人的损失。

4.2 托收的种类

根据托收时是否向银行提交代表物权凭证的货运单据,托收分为光票托收和跟单托收。

4.2.1 光票托收(Clean Collection)

1. 含义与特点

根据国际商会《托收统一规则》的规定,光票托收是仅使用金融单据(主要是汇票、本票、支票),不附带商业单据(主要指货运单据),委托银行代收款项的一种托收结算方式。光票托收并不一定不附带任何单据,有时也附有一些非货运单据,如发票、垫款清单等,这种情况仍为光票托收。光票托收时,货运单据由卖方直接寄给买方,汇票等则交银行委托收款。由于光票托收不涉及物权的转移或货物的处理,银行业务比较简单。

光票托收的单据,由收款人做成空白背书,托收行做成记名背书给代收行,并制作托收指示,随汇票寄给代收行托收票款。光票托收的汇票在期限上也应有即期和远期两种。但在实际业务中,由于一般金额不大,即期付款的汇票居多。

2. 业务流程

光票托收的流程与跟单托收没有太大的区别。首先由委托人填写托收申请书,开具托收汇票交付托收行,然后托收行依据托收申请制作托收指示,将托收指示、汇票及随附单据一并航邮给代收行。对于即期汇票,代收行收到汇票后应即刻联系付款人提示付款,付款人付款后代收行将汇票交与付款人入账;对于远期汇票,代收行收到汇票后应即刻联系付款人提示承兑，于到期日再次向付款人提示付款。如果遭遇付款人拒绝付款或承兑，除非另有指示，代收行应在法定期限内做成拒绝证书，并将拒付情况通知托收行。

光票托收对出口商风险很大，出口商只有在确信进口商能遵守合同和及时付款的情形下才采用这种支付方式，我国贸易人士很少在国际贸易中采用这种做法。但欧洲一些国家之间的贸易，由于货物到达目的地的时间要早于单据到达的时间，就给进口商及时办理报关、提货带来了不便，还可能会产生额外的仓储等费用。为了避免这种情况出现，这些国家之间的贸易较多使用不代表物权的货运单据，如空运单、海运单、铁路运单、邮局收据等，这些单据不能背书转让，也不是提货凭证，这就导致了光票托收的大量使用。

4.2.2 跟单托收(Documentary Collection)

1. 含义与特点

跟单托收是附有商业单据的托收，主要附有代表物权的货运单据。跟单托收下，卖方开具托收汇票，连同商业单据(主要是代表物权的货运单据)一起交给托收行。跟单托收也包括不使用金融票据如汇票的情况，如欧洲大陆国家使用汇票政府要收印花税，为了避免印花税负担，一般的即期付款托收不使用汇票。

2. 跟单托收的分类

根据代收行不同的交单方式，跟单托收可以分为付款交单和承兑交单。

1)付款交单(Documents against Payment, D/P)

付款交单是委托人指示代收行在付款人付清款项后将单据交出。付款交单按照委托人开出的汇票期限的不同可以分为即期付款交单和远期付款交单两种形式。

(1)即期付款交单(Documents against Payment at Sight, D/P at Sight)是代收行向进口商提示跟单汇票要求其付款，进口商见票后付款，代收行即交付单据给进口商。在即期付款交单中，付款人在代收行提示单据时即刻付款，因此汇票不是必需的。采用即期付款交单方式，出口商可以开立即期汇票，也可以不开立即期汇票。

(2)远期付款交单(Documents against Payment after Sight, D/P after Sight)是代收行向进口商提示跟单汇票要求其承兑，进口商承兑后代收行保管单据及汇票，于汇票到期日向进口商提示付款，进口商付款后代收行即放单给进口商。

对比上述两种付款交单方式，在远期付款交单中，出口商出具的是远期汇票，不同于即期付款交单中使用的是即期汇票。另外，远期付款交单在实务中存在一些操作上的问题。例如，严格地按照远期付款交单的定义操作，可能货物到港却由于汇票未到期进口商无法提货导致货物滞港产生一系列的费用，加重进口商的负担；一些国家的银行认为进口商的承兑行为已经使得进口商承担了付款义务却无法享有相应的获得单据的权利是不公平的行为，因此一些银行在处理此类业务时按照承兑交单来操作，但这样做可能会导致出口商对物权提前失去控制，加大了出口商的风险。由于国际商会的相关规定遵从地区的操作惯例，因此这些地方银行将远期付款交单改为承兑交单处理后，一旦汇票到期进口商没有付款，出口商是无法向该地区银行索赔的。为了避免地方惯例与定义产生的冲突，国际商会在URC522中明确规定：托收不应含有凭付款交付商业单据的远期汇票，其用意就在于提醒贸易商不要采取远期汇票付款交单的结算方式。

2)承兑交单(Documents against Acceptance,D/A)

承兑交单是代收行在付款人承兑远期汇票后,把货运单据交给付款人,于汇票到期日由付款人付款的一种交单方式。在承兑交单方式下,出口商面临的风险比付款交单要大,因为出口商实际没有收款却已经丧失对物权的控制。

虽然承兑交单与远期付款交单使用的都是远期汇票,但严格的远期付款交单与承兑交单对出口商的风险是不同的。前者凭付款人的承兑即可获得商业单据,后者仍然需要远期汇票到期付款后才能获得商业单据。为避免地方某些银行将远期付款交单处理为承兑交单的惯例发生,出口商应当在托收指示书中明确一定要付款才能交单,否则银行承担相应的责任,从而排除地方惯例的作用。同时,URC522 也明确:如果托收含有远期付款的汇票,托收指示书应注明商业单据是凭承兑交单还是付款交单。如果无此注明,则商业单据仅能凭付款交付,代收行对因延迟交付而产生的任何后果不负责任。

3)业务流程(图 4.1)

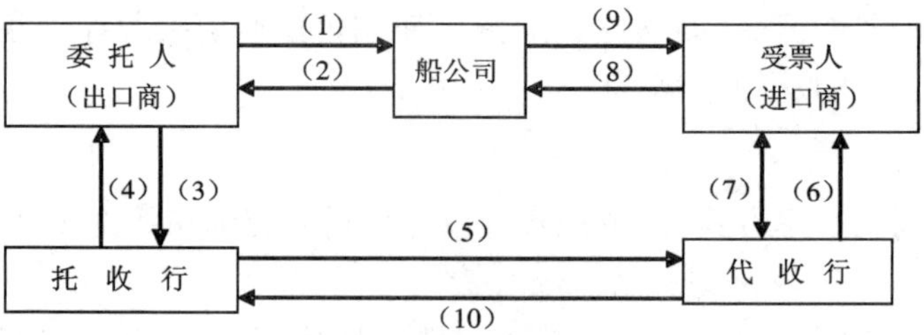

图 4.1 跟单托收业务流程

(1)进出口商确定合同支付方式为付款交单后,出口商将货物交给船公司发运。

(2)船公司收到货物后,签发代表物权凭证的海运提单给出口商。

(3)出口商填写托收申请书并将提单、发票等单据交付银行办理托收。

(4)托收行审核出口商提交的托收申请书,并审核出口商提交的单据数量及种类是否与托收申请书一致。

(5)托收行缮制托收面函,连同即期/远期汇票、货运单据等寄交代收行委托其代收货款。

(6)国外代收行收到单据后,审核其是否与托收面函一致。审核无误后向进口商提示承兑或付款(远期或即期汇票)。

(7)在承兑交单方式下,进口商承兑远期汇票即可获得代收行的放单;在付款交单方式下,进口商付款后即可获得代收行的放单。

(8)进口商取得商业单据后,凭海运提单向目的港船公司提货。

(9)船公司在运费结清的情况下,凭原始提单换取的提货单(盖有海关放行章)放货。

(10)代收行收到货款后扣除手续费偿付托收行。

4.3　托收结算方式的特点

托收结算方式仍然是一种商业信用,风险对于进出口商是不均衡的,因此比较适合于相互比较信任或有诚信的企业之间的货款结算。

4.3.1　出口商面临的风险

1. 汇率风险

在 D/P 远期或 D/A 方式下,货物发运距离收款有段时间,在该期间内如果合同标价的外币贬值则意味着出口商发生损失。

2. 交易风险

在托收方式下银行不提供任何信用或担保,仅仅提供代收货款的服务。如果货到目的地对方拒绝付款赎单或以货物有瑕疵要求降价,将使出口商面临困境。而在 D/A 方式下,如果进口商到期不付款则出口商面临钱货两空的局面。

3. 政策风险

某些进口国实行贸易管制或外汇管制,如果进口商没有取得进口许可证或没有申请到外汇,出口商贸然发货将会承担货物到港被没收或禁止进口的风险;或者由于政府管制导致进口商无法对外支付外汇。

4.3.2　进口商面临的风险

1. 交易风险

在 D/P 结算方式下,进口商付款赎单提货后,可能会遭遇货物品质与合同不符的情况。在 D/A 结算方式下,进口商承兑后将使得自己承担双重义务,票据的到期付款义务及合同下的买方义务。

2. 信用风险

在 D/P 结算方式下,进口商付款赎单后,如果发现出口商伪造单据,则不得不面临钱货两空的局面。

3. 汇率风险

汇率风险同样适用于进口商,与出口商面临的汇率风险相反,如果货物发运到收款期间合同标价的货币增值则进口商要支付更多的本币进口该货物。

4.4 托收方式下的资金融通

4.4.1 托收押汇(Collection Bill Purchased)

托收押汇是银行对进出口商的融资行为。托收行对出口商的融资称为出口托收押汇，指托收行在出口商办理委托收款时先行买下托收下的单据(按发票价值扣除预期利息及银行手续费)，尤其是代表物权凭证的海运提单，然后等收到款项后归还货款给托收行的融资行为。代收行对进口商的融资称为进口托收押汇，指代收行在进口商与代收行签订进口押汇协议后，购买托收行寄来的商业单据并交付进口商的资金融通行为。

无论是进口托收押汇还是出口托收押汇，银行均承担了较大的风险(进出口商的信用风险、国家风险、外汇风险等)。为规避某些风险，银行对押汇保留追索权。同时，银行提供的仅是资金融通，不承担合同项下的买卖纠纷。

4.4.2 信托收据(Trust Receipt)

在远期付款交单下，进口商承兑远期汇票后要等到汇票到期付款后才能取得托收项下的货运单据提货，这可能导致进口商错过销售旺季或产生仓储及滞港费用。为此，进口商向代收行申请凭信托收据赎单，向银行保证货物所有权仍属于银行，进口商仅代为销售货物，取得的销售货款首先用于支付货款。这种在远期付款交单下进口商凭信托收据提货就是托收行对进口商的融资行为。

在进口商凭信托收据提货的情况下，如果进口商违约不交付货款，而代收行并未从托收行的托收指示中获得凭信托收据放单的指令，意味着代收行要承担向托收行交付货款的责任。因此，凭信托收据放单仅适合于有诚信的进口商。

思考题

1. 为什么托收与汇付一样都是商业信用？银行在此业务中的作用是什么？
2. 托收的当事人有哪些？
3. 比较付款交单、承兑交单、货到付款、预付货款对出口商的风险大小。
4. 托收的工作流程如何？

Chapter 4

Collection

4.1 Introduction to collection

Collection is an arrangement whereby the goods are shipped and a relevant bill of exchange is drawn by the seller on the buyer, and/or shipping documents are forwarded to the seller's bank with clear instructions for collection through one of its correspondent bank located in the domicile of the buyer.

Uniform Rules for Collections mentions that collection means the handling by banks, on instructions received, of documents, in order to:

(1) obtain payment and/or acceptance;

(2) deliver documents against payment and/or against acceptance;

(3) deliver documents on other terms and conditions.

Collections do not give the exporter the security of advance payment or the relative peace of mind that comes from open account transactions with long-term customers in established relationships.

They require both exporter and buyer to exercise great care in agreeing the detail of the sales contract.

The transaction is initiated by the exporter, who dispatches the goods to the buyer's country. At the same time, they entrust the related documents (which may include negotiable bills of lading) to their bank, for collection of sale proceeds and the delivery of documents to the buyer according to the terms of the sales contract.

There are three types of collection:

(1) Clean collections;

(2) Documents against acceptance (D/A);

(3) Documents against payment (D/P).

4.2 Clean collections

For a clean collection, the exporter dispatches the goods and the related documents directly to the buyer and then sends his/her bank the bill of exchange for the value of the goods drawn according to the sales contract. The bank can then set in train the collection of the due amount from the buyer.

(1) The exporter sends goods first to the buyer.

(2) The exporter sends all documents except the bill of exchange to the buyer.

(3) The exporter sends the bill of exchange to his/her own bank.

(4) The exporter's bank sends the bill of exchange to the buyer's bank for it to be presented to the buyer.

(5) The buyer pays the money, which is remitted to the exporter's bank.

1. Advantages

All in favour of the buyer.

2. Disadvantages

All against the exporter. If the buyer does not pay, or if he/she does pay but his/her country blocks remittance of funds to the exporter:

(1) the exporter has neither the goods nor the money;

(2) the exporter may not get his/her goods back.

4.3 Documents against acceptance (D/A)

(1) The exporter sends goods first to the destination country.

(2) The exporter sends the required documents to his/her own bank.

(3) His/her bank sends the required documents to the buyer's bank.

(4) The buyer's bank obtains the buyer's acceptance of the bill of exchange, payable either at an agreed period after sight or on a fixed date in the future, and releases the required documents to the buyer.

(5) The buyer obtains delivery of the goods.

The documents referred to in a documentary collection D/A usually include:

(1) a bill of exchange drawn payable at a future date;

(2) the transport documents needed to obtain delivery of the goods along with other related documents.

For a documentary collection D/A, the exporter (through the bill of exchange) does not authorize release of the transport documents until the buyer accepts the bill of exchange for payment at a definite future date. Once the buyer accepts the bill of exchange, the buyer's bank releases the transport documents needed to obtain delivery of the goods and any other remaining documents.

The buyer can then take possession of the goods for which he/she has agreed to pay in terms of the accepted bill at a definite date in the future.

1. Advantages

All in favour of the buyer.

2. Disadvantages

All against the exporter. If the buyer does not pay on the due date, or if he/she does pay but his/her country blocks remittance of funds to exporter:

(1) the exporter has neither the goods nor the money;

(2) the exporter may not get the goods back.

4.4 Documents against payment (D/P)

The documents referred to in a documentary collection D/P usually include:

(1) a bill of exchange drawn payable at sight, at an agreed period after sight, or on a fixed date in the future;

(2) the transport documents needed to obtain delivery of the goods;

(3) together with other related documents.

The essential word in D/P collections is "payment". There are two types of D/P collection, according to when payment is made, but in both types the documents that give title to the goods are released to the buyer only upon payment. Unlike collections on D/A terms, collections on D/P terms leave the exporter in effective control of the goods until payment.

1. Payment at sight

(1) The exporter sends goods first to the destination country.

(2) The exporter sends the required documents to his/her own bank.

(3) The bank sends the required documents to the buyer's bank.

(4) The buyer's bank obtains the buyer's payment and releases the required documents to the buyer.

(5) The buyer obtains delivery of the goods.

For a documentary collection D/P with payment at sight, the terms of the sales contract stipulate that the buyer must pay as soon as the exporter presents the documents. Upon such payment, the exporter releases the transport documents (typically including bills of lading that grant title to the goods) to the buyer, who can then arrange for delivery of the goods.

1) Advantages

Mostly in favour of the exporter, who retains control over the goods until payment is made.

2) Disadvantages

If the buyer's country blocks remittance of funds to the exporter:

(1) the exporter has neither the goods nor the money;

(2) the exporter may not get the goods back, if the buyer does not pay.

2. Payment at an agreed period after sight or on a fixed date in the future

For a documentary collection D/P with payment at an agreed period after sight, the terms of the sales contract stipulate that the bills of exchange be drawn at say 30, 60, 90 or 120 days (or another agreed period) after sight.

Alternatively, the bill of exchange may be payable on a fixed date in the future. The buyer is required to accept the bill of exchange for payment at the defined future date, but the exporter does not immediately release the transport documents (which give title to the goods). Thus, the buyer does not immediately get delivery of the goods.

(1) The exporter sends goods first to the destination country.

(2) The exporter sends the required documents to his/her own bank.

(3) The bank sends the required documents to the buyer's bank.

(4) The buyer's bank obtains the buyer's acceptance of the bill of exchange payable on a defined future date, and retains all documents in its custody.

(5) On (or before) the defined future date, the buyer's bank obtains the buyer's payment and releases the required documents to the buyer.

(6) The buyer obtains delivery of the goods.

The buyer makes payment on the defined future payment date. The exporter then releases the documents to the buyer, enabling the buyer to take delivery of the goods. If the goods arrive before the defined future payment date, and if the buyer then wishes to take delivery of the goods, the buyer must still make payment before receiving the documents that enable him/her to take delivery of the goods.

1) Advantages

Mostly in favour of the exporter, who retains control over the goods until payment is made.

2) Disadvantages

If the buyer's country blocks remittance of funds to the exporter:

(1) the exporter has neither the goods nor the money;

(2) the exporter may not get the goods back, if the buyer does not pay.

第 5 章

信用证

5.1 信用证的含义及特点

5.1.1 含义

简单来理解，信用证是银行做出的有条件付款承诺。即开证行在申请人(进口商)的请求下向受益人(出口商)开出有条件付款的书面文件，承诺如果出口商能按照信用证及相关规则要求提交相关的单据(提单、发票、质检单等)，开证行保证支付信用证下的款项。因为信用证常常要求提交相符单据作为付款的条件，因此，信用证也被称为“跟单信用证(Documentary Credit)”。

《跟单信用证统一惯例》UCP600 对信用证的定义是：信用证指一项约定，无论其如何命名或描述，该约定不可撤销并因此构成开证行对于相符交单提示予以兑付的确定承诺。(UCP Article 2: Credit means any arrangements, however named or described, that is irrevocable and constitutes a definite undertaking of the issuing to honour a complying presentation.)

这里，相符交单指交单要符合信用证条款要求与 UCP600 及国际标准银行实务保持一致。(UCP Article 2: Complying presentation means a presentation is in accordance with the terms and conditions of the credit, the applicable provisions of the rules and the international standard banking practice.)

由上述定义可知，信用证下相符交单不仅仅是传统教材所说的“单证相符、单单相符”，而应该另外加上“单证与 UCP600 相符、单证与标准银行实务相符”。因此，学习信用证支付方式应该掌握这两个规则中对于信用证下制单审单的要求，这样才能避免由于不符交单而导致的损失。

5.1.2 特点

1. 信用证是银行信用，开证行承担第一性的付款责任

不同于汇款与托收的支付方式，信用证是银行信用。所谓银行信用，是指银行或其他金融机构以货币形式提供的信用。信用证支付方式是一种银行信用，表示银行以自己的信用做出付款承诺，该承诺被接受后，做出承诺的银行即承担第一性的付款责任。当然，这种付款承诺是有条件的，即满足四个条件：单据数量、内容与信用证要求相符，单据之间相符，单据符合 UCP600 要求，单据符合国际标准银行实务要求。信用证下的付款是出口商与银行之间的债权债务关系,其关系建立的基础是信用证,与进口商是无关的。双方的义务分别是:出口商交付相符单据、银行交付货款。所以,即便进口商破产,银行也要向交付了相符单据的出口商付款。这样,信用证支付方式就规避了汇款与托收方式下的企业商业信用的风险,即出口商由于进口商的不诚信或进口商由于出口商的不诚信而导致的损失。所以,信用证下开证银行的付款责任是一种独立的责任,与进口商无关。

2. 信用证是一种独立文件,不依附于贸易合同

信用证作为一种支付方式,其付款的基础是开证行向出口商(受益人)开出的信用证。信用证是怎么开出的呢?信用证是依据开证申请人(进口商)填写的开证申请书开出的,开证申请书是进口商依据贸易合同填写的。所以,归根到底,信用证还是贸易合同条款的反映。但是,根据信用证惯例,信用证一旦开出便脱离了贸易合同,即便信用证与合同不符,也将被视为对贸易合同的修改,意味着出口商如果在初次审核信用证时没有表示异议(出口商初次审核信用证时有权提出对不符合贸易合同的信用证条款进行修改),即视为对贸易合同修改的同意,其交单的义务也将按照信用证要求执行。如果无法做到交单的四个标准,开证行就有拒付的权利。所以,作为付款的开证行与收款的出口商之间的法律关系基础的信用证,其条款是否符合合同或是否隐藏有出口商交单无法控制的条款(又称"软条款"),将是信用证支付方式能否顺利执行的关键。

3. 信用证业务是单据业务,而非货物买卖

UCP600 第 5 条明确规定:银行处理的是单据,而不是单据可能涉及的货物、服务或履约行为。(UCP Article 5: The banks deal with documents, not goods, services or performance to which the documents may relate.)可见,信用证业务是一种纯粹的凭单据付款的业务,相符交单(四个相符)是银行付款的唯一依据,至于货物是否符合合同要求并不是银行付款的前提条件。因此,出口商要取得信用证下开证行的付款,一定要使得信用证下的单据达到此标准:符合信用证条款要求,不同单据之间互相吻合,符合 UCP 规则要求,符合国际标准银行实务要求。

5.2 信用证的当事人

5.2.1 开证申请人(Applicant)

开证申请人是向银行申请开立信用证的人,在国际贸易中通常是进口商或中间商。一旦开证行接受了开证申请,为其开出信用证,开证申请人就要承担开证行的开证及相关费用并且在相符交单下应向银行付款赎单。

开证申请人受到两个法律文书的约束:一个是与出口商签订的贸易合同;另一个是与开证行签订的开证申请书。首先,开证申请人应对合同负责,必须根据合同的规定及时申请开立符合合同条款的信用证,并保证信用证于合同规定的期限前送达出口商,以便后者有足够的时间安排生产、备货的事宜。另外,信用证是独立于合同的文件,开立信用证并不能解除进口商最终的付款义务。信用证付款方式下只不过是由开证行承担了第一性的付款责任,相符交单下开证行对出口商付款后需要进口商对银行履行付款赎单的义务;而一旦信用证下由于不符交单导致开证行拒付,进口商就要承担合同项下第一性的付款责任。

开证申请人必须遵守开证申请书的约定,并承担相应的义务。

1. 合理指示开证

为了提高信用证业务的效率,申请人在申请书中的措辞必须简洁和前后一致,避免开证行和申请人对信用证内容在理解上有出入,致使信用证内容无法执行。

2. 提供开证担保

信用证是开证行对出口商的付款承诺,是对进口商的授信,开证行为了避免风险通常要求申请人提供一定形式的担保,可以是现金、动产或不动产,也可以是第三人提供的担保。现金保证就是开证押金,可以高达开证金额的100%,也可以为0,开证押金的多少与申请人的资信直接关联。

3. 及时付款赎单

开证申请书是开证申请人与开证行之间的委托付款代理合同。开证行是付款代理人,申请人是承担付款责任的委托人。开证行在相符交单下向出口商履行付款义务后,进口商应及时向开证行付款赎单。当然,对于出口商的不符交单,开证申请人有拒绝付款赎单的权利,有权收回开证押金或担保。如果由于开证行的审单不慎,对出口商的不符交单支付货款,开证申请人在向开证行指出单据中的不符点后可以拒绝付款赎单,此后果将由开证行承担。在进口商付款赎单提货后,如果发现货物质量、数量等与合同不符,进口商无权要求开证行赔付(根据前述信用证业务的第三特点:信用证业务银行处理的是单据,而不是货物或服务),只能依据贸易合同向出口商追究违约责任。

5.2.2　开证行(Issuing Bank or Opening Bank)

开证行是应进口商的申请开出信用证的银行,通常是进口商的银行。开证银行的信誉、业务经验是进口商选择开证银行或是其他当事人参与信用证业务的主要考量因素。

开证行受到三个合同的约束:与申请人之间的开证申请书,与受益人之间的信用证,与通知行或议付行之间的业务代理协议。因此,开证行必须履行如下义务。

1. 根据开证申请书的内容,按照UCP规则的要求开证

开证行作为申请人的付款代理人,应当根据申请人的指示行事,按UCP规则处理信用证业务。UCP600规定:若信用证含有某些条件而未列明需要提交与之相符的单据,银行将认为未列如此条件,且对此不予理会。因此,首先开证申请人应当注意将合同条款单据化,并将所需单据在申请书上列明;其次,开证行应按照申请书列明的要求逐一列出单据及其内容要求。可见,单据是信用证内容的全部,是进口商对出口商履约行为的约束工具,出口商通过提交符合要求的单据来证明自己的履约行为。同时,符合信用证要求的单据也是出口商从开证行获得偿付的唯一依据。

2. 取得质押的权利

进口商在开证行对出口商相符交单付款后有对其付款赎单的义务,如果进口商违约或无力付款,开证行可以取得对货物的质押权。开证行取得对货物的质押,通常通过要求申请人在申请开证时出具质押书或者赔偿保证书来获得。在申请人无法支付货款后,开证行可以自由处理货物,可以通过出售货物来补偿自己的垫款,对不足部分有权向进口商追偿。

3. 第一性付款责任

开证行对受益人的付款责任受到信用证条款及 UCP 规则的约束。信用证是开证行对受益人的付款保证,它取代申请人在贸易合同中的付款责任而成为第一性付款责任,即以银行信用取代了商业信用。开证行对受益人的义务就是信用证下的相符交单付款,这种付款是确定的,不受其他条件或因素的影响,例如进口商拒绝付款赎单或破产,进出口商因合同或货物的某些纠纷等。而且,开证行的付款是终局性的,开证行不能以任何理由向受益人追索。当然,如果单据不符合信用证要求,开证行完全有权利拒付。尽管有时开证申请人做出放弃不符点的保证并承诺在付款赎单的情况下开证行仍可以对不符单据付款,但这不意味着开证行放弃了拒付的权利。需要特别指出的是,受益人相符交单下开证行一般是不可以拒付的,仅仅在一种情况下可以拒付:开证申请人向法院举证受益人欺诈,法院向银行下达了止付令,这叫"信用证欺诈的例外原则"。但是,即便是存在受益人欺诈,如果存在善意的第三人在止付令下达前议付了信用证款项,出于保护善意第三人的需要,法院不应当下达止付令,这叫"信用证欺诈例外的例外原则"。

5.2.3 受益人(Beneficiary)

受益人是信用证利益的享受者,信用证上规定有权使用信用证的人,也是开证行保证付款的对象,信用证项下汇票的出票人,即出口商。其享有如下的权利和义务。

1. 收到信用证后,有审核并要求修改信用证的权利

受益人在收到开证行开立的信用证后,应及时审核信用证,判断信用证条款是否与合同相符。如果发现有不相符的地方或不能接受的条款(例如信用证要求的单据不在自己的控制范围之内,需要进口商来人签发的客检证书,不合理的费用承担要求等),受益人有权要求进口商联系开证行对信用证进行修改,直至与合同相符。

2. 发货交单的义务

受益人在审核信用证无误后,意味着信用证发生效力,此后,信用证不可以单方面修改,任何对信用证的修改必须得到进口商、出口商和开证行的同意。并且,收到无误的信用证表示收到了开证行的付款承诺,出口商应该按照合同的规定及时发货并取得相关的货运单据及缮制商业单据,按照信用证的要求在交单期内向银行交单。如果单据与信用证要求不符,受益人可以在规定期限内及时更改。

3. 在相符交单下取得银行的付款

受益人按期发运货物并取得符合信用证要求的单据后,可以向开证行或保兑行(如果有的话)请求付款,如果不是银行倒闭的原因,银行不可以借口其他理由拒绝付款,因为信用证下付款的唯一依据是相符交单。如果受益人与开证行就是否相符交单产生争议,双方可以请国际商会予以仲裁。需要注意的是:开证行提出不符点的时限是收到单据后的 5 个工作日内,超过时限无权提出不符点,只能支付货款;如果单据在银行之间寄送的路途中遗失,开证行也失去了拒付的权利;开证行只有一次提出不符点的机会,如果提出的不符点没有一个是合理的,也失去了拒付权利;开证行或保兑行付款后又提出不符点(即便不符点是存在的),要求受益人退款,受益人可以置之不理,因为开证行与保兑行都没有追索权。

5.2.4 通知行(Advising Bank)

通知行是将开证行开立的信用证及信用证修改书通知受益人的银行,通知行通常是开证行位于受益人国家且同城的联行或代理行。通知行的权利和义务如下。

1. 审核信用证真伪并及时通知信用证

通知行在收到开证行以航邮或电信方式发来的信用证后,如接受委托通知信用证,需要通过核对印鉴或密押确认信用证的表面真实性,并立即通知受益人;如不接受委托通知该信用证,应毫不迟疑地通知开证行。经由通知行通知信用证是为了充分利用银行间的核对信用证真实性的手段来保护受益人的利益。

2. 收取通知费

通知行在履行了通知信用证的职责后,有权向委托人收取通知费用。一般在实务中,各自国家的银行向各自的当事人收取银行费用。因此,通知行是在通知信用证的同时向受益人收取通知费。

3. 兼具保兑行、议付行的角色

如果通知行接受了信用证中要求保兑的请求,则通知行兼具保兑行的角色,承担保兑行的权利及义务。如果通知行在受益人交单时付款议付了受益人的交单,则通知行也兼具了议付行的角色。

5.2.5 议付行(Negotiating Bank)

议付行是愿意买入或贴现受益人交来的汇票和单据的银行,通常为出口地银行。议付行可以是指定的(限制议付信用证),也可以是非指定的(自由议付信用证),这由信用证条款而定。议付行的权利和义务如下。

(1)在信用证的交单期内,接受受益人提交的信用证及单据并审核是否为相符交单。若确定为相符交单,可予以议付;若非相符交单,可拒绝议付。

(2)议付行是开证行委托议付信用证的银行,因此开证行有义务对议付行转交的相符交单予以偿付。若开证行审核单据发现为非相符交单,开证行可以拒付,同时议付行也可以转向受益人追索垫款。为避免这种垫款的风险,议付行应严格审单。

5.2.6 付款行(Paying Bank)

付款行是开证行指定的信用证项下汇票的付款人,一般是开证行自身或其指定的另外一家银行。付款行可以是出口地银行,也可以是进口地银行。付款行的权利与义务如下。

(1)付款行是开证行在信用证中指定的另外一家银行,它只是代为付款,在法律上没有必须对受益人付款的义务。付款行通常是开证行的分支机构或与开证行有业务往来的银行。如果它与开证行签订了代付合同,正常情况下,它应该对受益人提交的相符单据予以付款。

否则,它应该对开证行承担违约责任,但不对受益人负责。

(2)付款行一经确认单据无误并向受益人付款后,就无权向受益人追索,但有权拒付。

(3)付款行付款后有权根据代理合同向开证行要求偿还所付款项,并收取代付发生的一切费用。

5.2.7 偿付行(Reimbursing Bank)

偿付行是开证行在信用证中指定的、代开证行向议付行或付款行清偿垫款的银行。当结算货币是进出口国以外的第三国货币时,开证行为了头寸调拨的便利,可授权第三国货币清算中心的一家联行或代理银行作为偿付行。偿付行的权利和义务如下。

(1)偿付行只有在收到偿付授权书后,才有权对受益人偿付信用证金额。因此,开证行指定索偿行向偿付行索偿时,应当及时给偿付行下达偿付授权书。

(2)偿付行偿付款项后,有权向开证行索要垫款。

(3)偿付行与受益人无契约关系,不受理单据,也无审核单据的义务,因此偿付行对议付行、付款行等的偿付不能被视为开证行的最终付款。当开证行接到单据经审核为不符交单时,不能向偿付行追索,只能向议付行或付款行追回偿付行所付款项。

(4)若偿付行未能履行偿付义务,开证行不能解除其自行偿付的义务;若偿付行延迟偿付,开证行应负责赔偿议付行、付款行等的利息损失。

5.2.8 承兑行(Accepting Bank)

承兑行是对受益人签发的信用证下的远期汇票予以承兑,并到期付款的银行。承兑行的承兑和到期付款责任是根据开证行的指定和请求,通常它们之间有代理协议相互提供此类服务。承兑行的权利和义务如下。

(1)开证行如开立承兑信用证,该信用证的汇票付款人(Drawee)必须是银行,而不能是开证申请人。该付款人一般是开证行本身或其指定的一家银行。受益人必须到指定的承兑行提交单据,承兑行审核无误后承兑汇票,即在汇票正面加注“已承兑”字样,加注日期并加签,这时承兑行就成为汇票的主债务人,承担到期付款的责任。

(2)无论开证行倒闭或发生支付困难,承兑行都要履行到期付款的义务。所以银行被要求担当承兑行时都非常慎重。通常承兑行是开证行在汇票货币清偿地的分支机构或存款行。

5.2.9 保兑行(Confirming Bank)

保兑行是应开证行的要求和委托,对开证行开出的不可撤销信用证加具保兑的银行。保兑行对信用证加具保兑的行为构成了除开证行以外的另一家银行的确定付款承诺。保兑行的权利和义务如下。

(1)被要求加具保兑的银行一般要对开证行的资信状况及信用证条款进行严格的审核后,才能决定是否加具保兑。它有权不予照办,但必须毫不延迟地通知开证行。保兑行承担保兑责任后,对于受益人来说承担了与开证行同样的付款责任。无论开证行发生什么变化,保兑行都不能片面撤销其保兑责任。保兑行有权就保兑收取保兑费。

(2)保兑行付款后,只能向开证行索偿,若开证行无力或无理拒付,保兑行无权向受益人或其他前手银行进行追索。

5.3 信用证的业务流程

信用证的业务流程如图 5.1 和图 5.2 所示。

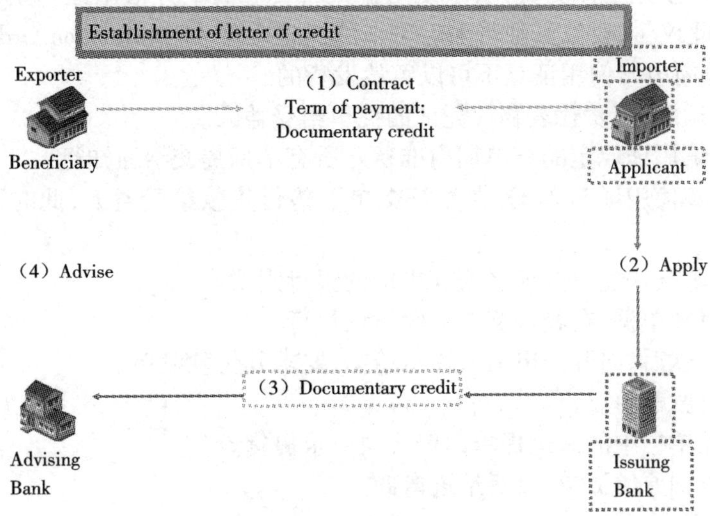

图 5.1　Establishment of letter of credit

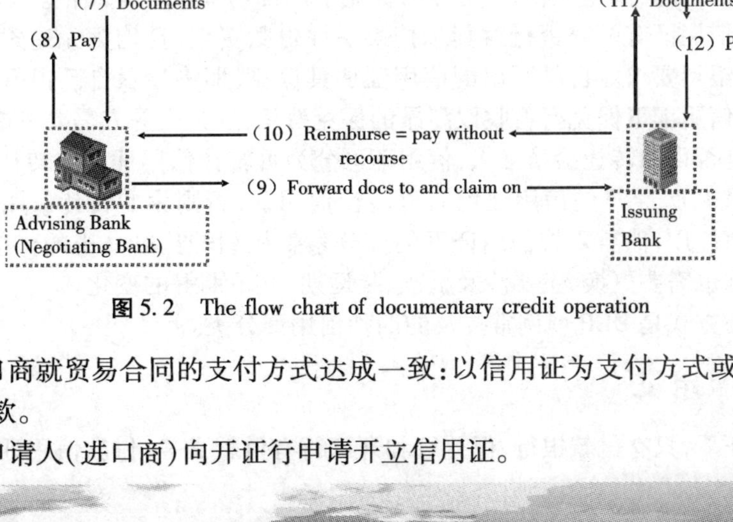

图 5.2　The flow chart of documentary credit operation

(1)进出口商就贸易合同的支付方式达成一致:以信用证为支付方式或信用证与其他方式结合支付货款。

(2)开证申请人(进口商)向开证行申请开立信用证。

(3)开证行将信用证以电开或信开方式发给出口商同城的通知行。

(4)通知行向受益人(出口商)通知信用证并收取通知费用。

(5)受益人(出口商)收到信用证后,审核信用证是否与合同相符,确认没有不符意味着信用证正式成立。出口商安排生产并通过承运人(船公司)发货。

注意:电开信用证作为常见的开证方式,又分为"全电开信用证"和"简电开信用证"。前者是将信用证的全部内容加注密押后发出,该电信文本就是正式的有效文本。后者是将信用证的主要内容发出,预先通知受益人,以便受益人备货。简电开信用证不是有效的信用证文本,受益人不能凭此议付,要以开证行随后寄来的"证实书"(Confirmation Order)为准。因此,如受益人收到的是简电开信用证是不可以贸然发货的。

(6)船公司装运后,签发代表物权凭证的提单给受益人。

(7)受益人在信用证规定的交单期内准备好所有单据提交给通知行。

(8)通知行审核信用证与单据,在相符交单下垫付货款给受益人,此时通知行转变为议付行。

(9)议付行将单据快递给开证行或其指定的银行索偿。

(10)开证行审核单据,在相符交单下偿付议付行。

(11)开证行付款后,向开证申请人提示单据,要求其付款赎单。

(12)申请人付款赎单。

(13)申请人凭单据中的海运提单向船公司要求提货。

(14)船公司收到原始提单,放货给进口商。

5.4 信用证的种类

根据信用证开出后开证行是否能收回其付款承诺,信用证可分为可撤销信用证与不可撤销信用证。然而由于可撤销信用证对受益人的权益没有保障,信用证支付方式出现至今都无人使用可撤销信用证。因此,UCP600 规定"凡依据 UCP600 开出的信用证均为不可撤销信用证,即便信用证中并未提及该信用证的类型"。

根据信用证是否加具保兑,信用证可分为保兑信用证与非保兑信用证。如果被指定银行同意加具保兑,该信用证有两家银行对其承担第一性付款责任,且均为无追索权的付款。但在实务中,很少有银行要求对自己开出的信用证加具保兑,那将显示自己银行的信誉是无保障的。另外,保兑信用证下保兑行将收取高昂的保兑费用,这是交易人需要考虑的问题。

根据信用证是否可以转让给第三人,信用证可分为可转让信用证与非转让信用证。凡是写有"TRANSFERABLE"字样的信用证均为可转让信用证,否则为非转让信用证。可转让信用证主要为中间商使用,他需要将信用证下的部分索款权利转让给真正的供应商。因此,在该信用证下的单据也需要更换,主要涉及金额、装运期、交单期等的变化。

另外一种分类方式是 UCP 惯例常提及的四种信用证分类。

5.4.1 付款信用证

在付款信用证下,只有付款银行、保兑行和开证行有付款义务,付款信用证下的单据应当

交到以上三家银行。一般来说,付款信用证下无须开出汇票,这样也可以避免印花税。付款信用证一般有以下条款:

AVAILABLE WITH…BY…;41A
CHINA MERCHANTS BANK
BY PAYMENT

5.4.2　议付信用证

议付信用证根据可兑付信用证银行的限制不同分为自由议付信用证和限制议付信用证。前者中有条款提示该信用证可以在任何银行议付,因此任何银行均可以为议付行,议付后即可取得善意持票人地位。后者中有条款提示该信用证只能交到指定的银行议付,也只有该银行议付后才能取得善意持票人地位。在议付信用证下,可以要求开出汇票,也可不要求开出汇票。议付信用证一般有以下条款:

AVAILABLE WITH…BY…;41A
ANY BANK　(CHINA MERCHANTS BANK)
BY NEGOTIATION

5.4.3　承兑信用证

承兑信用证要求被指定银行或开证行对信用证下的远期汇票先行承兑,再于到期后付款。因此,承兑信用证下一般要求开出汇票。承兑信用证一般有如下条款:

AVAILABLE WITH…BY…;41A
ANY BANK
BY ACCEPTANCE

5.4.4　延期付款信用证

在延期付款信用证下,被指定银行或开证行在信用证规定的时间在相符交单下对受益人付款。由于一些国家法律规定不允许开出超过半年期的远期汇票,因此,延期付款信用证是不需开出汇票的。由于与承兑信用证功能类似,它可以取代承兑信用证。延期付款信用证一般有如下条款:

AVAILABLE WITH…BY…;41A
CHINA MERCHANTS BANK
BY DEFERRED PAYMENT

5.5　信用证的内容及格式

信用证的内容包括:关于信用证本身的项目、关于汇票的项目、关于货运单据的项目、关于商品的项目、关于运输方面的项目及其他。目前,世界上开立信用证主要采用SWIFT金融系统,因此具有该系统统一的开证格式(MT700 格式)。

(1)必选 20 DOCUMENTARY CREDIT NUMBER(信用证号码)。

(2)可选 23 REFERENCE TO PRE-ADVICE(预先通知号码)。如果信用证采取预先通知方式,该项目填入“PREADV/”,再加上预先通知的编号或日期。

(3)必选 27 SEQUENCE OF TOTAL(电文页次)。

(4)可选 31C DATE OF ISSUE(开证日期)。如果没有此项,则开证日期为电文发送日期。

(5)必选 31D DATE AND PLACE OF EXPIRY(信用证有效期和有效地点)。

(6)必须 32B CURRENCY CODE, AMOUNT(信用证结算的货币和金额)。

(7)必选 39A PERCENTAGE CREDIT AMOUNT TOLERANCE(信用证金额上下浮动允许的最大范围)。例如:5/5 表示允许最大上下浮动 5%。

(8)可选 39B MAXIMUM CREDIT AMOUNT(信用证最大限制金额)。

39B 与 39A 不能同时出现。

(9)可选 39C ADDITIONAL AMOUNTS COVERED(额外金额)。

(10)必选 40A FORM OF DOCUMENTARY CREDIT(跟单信用证形式)。

跟单信用证有六种形式:① IRREVOCABLE(不可撤销跟单信用证);② REVOCABLE(可撤销跟单信用证);③ IRREVOCABLE TRANSFERABLE(不可撤销可转让跟单信用证);④ REVOCABLE TRANSFERABLE(可撤销可转让跟单信用证);⑤ IRREVOCABLE STANDBY(不可撤销备用信用证);⑥ REVOCABLE STANDBY(可撤销备用信用证)。

(11)必选 41A AVAILABLE WITH... BY...(指定的有关银行及信用证的兑付方式)。① 指定银行付款、承兑、议付。② 兑付的方式有 5 种:BY PAYMENT(即期付款);BY ACCEPTANCE(远期付款);BY NEGOTIATION(议付);BY DEFERRED PAYMENT(迟期付款);BY MIXED PAYMENT(混合付款)。③ 如果是自由议付信用证,对该信用证的议付地点不做限制,该项目代号为 41D,内容为:ANY BANK FOR NEGOTIATION。

(12)可选 42A DRAWEE(汇票付款人)。

(13)可选 42C DRAFTS AT(汇票付款期限)。必须与 42A 同时出现。

(14)可选 42M MIXED PAYMENT DETAILS(混合付款条款)。

(15)可选 42P DEFERRED PAYMENT DETAILS(迟期付款条款)。

(16)可选 43P PARTIAL SHIPMENT(分装条款)。

(17)可选 43T TRANSSHIPMENT(转船条款)。

(18)可选 44A LOADING ON BOARD/DISPATCH/TAKING IN CHARGE AT/FROM(装船、发运和接受监管的地点)。

(19)可选 44B FOR TRANSPORT TO...(货物发运的最终地)。

(20)可选 44C LATEST DATE OF SHIPMENT(最迟装船期)。

(21)可选 44D SHIPMENT PERIOD(船期)。

44C 与 44D 不能同时出现。

(22)可选 45A DESCRIPTION OF GOODS AND/OR SRVICES(货物描述:名称、规格、价格条款)。

(23)可选 46A DOCUMENTS REQUIRED(单据要求)。

(24)可选 47A ADDITIOANL CONDITIONS(特别条款)。

(25)可选 48 PERIOD FOR PRESENTATION(交单期限)。

(26)必选 49 CONFIRMATION INSTRUCTIONS(保兑指示)。

① CONFIRM:要求保兑行对该信用证加具保兑。

② MAY ADD:收报行可以对该信用证加具保兑。

③ WITHOUT:不要求收报行保兑该信用证。

(27)必选 50 APPLICANT(信用证开证申请人)。

(28)可选 51A APPLICANT BANK(开证行)。

(29)可选 53A REIMBURSEMENT BANK(偿付行)。

(30)可选 57A "ADVISING THROUGH "BANK(通知行)。

(31)必选 59 BENEFICIARY(信用证受益人)。

(32)可选 71B CHARGES(费用情况)。

标明费用是否由受益人出,如果没有这一条,表示除了议付费、转让费以外,其他各种费用由开出信用证的申请人承担。

(33)可选 72 SENDER TO RECEIVER INFORMATION(附言)。

(34)可选 78 INSTRUCTION TO THE PAYING/ACCEPTING/NEGOTIATION BANK(给付款行、承兑行、议付行的指示)。

5.6 信用证样本

信用证样本中文部分均为翻译。

2005MAY 23 14:49:12 Logical Terminal SWPP

MT S700 Issue of a Documentary Credit Page 00002

表示开证 跟单信用证的开立

Func

SWIFT 环银电协(环球银行金融电讯协会)信用证

MSGACK DWS7651 Auth OK, key B30407186423644D, BKCHCNBJ HSBCHKHH record875803

Basic Header F 01 BKCHCNBJA400 1274 311389

基本字号

Application Header 0 700 1411 050523 HSBCHKHHDHKH 0760 552387 050523 1411 N

开证行

汇丰银行 * THE HONGKONG AND SHANGHAI
* BANKING CORPORATION LIMITED,
* HONG KONG

各香港办事处及总部 * (ALL HK OFFICES AND HEAD OFFICE)

User Header	Service Code		103:
	Bank Priority		113:
	Msg User Ref.		108: 143090658
	Info. From CI		115:
Sequence of Total: 电文页次	*27	:	1/1
Form of Doc. Credit 跟单信用证形式	*40 A	:	IRREVOCABLE 不可撤销
Doc. Credit Number 跟单信用证号码	*20	:	DC NPH182503
Date of Issue 开证日期	31 C	:	050523 2005 年 5 月 23 日
Expiry 信用证有效期	*31 D	:	Date 050804 Place CHINA 日期:2005 年 8 月 4 日 地点:中国
Applicant 信用证开证申请人	*50	:	FUNDINS TORONTO, CANADA 56 TOWER STREET, TORONTO, CANADA 加拿大多伦多 FUNDINS 公司 加拿大多伦多托尔大街 56 号
Beneficiary 信用证受益人	*59	:	GUANGDONG WHOLE ARTS TRADING COMPANY FINANCE BUILDING 35 - 39, ZHONGSHAN ROAD 7, GUANGZHOU, CHINA 广东鸿艺贸易有限公司 中国广州中山路 7 号金融大厦 35 - 39 楼
Amount 信用证金额	*32B	:	Currency USD Amount 38,963.80 币种:美元 金额:38 963.80
Pos. / Neg. Tol. (5) 金额上下浮动允许的最大范围	39 A	:	05 / 05 上下浮动 5%
Available with/by 指定的有关银行及 信用证的兑付方式	*41A	:	ANY BANK BY NEGOTIATION 自由议付
Drafts at... 汇票付款期限	42 C	:	SIGHT FOR FULL INVOICE OF GOODS 金额为发票全额的即期汇票
Drawee 汇票付款人	42 A	:	ISSUING BANK 开证行
Partial Shipments 分批装运条款	43P	:	ALLOWED 允许分批装运

Transshipment 43 T : ALLOWED

转船条款 允许转船

Loading in Charge 44 A : ANY PORT IN CHINA

装船、发运和接受监管的地点 中国任意港口

For Transport to. . . 44 B : TORONTO, CANADA

货物发运的最终地 加拿大多伦多

Latest Date of Ship. 44 C : 050720

最迟装船期 2005 年 7 月 20 日

Descript. of Goods 45 A :CIF TORONTO, CANADA

货物描述 CIF 加拿大多伦多

1) 20,000 PCS OF CORN BASKET AT USD1. 40/PC
AS PER PURCHASE ORDER NO: 7980/05/FK
2 万个玉米篮子,每个 1. 40 美元,按 7980/05/FK 号订单

2) 12,182 PCS OF RATTAN BASKET AT USD0. 90/PC
AS PER PURCHASE ORDER NO: 7990/05/FK
12 185 个藤篮子,每个 0. 90 美元,按 7990/05/FK 号订单

Documents Required 46A :

单据要求

+ SIGNED COMMERCIAL INVOICE IN TRIPLICATE CONSIGNED TO(MADE OUT TO) FUNDINS TORONTO, CANADA AND CERTIFYING THAT GOODS ARE IN CONFORMITY WITH THOSE DESCRIBED ON THE PROFORMA INVOICE NO. E-11 13001/6 DATED FEB. 21, 2005.

已签署的以加拿大多伦多的 FUNDINS 为抬头人的商业发票一式三份,证明货物与 2005 年 2 月 21 日出具的第 E-11 13001/6 号形式发票中描述的一致。

+ PACKING LIST IN TRIPLICATE SHOWING NET WEIGHT, GROSS WEIGHT AND MEASUREMENT PER PACKAGE.

装箱单一式三份,注明每件包装的净重、毛重及体积。

+ FULL SET ORIGINAL CLEAN ON BOARD OCEAN BILLS OF LADING MADE OUT TO ORDER, BLANK ENDORSED, MARKED FREIGHT PREPAID AND NOTIFY APPLICANT WITH FULL ADDRESS.

全套清洁已装船海运提单做成空白抬头,空白背书, 注明运费预付,并通知开证申请人同时提供详细地址。

+ INSURANCE POLICY OR CERTIFICATE BLANK ENDORSED FOR FULL CIF VALUE PLUS 10 PERCENT COVERING W. A. AND SRCC INCLUDING W/W CLAUSE AS PER CIC. CLAIMS, IF ANY, WILL BE PAYABLE AT DESTINATION IN CURRENCY OF DRAFT.

保险单或保险凭证,空白背书,按 CIF 价的 110% 投保《中国保险条款》的水渍险和罢工、暴动、民变险,含仓至仓条款。如有索赔,将按汇票币种在目的港赔付。

+ CERTIFICATE OF ORIGIN

原产地证

+ BENEFICIARY'S CERTIFICATE CERTIFYING THAT ONE SET OF SHIPPING DOCUMENTS HAS BEEN FAXED TO APPLICANT WITHIN 1 DAY AFTER SHIPMENT.

受益人证明,证明一套运输单据已经在装船后 1 天内传真给开证申请人。

+ COPY OF TELEX/FAX SENT BY BENEFICIARY TO APPLICANT ON OR BEFORE B/L ON BOARD DATE CONTAINING ALL SHIPMENT DETAILS, INCLUDING: AMOUNT, GROSS WEIGHT, NET WEIGHT, CARTONS NO., VESSEL NAME AND B/L NO. NO. OF THIS L/C AND RELEVANT S/C TO BE MENTIONED.

受益人在 B/L 装船日当天或之前发送给开证申请人一份含所有装船详情的电传/传真的副本,包括:金额、毛重、净重、箱数、船名、B/L 号码、L/C 及相关 S/C 号码。

Additional Cond. 47A :

特别条款

+ SHIPMENT MUST BE EFFECTED THROUGH "ROCKWOOD SHENZHEN" CHINA AND B/L TO EVIDENCE THIS EFFECT IS REQUIRED.

货物装运须由"ROCKWOOD 深圳"承担,且须在提单中证实此事。

+ 5 PERCENT MORE OR LESS IN QUANTITY OF EACH ITEM ACCEPTABLE.

允许每种货物的数量溢短装 5%。

+ BILL OF LADING MUST SHOW ACTUAL NAME OF PORT OF LOADING.

提单必须指明装货港具体名称。

+ A DISCREPANCY FEE OF HKD 400.00 OR EQUIVALENT CHARGE PLUS ALL RELATIVE CABLE CHARGES WILL BE DEDUCTED FROM THE REIMBURSEMENT CLAIM FOR EACH PRESENTATION OF DISCREPANT DOCUMENTS UNDER THIS DC. NOTWITHSTANDING ANY INSTRUCTIONS TO THE CONTRARY, THESE CHARGES SHALL BE FOR THE ACCOUNT OF BENEFICIARY.

400 港元或相等的不符点费加上全部相关电报费将从本信用证项下每次提交的、含有不符点的单据的索偿中扣除。如果没有相反的指示,此项费用将由受益人承担。

WE WILL COLLECT FROM THE BENEFICIARY AN ADDITIONAL FEE EQUIVALENT TO HKD 200.00 PER MONTH OR PART THEREOF IF THE

DOCUMENTS REMAIN UNACCEPTED/UNPAID DUE TO DISCREPANCY FOR MORE THAN 1 MONTH AFTER OUR RECEIPT.

如果我行(开证行)接收的单据由于存在不符点仍然不被接受或兑付超过一个月,我行(开证行)将每月或一段时间从受益人处收取相当于200港币的额外费用。

+ DOCUMENTS TO BE PRESENTED WITHIN 15 DAYS AFTER THE SHIPMENT DATE BUT WITHIN THE VALIDITY OF THE CREDIT.

所有单据必须在装船后15天内提交议付,但不得超过信用证有效期。

+ NOTWITHSTANDING THE PROVISIONS OF UCP 500, IF WE GIVE NOTICE OF REFUSAL OF DOCUMENTS PRESENTED UNDER THIS CREDIT WE SHALL, HOWEVER RETAIN THE RIGHT TO ACCEPT A WAIVER OF DISCREPANCIES FROM THE APPLICANT AND, SUBJECT TO SUCH WAIVER BEING ACCEPTABLE TO US, TO RELEASE DOCUMENTS AGAINST THAT WAIVER WITHOUT REFERENCE TO THE PRESENTER PROVIDED THAT NO WRITTEN INSTRUCTION TO THE CONTRARY HAVE BEEN RECEIVED BY US FROM THE PRESENTER BEFORE THE RELEASE OF THE DOCUMENTS. ANY SUCH RELEASE PRIOR TO RECEIPT OF CONTRARY INSTRUCTIONS SHALL NOT CONSTITUTE A FAILURE ON OUR PART TO HOLD THE DOCUMENTS AT THE PRESENTER'S RISK AND DISPOSAL, AND WE WILL HAVE NO LIABILITY TO THE PRESENTER IN RESPECT OF ANY SUCH RELEASE.

不考虑《跟单信用证统一惯例》(第500号)的规定,如果我行发出拒收此证下单据的通知,我行将仍保留接受开证申请人对不符点加以放弃的权利,只要这种放弃为我行所接受。除非在放单之前收到来自交单人的相反的书面通知,我行即根据这种放弃在不征求交单人意见的情况下向开证申请人放单。在收到该相反的指示之前,放单将不构成我行为交单人的风险和指示持有单据之责任的失职,对于此种放单,我行对交单人将不负任何责任。

+ EXCEPT SO FAR AS OTHERWISE EXPRESSLY STATED THIS DOCUMENTARY CREDIT IS SUBJECT TO UNIFORM CUSTOMS AND PRACTICE FOR DOCUMENTARY CREDITS (1993 REVISION) INTERNATIONAL CHAMBER OF COMMERCE PUBLICATION NO. 500.

除非另有明文规定,此跟单信用证遵照国际商会第500号出版物《跟单信用证统一惯例》(1993年修订版)。

Details of Charges	71B	: ALL CHARGES OUTSIDE COUNTRY OF ISSUE FOR ACCOUNT OF BENEFICIARY/EXPORTER
费用情况		开证行所在国家以外的所有费用由受益人/出口商承担
Confirmation	*49	: WITHOUT

保兑指示　　　　　　　　　　　　无

Instructions　　　　78　　:

给付款行、承兑行、议付行的指示

ON RECEIPT OF DOCUMENTS CONFORMING TO THE TERMS OF THIS DC AT OUR COUNTER, WE UNDERTAKE TO REIMBURSE YOU IN THE CURRENCY OF THIS CREDIT IN ACCORDANCE WITH YOUR PAYMENT INSTRUCTION AFTER DEDUCTING ALL RELATIVE REIMBURSING CHARGES INCURRED.

一旦收到符合此证要求的各项单据,我行在扣除所有相关索偿费用后,即刻按照你方的付款方式以此信用证项下的币种偿付。

DOCUMENTS MUST BE DISPATCHED BY COURIER IN ONE COVER TO HSBC ESD DIV. L5 HSBC BLDG MONG KOK 673 NATHAN RD, MONGKOK, KLN, HONG KONG.

所有单据必须由快递公司一次送往以下地址:HSBC ESD DIV. L5 HSBC BLDG MONG KOK 673 NATHAN RD, MONGKOK, KLN, HONG KONG.

Send. To Rec. Info.　　72　　: BENEFICIARY'S TEL NO: 086 - 020 - 86479522
FAX NO:086 - 020 - 86479518

附言

受益人电话号码:086 - 020 - 86479522
传真号码:086 - 020 - 86479518

Trailer　　: MAC : 46064EE8
CHK : 86746F06C529

5.7 信用证支付方式下进出口商的风险

5.7.1 进口商可能面临的风险

(1)由于出口商的欺诈,进口商可能由于出口商的相符交单(伪造的单据)而不得不付款,但却没有能够得到合同项下的货物。类似的情形,货物短装、质量不合格、货物延迟到港,都会给进口商带来损失,但由于出口商的相符交单无法阻止开证行全额支付货款。所以,在交易前通过资信调查公司了解交易对象的信誉和财务状况是有必要的。

(2)在近海运输中,货物往往较早到港,但信用证下的相关单据却由于业务流程的需要迟滞到港。为了避免滞港费用,进口商不得不凭银行出具的提货担保向船公司提货。这样,即便出口商交来的单据存在不符点,进口商也不得不付款赎单(要将原始提单交给船公司换回提货担保函),失去了因不符点拒付的权利。

(3)国际贸易的长途运输使得货物有损毁的风险,如果出口商未能对货物进行合理的投保,进口商也可能遭受损失。所以,进口商应对合同条款十分清晰,并在信用证中提出风险防范的单据化条款。

(4)由于签订合同或者信用证开立到偿付货款有一段时间，如果在此期间汇率发生较大的变化，特别是远期的信用证，进口商可能遭受汇率的损失。

(5)如果开证行破产，进口商仍然需要履行合同项下的付款义务，尽管为了开证进口商向开证行交纳了开证押金或全额的货款。

5.7.2 出口商可能面临的风险

(1)尽管信用证支付方式对出口商是有保障的(银行信用取代了商业信用)，但这种支付方式对进口商最大的问题是“相符交单”。由于银行对信用证下的审单采取的是严格相符的原则，任何细微的纰漏都将导致银行的拒付。根据国际商会的统计，百分之八十以上的初次交单都遭到了拒付。因此，出口商首先需要严格审核开证行的来证，任何与合同不符或存在软条款的地方都需要向对方提出修改信用证。如果没有收到合格的修改通知书，出口商不能贸然发货，否则可能因为无法相符交单而被拒付。

(2)如果信用证是不可撤销的，无保兑的，开证行可能由于政府的外汇管制政策原因导致银行无法汇出外汇，这样，即便是相符交单出口商也无法获得偿付。为了避免这种国家的风险，出口商可以要求对方对信用证加具保兑，并且保兑行为出口商本国的银行。

(3)由于国外信用证可以由非银行的机构开具，如果出口商无法辨别开证单位是否为银行，将会导致收款的风险加大。因为这样的信用证提供给出口商的不是银行信用，而是商业信用。

思考题

1. 什么是申请人公司？
2. 什么是受益人公司？
3. 信用证到期时间和地点分别指什么？
4. 受益人开立汇票的要求有哪些？
5. 单据种类、份数、要求分别指什么？
6. 货物装运港、目的港、最迟装运期分别指什么？
7. 货物能否分运？能否转运？
8. 银行费用如何负担？
9. 交单期指什么？
10. 开证行处理信用证业务的依据是什么？
11. 开证行除审查申请书外，还应该处理哪些事宜？
12. 开证行在什么情况下可以免责？

Chapter 5

Letter of Credit

5.1 Definition of L/C

L/C is a letter from a bank guaranteeing that a buyer's payment to a seller will be received on time and for the correct amount. In the event that the buyer is unable to make payment on the purchase, the bank will be required to cover the full or remaining amount of the purchase.

Letters of credit are often used in international transactions to ensure that payment will be received. Due to the nature of international dealings including factors such as distance, differing laws in each country and difficulty in knowing each party personally, the use of letters of credit has become a very important aspect of international trade. The bank also acts on behalf of the buyer (holder of letter of credit) by ensuring that the supplier will not be paid until the bank receives a confirmation that the goods have been shipped.

5.2 Legal principles governing documentary credits

One of the primary peculiarities of the documentary credit is that the payment obligation is independent from the underlying contract of sale or any other contract in the transaction. Thus the bank's obligation is defined by the terms of the letter of credit alone, and the sale contract is irrelevant. The defenses available to the buyer arising out of the sale contract do not concern the bank and in no way affect its liability. Article 4(a) UCP states this principle clearly. Article 5 the UCP further states that banks deal with documents only, they are not concerned with the goods (facts). Accordingly, if the documents tendered by the beneficiary, or his or her agent, appear to be in order, then in general the bank is obliged to pay without further qualifications.

Policies behind adopting the abstraction principle are purely commercial, and reflect a party's expectations. First, if the responsibility for the validity of documents was thrown onto banks, they would be burdened with investigating the underlying facts of each transaction, and less inclined to issue documentary credits as the transaction would involve great risk and inconvenience. Second, documents required under the letter of credit could in certain circumstances be different from those required under the sale transaction. This would place banks in a dilemma in deciding which terms to follow if required to look behind the credit agreement. Third, the fact that the basic function of the credit is to provide a seller with the certainty of payment for documentary duties suggests that banks should honour their obligation notwithstanding allegations of misfeasance by the buyer. Finally, courts have emphasized that buyers always have a remedy for an action upon the contract of sale, and that it would be a calamity for the business world if, for every breach of contract between the seller the buyer, a bank were required to investigate said breach.

The "principle of strict compliance" also aims to make the bank's duty of effecting payment against documents easy, efficient and quick. Hence, if the documents tendered under the credit deviate from the language of the credit the bank is entitled to withhold payment even if the deviation is purely terminological. The general legal "maximde minimis non curat lex" (the law cares not for small things) has no place in the field of documentary credits.

5.3 Parties of L/C

5.3.1 LC applicant

LC applicant is normally the buyer under the sales contract and the party that initiates the request to the issuing bank to issue an LC on its behalf. The LC applicant normally maintains banking facilities with the issuing bank.

5.3.2 LC beneficiary

LC beneficiary is normally the seller under the sales contract and the party who will receive payment under the LC if it can fulfill all the terms and conditions of the credit.

5.3.3 Issuing bank

An issuing bank (or LC opening bank) is the bank that issues the LC in favor of a seller at the request of the LC applicant. The issuing bank is normally located in the applicant's country with established banking relationship with the applicant.

By issuing an LC, the issuing bank undertakes to pay the beneficiary the value of the draft and/or other documents if all the terms and conditions of the LC are complied with.

5.3.4 Advising bank

An advising bank (or sometimes known as notifying bank) is the bank that advises the LC beneficiary that there is an LC issued in his favour. Advising bank is normally located in the seller's country and is either appointed by the issuing bank or LC applicant. Its primary responsibility is to authenticate the LC to ensure that the LC comes from genuine source.

5.3.5 Confirming bank

A confirming bank (normally also the advising bank) is the bank that adds its own undertaking to pay the LC beneficiary if all terms and conditions of the credit are complied with. Such undertaking is in addition to that given by the issuing bank at the request of the issuing bank.

The confirming bank will only confirm an LC upon satisfactory evaluation on the conditions of the issuing bank and its domicile country.

5.3.6 Nominated bank

A nominated bank is a bank authorized by the issuing bank in the credit to pay, negotiate, issue a deferred payment undertaking or accept drafts under the LC. If the LC does not specify a nominated bank, the LC is deemed as freely negotiable and any banks that receive documents from the LC beneficiary are qualified to be a nominated bank.

A nominated bank is not responsible to pay under the credit unless it has added its confirmation to the credit. In such a case, it will become a confirming bank.

5.3.7 Negotiating bank

A negotiating bank is the bank that examines the drafts and/or documents presented by the LC beneficiary and gives values to such drafts and/or documents. Negotiation could be in the form of purchasing or agreeing to purchase the drafts and/or documents presented.

5.3.8 Reimbursing bank

A reimbursing bank is the paying agent appointed by the issuing bank to honour claims submitted by the nominated or negotiating bank.

5.4 The flow of letter of credit

Stage 1. Letter of credit issuance and advising/confirmation (Figure 5.1)

Step 1. Buyer and seller conclude the sales contract and agree to use an LC as the method of payment.

Step 2. Buyer approaches the issuing bank to issue an LC on his behalf in favour of the seller with all the terms and conditions specified.

Step 3. Issuing bank issues the LC and requests the advising bank to advise or confirm the credit to the LC beneficiary (seller).

Step 4. Advising/confirming bank authenticates the LC and sends the LC to the LC beneficiary.

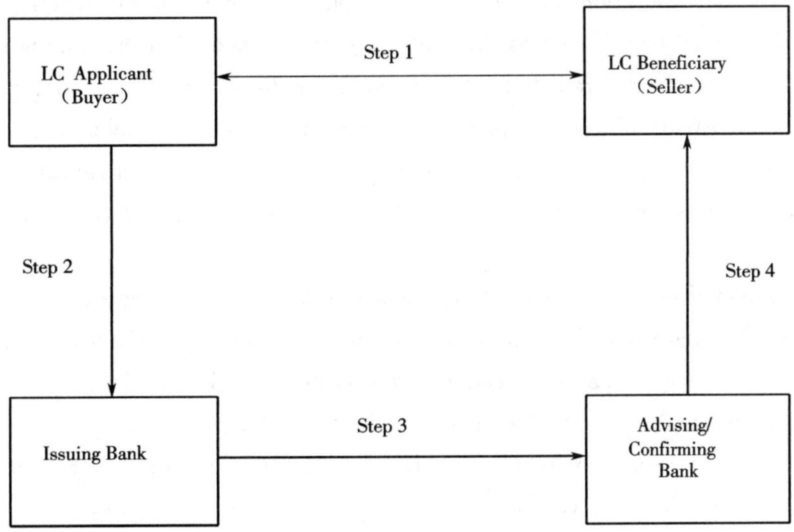

Figure 5. 1 Letter of credit issuance and advising/confirmation

Stage 2. Presentation of documents and settlement (Sight LC with reimbursing bank) (Figure 5. 2)

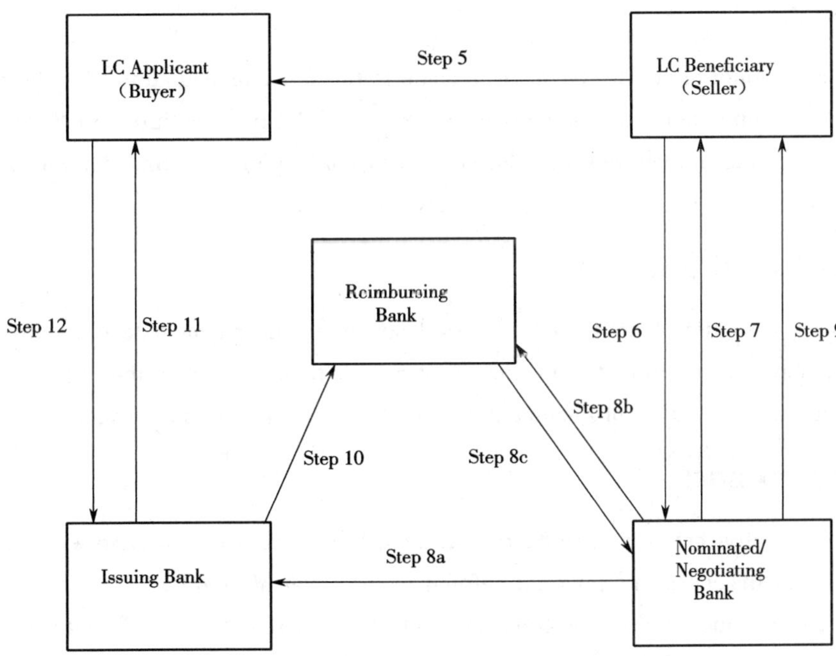

Figure 5. 2 Presentation of documents and settlement

Step 5. Seller prepares and dispatches the goods to the buyer's country.

Step 6. Seller presents the drafts and/or documents to the nominated bank.

Step 7. Nominated (nominated as the negotiating bank) bank checks documents presented against the LC terms and conditions and seeks instructions from seller on documentary discrepancies.

Step 8a. Nominated bank forwards the drafts and/or documents to the issuing bank.

Step 8b. If documents are free from discrepancies or discrepancies are supported by seller's indemnity, nominated bank claims reimbursement from the appointed reimbursing bank.

Step 8c. Reimbursing bank pays the nominated bank against a valid reimbursement authority received from the issuing bank and statement from negotiating bank that the documents complied with LC terms.

Step 9. Nominated bank credits the net proceeds into the seller's account.

Step 10. Issuing bank checks documents presented against the LC terms and conditions. If documents are free from discrepancies, issuing bank reimburses the reimbursing bank.

Step 11. Issuing bank presents documents to the buyer for payment.

Step 12. Once payment is received from the buyer, issuing bank releases documents to the buyer for the buyer to collect his goods.

5.5 Types of L/C

5.5.1 Sight

Under a sight letter of credit, payment is made to the seller immediately after the required documents have been submitted to the authorized bank, provided the conditions in the letter of credit have been met. Banks are, however, allowed a reasonable period of time for checking purposes (not more than five working days after they receive the documents).

5.5.2 Deferred payment

In the case of a letter of credit with deferred payment, the payment to the seller is not made when the documents are submitted, but instead at a later time defined in the letter of credit.

In the Far East, this kind of documentary credit is also known as a "usance L/C."

5.5.3 Acceptance

In the case of an acceptance credit, the payment to the seller is not made when the documents are submitted, but instead at a later time defined in the letter of credit.

The seller can request a discount from the bank that accepted the bill of exchange, or from another bank, and thus draw the amount of the bill minus the discount at any time after the documents have been submitted.

5.5.4 Commercial letters of credit

Commercial letters of credit are mainly used as a primary payment tool in international trade such as exporting and importing transactions. Majority of commercial letters of credit are issued subject to the latest version of UCP (Uniform Customs and Practice for Documentary Credits). The ICC publishes UCP, which are the set of rules that governs the commercial letters of credit procedures.

5.5.5 Standby letters of credit

Commercial letters of credit are a means of payment to be utilized when the principal perform its duties. As an example, let us consider an exporter who ships the goods according to the sales contract and apply to the nominated bank for the payment. If the nominated bank decides that the presentation is conforming to the terms and conditions of the credit and the UCP rules then exporter will be paid. This situation is just contrary in standby letters of credit.

A payment is made to the beneficiary of a standby letter of credit when there is a breach of the principal's obligation. As an example, let us consider a construction company that has been awarded with a tender. If this construction company cannot fulfill its obligations under the project contract, beneficiary of the standby letter of credit can apply to the nominated bank for the payment. However, the nominated bank considers only the terms and the conditions of the standby letter of credit and the rules governing the credit when deciding a complying presentation. One point that needs to be stressed is that standby letters of credit have their own rules, which are called The International Standby Practices 1998 (ISP98). They are also published by ICC. However, a standby letter of credit can be issued subject to either UCP or ISP.

5.5.6 Revocable letters of credit

Revocable letters of credit give issuer the amendment or cancellation right of the credit any time without prior notice to the beneficiary. Since revocable letters of credit do not provide any protection to the beneficiary, they are not used frequently. In addition, UCP 600 has no reference to revocable letters of credit. All credits issued subject to UCP 600 are irrevocable unless otherwise agreed between the parties.

5.5.7 Irrevocable letters of credit

Irrevocable letters of credit cannot be amended or cancelled without the agreement of the credit parties. Unconfirmed irrevocable letters of credit cannot be modified without the written consent of both the issuing bank and the beneficiary. Confirmed irrevocable letters of credit need also confirming bank's written consent in order any modification or cancellation to be effective.

5.5.8 Confirmed letters of credit

It would be easier to understand the confirmed letters of credit if we start from the definition of the confirmation.

Confirmation means a definite undertaking of the confirming bank, in addition to that of the issuing bank, to honour or negotiate a complying presentation.

If a letter of credit's payment undertaking is guaranteed by a second bank, in addition to the bank originally issuing the credit this kind of credit is called confirmed letter of credit. The confirming bank agrees to pay or accept drafts against the credit even if the issuer refuses to do so. Only irrevocable credits can be confirmed.

5.5.9 Unconfirmed letters of credit

Unconfirmed letters of credit can be described as a letter of credit, which has not been guaranteed or confirmed by any bank other than the bank that opened it. In these types of credits, the only bank that undertakes to honour a complying presentation is the issuing bank.

5.5.10 Clean letters of credit

Below two different definitions of clean letters of credit are given.

A letter of credit payable upon presentation of the draft, without any supporting document being required.

L/C that does not require any document other than a written demand for payment by its beneficiary. In effect, a draft.

Clean letters of credit are issued only by the request of the highest credit standing companies. It is suitable for variety commercial situations where no movement of goods is expected. Historically these types of credits have been used in traveler's letters of credit. Today direct pay standby letter of credit can be given as an example of clean letters of credit.

There are also some other forms of letters of credit which deserve special attention. We will discuss them by one by more in detail however; you can find short description of each of them below.

5.5.11 Transferable letters of credit

Transferable letter of credit gives the intermediary (the first beneficiary of the letter of credit) an opportunity to apply to the bank for a transfer of the documentary credit for the benefit of the supplier (seller, the second beneficiary of the letter of credit). Thus, the intermediary buys the goods from the supplier with the same documentary credit that the intermediary sells the goods with to the buyer. The intermediary transfers its right to the documentary credit amount paid against documents that are in accordance with the conditions of the documentary credit to the supplier.

The conditions of the documentary credit, specified by the buyer i. e. the party opening the letter of credit, have to be fulfilled and the documents have to be submitted by the supplier. The intermediary exchanges only the supplier's invoice and the bill of exchange upon receipt of the documentation to the transferring bank (provided that the bill of exchange is required under the letter of credit). Therefore, the main task of the intermediary is to agree upon similar terms and conditions with both its buyer and the seller (with the exception of price), as the second beneficiary of the letter of credit or the seller must meet the terms stated by the buyer in the letter of credit.

The letter of credit is transferred in its original form. The first beneficiary of the letter of credit (the intermediary) has the right to change only the following terms upon the transfer of the documentary credit:

(1) documentary credit amount;

(2) price charged for goods (unit price);

(3) expiry date of the letter of credit;

(4) last date for the delivery of goods;

(5) date for presentation of documents.

All the aforementioned amounts can be decreased and the deadlines shortened. Also, the intermediary may increase the insurance amount so as to assure the compliance of the insurance with the provisions stated in the original documentary credit.

What are the benefits of transferable documentary credit for the intermediary?

(1) Transferable documentary credit is an opportunity to intermediate large trade transactions without having to use one's own funds (no need for credit decision);

(2) If the terms stated in the documentary credit allow partial shipments, the intermediary may transfer the documentary credit to a number of other beneficiaries of the documentary credit.

5.5.12 Untransferable letters of credit

It is said to the credit that seller cannot give a part of or complete right of assigned credit to somebody or to the persons he wants. In international commerce, it is required that the credit will be untransferable.

5.5.13 Back-to-back letters of credit

Arrangement in which one irrevocable letter of credit serves as the collateral for another; the advising bank of the first letter of credit becomes the issuing bank of the second L/C. Unlike transferable letters of credit, there are two separate letters of credit exist in back-to-back letter of credit transactions.

5.5.14 Advance payment (red clause) letters of credit

Letter of credit that carries a provision (traditionally written or typed in red ink) which allows a seller to draw up to a fixed sum from the advising or paying bank, in advance of the shipment or before presenting the prescribed documents.

5.6 How to read a L/C

You should understand the form of documentary credit. In order to do that you should look at field 40A: *Form of Documentary Credit* on the swift message.

You should find out the applicant of the documentary credit. Please look at field 50 : *Applicant* on the swift message.

You should find out the beneficiary of the documentary credit. Please look at field 59 : *Beneficiary - Name & Address* on the swift message.

You should find out the applicable rules of the documentary credit. Please look at field 40E : *Applicable Rules* on the swift message.

You should find out the date of issue of the documentary credit. Please look at field 31C : *Date of Issue* on the swift message.

You should find out the date and place of expiry of the documentary credit. Please look at field 31D : *Date and Place of Expiry* on the swift message.

You should find out the currency code and amount of the documentary credit. Please look at field 32B : *Currency Code, Amount* on the swift message.

You should find out whether letter of credit allows any tolerance level or not. Please look at field 39B : *Maximum Credit Amount* on the swift message.

You should find out the payment terms of the documentary credit as well as by whose counters letter of credit is payable. Please look at field 41A : *Available with... by...* on the swift message.

You should find out whether partial shipments and transhipments are allowed or not on the documentary credit. Please look at field 41P : *Partial Shipments* and field 43T : *Transhipment* on the swift message.

You should find out port of loading and port of discharge of the documentary credit. Please look at field 44E : *Port of Loading* and field 44F : *Port of Discharge* on the swift message.

You should find out the latest date of shipment of the documentary credit. Please look at field 44C : *Latest Date of Shipment* on the swift message.

You should find out how goods and services are defined on the documentary credit. Please look at field 45A : *Description of Goods &/or Services* on the swift message.

You should find out which documents are required under the documentary credit. Please look at field 46A : *Documents Required* on the swift message.

You should find out what kind of additional conditions are stated on the documentary credit. Please look at field 47A : *Additional Conditions* on the swift message.

You should find out which party is responsible for the charges of the documentary credit. Please look at field 71B : *Charges* on the swift message.

You should find out period for presentation of the documents required under the documentary credit. Please look at field 48 : *Period for Presentation* on the swift message.

You should find out whether the documentary credit is confirmed or not. Please look at field 49: *Confirmation Instructions* on the swift message.

You should find out whether any reimbursing bank defined under the documentary credit or not. Please look at field 53A : *Reimbursing Bank - BIC* on the swift message.

You should find out what sort of instructions given by the issuing bank to the paying/accepting/negotiating bank under the documentary credit. Please look at field 78 : *Instructions to Paying/Accepting/Negotiating Bank* on the swift message.

You should find out the advising bank of the documentary credit. Please look at field 57D : *Advise Through Bank – Name & Address* on the swift message.

5.7 Advantages and disadvantages of L/C

5.7.1 Advantages of letter of credit to exporter

One of the best methods after advance mode of payment for any business transaction is letter of credit (LC) mode, as buyer's bank guarantees payment to seller through seller's bank on presentation of required documents as per LC.

The major advantage of letter of credit to a supplier is minimizing of credit risk. In an import and export trade, the geographical distance between importer and exporter is very far; hence ascertaining credit worthiness of buyer is a major threat. In the mode of letter of credit, such risk can be avoided.

Buyer can not deny payment by raising dispute on quality of goods, as letter of credit terms and conditions are based on documentation. This is a major advantage of letter of credit in terms of seller point of view. Some of the fraudulent buyers deliberately delay or hold payments by complaining on quality of goods. In a letter of credit terms of business transactions, rejection of export payment by raising complaint on quality of goods can not be effected.

LC provides a security to exporter which is another advantage of a letter of credit. Based on such security, the exporter can preplan his further business activities to strengthen his business world.

In a letter of credit, any dispute in transaction can be settled easily, as LC terms and conditions are under the guidelines of uniform customs and practice of documentary credit. This is another advantage of a LC for an exporter.

In a letter of credit, all required documents have been mentioned well in advance of shipment and there is no confusion or misunderstanding to the importer (buyer) to inform supplier to act in between. This is a good advantage for a supplier to preplan efficiently which saves time.

Against a letter of credit, an exporter can avail pre shipment finance from banks or other financial institutions. This is another advantage of letter of credit for a seller. Many banks extend financial assistance with minimum bank interest, as letter of credit is a "safe export order".

Assurance to receive money in full is another advantage of letter of credit. In a letter of credit, an exporter can ensure that he receives full amount as per LC which helps seller to plan future business ideas.

Another advantage under a letter of credit transaction is that the exporter receives money on time. As you know, "finance at right time" is a prime factor for any business transaction. So if a business man receives his anticipated amount on time, he can plan his business activities smoothly without wasting time. This is one of the major advantages of letter of credit. Assurance to receive money on time is one of the major advantages to supplier/exporter in a letter of credit terms.

Normally and widely, a confirmed irrevocable LC is opened by buyer and seller which is suitable for both. A "confirmed irrevocable letter of credit" is a "confirmed order" for any exporter concerned. So the exporter need not worry on cancellation of his export order or changes in said order. This helps a lot for an exporter for his business plans in various levels including financial plans, minimizing production risk, saving time etc.

Meeting delivery schedule by proper production plan is one of the major advantages under a letter of credit terms of business. Normally, under a non LC business terms, the buyer may keeps on changing delivery schedule as per their requirements time to time. So this change of delivery schedule at importer's interest leads exporter to rearrange his overall daily business activities.

5.7.2 Advantages of letter of credit to importer

While accepting a LC, the supplier guarantees to meet the terms and conditions of letter of credit with documentary proof. This is one of the major advantages of LC to an importer/buyer. This assurance provides security to buyer for future business plan.

Since buyer is the holder of letter of credit, bank acts on behalf of buyer. Opening bank remits amount only after satisfaction of all terms and conditions of letter of credit with documentary proof. This arrangement protects importer and minimizes time, as bank acts on behalf of him.

A letter of credit transaction reduces the risk of non performance by the supplier, as the supplier prefers LC than other transactions due to various reasons which protect him than the buyer. This is an advantage for the buyer on fulfillment of meeting commitments on shipments.

Another advantage of letter of credit to a buyer/importer is that the exporter/seller receives payment of exported goods only after shipment and meeting of all necessary requirements under LC terms and conditions with presentation of documentary proof including evidence of shipment.

Unlike other shipments, a shipment under letter of credit is treated with most care to meet delivery schedule and other required parameters by the exporter. The buyer will receive the documents. Unless meeting delivery schedule and prompt documentation, the supplier does not get his payment from opening bank. This is one of the major advantages of LC for an importer concerned.

An importer/buyer is concerned; he can plan his payment schedule properly by anticipating the requirements under letter of credit. This arrangement makes importer for easier planning.

Based on timely delivery schedule, buyer receives goods on time thereby he can execute his business plan smoothly and efficiently, in turn satisfying his clients promptly and effectively.

5.7.3 Disadvantages of letter of credit to exporter

While accepting a letter of credit, the exporter guarantees to meet the requirements of buyer as mutually agreed as per the terms and conditions mentioned in letter of credit. So the liability of meeting all required parameters are with supplier failing which bank may not accept documents under such transaction. Bank may debit certain charges against the discrepancy of documents also if proper documentary proof has not been submitted along with other shipping documents. So, if the exporter does not follow strictly with the terms and conditions of letter of credit with 100% compliance of documentation, the payment will not be effected by bank.

Under letter of credit opening procedures, there are certain bank charges and other costs. If buyer insists seller to pay such costs, the said charges will be additional expenses for the supplier.

If exporter is aware that the credit worthiness of buyer is favorable and sound, he does not need to open a letter of credit to transact with such buyers. However, he agrees on opening LC based on the requirements of buyer to enjoy the advantage of opening LC by buyer. In such cases, meeting of all terms and conditions under letter of credit is the major responsibility of exporter. Apart from meeting additional documentation procedures, exporter needs to spend additional expenses also.

An exporter must verify the authenticity of opening bank. The opening bank of letter of credit should be a prime banker. There are many cases of fraudulent LC opening bank who are not prime bankers and do not have proper "stand" to follow the guidelines of uniform customs and practice of documentary credit. So the strength and stability of LC issuing bank is a prime factor while discussing about the demerits of letter of credit.

Policy of a country may effect the business transaction between countries. If a cold ware is being continued between two countries, due to political reason, the trade bilateral agreement between such countries may become void, resulting to effect the guidelines of uniform customs and practice of documentary credit.

A best caliber of personnel is required to monitor and navigate the process of letter of credit to provide no room for even minute discrepancy of documents.

Compared to other modes of payment, the expenses for opening, negotiating and other procedures of letter of credit is high. This is another disadvantage of letter of credit for an exporter. This is another disadvantage of letter of credit for an exporter.

Currency fluctuation is another disadvantage of letter of credit. Normally buyer/importer places purchase orders once in a year and opens letter of credit accordingly. The exchange rate may differ at the time of shipping goods, from the time of opening LC. The exporter receives payment after shipment. So, if any loss due to fluctuations in foreign currency contracted under letter of credit, needs to be beard by him. This is also one of the major demerits of LC.

Currency fluctuations may also effect on price variation to procure raw materials for the buyer/exporter, resulting hike of cost of production in turn the exporter/seller can not hike the selling price, as the purchase order agreement already signed by accepting letter of credit for whole shipments under one LC. So currency fluctuation is also a threat under letter of credit which is treated as other disadvantages of letter of credit.

5.7.4 Disadvantages of letter of credit to importer

One of the major disadvantages of letter of credit is that LC is operated on the basis of documentation and not on the basis of physical verification of goods on its quality, quantity or other parameters. In other words, an LC issuing bank can effect payment to beneficiary of LC on the basis of documentation produced as per the terms and conditions of letter of credit. The parties under letter of credit do not have any right to physically verify the contents of goods. So, if the buyer needs to confirm and satisfy on the quality of goods he buys, he can appoint an inspection agency of international repute and instruct exporter to enclose certificate of such inspection by mentioning a condition in letter of credit.

Once opened a confirmed and irrevocable letter of credit, the importer/buyer already tied up with the said business credit line and can not change in between. Due to various reasons, especially on selling price variation, if buyer needs to stop his export order he can not do so.

Compared to other payment mode of transactions, cost of operating letter of credit procedures and formalities are more, which may be an additional expenses to an importer especially on amendment, negotiation etc.

第 6 章

银行保函、国际保理与福费廷

6.1 银行保函

6.1.1 银行保函的含义

银行保函或银行保证书是指商业银行根据申请人的要求向受益人开出的担保申请人正常履行合同义务的书面证明，它是银行有条件承担一定经济责任的法律文件。当申请人未能履行其承诺的义务时，银行负有向受益人赔偿经济损失的责任。

作为第三方的信用凭证，银行保函以银行信用提供保证，消除了受益人对申请人履约能力的疑虑，从而促进了交易的进行，这是保函的基本功能之一。此外，保函还用于保证预付货款的归还、贷款及利息的偿还、合同标的质量完好等。

概括来说，保函具有两个基本的功能：一是保证合同价款的支付；二是当发生违约时，对受害人进行补偿并对违约方进行经济处罚。根据这两个基本功能，保函既可以用来充当交易的一种支付手段，也可以当作制约当事人履约的手段或是违约的补偿保证手段。

6.1.2 银行保函的当事人

1. 申请人(Applicant)

申请人即向担保行申请开立保函的人。他应该按照合同的规定履行其应尽的责任义务，具体来说就是负担保函项下的费用和利息，并在担保行依据保函条款的规定履行担保责任向受益人赔付款项时，立即对其进行补偿。此外，在保函实务中，担保行为了减少风险，往往还要求申请人提交反担保或财产抵押，在这种情况下，申请人必须按担保行的规定提供他认可的反担保或财产抵押。

保函的申请人因业务不同，可以是投标人(Tenderer)、供货人(Supplier)、买方(Buyer)、卖方(Seller)、签约人(Contractor)、承租人(Lessee)等，不一而足。从这一点可以看出保函的适应范围是十分广泛的。

2. 受益人(Beneficiary)

受益人即接受保函并有权按保函条款的规定向担保行索赔的人。具体来说，受益人按照合约的规定提供货物或劳务等，在保函规定的索赔条件具备时，可凭索赔文件或连同有关单据，要求担保行赔付。因而，受益人的责任是履行他在有关合约项下的义务，他的权益即为凭合格的索赔单据向担保行提出索赔要求。

3. 担保行(Guarantor Bank)

担保行即受申请人的委托向受益人开立保函的商业银行。担保行的责任是促使申请人履行合同的各项义务;在申请人违约时,根据受益人提出的索赔文件和保函的规定向受益人做出赔偿;并有权在赔偿后向申请人或反担保人索赔。

4. 通知行(Advising Bank)

通知行即受担保行的委托将保函通知或传递给受益人的银行,通常是受益人所在地的银行。通知行的责任是:负责核实保函表面的真实性,并严格按照担保行的要求和指示及时将保函通知给受益人;如果因某种原因不能传递给受益人,应将情况及时告知担保行,以便担保行采取其他措施。通知行对保函内容是否正确,保函在寄递过程中可能出现的延误、遗失等均不负责,也不承担任何的支付保证责任。

5. 转开行(Reissuing Bank)

转开行是根据原担保行的要求,向受益人开立以原担保行为申请人,反担保行为担保行的保函的银行。转开行一般是指示行(反担保行)的联行或代理行。转开行转开保函后,成为新的担保行,原担保行便成为保函的指示行(Instructing Bank)。转开行一般为受益人所在地银行,而指示行一般为申请人所在地银行。在跨国交易中,受益人出于对申请人所在国银行的不了解、不信任以及保函签发所在国的法律约束等原因,往往只接受以本国银行为担保的保函。因此,原担保行不得不在受益人国内寻找转开行转开保函,以保证交易正常进行。

6. 反担保行(Counter Guarantor Bank)

反担保行是接受申请人的委托向担保行出具不可撤销反担保,并承诺在申请人违约且无法付款时,负责赔偿担保行所做出的全部支付的银行。反担保行是与申请人有经济业务往来的其他银行。反担保行负有向担保行(或转开行)赔偿的责任,同时有权向申请人索偿。

7. 保兑行(Confirming Bank)

保兑行是根据担保行的请求,在保函上加具保兑,承诺当担保行无力赔偿时,代其履行付款责任的银行,也称第二担保行。当受益人认为担保银行的资信不足以信任时,可要求担保行寻找一家国际知名银行作为保兑行对保函加具保兑,相当于双重担保。保兑行在替担保行赔付后,有权向其索偿。

6.1.3 银行保函的内容

世界上银行保函没有统一的格式,但出于功能的需要,其基本内容大致相同。

1. 保函当事人(申请人、担保行、受益人、通知行等)的完整名称与详细地址

保函当事人的完整信息对于明确双方的权利、义务及产生争议时的法律诉讼有重要的意义。

2. 基础合同的内容

保函的开立是为了担保申请人履行基础合同。因此,保函中应当说明交易合同的内容、编号、开立日期、签约双方和有无修改等,从而明确担保行的责任范围。

3. 保函的编号、开立日期和种类

保函的编号是为了便于银行内部管理工作，保函的开立日期一般即为保函的生效日期，注明保函的开立日期有利于确定担保行的责任，对于不同性质和用途的保函，必须注明其种类。

4. 保函的金额和货币

保函的金额和货币影响到银行的担保限额，因此必须明确。保函金额的大小根据保函种类不同而不同，大小写应该一致。如果受益人的索偿金额按照申请人已履约部分的比例递减，则保函中应加以说明。

5. 保函的担保期限

保函的担保期限即保函的有效期，即从保函的生效日至到期日。只有在保函的有效期内，担保行才承担保证责任。所以受益人必须在规定的期限内向担保行提出赔付的要求，否则担保行可以不付款或不履行赔偿义务。同时，明确规定保函的期限也是担保行向申请人收取担保费用的依据之一。保函中明确规定担保期限对担保行和申请人都是有利的。

6. 保函的担保责任

保函的担保责任是银行保函的主体内容和核心，必须明确而详细地陈述。重点是担保行所承诺的担保责任，包括对履行条件和环境的变化的预测方式，都要在责任条款中明确。如："We undertake as a principal and not as an accessory debtor, to make payment of any amount due hereunder upon our receipt of written demand from the beneficiary..."

7. 保函索偿的条件和办法

索偿条件是说明受益人在什么条件下才能向担保人索偿，需要提交什么必要的证明文件。索偿办法是指受益人向担保行提出索偿的方式（如信索或电索）和途径（是否通过通知行）等。

除此以外，保函中还可能有鉴定条款、自动延展条款、担保责任不变条款、责任连带条款、不可转让条款等附加条款。

银行保函实例如图6.1所示。

Arabian International Company
For steel Structures

الشركة العربية الدولية للإنشاءات الحديدية

الرقم: ٠٨/٣٩٩/ف

التاريخ: ٢٤/٠٣/١٤٢٩هـ

الموافق: ٠١/٠٤/٢٠٠٨م

April 01st, 2008

To,
The Dept. Of Labour and Employment Promotion
Ministry Of Labour
HMG of Nepal

Dear Sir,

Sub: **Letter of Guarantee**

With due respect, we hereby guarantee that we will provide employment to all 260 Nepalese worker recruiting for the position of " Helper and Erector" by our local agent The River Overseas Pvt. Ltd. License No. 406/060/061, Ratopul, Gausala, Kathmandu, Nepal PO Box No. 2223 Tel No. 00977-01-4483015 / 4480639, in our company in RAS AL KHAIMAH in the territory of UAE During their contract period of three years.

Assuring you of our best attention at all times, we remains.

Thanks and best regards,

Wasim Attieh

Serial No. 1079
Ras Al Khaimah Chamber of Commerce & Industry certifies that
Arabian International For Steel Structure
Is registered under Membership No. 23353 and Commercial Registration No 66493
Date 9/4/2008
Director General

Ahmad M. Attieh & Sons Group

مجموعة أحمد محمد عطية وأولاده

Saudi Arabia (H.O.) P. O.Box 41017 Jeddah 21521 Tel.: 966-2-59-0999 Fax: 966-2-591-0099 E-mail: aic@aicsteel.com, www.aicsteel.com aic@aicsteel.com
Egypt Branch , Tel.: 002 22 63 1404, Fax: 0020 22 63 1406
U.A.E. Branch P.O.Box 6256, RAS AL KHAIMAH Tel.: 971-7-244 7372, Fax: 971-7-244 7375
Bahrain Branch P.O.Box 11375, Tel.: 973-241-472, Fax: 973-241-412

图 6.1 银行保函实例

6.1.4 保函的种类

1. 根据保函与基础交易合同的关系划分

1)从属性保函

其效力依附于基础交易合同,担保行依据保函所承担的付款责任成立与否,即基础合同的执行情况来加以确定。所以,此类保函是基础合同的附属性合同,两者是从合同与主合同的关系。

2)独立保函

其开立依据基础交易合同,但一旦开立便脱离合同,其效力不依附于基础交易合同而独立存在。其付款责任以自身的条款为准。目前,国际银行界的保函大多属于独立保函,而不是传统的附属性保函。

2. 根据保函支付的前提划分

1)付款类保函

付款类保函指银行为有关合同价款的支付义务提供担保所出具的保函。付款类保函担保行付款行为的发生与否,是以受益人能否按照保函中确定的要求去履行自己的职责和义务为条件的。只要受益人履行了自己应尽的合同义务,从而获得了求索的权利,他就可以在保函项下提出索赔并取得自己应得的合同款项。因此,付款类保函支付的前提是受益人履约。

2)信用类保函

信用类保函指银行为合同一方有违约行为从而使其承担在合同项下的赔偿责任时,支付才可能发生所开立的保函。只要不出现保函的申请人作为合同一方违约的事件,担保行就不会有支付行为。所以,信用类保函支付的前提是申请人违约。

3. 根据保函索赔条件划分

1)有条件保函

有条件保函指担保行在保函中对索赔的发生与受理设立了若干条件,只有当这些条件得以满足的时候,担保行才履行支付赔偿的义务。这类保函有利于保护申请人的利益,防止受益人无理索赔和欺诈。

2)无条件保函

无条件保函也称为“见索即付”保函。在这类保函项下,担保行在受益人的简单书面索偿面前承担无条件支付义务,不论基础合同执行情况如何,也不论受益人本身是否履行合同中规定的义务,只要担保行在有效期内收到受益人提交的符合保函索赔条款的书面请求,就立即付款。在这种保函下,申请人及担保行承担的风险很大,有时遭遇受益人无理的索赔。不过,从国际银行保函业务看,无条件保函占了很大的比例。

4. 根据担保行付款责任的属性划分

1)第一性责任保函

此类保函中只要受益人的索赔满足保函规定的条件,担保行就承担第一性的付款责任,无须受益人先向申请人索要,也无须理会申请人是否愿意支付。

2)第二性责任保函

此类保函与第一性责任保函相反，担保行只有在受益人向申请人提出索赔而申请人予以拒付时才能向担保行提出索赔，所以担保行在此承担的是第二性的付款责任。

5. 根据业务范围划分

1）履约保函

履约保函的应用范围很广。在进出口贸易中，履约保函可以分为进口履约保函与出口履约保函。前者是在出口商履行交货义务后，担保进口商履行付款的义务；后者是担保出口商履行交货的义务，如果出口商违约，将由担保行负责赔偿进口商的损失。在招投标业务中，履约保函是担保行应中标方（承包商）的请求向招标方（发包方）出具的保证文件，担保受益人保证履行标书项下的合同义务。

2）预付款保函

在进出口贸易中，有时进口商在合同项下提前支付货款给出口商，但为了防止对方不履约所导致的货款损失的风险，要求出口商提供预付货款的担保。担保的金额即进口商的预付货款金额加相应的利息。

3）关税保付保函

暂准进口货物为了不交纳关税，需要向进口国海关提供税费担保，关税保付保函就是起这个作用的。如果暂准进口货物到期不返运出国，海关就向担保行收取关税费用。关税保付保函一般在施工机械或参加展会的产品进入别国关境时提供给该国的海关。

银行保函的种类很多，以上仅仅就常见种类做一介绍。还有其他功能和用途的保函，例如：投标保函、补偿贸易保函、来料加工保函、技术引进保函、维修保函、融资租赁保函等。

6.1.5 保函的业务流程

一笔保函业务大概经过如下几个环节。

1. 申请人申请出保

申请人要求银行出具保函，一般要履行三个手续：填写开立保函申请书或签订委托担保协议；提交一定的保证金或提供反担保；提供业务的有关资料，以便银行对项目进行审查。

2. 担保行签发保函

银行对申请人提供的资料及申请人的资信审核通过后，便可以正式签发保函，这对担保行来说是一笔或有负债。因此，担保行出于风险考虑，在签发保函之前往往要对申请人的资信及财务状况、担保品及反担保措施、项目的可行性及效益、保函申请书或委托协议书等内容做详尽审查。在各项审核结果满意的情况下，银行会按照申请人的要求对外开出保函，并发往国外银行，请其代为通知或传递，或以信函方式开立后交由申请人直接寄往或转交国外受益人。

3. 保函的修改

银行保函可以在有效期内进行修改，但修改必须得到当事人一致同意才能进行，任何一方单方面对保函进行修改都是无效的。当各方同意修改后，由申请人向担保行提出书面申请并加盖印章，注明原保函编号、开立日期、金额等内容以及修改的详细条款和由此产生的责任条款，同时应出具受益人要求或同意修改的意思表示，供担保行参考。担保行在审查申请并同意修改后,向受益人发出修改函电,由负责人签字后发出。

4. 保函项下的索赔和理赔

担保行在保函有效期内,若收到受益人提交的索赔单据及有关证明文件,应以保函的索赔条款为依据对该索赔是否成立进行严格审核,并在确认索赔单据及有关证明文件完全与保函的索赔条款相符时及时对外付款,履行其在保函项下的付款责任。

通常,保函项下的索赔有三种。

1)受益人凭保函进行索赔

如果申请人在履行基础合同义务时违约,受益人就可以提出索赔。受益人必须准备好保函所规定的索赔文件或单据,并在保函失效前送达担保行,由担保行审核后进行相应的赔付。

2)担保行根据反担保协议向反担保行索赔

担保行在收到受益人的合格索赔单据时,在存在反担保协议的情况下,应立刻通知反担保行。担保行在对受益人做出赔付后,将受益人提交的单据或文件以及担保人出具的说明已收到合格索赔要求的书面声明转交反担保行,并根据反担保协议获得补偿。

3)反担保行向申请人索赔

反担保行在收到担保行的通知后,应立刻通知申请人,由其准备赔付资金。反担保行在有效期内收到担保行寄来的书面声明及受益人提供的索赔文件或单据时,应在合理的时间内根据反担保要求进行审核。若发现不符点,可以立即通知担保行拒付,并留存文件或单据听候处理;若审核无误,应立即做出赔付,并从申请人处获得相应资金。

5. 保函的撤销

一般来说,保函失效即可注销。但是,保函到期注销有两个条件:一是受益人在合同完结后立即将保函正本退回;二是由受益人签署文件,明确放弃保函项下的一切权利,凭此担保才能有权办理保函的撤销。此外,保函项下担保余额的全部支付也意味着保函的完结,担保行也可据此办理撤销手续。

6.2 国际保理

6.2.1 国际保理的含义

国际保理是指在国际贸易中,出口商在采用赊销、承兑交单等信用方式向进口商销售货物或提供服务时,由出口保理商和进口保理商共同提供的一项集商业资信调查、应收账款催收与管理、保理融资及信用风险控制与坏账担保于一体的综合金融服务。在保理业务中,保理商承担第一性的付款责任。保理业务也称保付代理、托收保理、承购应收账款。

6.2.2 国际保理对国际贸易的影响

1. 有利于出口商加快回收资金

出口商将货物装运完毕,即可获得不超过发票金额80%的有追索权的贸易融资,缩短资金回收周期,保证了较为充足的营运资金,加速了资本的周转。

2. 有利于出口商转移风险

只要出口商的商品品质和交货条件符合贸易合同的规定,在保理商无追索权地购买其出口债权后,出口商就可以将商业风险和汇价风险转嫁给保理商,潜在的坏账风险大大减小,债款的回收率明显提高。

3. 有利于出口商获取有关的信息

由于保理商熟悉海外市场和商业交易环境,很大程度上保证了对进口商资信调查的准确性和真实性,为出口商决定是否向进口商提供商业信用提供了可靠的依据。保理商还经常向中小出口商就海外市场情况和进口国的有关法规提出出口建议,替他们寻找买主和代理商,协助其打入国际市场,增强其竞争力。

4. 会增大企业出口成本

保理业务依据业务性质、地域不同来评估风险,从而收费也不同,但都会直接提高出口商的出口成本,导致出口价格上升或利润下降。但对于出口商品利润较大,收款风险也较大的地区,保理业务不失为一个较好的选择。

6.2.3 国际保理的服务项目

1. 销售分户账的管理(Maintenance of the Sales Ledger)

对出口企业销售分户账的管理是指出口商发出货物后,将有关的售后账务管理交给保理商。销售分户账的管理是确保出口企业正常生产、经营和销售的必要手段;是出口企业减少经营开支、提高经济效益的最基本的财务管理工作。

具体做法是:保理商收到客户(出口商)交来的销售发票后,在电脑中设立分户账,输入必要的信息和参考数据,如债务人、金额、支付方式、付款期限等,然后由电脑进行自动处理,诸如记账、催收、清算、计息、收费、统计报表的打印等工作,保理商可根据客户的要求,随时或定期提供各种数字和资料。

2. 收取应收账款(Collection from Debtors)

收取应收账款及债款回收是一种技术性、法律性较强的工作。一般出口商甚至畅销产品的卖主因缺乏这种回收债权的技术,常常导致营运资金周转不灵、应收账款不能及时回收、应付账款不能及时偿付,给出口企业带来生产、经营、销售链条上的障碍。而保理商拥有专门的法律部门,提供有效的法律服务。

债款回收的具体做法为:客户首先与保理商商议收债方式、程序和最后手续;然后,双方签订保付代理协议,各自按照协议规定享受权利与履行义务。

3. 信用销售控制(Credit Control)

信用销售控制是通过对进口商的资信调查及评估核定信用额度,掌握进口商资信的变化并调整其信用额度。国际贸易渠道和网络错综复杂,国际市场千变万化。出口企业了解和掌握客户资信的变化情况,制定出切实可行的信用销售限额和采取必要的防范措施,避免和减少潜在风险是至关重要的。然而,一般的中小企业很难做到这一点。保付代理商以独特的优势，利用保理商联合会广泛的代理网络和官方或民间的资信机构，利用其母行在国外的广泛分支机构和代理网络，通过现代化手段获得最新的动态资料，依据所掌握的客户资信情况的变化，为出口商提供其客户的信用销售额度，从而将应收账款的风险降到最低。

4. 坏账担保(Full Protection Against Bad Debts)

保理商对坏账担保的服务项目是有限制条件的。通常，保理商对其客户并非提供100%的坏账担保，而只对已核准的应收账款提供100%的坏账担保。这就是说，只要供应商对其每个客户的销售控制在保理商核定的信用销售限额内，就能有效消除因买方信用造成的坏账风险。但对因供应产品的质量、服务水平、交货期等引起的贸易纠纷而造成的坏账和呆账，保理商不负赔偿之责。

5. 贸易融资(Trade Financing)

保理商在促进企业改善经营管理、提高经济效益、提供贸易融资服务等方面起着不可忽视的作用。保理商可以向供应商提供无追索权的贸易融资，而且手续简单。它不像信用放款那样需要复杂的手续，也不像抵押放款那样需要办理抵押品的移交和过户手续。供应商在发货或提供技术服务后，将发票通知保理商，即可立即获得不超过80%发票金额和无追索权的预付款融资，基本解决了在途和信用销售的资金占用问题。

根据国际保理公约的规定，保理商的职责主要是履行上述五项中的至少两项。

6.2.4 国际保理的当事人

1. 出口商(Exporter)

出口商对所提供的货物和服务出具发票，将商业发票表示的应收账款转让给保理商叙做保理业务。

2. 债务人(Debtor)

债务人是国际贸易的进口商，对出口商提供的产品或服务所产生的应收账款负有付款责任的一方。

3. 出口保理商(Exporter Factor)

出口保理商是与出口商签订保理协议，从而为出口商对进口商进行资信调查，进而提供相应的信用担保，在担保的进口商信用额度内，对由出口商出具商业发票表明的应收账款做保理业务的一方。出口保理商在出口商所在地。

4. 进口保理商(Import Factor)

进口保理商是根据与出口保理商的协议，为出口保理商就近调查进口商的资信，并根据调查情况提出进口商的信用额度，在该额度内代收已由出口保理商转过来的应收账款，并有义务支付该款项的一方。根据《国际保理业务惯例规则》，进口保理商对出口保理商过户给它的并已承担信用风险的应收账款必须付款。进口保理商对出口商承担担保付款的责任。

出口商以商业信用形式出卖商品，在货物装船后即将应收账款无追索权地转卖给保理商，从而使出口商的部分或全部应收账款立即转换成现金，实际上是将出口应收账款贴现，或者说将出口应收账款卖断给出口保理商。因此，保理业务从保理商的角度也被称为承购应收账款。

6.2.5 国际保理的业务流程

根据《国际保理管理规则》的规定,每一笔国际保理业务一般都牵涉四个当事人:出口商、进口商、出口保理商和进口保理商。其业务流程包含如下七个阶段。

1. 出口商向出口保理商提出保理申请

出口商向出口保理商提出申请,填写保理商提供的“信用额度申请表”,此表的主要内容包括准备达成的买卖合同,进口商名称、地址以及申请的信用额度。

2. 出口保理商委托进口保理商核定“买方信用额度”

出口保理商向进口保理商寄出“信用额度申请表”和“出口商信息表”。进口保理商对指定的进口商的资信情况、经营作风等进行调查和评估,并在收到申请后的14天内将结果及该进口商的信用额度汇报给出口保理商。

3. 签订保理协议

出口保理商将进口保理商的调查结果和批准的信用额度告知出口商,在出口商接受该信用额度的基础上双方签订保理协议。其主要内容为:出口业务的范围、信用额度、所提供的保理服务的种类和手续以及费用等。出口商需将保理协议通知进口保理商并取得进口保理商的正式批准。根据《国际保理业务惯例规则》的规定,进口保理商将承担债务人未能按照有关销售或服务合同条款在到期日全额支付已核准应收账款所产生的损失风险。

4. 进出口商签订贸易合同

出口商和进口商签订以汇款中的赊账或托收作为支付方式的国际货物买卖合同,金额以保理商提供的信用额度为最高限额。

5. 出口商装货、制单并交单

合同签订后,出口商按照合同备货、装运并向出口保理商交单,请其依据保理委托协议通过进口保理商向进口商提示单据,要求付款。当出口商提出融资时,出口保理商可按照双方的保理协议在此时向出口商提供一定金额的资金融通。一般情况下,保理商提供的预支金额不超过全部贷款的90%,但对一些信用特别可靠的出口商,有全额预支的。

6. 出口保理商向进口保理商提出委托

出口保理商在收到出口商交付的单据并检验合格后,将单据寄给进口保理商,委托进口保理商向进口商提示,要求付款或承兑后付款。

7. 进口保理商向进口商提示单据,付款人付款或拒付

如在被提示单据后,进口商及时按合同规定付款,则由进口保理商将款项通过出口保理商交出口商,从而顺利完成一笔收款业务;如果在要求付款时遭到进口商拒付,则进口保理商应依约承担付款责任,并在付款后获得向进口商索偿的权利。

出口商需要保理商的服务时,需交纳一定的保理手续费,一般是所收账款的1%~3%不等,由保理商视实务繁简及风险大小而定。出口商在向保理商交单时还可以要求保理商给予融资便利,但要承担融资利息。

需要注意的是,出口商应在保理商确定的进口商信用额度内与进口商签订合同、发运货物。如因超过此额度而导致进口商拒付,保理商不予负责;出口商要严格执行合同交货,如由于货物问题而导致进口商拒付,保理商不予负责。

6.3 福费廷

6.3.1 福费廷的含义

福费廷(Forfaiting)属于担保业务的一种类型,是票据担保业务的最常见形式。它通常是因买进商品和劳务转让(主要是出口交易)而产生的将来某一个日子到期的债务,这种购买对原先的票据持有人无追索权。通常这些应收款项采用商业汇票或本票的形式,担保人应进口商之请求,在延期付款票据(远期汇票等)上加签担保,以便出口商向当地银行或金融机构进行贴现融资,且贴现机构对出口商无追索权。

6.3.2 福费廷的特点

(1)福费廷票据应产生于销售货物、技术或劳务服务的正当贸易。在大多数情况下,票据的开立都是以国际贸易为背景的。但随着同业竞争的加剧和业务技术的改进,少部分国内贸易也进入了福费廷业务的范畴。

(2)在福费廷业务中,出口商向包买商出卖票据时,包买商须声明无追索权,从而票据权利由出口商转让给包买商。与此同时,票据的风险也转让给了包买商。

(3)福费廷业务是一种中长期融资业务,融资期限至少是半年以上,以5~6年较多,也有长达10年之久的。包买商往往会对该笔包买业务进行风险评估,从而决定自己的时间期限。

(4)福费廷业务有三种叙做方式:①投资,购买票据后保留至到期日;②交易,购买票据后准备将来再出手获利;③ 经纪,即买卖同时进行。大多数银行都希望将其活动集中在一种业务上,不管是直接从出口商还是从其他银行买进票据。资金雄厚的大银行仅把福费廷作为一种投资。

(5)出口商叙做福费廷,实际上是将赊销变成了一次现金交易。其仅有的责任就是生产和提供符合贸易合同规定的货物或劳务,并正确开立票据(远期汇票)。

6.3.3 福费廷当事人

1. 包买商(银行)

包买商多为出口商所在国的银行及有中长期信贷能力的大金融公司。当包买商与出口商达成包买业务协议,并购入出口商转让的票据后,即成为该延期付款交易的信贷机构,并承担了向进口商分期收回货款及利率、汇率变动的风险。

2. 出口商

出口商为资本货物交易中的供货方。当出口商以延期付款方式与进口商达成交易而需要资金支持时，可向包买商申请包买票据融资。当出口商将表明交易金额的若干票据全部转售给包买商并支付贴息后，即可取得贴现净额，提前收回货款。

3. 进口商

进口商为资本货物交易中的进货方。当进口商在包买商的资助下以延期付款方式购入货物后，在作为正当持票人的包买商向其提出付款要求时，应无条件履行其在票据上的债务责任，按期归还货款。

4. 担保人

担保人虽不是包买票据的直接当事人，但担保人及其担保对包买业务至关重要。包买商为了转移及规避风险，只购入经担保人担保的票据。若进口商不能按期偿还货款，担保人有责任代其偿还。担保人多为进口地银行，在履行付款责任后，担保人有权向进口商追索，但追索能否成功取决于进口商的资信状况，故担保人承担追索不能成功的风险。

6.3.4 福费廷的业务流程

福费廷可以是无证项下的融资，也可以是远期信用证项下的业务。以下对福费廷的一般业务流程做一些介绍。

1. 申请

如果出口商打算利用福费廷来取得资金融通，就要尽早与包买商取得联系，甚至在和进口商签订贸易合同之前就要打招呼。包买商一般会原则上表明是否提供福费廷以及其他具体的要求。在此基础上，出口商提出正式申请。

2. 审查

包买商在收到出口商的申请时，要进行一番调查及风险分析，以决定是否承做这笔业务。调查的内容包括出口商的详细情况，如资信状况、经营业绩等，以确定出口商有履行合同的能力，进口商的经营地点、资信状况，担保人的信誉，融资的币种、金额，商品的类别，有关的进出口许可证是否办妥，票据的付款地等。只有包买商确信在合同的履行中没有明显的阻碍，才能接受出口商的申请。若包买商同意承做这笔业务，就会立即对出口商提供相应的报价，如果出口商接受了报价，在包买商确认后，包买商即开始承担将来按这种价格向出口商购买某种票据的责任和义务。此项确认也叫承诺函，是叙做福费廷双方的合同，如果任何一方违约或单方面终止交易，违约一方必须赔付对方因此而造成的一切损失和费用。出口商接受了报价，就要按规定在约定的时间将债权凭证出售给包买商。一般的，为使贴现尽早进行，一些单据可预先出具。由于货物还没发运，所以单据的出具日和到期日可暂不填，并将这些单据存放在出口商或包买商所在地的一家银行(远期信用证项下的票据不能用这种方法)。出口商发货后，立即将运输单据交给寄存银行，由寄存银行根据出口商的授权在票据上加注出票日期，至到期日交给出口商，出口商直接交给包买商进行贴现。

3. 付款

包买商对出口商所提交的单据审核无误后，即按原承诺函中的贴现率向出口商付款。同时向出口商和担保人各提交一份清单，前者列明贴现率、每期票据的面额及贴现后的净额，后者列明每期票据的到期日、金额和币别等。

4. 清算

票据到期时，包买商对进口商提示付款，进口商付款后，此笔交易即告结束。

以上过程的具体步骤可以用图 6.2 简示。

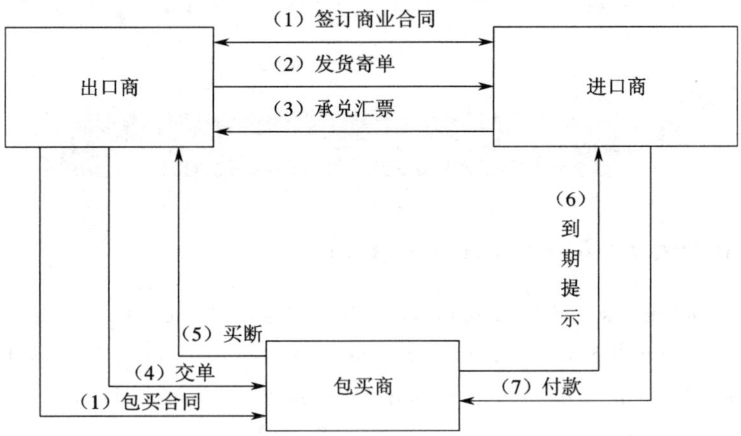

图 6.2　福费廷的业务流程

目前国内各银行大多对远期信用证下的已承兑汇票做福费廷业务，其流程如图 6.3 所示。

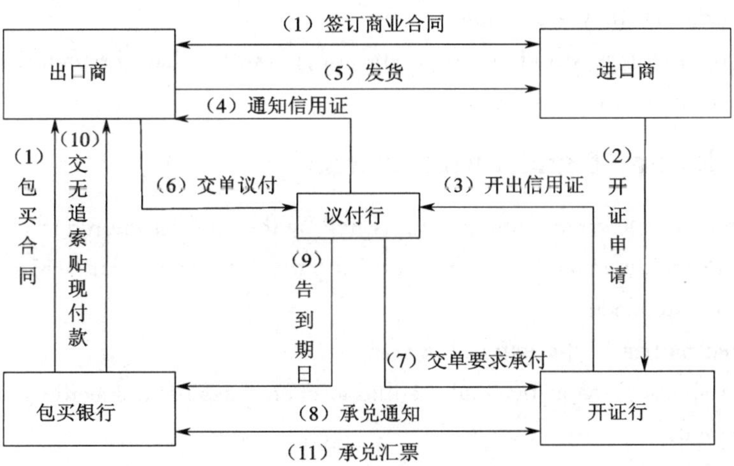

图 6.3　国内银行做福费廷业务的流程

Chapter 6

Letters of Guarantee, International Factoring and International Forfeiting

6.1 Letters of guarantee

6.1.1 Definition of letters of guarantee

It is a type of contract issued by a bank on behalf of a customer who has entered a contract to purchase goods from a supplier and promises to meet any financial obligations to the supplier in the event of default and also it is a document issued by a bank on behalf of a call writer guaranteeing that the writer owns the underlying asset and that the bank will deliver the underlying securities should the call be exercised.

A letter of guarantee often helps firms conduct business with parties they would never normally get the chance to deal with. Many suppliers will often choose to do business with customers that have a letter of guarantee because it eliminates the risk that they will not receive the appropriate payment for the goods that they are selling.

Additionally, call writers will often use a letter of guarantee when the underlying asset of a call option is not held in their brokerage account.

6.1.2 How letter of guarantee works

Letter of guarantee is a written undertaking issued by the bank at the request of his client (businessman) to pay a specific amount of cash to a third party (the beneficiary) within a specified period (which may be extended).

There are three parties in the letter of guarantee.

(1) Bank: (a sponsor) as a financial institution charge against a specific guarantee of a commission from the client.

(2) Client: (which is guaranteed), which requires the bank issuing the letter of guarantee.

(3) Beneficiary: (which guaranteed him) any entity or person who issued the letter for him.

That the issuance of the letter of guarantee means banking join the bank client to ensure the fulfillment of its obligations to a third party (i. e. the beneficiary).

Let's assume XYZ Company has a subsidiary named ABC Company. ABC Company would like to build a new plant and thus would like to borrow $10 million from a bank. The bank will probably require XYZ Company to guarantee the loan in writing by issuing a letter of guarantee. By doing so, XYZ Company agrees to repay the loan using cash flows from other parts of its business if ABC Company is unable to generate enough cash on its own to repay the debt.

Often a parent company will guarantee bonds issued by one of the parent's subsidiaries, but there are plenty of other situations that might involve letters of guarantee. For example, vendors sometimes require letters of guarantee from their customers if the vendor is uncertain about the customer's ability to pay (this most often happens in transactions involving expensive equipment or other physical property). In these situations, the customer's bank might issue a letter of guarantee for the customer's payment, meaning that the bank will pay the vendor if the customer does not.

Letters of guarantee don't always guarantee the entire amount of a liability. In bond issues, for example, the letter might only guarantee the repayment of interest or principal, but not both. Sometimes more than one company might guarantee a security; in these cases, each letter of guarantee pertains to a pro rata portion of the issue, but in other cases, a letter of guarantee may make a guarantor responsible for the other guarantors' portions if they also default on their responsibilities.

6.1.3 General issuing process for letters of guarantee

1. Examination and issuance of letter of guarantee

(1) The bank examines the customer qualification, underlying transaction and relevant materials.

(2) The bank confirms the customer's margin or credit line and other mortgage.

(3) The bank examines the written application and form of letter of guarantee.

(4) The bank issues the letter of guarantee.

2. Letter of guarantee fees

The letter of guarantee fees should be charged by the charging principles and rates determined in accordance with relevant rules of the head office of Bank of China.

3. Amendment to letter of guarantee

The clauses of the letter of guarantee can be amended on request of the guaranteed party and the beneficiary, such as extension of the validity period.

4. Payment/compensation against letter of guarantee

In case the beneficiary claims compensation within the validity period of the guarantee, the applicant shall be notified in time. The payment should be made after the guaranteeing bank examines the claim documents and confirms that the documents are in compliance with the claim clauses of the guarantee.

5. Guarantee final-period management

(1) The bank updates the customer records for any major change of customers.

(2) The bank stores all the letter of guarantee records in a centralized way, and checks them, ensuring that the records reflect the whole process of operation.

(3) Upon confirmed relief from the letter of guarantee liability, the bank revokes the guarantee, and accordingly recovers the credit line of the guarantee applicant or refunds the margin.

6.1.4 Risk and concern

Letters of guarantee can mitigate risk, but it is important to note that they do not make a security risk-free. After all, it is still possible that even the guarantor can default on the liability if the liability is too large or if the guarantor is already struggling for other reasons. Regardless, letters of guarantee provide an extra layer of security, which is why guaranteed securities often get higher credit ratings.

Historically, guarantors disclosed the nature and size of their written guarantees in the notes to their financial statements. But in 2002, the Financial Accounting Standards Board (FASB) issued Interpretation 45, stating that guarantors must book the fair value of the guaranteed obligation as a liability on the balance sheet and that they must do so at the inception of the guarantee. Some guarantees, such as those accounted for as derivatives, those issued by insurance companies, and some guarantees issued by leasing companies, are exempt from this rule. It is important to note that guarantees issued between parents and their subsidiaries do not have to be booked as balance sheet liabilities. Examples of this include the parent's guarantee of a subsidiary's debt to a third party or a subsidiary's guarantee of the parent's debt to a third party or another subsidiary.

All guarantees must, however, be disclosed. The guarantor must disclose the nature of the guarantee (terms, history, and events that would put the guarantor on the hook), the maximum potential liability under the guarantee, and any provisions that might enable the guarantor to recover any money paid out under the guarantee.

6.1.5 Types of letters of guarantee

1. Accessory guarantees

An accessory guarantee is inherently linked to the underlying contract between the principal and the beneficiary. Under this type of guarantee, neither the principal nor the bank is required to make payment to a beneficiary's claim unless the beneficiary has proven the validity of his claim and presents a court decision, arbitration agreement or written consent from the principal allowing payment.

2. Non-accessory guarantees

Non-accessory guarantees do not have ties to the underlying business agreement between the principal and the beneficiary and instead of requiring the beneficiary to prove the validity of his claim, payment is made first and questioned later; this is a more secure form of guarantee for the beneficiary. Standby letter of credit and demand guarantees fall under the non-accessory category. The demand or simple demand guarantees, in most cases, do not require documentation to back up a claim for payment.

3. Direct and indirect guarantees

Direct guarantees are set up and executed through one bank, the bank at which the principal applies for the guarantee, known as the issuing bank. Indirect guarantees are set up through one bank and then executed through another bank that is local to the benefactor. The local bank then gets a guarantee from the issuing bank to cover any claims. Direct guarantees are typically less expensive and more secure for the principal, whereas indirect guarantees are more secure for an out-of-country beneficiary.

4. Supporting the principal

There are several types of guarantees designed to support the principal's contractual obligations to the beneficiary of the guarantee. These principal supporting guarantees include tender and bid, advanced payment, and performance and retention guarantees are designed to assist the principal either in meeting his contractual obligations or in making remands for the inability to meet him.

5. Supporting the beneficiary

Some guarantees are designed to assist the beneficiary in meeting his contractual obligations or recovering losses for the inability of the principal to live up to his end of the deal. Warranty, loan and payment guarantees are all structured to support the beneficiary in making payments or recovering funds from an unsatisfied contract. These types of guarantees usually guarantee a certain percentage of the value of the contract, for instance 5 percent, but may cover the full value.

6.1.6 The differences between letters of guarantee and letter of credit

A bank guarantee and a letter of credit are similar in many ways but they're two different things. Letters of credit ensure that a transaction proceeds as planned, while bank guarantees reduce the loss if the transaction doesn't go as planned.

A letter of credit is an obligation taken on by a bank to make a payment once certain criteria are met. Once these terms are completed and confirmed, the bank will transfer the funds. This ensures that the payment will be made as long as the services are performed.

A bank guarantee, like a line of credit, guarantees a sum of money to a beneficiary. Unlike a line of credit, the sum is only paid if the opposing party does not fulfill the stipulated obligations under the contract. This can be used to essentially insure a buyer or seller from loss or damage due to nonperformance by the other party in a contract.

For example a letter of credit could be used in the delivery of goods or the completion of a service. The seller may request that the buyer obtain a letter of credit before the transaction occurs. The buyer would purchase this letter of credit from a bank and forward it to the seller's bank. This letter would substitute the bank's credit for that of its client, ensuring correct and timely payment.

A bank guarantee might be used when a buyer obtains goods from a seller then runs into cash flow difficulties and can't pay the seller. The bank guarantee would pay an agreed-upon sum to the seller. Similarly, if the supplier was unable to provide the goods, the bank would then pay the purchaser the agreed-upon sum. Essentially, the bank guarantee acts as a safety measure for the opposing party in the transaction.

6.2 International factoring

6.2.1 Definition of international factoring

Factoring is a form of financing in which a business sells its receivables to a third party or "factor company" at a discounted price. Under this arrangement, a factoring company agrees to provide financing and other services to the selling business in return for interest and fees on the money that it advanced against the seller's accounts receivables. Businesses in need of cash can thus secure about 80 percent of their accounts receivables' face value. In rare cases, a higher percentage can be secured, but in most instances 20 percent of the value of the accounts receivable is held in reserve until the accounts are collected.

Factoring is a tool used by many established firms to avoid the sorts of cash flow problems that arise because of a customer's slow payment patterns. Economic downturns are often accompanied by an elongating of the average invoice payment time. Cash is the lifeblood of a business. Managing it efficiently is essential for success. It is often a lack of cash flow rather than a lack of sales that prevents companies from developing beyond their initial stages. Factoring agreements are one way that businesses with established sales can, for a price, guarantee smooth cash flow. Since factoring is a practice based on lending against accounts receivable, it is not a realistic source of capital for start-ups.

There are two primary financing agreements entered into by factoring companies, recourse and nonrecourse financing. Recourse financing is an agreement under which the borrower maintains the responsibility for any bad debt or uncollectible invoices that it has issued. Nonrecourse financing is the term used when the factoring company bears the risk of collecting from its client's clients. It takes on the responsibility for collecting and covers uncollectible invoices.

As for the international factoring, it is a comprehensive financial instrument that combines cash flow management and credit risk management in cross-border trade. It includes financing granted to the exporter, receivables management, receivables collection, and the buyer's credit guarantee.

6.2.2 How factoring works

The factoring process varies from agreement to agreement but the basics are similar in most situations. A business that is working with a factoring company, upon invoicing its clients, will send a copy of each invoice issued to the factoring company. On receipt of the invoices, the factoring company immediately provides its client with 80 to 85 percent of the value of the invoices received.

Once the outstanding invoices are paid by the business's customers to the factoring company it pays the business the remaining 20 percent of the value of those invoices less prearranged charges. Factoring charges include a fee and interest on the 80 to 85 percent paid in advance of collections.

In some respects, the factoring process is roughly comparable to credit card arrangements. Just as MasterCard buys a retailer's receivables and pays the store as soon as a sale is made, factoring companies do much the same thing on the wholesale level. For example, assume a toaster manufacturer ships a $150,000 order to one of its customers. Rather than waiting for the customer to pay, the manufacturer can sell the receivables to a factor, receiving up to 85 percent of the $150,000 total as soon as the goods leave the shipping dock and an invoice is sent. This speeds the collection process. The balance is paid, less factoring charges, when the factor collects from the toaster manufacturer's customer.

Small business owners should be aware that factoring is different in several fundamental respects from bank financing. For one thing, it is much more expensive. Factoring charges can cost between 2 percent and 10 percent of sales. Arrangements for fees vary widely, depending on the credit quality of the borrower's customer account balances and the range of services that are purchased from the factor. In addition, small business owners should recognize that utilizing a factoring company is an all-or-nothing proposition. Factors generally demand 100 percent of a client's receivables. They will not limit their efforts to those receivables considered marginal or high risk.

6.2.3 Growth of factoring

Factor companies are an increasingly mainstream choice for small business owners seeking capital. According to the World Bank, in its report entitled financing small and medium-size enterprises with factoring, the volume of business handled by factors in the United States increased 15.2 percent between 1998 and 2003. Indeed, even though factoring carries some risks for small enterprises, it is regarded as a viable short-term cash management tool.

Factoring companies usually include a range of accounts receivable services as a part of their overall service. These services include such things as bookkeeping, collections, and credit verification. By reducing the in-house cost of managing these tasks it is more likely that a business will be able to justify the cost of working with a factoring company.

Although the cost of working with a factoring company is high, it may still be more cost effective than offering customers a 6 percent early payment discount in order to encourage the early payment of invoices. A factor will provide a business with cash almost immediately upon shipping a product whereas early payment discounts will usually only bring in payments marginally sooner than would be the case without the discount. Working with a factor is far more likely to offer substantial cash flow benefits than simply speeding up the collection period. The growth of factoring suggests that many companies are finding it a profitable way in which to help manage cash flow.

6.2.4 Selecting a factor

Selecting a factor is much like selecting any other service provider. The objective is to find the best price for the services provided. Several considerations should be weighed by the small business owner in making fee arrangements with a factor.

Recourse—small business enterprises that elected to go with a recourse factor (in which they bear final responsibility for collecting monies owed) over nonrecourse factors (where the factoring company bears that responsibility) will find that they may gain lower fees and more money from the factor in return for increasing their risk.

Customer base—the larger the number of customers a business has, the more cost advantages the factor can offer the business. Automation provides factors with significant economies of scale when a large number of customers are involved.

Creditworthiness of customers—factoring companies will assess the credit worthiness of a business's clients and use this as an important element in pricing the factoring services for that business. Factors will not purchase substandard customer balances.

Size and age of the average invoice—smaller receivables that have been on the books for a while will result in less advantageous factoring arrangements for small business owners than will large, current receivables.

Factor preferences—some factors tend to work with larger businesses, while others concentrate their efforts on smaller enterprises. Large factoring companies tend to focus their attentions on companies that have at least \$10 million in annual sales, while smaller factoring companies—sometimes known as "re-factors"—may provide services to companies with annual sales as low as \$300,000.

Industry knowledge—most factors that reach agreements with small businesses will have a fairly solid understanding of the industry and competitive environment in which those businesses operate. Such factoring companies can provide help to small businesses in determining who they should (and should not) extend credit to. In addition, factoring companies can be helpful in settling upon credit limits for both new and existing customers.

System compatibility—most businesses in today's environment have implemented automated processes to calculate and monitor accounts receivable and cash applications of cash received. Small business owners should make sure that their systems are compatible with those of the factor before agreeing to a factoring arrangement.

Collections—as indicated above, this can be a tricky area for the small business owner. Handing over collection duties to a factoring company is expensive, and over-aggressive collection efforts on their part can damage a small business's relations with legitimate clients. However, factoring companies often have better luck in collecting money owed than do small business enterprises, which have more limited resources to dedicate to the collections process. Business owners should recognize, however, that the factor is only interested in business transactions in which their client is owed money. Factors will not be responsible for non-payment that is attributed to other issues, such as vendor disputes or defective merchandise.

A variety of institutions, including bank subsidiaries and finance companies, provide factoring services. These companies can be found via several different methodologies. The Commercial Finance Association offers a list of its members and their service offerings online at www. cfa. com. Many factoring businesses also advertise in local yellow pages under such headings as "factors" "financing commercial" "accounts receivable financing" or "billing service".

Procedures are as follow.

(1) The customer applies to the factor for pre-application for a factoring limit.

(2) The factor replies with the approved factoring limit and quotation within 10 working days.

(3) The exporter confirms the factoring limit and the quotation and then signs the factoring agreement.

(4) The exporter applies to the factor formally for the factoring limit.

(5) The factor replies with the final approved factoring limit.

(6) The exporter ships the goods and assigns the receivables under the invoice to the factor.

(7) The exporter receives the financing funds for up to 80% of the invoice value assigned.

(8) The factor collects payment from the importer upon maturity of the invoice and pays to the exporter the received payment minus the interest and other fees. The factor provides 100% indemnity to the exporter for any unpaid funds caused by the importer's bankruptcy or insolvency.

6.2.5 Benefits of factoring

One of the greatest advantages of export and import factoring is that it allows exporters to trade on open account terms without risk.

Commissions paid are based on sales volume. This means that costs fluctuate with actual sales giving lower operating costs during slow sales periods.

1. Benefits to the exporter

(1) The most secure and competitive method of settlement.

(2) Investigation of the credit standing of the importer to avoid credit risk.

(3) Flexible and convenient financial instrument.

(4) Earlier write-off and export tax refund.

(5) Collection and settlement of receivables.

2. Benefits to the importer

(1) Higher utilization efficiency of the importer's credit.

(2) Payment by credit to minimize the pressure on working capital.

(3) Consolidation of cooperation between the buyer and the seller.

6.3 International forfaiting

6.3.1 What is international forfaiting

Forfaiting is a method of trade finance that allows exporters to obtain cash by selling their medium and long-term foreign accounts receivable at a discount on a "without recourse" basis. A forfaiter is a specialized finance firm or a department in a bank that performs non-recourse export financing through the purchase of medium and long-term trade receivables. "Without recourse" or "non-recourse" means that the forfaiter assumes and accepts the risk of non-payment. Similar to factoring, forfaiting virtually eliminates the risk of non-payment, once the goods have been delivered to the foreign buyer in accordance with the terms of sale. However, unlike factors, forfaiters typically work with exporters who sell capital goods and commodities, or engage in large projects and therefore need to offer extended credit periods from 180 days to seven years or more. In forfaiting, receivables are normally guaranteed by the importer's bank, which allows the exporter to take the transaction off the balance sheet to enhance key financial ratios. The current minimum transaction size for forfaiting is $100,000. In the United States, most users of forfaiting are large established corporations, but small and medium-size companies are slowly embracing forfaiting as they become more aggressive in seeking financing solutions for exports to countries considered high risk.

6.3.2 Characteristics of forfaiting

Forfaiting is an international trade finance tool. It helps exporters or international manufacturing companies to reach cash flow by selling their debts which are mostly supported by a bank guarantee with a discounted price to forfaiting companies. Good thing is that selling debts under a forfating agreement is made without recourse basis, which means that once you sell your debt you will be passing the non-payment risk to the forfaiter. What would be happening to original?

(1) Payment obligation will not be your concern any more.

(2) Forfaiting can be applied to a wide range of trade related and purely financial receivables typically have maturities from 3 months to 10 years.

(3) Forfaiting can be applied to both international and domestic transactions.

(4) 100% financing without recourse to the seller of the debt.

(5) The payment obligation is often but not always supported by a bank guarantee.

(6) The debt is usually evidenced a legally enforceable and transferable payment obligation such as a bill of exchange, promissory note or letter of credit.

(7) Transaction values can range from US $100,000 to US $200 million.

(8) Debt instruments are typically denominated in one of the world's major currencies, with Euro and US Dollars being most common.

6.3.3 How forfaiting works

The exporter approaches a forfaiter before finalizing the transaction's structure. Once the forfaiter commits to the deal and sets the discount rate, the exporter can incorporate the discount into the selling price. The exporter then accepts a commitment issued by the forfaiter, signs the contract with the importer, and obtains, if required, a guarantee from the importer's bank that provides the documents required to complete the forfaiting. The exporter delivers the goods to the importer and delivers the documents to the forfaiter who verifies them and pays for them as agreed in the commitment. Since this payment is without recourse, the exporter has no further interest in the financial aspects of the transaction and it is the forfaiter who must collect the future payments due from the importer.

6.3.4 When to contact a forfaiter

Forfaiting is widely used by exporters and financial institutions throughout Europe because their sales and financing professionals work very closely together to develop a contract price proposal that makes the cost of financing competitive and attractive to foreign buyers, an approach not widely embraced and practiced in the United States. Thus, exporters should contact a forfaiter at the earliest possible point in formulating their sales and financing proposals so that they might better understand the subtleties and complexities of dealing in certain markets, including how to create a medium-term financing proposal at interest rates that are competitive, without reducing the margin on the sale.

6.3.5 Costs and benefits of forfaiting

The cost of forfaiting to the exporter is determined by the rate of discount based on the aggregate of the LIBOR (London inter bank offered rate) for the tenor of the receivables and a margin reflecting the risk being sold. In addition, there are certain costs that are borne by the importer that the exporter should also take into consideration. The degree of risk varies based on the importing country, the length of the loan, the currency of the transaction, and the repayment structure-the higher the risk, the higher the margin and therefore the discount rate. However, forfaiting can be more cost-effective than traditional trade finance tools because of the many attractive benefits it offers to the exporter.

Three additional major advantages of forfaiting are as follow.

(1) Volume: Forfaiting can work on a one-off transaction basis, without requiring an ongoing volume of business.

(2) Speed: Commitments can be issued within hours or days depending on details and country.

(3) Simplicity: Documentation is usually simple, concise, and straightforward.

6.3.6 Forfaiting industry profile

Forfaiting was developed in Switzerland in the 1950s to fill the gap between the exporter of capital goods, who would not or could not deal on open account, and the importer, who desired to defer payment until the capital equipment could begin to pay for itself. Although the number of forfaiting transactions is growing worldwide, there are currently no official statistics available on the size of the global forfaiting market. However, industry sources estimate that the total annual volume of new forfaiting transactions is around $30 billion and that forfaiting transactions worth $60 to $75 billion are outstanding at any given time. Industry sources also estimate that only 2 percent of world trade is financed through forfaiting. U. S. forfaiting transactions account for only 3 percent of that volume. Forfaiting firms have opened around the world, but the Europeans maintain a hold on the market, including in North America. Although these firms remain few in number in the United States, the innovative financing they provide should not be overlooked as a viable means of export finance for U. S. exporters.

第 7 章

国际结算单据

7.1 国际结算单据概述

国际贸易中,绝大部分的货物交货都是以象征性交货完成的。卖方交货义务的完成是以提交相关的贸易单据为标志的,尤其是提交代表物权凭证的单据。基本上所有的单据可以分为两类:金融单据与货运单据。主要的金融单据包括三种:汇票、本票和支票。货运单据包括金融单据之外所有的国际贸易中使用到的单据:商业发票、提单、装箱单、产地证、许可证、商品品质检验证明、保险单、重量单、形式发票、动植物检疫证明等。货运单据作为国际贸易的重要单证,大致分为基本单据和随附单据。基本单据主要有三种:运输单据(海运提单、海运单、空运单、快递收据等)、发票和保险单。随附单据涵盖三种基本单据外的所有货运单据:产地证、许可证、装箱单、重量单、品质证明等。

7.2 基本单据

7.2.1 运输单据

运输单据有多种,包括:海运提单、海运单、空运单、快递收据等。其中,最重要的运输单据是海运提单,它具有物权凭证的性质,即持有原始提单就等于拥有了在目的港提货的权利,从某种意义上说,国际贸易也是提单的买卖交易。

根据收货人栏目填写的不同,提单分为记名提单、不记名提单和指示提单。不记名提单无须背书即可转让;指示提单必须经过记名背书或空白背书才可以转让。

根据提单签发日期与实际装船日期的前后不同,提单可以分为倒签提单、过期提单、预借提单。倒签提单是货物装船后,承运人应托运人要求,将提单的签发日期提前到实际装船日期之前,以符合信用证装运期的要求。过期提单是指出口商取得提单后没能及时到银行交单议付(过了交单期)或过了信用证有效期的提单。另外,UCP600 规定,超过装运日期 21 天的提单也是过期提单。因此,信用证下的提单不过期须满足以上三个时间的限制。预借提单指信用证装运期将到而货物因故尚未装船,或已经开始装船但尚未完毕,托运人为了交单结汇向承运人提出预先签发装船提单。

根据提单是否附有关于货物状况的不良批注,提单分为清洁提单与不清洁提单。清洁提单指所承载货物状况完好,提单表面没有不良批注的提单;不清洁提单是因为货物包装不好,货物存在缺陷,承运人在提单上加注货物残损、锈蚀等不良批注的提单。在信用证业务中,银行只接受清洁提单,不接受不清洁提单。

7.2.2 发票

在国际贸易中常用到三种发票:商业发票、海关发票和形式发票。商业发票是出口商开给进口商的记账凭证,也是进出口报关纳税的证明文件,信用证下商业发票是所有单据的核心,很多单据都是参照商业发票制作的,它反映了该笔交易的全貌。海关发票是出口商根据进口国海关的要求制作的一种特定格式的发票,它的主要用途是供进口商办理报关纳税等手续使用。形式发票是出口商向进口商发出的有关货物名称、规格、单价等内容的非正式的参考性发票,供进口商申请进口批汇之用。它只能算是一种简式合同,不能用于托收和议付。

7.2.3 保险单

国际贸易货物要以各种不同的运输方式长途跋涉从出口国运送到进口国,在货物运送途中,有可能遇到各种各样的风险,从而使货物遭受到不同程度的损失。为了避免这种风险引起的损失,进出口商往往会在合同中协商安排保险事宜,将货物的风险转嫁给保险公司,一旦货物发生承保风险内损失,保险公司将予以相应的赔偿。

注意在投保时,首先要明确使用哪种保险条款。在我国,主要使用《中国保险条款》,它主要包括海洋、陆地、航空等多种运输方式的货物运输保险条款,其保险险别按照能否单独投保分为基本险和附加险。基本险可以单独投保,附加险不能单独投保,只能在基本险的基础上加投附加险。目前,我国国际贸易货物绝大部分以海洋运输方式完成运送,因此《中国保险条款》的《海洋货物运输保险条款》运用广泛,但与之类似的英国《伦敦保险协会货物保险条款》由于历史长久,在国际范围内更具有影响力。如果有客户要求按照《伦敦保险协会货物保险条款》投保,我方也是可以接受的。

常见的保险单分为以下几种。

1. 保险单

保险单又称大保单,是使用最广泛的一种保险单据。一般内容有:当事人名称和地址,保险标的名称、数量与重量,唛头,运输工具,保险险别,保险责任起讫时间与地点,赔付地点等。保险单背面写有保险人与被保险人之间的权利和义务的条款,这也是保险单的重要内容,特别涉及保险人的免责条款应当仔细阅读。

2. 保险凭证(Insurance Certificate)

保险凭证又称小保单,是一种简化的保险合同。这种单据正面与保险单相同,但背面没有写明保险人与被保险人之间的权利义务的条款。但它与大保单具有同等法律效力。在信用证业务中,有时保险凭证是不被银行接受的。但如果信用证要求提供保险凭证,受益人提供大保单来代替小保单是可以接受的。

3. 联合凭证(Combined Certificate)

联合凭证是一种更为简化的保险单据。由保险公司在出口公司提交的发票上加上保险编号、承保险别、保险金额并加盖保险公司的印章。

4. 批单(Endorsement)

保险单开立后,投保人如果需要变更保单内容,可根据保险公司的规定向保险公司提出申请,经同意后另出一种凭证,注明变更内容,此凭证称为批单。批单原则上须粘贴在保险单上,并加盖骑缝章,作为保险单不可分割的一部分。

5. 预约保险单(Open Policy)

预约保险单是一种长期的货物运输保险合同。合同内容主要包括:承保险别、承保范围、费率、责任赔偿等。凡是属于合同约定的运输货物,在合同有效期内自动承保。预约保险单的优点是减少了逐笔签订保险合同的手段,并可以防止因漏保或迟保造成的损失。一般保险公司对此种保单的投保人会给予一定的费率优惠。

7.3 随附单据

7.3.1 装箱单

装箱单(Packing List/Packing Slip)又称包装单,是表明出口货物的包装形式、包装内容、数量、质量、体积或件数的单据。其主要作用是作为海关、进出口商等验货的凭据以及商业发票的补充。是最常用的附属单据,是发票内容的补充。在进出口业务中,除了散装货物外,一般都要求提供装箱单。它是记载一批货物每一件包装内容的清单。

7.3.2 原产地证

原产地证明书(Certificate of Origin)是卖方应进口商的要求,自行签发或向特定的机构申请后由其签发的,证明出口商品的产地或制造地的一种证明文件。它是决定出口产品在进口国受何种关税待遇的重要证明文件,也是进口国对某些国家或某种商品采取控制进口额度和进口数量的依据。我国国家质量监督检验检疫总局(CIQ, CCIB, CCIC)和贸促会(CCPIT, CCC)分别代表官方和民间机构对外签发产地证(CIQ, China Inspection & Quarantine;CCIB, China Commodity Inspection Bureau;CCIC, China Commodity Inspection Company;CCPIT, China Council for Promotion of International Trade;CCC, China Chamber of Commerce)。

常见的原产地证明书有一般原产地证明书和普惠制原产地证明书。前者在中国由国际商会或者贸促会签发;后者由于涉及普惠制的适用,只能由国家质量监督检验检疫总局在各地的分局签发。

7.3.3 受益人证明

受益人证明(Beneficiary's Certificate)是一种由受益人自己出具的证明,以便证明自己履行了信用证规定的任务或证明自己按信用证的要求办事,如证明所交货物的品质、证明运输包装的处理、证明按要求寄单等。

7.3.4 装船通知

成交条件为 FOB/FCA,CFR/CPT 等还需要向进口国保险公司发出该通知以便其为进口商办理货物保险手续,出口装船通知应按合同或信用证规定的时间发出,该通知副本(Copy of Telex/Fax)常作为向银行交单议付的单据之一;在进口方派船接货的交易条件下,进口商为了使船、货衔接得当也会向出口方发出有关通知;通知以英文制作,无统一格式,内容一定要符合信用证的规定,一般只提供一份。

7.3.5 报检单

进出口商品报检是指进出口商品的收发货人或其代理人,根据《中华人民共和国商检法》等有关法律、法规,对法定检验的进出口商品,在检验检疫机构规定的时限和地点,向检验检疫机构申请检验、配合检验、缴费、取得商检单证等手续的全过程。

Chapter 7

Export documentation

7.1 Introduction to export documentation

The export process is made more complex by the wide variety of documents that the exporter needs to complete to ensure that the order reaches its destination quickly, safely and without problems. These documents range include those required by authorities (such as bills of entry, foreign exchange documents, export permits, etc.), those required by the importer (such as the proforma and commercial invoices, certificates of origin and health, and pre-shipment inspection documents), those required for payment (such as the letter of credit and the bill of lading) and finally, those required for transportation (such as the bill of lading, the airway bill or the freight transit order). Documentation requirements for export shipments also vary widely according to the country of destination and the type of product being shipped. Most exporters rely on an international freight forwarder to handle the export documentation because of the multitude of documentary requirements involved in physically exporting goods and it is strongly recommended that you also make use of a freight forwarder to help you work your way through the maze of documentation.

7.1.1 The benefits of documentation

Documentation is a key means of conveying information from one person or company to another, and also serves as permanent proof of tasks and actions undertaken throughout the export process. Documentation is not only required for your own business purposes and that of your business partner, but also to satisfy the customs authorities in both countries and to facilitate the transportation of and payment for goods sold.

One value of documentation is that copies can be made and shared with the parties involved in the export process. If the documentation is complete, accurate, agreed upon by the parties involved and signed by each of these parties (or their representatives), the document will represent a legally binding document.

7.1.2 Function of export documentation

Export documentation may serve any or all of the following functions.

(1) An attestation of facts, such as a certificate of origin.

(2) Evidence of the terms and conditions of a contract if carriage, such as in the case of an air-

way bill.

(3) Evidence of ownership or title to goods, such as in the case of a bill of lading.

(4) A promissory note; that is, a promise to pay.

(5) A demand for payment, as with a bill of exchange.

(6) A declaration of liability, such as with a customs bill of entry.

(7) A receipt for goods received.

7.2 Common export documents

7.2.1 Commercial invoice

A commercial invoice is a bill for the goods from the seller to the buyer. These invoices are often used by governments to determine the true value of goods when assessing customs duties. Governments that use the commercial invoice to control imports will often specify its form, content, and number of copies, language to be used, and other characteristics.

7.2.2 Export packing list

Considerably more detailed and informative than a standard domestic packing list, an export packing list lists seller, buyer, shipper, invoice number, date of shipment, mode of transport, carrier, and itemizes quantity, description, the type of package, such as a box, crate, drum, or carton, the quantity of packages, total net and gross weight (in kilograms), package marks, and dimensions, if appropriate. Both commercial stationers and freight forwarders carry packing list forms. A packing list may serve as conforming document. It is not a substitute for a commercial invoice. In addition, U. S. and foreign customs officials may use the export packing list to check the cargo.

7.2.3 Pro forma invoice

A pro forma invoice is an invoice prepared by the exporter before shipping the goods, informing the buyer of the goods to be sent, their value, and other key specifications. It also can be used as an offering of sale or price quotation.

7.3 Transportation documents

7.3.1 Airway bill

Air freight shipments require airway bills. Airway bills are shipper-specific (i.e., USPS, Fed-Ex, UPS, DHL, etc.).

7.3.2 Bill of lading

A bill of lading is a contract between the owner of the goods and the carrier (as with domestic shipments). For vessels, there are two types: a straight bill of lading, which is non-negotiable, and a negotiable or shipper's order bill of lading. The latter can be bought, sold, or traded while the goods are in transit. The customer usually needs an original as proof of ownership to take possession of the goods. See also: straight bill of lading and liner bill of lading.

7.3.3 Electronic export information filing (formerly known as the shipper's export declaration)

Electronic export information (EEI) is the most common of all export control documents. It is required for shipments above $2,500 and for shipments of any value requiring an export license. It has to be electronically filed via the AES Direct online system, which is a free service from Census and Customs.

Note: The EEI is required for shipments to Puerto Rico, the U.S. Virgin Islands and the former Pacific Trust Territories even though they are not considered exports (unless each "Schedule B" item in the shipment is under $2,500).

Shipments to Canada do not require an EEI except in cases where an export license is required. (Shipments to the third countries passing through Canada do need an EEI.)

7.4 Export compliance documents

An export license is a government document that authorizes the export of specific goods in specific quantities to a particular destination. This document may be required for most or all exports to some countries or for other countries only under special circumstances.

7.5 Certificates of origin

The Certificate of Origin (CO) is required by some countries for all or only certain products. In many cases, a statement of origin printed on company letterhead will suffice. The exporter should verify whether a CO is required with the buyer and/or an experienced shipper/freight forwarder or the Trade Information Center.

Note: Some countries (i. e., numerous Middle Eastern countries) require that certificate of origin be notarized, certified by local chamber of commerce and legalized by the commercial section of the consulate of the destination country. For certain Middle Eastern countries, the National U. S. - Arab Chamber of Commerce may also provide such services.

For textile products, an importing country may require a certificate of origin issued by the manufacturer. The number of required copies and language may vary from country to country.

7.6 Other certificates

7.6.1 Certificate of analysis

A certificate of analysis can be required for seeds, grain, health foods, dietary supplements, fruits and vegetables, and pharmaceutical products.

7.6.2 Certificate of free sale

Certificate of free sale may be issued for biologics, food, drugs, medical devices and veterinary medicine. More information is available from the Food and Drug Administration. Health authorities in some states as well as some trade associations also issue certificates of free sale.

7.6.3 Dangerous goods certificate

Exports submitted for handling by air carriers and air freight forwarders classified as dangerous goods need to be accompanied by the Shipper's Declaration for Dangerous Goods required by the International Air Transport Association (IATA). The exporter is responsible for accuracy of the form and ensures that requirements related to packaging, marking, and other required information by IATA have been met.

For shipment of dangerous goods it is critical to identify goods by proper name, comply with packaging and labeling requirements, which vary depending upon the type of product shipper and the country shipped to. For ocean exports, hazardous material regulations are contained in the International Maritime Dangerous Goods Regulations.

7.6.4 Fumigation certificate

The fumigation certificate provides evidence of the fumigation of exported goods (especially agricultural products, used clothing, etc.). This form assists in the quarantine clearance of any goods of plant or animal origin. The seller is typically required to fumigate the commodity at his or her expense a maximum of 15 days prior to loading.

7.6.5 Halal certificate

Required by most countries in the Middle East, this certificate states that the fresh or frozen meat or poultry products were slaughtered in accordance with Islamic law. Certification by an appropriate chamber and legalization by the consulate of the destination country is usually required.

7.6.6 Health certificate

For shipment of live animals and animal products (processed foodstuffs, poultry, meat, fish, seafood, dairy products, and eggs and egg products). Note: some countries require that health certificates be notarized or certified by a chamber and legalized by a consulate.

7.6.7 Ingredients certificate

A certificate of ingredients may be requested for food products with labels that are inadequate or incomplete. The certificate may be issued by the manufacturer and must give a description of the product, contents, percentage of each ingredient, chemical data, microbiological standards, storage instructions, shelf life, and date of manufacture. If animal fats are used, the certificate must state the type of fat used and that the product contains no pork, artificial pork flavor, or pork fat. All foodstuffs are subject to analysis by Ministry of Health laboratories to establish their fitness for use.

7.6.8 Pre-shipment inspections

The governments of a number of countries have contracted with international inspection companies to verify the quantity, quality, and price of shipments imported into their countries. The purpose of such inspections is to ensure that the price charged by the exporter reflects the true value of the goods, to prevent substandard goods from entering the country, and to deflect attempts to avoid payment of customs duties. Requirements for pre-shipment inspection are normally spelled out in letter-of-credit or other documentary requirements. Some countries require pre-shipment inspection certificates for shipments of used merchandise.

7.6.9 Insurance certificate

Insurance certificates are used to assure the consignee that insurance will cover the loss of or damage to the cargo during transit. These can be obtained from the freight forwarder or publishing house. Note: an airway bill can serve as an insurance certificate for a shipment by air. Some countries may require certification or notification.

7.6.10 Phytosanitary certificate

All shipments of fresh fruits and vegetables, seeds, nuts, flour, rice, grains, lumber, plants, and plant materials require a federal phytosanitary certificate. The certificate must verify that the product is free from specified epidemics and/or agricultural diseases.

7.6.11 Radiation certificate

Some counties including Saudi Arabia may require this certificate for some plant and animal imports. The certificate states that the products are not contaminated by radioactivity.

7.6.12 Other (product-specific) certificate

Shaving brushes and articles made of raw hair must be accompanied by a recognized official certificate showing the consignment to be free from anthrax germs. Used clothing requires a disinfection certificate. Grain requires a fumigation certificate, and grain and seeds require a certificate of weight. Many countries in the Middle East require special certificates for imports of animal fodder additives, livestock, pets, and horses.

7.6.13 Weight certificate

A certificate of weight is a document issued by customs, certifying gross weight of the exported goods.

7.6.14 Consular invoice

Required in some countries, a consular invoice describes the shipment of goods and shows information such as the consignor, consignee, and value of the shipment. If required, copies are available from the destination country's embassy or consulate. The cost for this documentation can be significant and should be discussed with the buyer.

7.6.15 Dock receipt and warehouse receipt

Dock receipt and warehouse receipt are used to transfer accountability when the export item is moved by the domestic carrier to the port of embarkation and left with the ship line for export.

第 8 章

国际支付业务实务

8.1 汇款业务实务

8.1.1 境外汇款申请书

境外汇款申请书实例如图 8.1 所示。其填写说明如下。

(1)境外汇款申请书:凡采用电汇、票汇或信汇方式对境外付款的机构或个人(统称“汇款人”),须逐笔填写此申请书。

(2)日期:指汇款人填写此申请书的日期。

(3)申请号码:根据国家外汇管理局有关申报号码的编制规则,由银行编制(此栏由银行填写)。

(4)银行业务编号:指该笔业务在银行的业务编号(此栏由银行填写)。

(5)收电行/付款行:(此栏由银行填写)。

(6)汇款币种及金额:指汇款人申请汇出的实际付款币种及金额。

(7)现汇金额:汇款人申请汇出的实际付款金额中,直接从外汇账户(包括外汇保证金账户)中支付的金额,汇款人将从银行购买的外汇存入外汇账户(包括外汇保证金账户)后对境外支付的金额应作为现汇金额;汇款人以外币现钞方式对境外支付的金额作为现汇金额。

(8)购汇金额:指汇款人申请汇出的实际付款金额中,向银行购买外汇直接对境外支付的金额。

(9)其他金额:指汇款人除购汇和现汇以外对境外支付的金额。包括跨境人民币交易以及记账贸易项下交易等的金额。

(10)账号:指银行对境外付款时扣款的账号,包括人民币账号、现汇账号、现钞账号、保证金账号、银行卡号。如从多个同类账户扣款,填写金额大的扣款账号。

(11)汇款人名称及地址:对公项下指汇款人预留银行印鉴或国家质量监督检验检疫总局颁发的组织机构代码证或国家外汇管理局及其分支局(以下简称“外汇局”)签发的特殊机构代码赋码通知书上的名称及地址;对私项下指个人身份证件上的名称及住址。

(12)对公组织机构代码:按国家质量监督检验检疫总局颁发的组织机构代码证或国家外汇管理局签发的特殊机构代码赋码通知书上的单位组织机构代码或特殊机构代码填写。

(13)个人身份证件号码:包括境内居民个人的身份证号、军官证号等以及境外居民个人

境外汇款申请书

APPLICATION FOR FUNDS TRANSFERS (OVERSEAS)

致：中国银行 日期
TO: BANK OF CHINA Date

■电汇□ T/T □票汇 D/D □信汇 M/T 发电等级 □普通NOMAL□加急 Urgent

申报号码 BOP REPORTING NO.	□□□□□□□ □□□□ □□ □□□□□□□ □□□□		
20 银行业务编号 Bank Transac.Ref.No	T/T	收电行/付款行 Receiver/Drawn on	HSBC Hong Kong
32A 汇款币种及金额 currency&interbank settlement amont	USD $2000	金额大写 Amount in words	美元贰仟元整
其中 现汇金额 Amount in FX		帐号Account no.	
其中 购汇金额Amount of purchase		帐号Account no.	
其中 其他金额 Amount of others		帐号Account no.	
50a 汇款人名称及地址 Remitter's Name &address	（您的姓名，请用拼音填写）+中文地址		
		■对私	个人身份证件号码 individual ID NO.
□对公 组织机构代码 Unit code	□□□□□□□□□-□	■对私	■中国居民个人 □中国非居民个人
54/56A 收款银行之代理行名称及地址 Correspondent of beneficiary's Bank Name &Address			
57a 收款人开户银行名称及地址 Beneficiary's bank name &Address	收款人开户银行在其代理行帐号 Bene's bank a/c no.		
	HSBC Hong Kong		
	HSBC, No. 1 Queen' s Road Central, Central, Hong Kong		
59a 收款人名称及地址 Beneficiary's name &Address	收款人帐号Bene's A/c NO. 168-708535-838		
	Robbins Investment International Group Limited		
70 汇款附言 Remittance Information	只限140个字位 Not exceeding 140 characters	71A	国内外费用承担
	（您的交易账号）	All bank's charges if any are to be borne by ■汇款人our □收款人 ben□共同sha	
收款人常驻国家（地区）名称及代码 Resident country/region name &code	香港	Hong Kong	□□□
请选择：□预付货款 □货到付款 □退款 □其他		最迟装运日期	
交易编码 BOPTransac code	相应币种及金额 Currency &Amount	交易附言 Transac.remark	（用途）
是否为进口核销项下付款	□是 □否	合同号	发票号
外汇局批件/备案表号		报关单经营单位代码	
报关单号	报关单币种及总金额	本次核注金额	
报关单号	报关单币种及总金额	本次核注金额	

银行专用栏		申请人签章	银行签章
购汇汇率		请按照贵行背页所列条款代办以上汇款并进行申报	
等值人民币			
手续费			
电报费			
合计			
支付费用方式	□ 现金 □ 支票 □ 账户	申请人姓名 签名 电话	核准人签字 日期
核印		经办	复核

图 8.1 境外汇款申请书实例

的护照号等。

(14)中国居民个人/中国非居民个人：根据《国际收支统计申报办法》中对中国居民/中

国非居民的定义进行选择。

(15)收款银行之代理行名称及地址:为中转银行的名称,所在国家、城市及其在清算系统中的识别代码。

(16)收款人开户银行名称及地址:为收款人开户银行名称,所在国家、城市及其在清算系统中的识别代码。

(17)收款人开户银行在其代理行账号:为收款银行在其中转行的账号。

(18)收款人名称及地址:指收款人全称及其所在国家、城市。

(19)汇款附言:由汇款人填写所汇款项的必要说明,可用英文填写且不超过 140 个字符(受 SWIFT 系统限制)。

(20)国内外费用承担:指由汇款人确定办理对境外汇款时发生的国内外费用由何方承担,并在所选项前的□中打√。

(21)收款人常驻国家(地区)名称及代码:指该笔境外汇款的实际收款人常驻的国家或地区。名称用中文填写,代码根据"国家(地区)名称代码表"填写。

(22)交易编码:应根据本笔对境外付款交易性质对应的"国际收支交易编码表(支出)"填写。如果本笔付款为多种交易性质,则在第一行填写最大金额交易的国际收支交易编码,第二行填写次大金额交易的国际收支交易编码;如果本笔付款涉及进口付汇核销项下交易,则核销项下交易视同最大金额交易处理;如果本笔付款为退款,则应填写本笔付款对应原涉外收入的国际收支交易编码。

(23)相应币种及金额:应根据填报的交易编码填写,如果本笔对境外付款为多种交易性质,则在第一行填写最大金额交易相应的币种和金额,第二行填写其余币种及金额。两栏合计数应等于汇款币种及金额;如果本笔付款涉及进口付汇核销项下交易,则核销项下交易视同最大金额交易处理。

(24)交易附言:应对本笔对境外付款交易性质进行详细描述。如果本笔付款为多种交易性质,则应对相应的对境外付款交易性质分别进行详细描述;如果本笔付款为退款,则应填写本笔付款对应原涉外收入的申报号码。

(25)外汇局批件/备案表号:指国家外汇管理局签发的,银行凭以对外付款的各种批件或进口付汇备案表号。

(26)报关单经营单位代码:指由海关颁发给企业的"自理报关单位注册登记证明书"上的代码。

(27)报关单号:指海关报关单上的编码,应与海关报关数据库中提示的编码一致。若有多张报关单,表格不够填写,可附附页。

(28)最迟装运日期:指货物的实际装运日期。境外工程物资和转口贸易项下的支付中最迟转运日期应为收汇日期。

8.1.2 范例:中国银行汇款业务实务

1. 汇出汇款(Outward Remittance)

1)产品说明

我行接受汇款人的委托,以约定汇款方式委托海外联行或代理行将一定金额的款项付给指定收款人的业务。用于满足国际资金汇划结算需求。汇款方式包括电汇、信汇和票汇,目前常用的是电汇和票汇。

2)产品特点

(1)费用少。与信用证和托收方式相比,汇款具有手续简便、费用低廉的特点。

(2)速度快。电汇速度较快,有利于出口商及时收款,加快资金周转速度。

(3)操作简便。操作简单易行,适用范围较广。

3)适用范围

(1)进口商流动资金充足,当前的主要目标是控制财务费用而不是取得融资便利。

(2)贸易结算项下,出口商接受货到付款的条件,但对收款速度有较高要求。

(3)进口商与出口商有良好合作关系且对其充分信任,愿意接受预付货款的条件。

(4)资料费、技术费、贸易从属费用(包括运费保费)等宜采用汇出汇款方式。

(5)贸易项下的尾款一般宜采用汇出汇款方式。

4)提交材料

(1)办理各类汇出汇款均需向银行提供:汇出汇款申请书、现汇账户的支款凭证、用于购汇的人民币支票。

(2)办理汇出汇款需符合国家有关外汇管理规定,提交外汇管理办法要求的有效凭证,例如有关批汇文件、国际收支申报表(如需)、贸易进口付汇核销单(如需)。

5)申请条件

(1)依法核准登记,具有经年检的法人营业执照或其他足以证明其经营合法性和经营范围的有效证明文件。

(2)拥有贷款卡。

(3)拥有开户许可证,并在我行开立结算账户。

(4)具有进出口经营资格。

(5)在我行有授信额度。

6)业务流程

汇出汇款业务流程如图8.2所示,图中电汇和信汇以实线表示,票汇以虚线表示。

(1)汇款人向我行提交"汇出汇款申请书"以及现汇账户支款凭证或用于购汇的人民币支票。

(2)我行经审核后向海外联行或代理行发出汇款指示电报(电汇项下)或指示信函(信汇项下),或开具汇票(票汇项下)交付汇款人。

(3)电汇或信汇项下,海外联行或代理行按我行指示向收款人解付汇款。

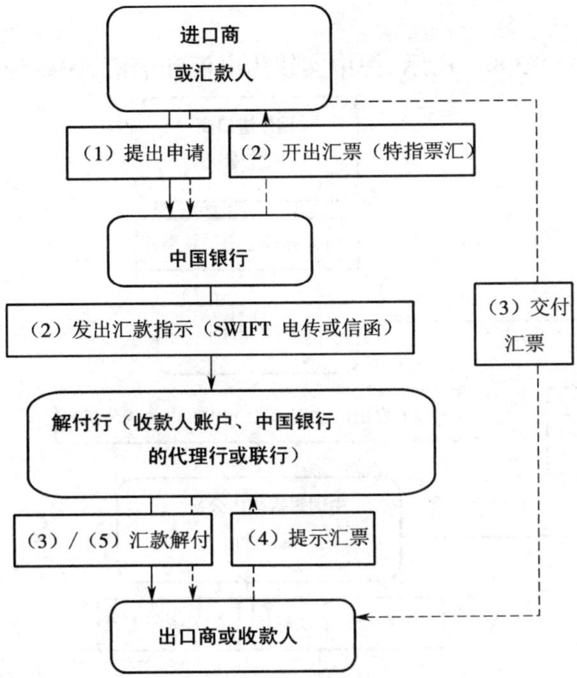

图 8.2　汇出汇款业务流程

(4)票汇项下,汇款人将汇票自行交付收款人,收款人向汇票注明的付款银行提示汇票,付款银行向收款人解付汇款。

2. 汇入汇款(Inward Remittance)

1)产品说明

我行根据国外汇出行指示将款项解付给指定收款人的业务。

2)产品分类

用于满足国际资金汇划结算需求。汇款方式包括电汇、信汇和票汇,目前常用的是电汇和票汇。

3)产品特点

(1)费用少。与信用证和托收方式相比,汇款具有手续简便、费用低廉的特点。

(2)速度快。电汇速度较快,有利于出口商及时收款,加快资金周转速度。

(3)操作简便。操作简单易行,适用范围较广。

4)适用范围

(1)若客户对资金周转速度或控制财务费用有较高要求,宜选择汇入汇款。

(2)对于非贸易以及资本项下的结算,需采用汇款方式。

5)申请条件

依法核准登记,具有经年检的法人营业执照或其他足以证明其经营合法性和经营范围的有效证明文件。

6)业务流程

汇入汇款业务流程如图 8.3 所示,图中实线为电汇和信汇,虚线为票汇。

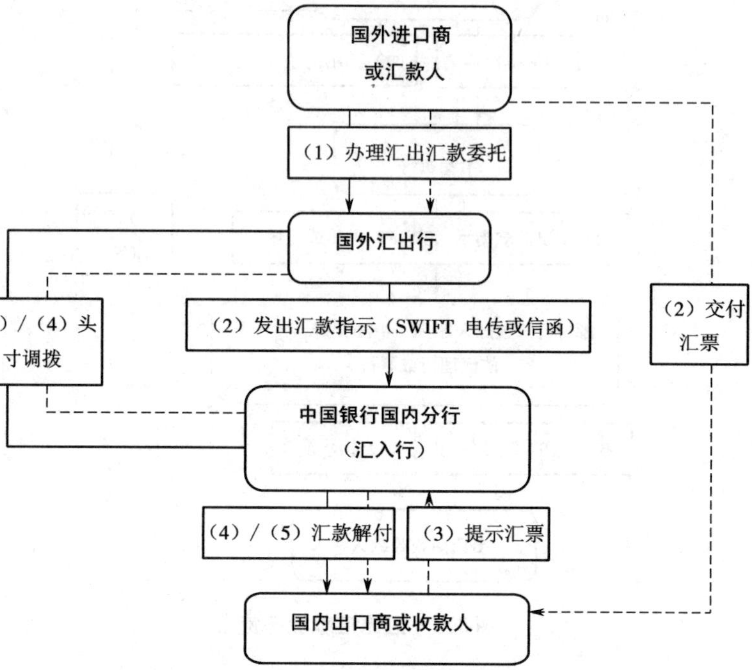

图 8.3 汇入汇款业务流程

(1)我行收到国外汇出行发出的汇款指示电报(电汇项下)或指示信函(信汇项下),或收到收款人向我行提示的汇票(票汇项下)。

(2)我行对上述指示电报、信函或汇票审核无误并收妥头寸后,向收款人解付汇款。

7)温馨提示

(1)如果在汇入行开有账户,银行将汇入的款项直接记入账户;如果在汇入行没有开立账户,银行将以合理的方式办理转汇。

(2)如果没有及时收到汇入款项,最好及时向银行查询。

8.2 托收业务实务

8.2.1 托收申请书的填写

托收申请书范本如图 8.4 所示。

中国农业银行
AGRICULTURAL BANK OF CHINA

跟单托收申请书

APPLICATION FOR DOCUMENTARY COLLECTION

Date 日期＿＿＿＿＿＿

To: Agricultural Bank of China Branch 致：中国农业银行 We enclose the following draft(s) □documents as specified hereunder which please collect in accordance with the instructions indicated herein. 兹附上汇票和单据如下，谨请贵行依照本申请书的要求为我公司办理托收。 This collection is subject to URC 522. 此托收遵循国际商会第 522 号出版物《托收统一规则》。	Collecting Bank (Full name & address) 代收行(全称和地址)	
Drawer (Full name & address) 收款人(全称和地址)	Tenor(期限)	
	Draft/Inv. No. 汇票/发票号码	Currency and Amount 币种及金额
Drawee(Full name & address) 付款人(全称和地址)		

DOCUMENTS 单据

DRAFT	COM. INV.	PACKING LIST	B/L	N/N B/L	AWB.	ORIGIN CERTI.	INS. POL.	INSP. CERT.	CERT.	CABLE COPY			

Special Instructions(See box marked "×") 特殊条款(用"×"在方框中表明)：

□ Please deliver documents against □payment at sight /□payment ＿＿ after sight /□acceptance.
请办理□即期付款交单/□远期付款交单/□承兑交单。

□ All your charges are to be borne by □the drawee /□us.
你行所有费用由□付款人/□我公司承担。

□ In case of a time bill, please advise us of acceptance giving maturity date.
如果托收包含远期汇票，请通知我公司承兑到期日。

□ In case of dishonour, please do not protest but advise us of non-payment □non-acceptance giving reasons.
如果发生拒付，无须拒绝证书，但应该通知我公司拒绝付款或拒绝承兑的原因。

□ Please instruct the Collecting Bank to deliver documents only upon receipt of all their banking charges.
请指示代收行收妥全部银行费用后再提示单据。

□ We will take on all the results caused by choosing the above bank as the collecting bank.
请选择我公司选定的代收行，由此引起的问题和其他后果由我公司负责。

Disposal of proceeds upon collection(款项收妥后，请按照以下要求办理)

联系人：　　　　　　　　　　电话：

申请人(盖章)

图 8.4　托收申请书

托收申请书填写说明。

1)代收行的选择

代收行可以由委托人选择指定,若未指定,托收行可以自行选择代收行。如果委托人指定的代收行资信较差或与托收行无业务往来,托收行无法接受,也可以自行选择代收行,在征得委托人同意后确定。

2)交单条件的选择

可供选择的交单条件有三种:即期付款交单、远期付款交单、承兑交单。注意在选中的交单方式前的方框内打叉,而不是打钩。

3)是否委托代收行做"需要时的代理"及其权限

在远期付款交单条件下,往往货已经到达目的港,但付款交单日期未到,进口商未能前来提货,或者在进口商拒付的情况下,货物及货权仍在代收行手中,委托人应明确指示此种情况下如何处理货物,是否请代收行凭单提货,代为存仓、保险等。按照惯例,出口商必须在托收申请书中明确"需要时的代理"的权限,如是否有权提货、重新议价、修改交单条件、更换付款对象等,如未注明,银行将不接受"需要时的代理"的任何指示。

4)是否要做拒绝证书

按照惯例,如果委托人没有指示,遇到拒付或拒绝承兑,代收行一般只通知托收行即可,没有义务去做拒绝证书,除非托收指示书有此要求。

5)付款时间的附加规定

这些附加规定包括:付款交单条件下是否准许付款人按比例分期付款、分批提货;付款人延期付款是否要加利息,提前付款是否给予贴息等。

6)利息的处理

如果出口商明示要收取利息,必须在托收申请书中注明利息的计算方式。但付款人拒付该利息时,代收行可视情况决定不必收取该款的利息,除非进口商在托收申请书中特别注明不得放弃利息。

7)银行费用的处理

银行费用包括银行办理托收业务的手续费和其他费用。托收费用应由委托人负担,但如果贸易合同对银行费用有规定,应在托收申请书中明确相应的条款。若是付款人拒付,代收行的手续费只能从货款中扣除,相当于出口商支付。所以出口商应在托收申请书中特别注明手续费或其他费用不得放弃。如果进口商拒付,代收行将不予交单并尽快通知托收行。

8)货款收妥后的处理

委托人应明确指示货款收妥后的付款方式和通知付款方式。一般来说,托收行是在收到代收行的付款通知书确定收妥的货款已划入托收行账户后才对委托人结汇。因此,对于大额款项,如果托收人希望尽快收款以减少利息损失,就必须指示银行以 T/T 汇款并以电信方式通知。如:

(1)托收申请书上关于见票即付的 D/P 下延迟付款加利息条款:In case of the draft being not only honored by the drawee at first presentation, kindly collect form the drawee an overdue interest at the rate of ××% per annul from the first presentation to the date of actual payment.

(2)远期付款交单托收申请书上关于提请付款情况下允许在票款中减除利息条款:In

case of the draft being effected payment before the date of maturity, kindly deduct form the payment a discount interest at the rate of ××% per annul form the date of actual payment to the date of maturity.

8.2.2 托收项下汇票的填写

托收项下汇票范本如图8.5所示。

BILL OF EXCHANGE

号码 汇票金额 上海

No. HLK356 Exchange for USD 56,000 Shanghai, Jan 1st, 2010

见票 日后(本汇票之副本未付)付交

At 90 DAYS sight of this First of Exchange (Second of Exchange being unpaid)

pay to the order of BANK OF CHINA

金额

The sum of SAY US DOLLARS FIFTY SIX THOUSAND ONLY

此致

To MITSUBISHI TRUST & BANKING CO. LTD.,

INTERNATIONAL DEPARTMENT,4—5

CHIYODA-KU,TOKYO 100,JAPAN

CHINA NATIONAL ANIMAL BYPRODUCTS

IMP. & EXP. CORP. TIANJIN BRANCH

66 YANTAI STREET,TIANJIN, CHINA

图8.5 托收项下汇票

托收项下汇票填写说明如下。

(1)出票根据、信用证号码和开证日期三栏是不需要填写的(这是信用证下汇票要填写的内容),或者在"Draw under"后的空栏内打上"For Collection"字样,或者在缮制托收汇票时不缮制这三项。

(2)号码:填写汇票号码,一般与发票号相同。

(3)小写金额:Exchange for 后面填写托收金额,用阿拉伯数字表示,并加上币种。

(4)汇票地点与时间:一般地点按实际地点打印;时间月份用英文表示,日及年份可以用阿拉伯数字表示。例如:Jan 1,2013.

(5)付款期限:即期汇票填写 D/P AT SIGHT(即期付款交单);远期汇票填写 D/P ×× days (××天远期付款交单);D/A ×× days (××天承兑交单)。

(6)收款人:填写收款的具体公司或银行名称。

(7)付款人:填写托收行名称。

(8)出票人:填写出口商名称。

托收汇票也是一式两份,两联汇票起相同的法律作用。当第一联汇票生效时,第二联自动作废(Second of Exchange being unpaid);当第二联汇票生效时,第一联汇票自动作废(First of Exchange being unpaid)。

8.2.3 范例:中国银行托收业务实务

1.出口跟单托(Outward Collection)

1)产品说明

我行受出口商委托,凭其提交的出口商业单据和金融票据通过国外代收行向进口商收取款项。

2)产品功能

用于满足国际贸易结算需求。较汇款方式而言,有一定的付款保证,可分为付款交单(D/P)和承兑交单(D/A)两种方式。

3)产品特点

(1)费用低廉。银行费用较低,有利于企业节约财务费用、控制成本。

(2)简便易行。与信用证方式相比,手续简单,易于操作。

(3)风险较小。进口商只有承兑或付款后才能提取货物,与赊销方式相比,出口商承担的风险较小。

4)适用客户

(1)出口商了解进口商的资信状况,并且有足够的资金用于备货和发运。

(2)当处于卖方市场的时候,出口商宜选择 D/P 方式;当处于买方市场且进口商要求给予融资便利时,出口商可选择 D/A 方式。

5)申请条件

(1)依法核准登记,具有经年检的法人营业执照或其他足以证明其经营合法性和经营范围的有效证明文件。

(2)有进出口经营权。

6)提交材料

(1)向银行申请办理出口托收时应提交:托收委托书、跟单托收的全套单据。

(2)如系首次办理委托业务,还应提交:工商营业执照(副本)原件、进出口业务的营业许可、法定代表人授权书。

7)业务流程

出口跟单托业务流程如图 8.6 所示。

(1)出口商备货发运后,将有关单据提交我行办理托收。

(2)我行将托收单据寄至国外代收行进行索汇。

(3)国外代收行收到单据后提示给进口商。

(4)进口商到期通过代收行向我行付款,我行向出口商解付。

8)温馨提示

(1)进口商拒付或拒绝承兑时,最好及时授权托收行协助安排货物。

(2)在 D/A 方式下,实际上延长了进口商付款的时间,建议制定价格时考虑利息等相关成本。

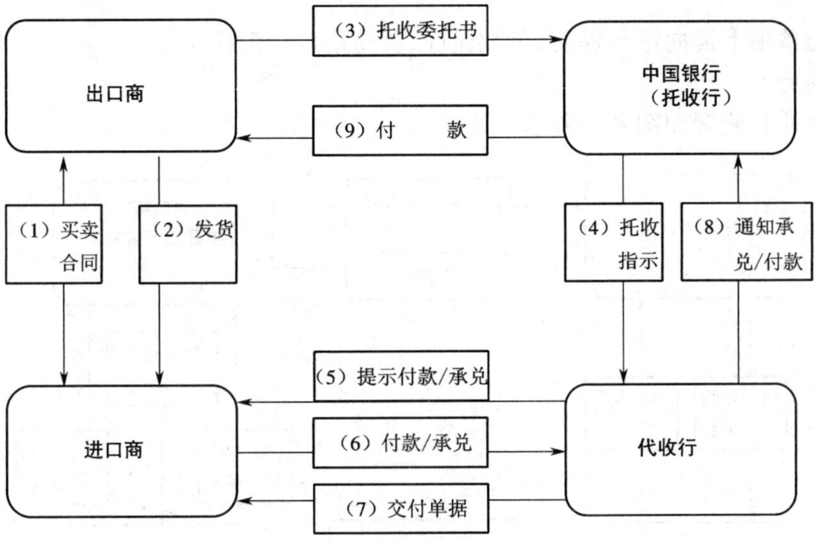

图8.6　出口跟单托业务流程

2. 进口代收（Inward Collection）

1）产品说明

我行接受国外代理行或联行委托，按照代理行或联行的指示向进口商收取进口款项，并向进口商交付有关商业单据。

2）产品分类

进口代收可分为付款交单（D/P）和承兑交单（D/A）两种方式。

3）产品特点

（1）费用低廉。银行费用较低，有利于节约财务费用、控制成本。

（2）简便易行。与信用证方式相比，手续简单，易于操作。

（3）资金占压少。在出口商备货和装运阶段不必预付货款、占压资金，支付货款或做出承兑后可立即取得货物单据并处置货物。

（4）改善现金流。在承兑交单项下，进口商承兑后即可以取得货物单据并处置货物，在售出货物并有现金流入后才对外支付，资金占压近乎为零，财务状况和偿债能力得到有效改善。

4）适用客户

（1）进口商希望以较信用证更为简便且低成本的办法向出口商支付货款。

（2）如进口商流动资金充足，可采用付款交单（D/P）方式。

（3）如进口商流动资金不足，需要出口商给予远期付款的融资便利，且与出口商有良好的合作关系，可采用承兑交单（D/A）方式。

5）申请条件

（1）依法核准登记，具有经年检的法人营业执照或其他足以证明其经营合法性和经营范围的有效证明文件。

（2）有进出口经营权。

6)提交材料

在付款交单项下需向银行提交:付款凭证、贸易进口付汇核销单。

7)业务流程

进口代收业务流程如图 8.7 所示。

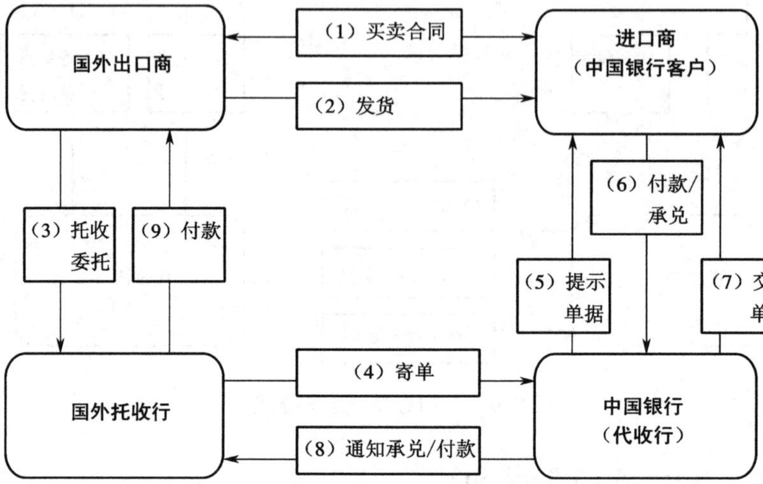

图 8.7 进口代收业务流程

(1)国外出口商备货发运后,将有关单据提交所在地银行办理托收。

(2)出口商所在地银行将托收单据寄至我行,我行按照指示通知进口商付款(D/P)或承兑(D/A)。

(3)进口商通过我行向出口商付款或承兑后,我行将单据交付进口商。

(4)在 D/A 项下承兑到期后,进口商通过我行向出口商付款。

8)温馨提示

(1)在承兑交单项下,须按规定办理远期汇票的承兑手续,并在汇票到期日及时付款。

(2)亦可向我行申请办理进口托收押汇、海外代付等贸易融资。

3. 光票托收(Clean Collection)

1)产品说明

光票托收是指中国银行受客户委托办理的不附带任何商业单据的金融单据的托收业务。

2)产品功能

用于满足国际贸易结算需求,可分为付款交单 D/P 和承兑交单 D/A 两种方式。

3)产品特点

(1)费用低廉。光票托收的银行费用相对较低。

(2)安全稳妥。与直接向付款人邮寄收款存在较大风险相比,通过银行间的国际网络收款可以避免这些风险,是较安全的收款方式。

(3)服务便捷。如托收行与付款行/代收行签有"立即贷记"协议,则可大大缩短收款时间。

4)适用客户

(1)贸易、非贸易项下的小额支付。

(2)在国内不能兑换的外币现钞(含残币)。

(3)外汇支票、本票,国外债券、存单等有价凭证的托收业务。

(4)不能或不便提供商业单据的交易,如寄送样品、软件等高科技产品交易、时令性商品交易以及服务、技术转让等无形贸易。

5)申请条件

依法核准登记,具有经年检的法人营业执照或其他足以证明其经营合法性和经营范围的有效证明文件。

6)业务流程

光票托收业务流程如图8.8所示。(直接向付款行托收时以实线表示)

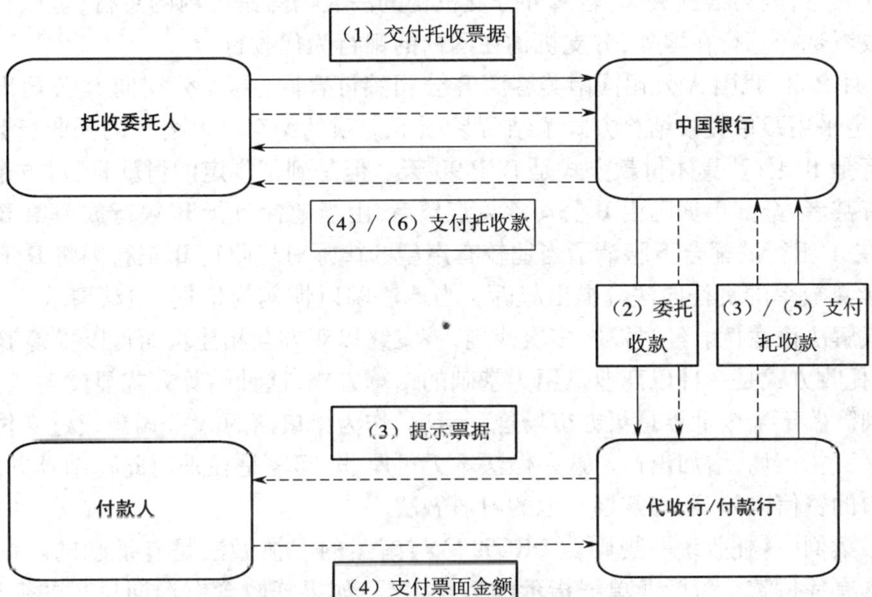

图8.8　光票托收业务流程

(1)收款人将托收单据提交我行。

(2)我行将托收单据寄至国外代收行委托收款。

(3)国外代收行向付款人提示票据,付款人按票面金额付款。

(4)国外代收行将托收款项付至我行,我行向收款人解付。

7)温馨提示

(1)光票托收适用于各类贸易和非贸易项下的票据及有价凭证托收。

(2)托收票据的标价货币一般应为可兑换货币。

(3)表面注明流通地区限制的票据难以办理托收。

(4)已背书转让的票据易存在伪造、变造等欺诈风险,应注意防范。

(5)陌生的、金额特别巨大或出票行资信有疑问的票据,易发生欺诈行为。

(6)用于投资、贷款、抵押等目的的大额票据易发生欺诈行为。

8.2.4 托收案例分析

(1)甲公司与国外的乙公司签订合同,确定 D/P 结算方式。甲公司放货,将单据交 C 银行托收。C 选择 F 为代收行。半月后,甲公司得知乙公司已经提货,但货款未收到。经 C 银行联系,F 银行回电称进口商拒绝付款。C 银行回电指出 F 在 D/P 方式下不应在进口人未付款的情况下就放单,要求 F 立即付款,但 F 未回电。甲公司指责 C 银行选择代理行负有责任。最后进口商降价 20% 了结。

分析:根据《托收统一规则》第 11 条,为执行委托人的指示,银行使用另一家银行或其他银行服务,是代委托人办理的,其风险由委托人承担。托收是商业信用,银行不承担任何责任。为避免 D/P 项下放单又拒付,选择进口地代收行十分重要。一般选择账户行的海外分支机构作为代收行,因为根据法律,若海外分支机构的法人仍然是国内的总行,可以在国内起诉其总行。或者选择总行在国外,分支机构在国内的银行为代收行。

(2)×月×日,我国 A 公司同南美客商 B 公司签订合同,由 A 公司向 B 公司出口货物一批,双方商定采用跟单托收结算方式了结贸易项下款项的结算。A 公司的托收行是 A′银行,南美代收行是 B′银行,具体付款方式是 D/P 90 天。但是到了规定的付款日,对方毫无付款的动静。更有甚者,全部单据已由 B 公司承兑汇票后,由当地代收行 B′银行放单给 B 公司。于是 A 公司在 A′银行的配合下聘请了当地较有声望的律师对代收行 B′银行因将 D/P 远期作为 D/A 方式承兑放单的责任向法院提出起诉。当地法院以惯例为依据,主动请求 A 公司撤诉,以调解方式解决该案例。经过双方多次谈判,该案终以双方互相让步而得以妥善解决。

分析:托收方式是一种以商业信用为基础的结算方式,这种结算方式显然对一方有利,对另一方不利。鉴于当今世界是买方市场这一情况,作为出口商的 A 公司想通过支付方式给予对方优惠来开拓市场,增加出口。这一做法本无可厚非,问题是在采用此种结算方式时,除了要了解客户的资信以外,还应掌握当地的习惯做法。

在这一案例中《托收统一规则》(URC522)与南美的习惯做法是有抵触的。据 URC522:托收不应含有凭付款交付商业单据指示的远期汇票;如果托收含有远期付款的汇票,托收指示书应注明商业单据是凭承兑交付款人(D/A)还是凭付款交付款人(D/P),如果无此项注明,商业单据仅能凭付款交单,代收行对因迟交单据产生的任何后果不负责任;如果托收含有远期付款汇票,且托收指示书注明凭付款交付商业单据,则单据只能凭付款交付,代收行对于因迟交单据引起的后果不负任何责任。

从中不难看出,国际商会的《托收统一规则》不主张使用 D/P 远期付款方式,但是没有把 D/P 远期从 URC522 中绝对排除。倘若使用该方式,根据 URC522,B′银行必须在 B 银行付款 90 天后才能将全套单据交付给 B 公司。故 B′银行在 B 公司承兑汇票后即行放单的做法是违背 URC522 的。

但从南美的习惯做法看,南美客商认为,托收方式既然是种对进口商有利的结算方式,就应体现其优越性。D/P 远期的本意是出口商给进口商的资金融通,而现在的情况是货到南美后,若按 D/P 远期的做法,进口商既不能提货,又要承担因货压港而产生的滞迟费。若进口商想避免此种情况的发生,就必须提早付款从而提早提货,那么这 D/P 远期还有什么意义?故南美的做法是将所有的 D/P 远期均视作 D/A 对待。在此情况下，B′银行在 B 公司承兑后放单给 B 公司的做法也就顺理成章了。

此案给我们的启示是：在处理跟单托收业务时，原则上应严格遵守 URC522。托收行在其托收指示中应明确表明按 URC522 办理，这样若遇当地习惯做法与 URC522 抵触时，可按 URC522 办理。

当然在具体操作时也应尊重当地的习惯做法。凡货运南美地区的托收业务，可采用 D/P 即期或 D/A 的付款方式，避免使用 D/P 远期，以免引起不必要的纠纷。倘若非用 D/P 远期不可，远期的掌握应该从起运地到目的地运输所耗费的时间为准。

(3)1995 年 11 月，荷兰 A 银行通过国内 B 银行向 C 公司托收贷款，B 银行收到单据后，将远期汇票提示给付款人承兑。据付款人称，出票人告知货物已抵达香港，必须承兑汇票后才肯交货。付款人为尽快取得货物，遂承兑了汇票。1996 年 1 月，B 银行收到已承兑的汇票后遂对外发出承兑电，称汇票业经付款人承兑，到期我行将按贵行指示付款。

1996 年 5 月，汇票到期，B 银行要求付款人(C 公司)付款，C 公司称，由于未完全收到货物，不同意付款，B 银行就此电告 A 银行，付款人不同意付款。

几天后，A 银行回电称，在我行的托收指示中，我们要求贵行：①承兑交单(汇票期限为出票后 180 天)；②承兑的汇票由贵行担保；③如果已承兑的汇票没有由贵行担保，请不要放单。贵行 1996 年 1 月来电通知，客户已承兑汇票，到期将按我行指示付款。因此，请贵行立即安排付款。

分析：B 银行收到 A 银行寄交的托收单据，必须按托收指示中的指示和国际商会 522 号出版物《托收统一规则》行事，对不能履行或不愿履行的指示，必须毫无延误地通知寄单行。国际商会 522 号出版物《托收统一规则》规定，无论出于何种原因，如果银行决定不办理它收到的托收或任何有关指示，必须无延误地以电信或在不可能采用电信方式的情况下，以其他快捷的方式通知向其发出托收指示的一方。B 银行收到 A 银行寄交的托收单据，既没有执行托收指示中的指示，又没有将不执行的决定及时通知寄单行，这种做法是不对的。

(4)提示行能否根据付款人(受票人)的授权部分付款交单？

1995 年 4 月，香港某公司委托当地 A 银行通过内地 B 银行向某进出口公司托收货款。B 银行收到单据后向某进出口公司(付款人)提示，要求其按托收金额 USD205,020.00 付款。同年 12 月，付款人通知 B 银行，该公司已将 USD165,020.00 直接汇给出票人，授权 B 银行将剩余的货款 USD40,000.00 通过 A 银行付给出票人。付款人支付了余款后，B 银行遂将单据交给了付款人。

1996 年 5 月，香港某公司(出票人)致函 B 银行称，这种做法严重伤害了该公司的正当权益，违背了国际惯例及 URC522 准则。

分析：国际商会 URC522 规定，跟单托收时，部分付款只有在托收指示特别授权时才被接受。除非另有指示，提示行只有在全部款项收讫时才能把单据交予受票人。本案例中，托收指示没有授权指示行(代收行)可部分付款交单，提示行也没有征得委托人的同意，而是根据付款人的授权执行部分付款交单，这种做法是错误的。

8.3 信用证业务实务

8.3.1 信用证开证申请书填写

图 8.9 所示为信用证开证申请书范本。

IRREVOCABLE DOCUMENTARY CREDIT APPLICATION

TO:BANK OF CHINA　　　　Place/date:Sept. 25th, 2001　NEW YORK

Beneficiary(fullname and address)	
SHANGHAI TEXTILES I&E CORP. 27CHUNGSHAN ROAD E.1, SHANGHAI CHINA	**Date and place of expiry of credit** Dec. 5th, 2001 in Shanghai
Partial shipments [×] allowed　□not allowed **Transhipment** □allowed　[×] not allowed	**Issue by airmail** [×] Issue by teletransmission
Loading on board/dispatch/taking in charge at/from SHANGHAI not later than NOV. 20TH, 2001 for transportation to NEW YORK	**Amount(both in figures and words)** USD23,522.50(SAY UNITED STATES DOLLARS TWENTY THREE THOUSAND FIVE HUNDRED TWENTY TWO AND 50/100 ONLY)
Description of goods: LADIES' 55% ACRYLIC 45% COTTON KNITTED BLOUSE USD 48.5 PER DOZ CIFC3% NEW YORK Packing: IN 120 CARTON	**Credit available with** [×] by sight payment □by acceptance □by negotiation □by deferred payment at against the documents detailed herein [×] and beneficiary's draft for 100% of the invoice value □FOB　□C&F　[×] CIF

Documents required:(marked with ×)

1. (×) Signed Commercial Invoice in 4 copies indicating L/C No. and Contract No.
2. (×) Full set of clean on board ocean Bills of Lading made out to order and blank endorsed, marked "freight [ ] to collect/[×] prepaid[ ] showing freight amount" notifying CRYSTAL KOBE LTD. 1410 BROADWAY, ROOM 300 NY 10018 U.S.A.
3. ( ) Air Waybills showing "freight [ ] to collect/[ ] prepaid[ ] indicating freight amount" and consigned to ______
4. ( ) Memorandum issued by ______ consigned to ______
5. (×) Insurance Policy/Certificate in 2 copies for 110% of the invoice value showing claims payable in China in currency of the draft. Blank endorsed, covering[×] Ocean Marine Transportation All Risks, War Risks.
6. (×) Packing List/Weight Memo in 3 copies indicating quantity/gross and net weight of each package and packing condition as called for by the L/C.
7. (×) Beneficiary's certified copy of cable/telex dispatched to the accountees within 24 hours after shipment advising[×] name of vessel/[ ] No./[ ] wagon No., date, quantity, weight and value of shipment.
8. (×) Beneficiary's Certificate certifying that extra copies of the documents have been dispatched according to the contract terms.
9. ( ) Other documents, if any.

Additional instructions:

1. (×) All banking charges outside the opening bank are for beneficiary's account.
2. (×) Documents must be presented within 15 days after the date of issuance of the transport documents but within the validity of this credit.
3. (×) The third party as shipper is not acceptable. Short form/Blank Back B/L is not acceptable.
4. ( ) Both quantity and amount % more or less are allowed.
5. (×) All documents to be forwarded in one cover, unless otherwise stated above.

Your correspondents to advise beneficiary □adding their confirmation [×] without adding their confirmation

Payments to be debited to our U.S. Dollars　Accounf No. 10-668855368

Signature: CRYSTAL KOBE LTD.

图 8.9 信用证开证申请书

8.3.2 根据合同填写开证申请书范例

合同范本如图 8.10 所示。

上海市纺织品进出口公司

SHANGHAI TEXTILES IMPORT & EXPORT CORPORATION

27 Chungshan Road E. 1 SHANGHAI CHINA

TEL:8621 - 65342517 FAX:8621 - 65124743

编号

TO:CRYSTAL KOBE LTD. No. 21SSG - 017

售货确认书

日期

SALES CONFIRMATION

Date:AUG. 26,2001

货号 ART. NO.	品名及规格 COMMODITY AND SPECIFICATION	数量 QUANTITY	单价及价格条款 UNIT PRICE & TERMS	金额 AMOUNT
H32331SE	LADIES' 55% ACRYLIC 45% COTTON KNITTED BLOUSE	120 CARTON	USD 48. 5 PER DOZ CIFC3% NEW YORK	USD24,250
			总金额 TOTAL AMOUNT	USD24,250

装运条款

SHIPMENT: SHIPMENT ON OR BEFORE NOV. 20,2001 WITH PARTIAL SHIPMENTS ARE NOT ALLOWED. TRANSHIPMENT IS ALLOWED FROM SHANGHAI TO NEW YORK.

付款方式

PAYMENT: THE BUYER SHALL OPEN THOUCH A BANK ACCEPTABLE TO THE SELLER AN IRREVOCABLE L/C AT SIGHT TO REACH THE SELLER 30 DAYS BEFORE THE MONTH OF SHIPMENT REMAINED VALID FOR NEGOTIATION IN CHINA UNTIL THE 15TH DAY AFTER THE DATE OF SHIPMENT.

保 险

INSURANCE:THE SELLER SHALL COVER INSURANCE AGAINST ALL RISKS FOR 110% OF THE TOTAL INVOICE VALLUE AS PER THE RELEVANT OCEAN MARINE CARGO CLAUSE OF P. I. C. C. DATED JAN. 1ST,1981.

注 意 请完全按本售货确认书开证并在证内注明本售货确认书号码。

IMPORTANT:PLEASE ESTABLISH L/C EXACTLY ACCORDING TO THE TERMS AND CONDITIONS OF THIS S/C AND WITH THIS S/C NUMBER INDICATED.

CRYSTAL KOBE LTD. SHANGHAI TEXTILES I&E CORPORATION

买方 (The Buyers) 卖方 (The Sellers)

图 8.10 合同

开证申请书范本如图 8.11 所示。

IRREVOCABLE DOCUMENTARY CREDIT APPLICATION

TO: BANK OF CHINA

Place/date: Sept. 25th, 2001 NEW YORK

Beneficiary (fullname and address)
SHANGHAI TEXTILES I&E CORP.
27CHUNGSHAN ROAD E.1, SHANGHAI CHINA

Date and place of expiry of credit
Dec. 5th, 2001 in Shanghai

Partial shipments
[×] allowed [ ] not allowed

Transhipment
[ ] allowed [×] not allowed

Issue by airmail
[×] Issue by teletransmission

Amount (both in figures and words)
USD23, 522.50 (SAY UNITED STATES DOLLARS TWENTY THREE THOUSAND FIVE HUNDRED TWENTY TWO AND 50/100 ONLY)

Loading on board/dispatch/taking in charge at/from
SHANGHAI not later than NOV. 20TH, 2001
for transportation to NEW YORK

Description of goods:
LADIES' 55% ACRYLIC 45%
COTTON KNITTED BLOUSE
USD 48.5 PER DOZ
CIFC3% NEW YORK
Packing: IN 120 CARTON

Credit available with
[×] by sight payment [ ] by acceptance [ ] by negotiation
[ ] by deferred payment at
against the documents detailed herein
[×] and beneficiary's draft for 100% of the invoice value
[ ] FOB [ ] C&F [×] CIF

Documents required: (marked with ×)

1. (×) Signed Commercial Invoice in 4 copies indicating L/C No. and Contract No.
2. (×) Full set of clean on board ocean Bills of Lading made out to order and blank endorsed, marked "freight [ ] to collect/[×] prepaid [ ] showing freight amount" notifying CRYSTAL KOBE LTD. 1410 BROADWAY, ROOM 300 NY 10018 U.S.A.
3. ( ) Air Waybills showing "freight [ ] to collect/[ ] prepaid [ ] indicating freight amount" and consigned to ________
4. ( ) Memorandum issued by ________________ consigned to: ________________
5. (×) Insurance Policy/Certificate in 2 copies for 110% of the invoice value showing claims payable in China in currency of the draft. Blank endorsed, covering [×] Ocean Marine Transportation All Risks, War Risks.
6. (×) Packing List/Weight Memo in 3 copies indicating quantity/gross and net weight of each package and packing condition as called for by the L/C.
7. (×) Beneficiary's certified copy of cable/telex dispatched to the accountees within 24 hours after shipment advising [×] name of vessel/[ ] No./[ ] wagon No., date, quantity, weight and value of shipment.
8. (×) Beneficiary's Certificate certifying that extra copies of the documents have been dispatched according to the contract terms.
9. ( ) Other documents, if any.

Additional instructions:

1. (×) All banking charges outside the opening bank are for beneficiary's account.
2. (×) Documents must be presented within 15 days after the date of issuance of the transport documents but within the validity of this credit.
3. (×) The third party as shipper is not acceptable. Short form/Blank Back B/L is not acceptable.
4. ( ) Both quantity and amount % more or less are allowed.
5. (×) All documents to be forwarded in one cover, unless otherwise stated above.

Your correspondents to advise beneficiary [ ] adding their confirmation [×] without adding their confirmation

Payments to be debited to our U.S. Dollars Amount No. 10-668855368

Signature: CRYSTAL KOBE LTD.

图 8.11 开证申请书

根据图8.12所示的合同审核图8.13所示的信用证。

合 同
CONTRACT

ORIGINAL

THE SELLER: SHANGHAI TEXTILES IMP. & EXP. CORP. SHANGHAI
27 ZHONGSHAN ROAD E. 1, SHANGHAI, CHINA
TELEPHONE: 86-21-63218467 FAX: 86-21-63291267

CONTRACT NO.: GL0082
DATE: Oct. 5, 2000
PLACE: SHANGHAI

THE BUYER: SUPERB AIM (HONG KONG) LTD.,
RM. 504 FUNGLEE COMM BLDG. 6-8A PRATT AVE., TSIMSHATSUI,
KOWLOO, HONG KONG

THE BUYER AND THE SELLER HAVE AGREEE TO CONCLUDE THE FOLLOWING TRANSACTIONS ACCORDING TO THE TERMS AND CONDITIONS STIPULATED BELOW:

1. COMMODITY & SPECIFICATION PACKING & SHIPPING MARK	2. QUANTITY (PCS)	3. UNIT PRICE	4. AMOUNT
80% COTTON 20% POLYESTER LADIES KNIT JACKET		CIF H. K.	
ART. NO. 49394 (014428)	600	US $14.25	USD 8,550.00
ART. NO. 49393 (014428)	600	US $14.25	USD 8,550.00
ART. NO. 55306 (014429)	600	US $14.25	USD 8,550.00
REMARKS: 1) EACH IN PLASTIC BAGS, 24 BAGS TO A CARTON TOTAL 75 CARTONS 2) SHIPPING MARK: SUPERB H K NO. 1-75 MADE IN CHINA		TOTAL:	USD 25,650.00

TOTAL VALUE: SAY US DOLLARS TWENTY-FIVE THOUSAND SIX HUNDRED AND FIFTY ONLY.

TIME OF SHIPMENT: Within 45 days of receipt of letter of credit and not later than the month of Dec. 2000 with partial shipments and transhipment allowed.

PORT OF LOADING & DESTINATION: FROM SHANGHAI TO HONG KONG.

TERMS OF PAYMENT: By 100% Confirmed Irrevocable Sight Letter of Credit opened by the buyer to reach the Seller not later than Oct. 31th 2000 and to be available for negotiation in China until the 15th day after the date of shipment. In case of late arrival of the L/C, the seller shall not be liable for any delay in shipment and shall have the right to rescind the contract and/or claim for damages.

INSURANCE: To be effected by the seller for 110% of the CIF invoice value covering ALL RISKS AND WAR RISK as per China Insurance Clauses.

TERMS OF SHIPMENT: To be governed by "INCOTERMS 2000". For transactions concluded on CIF terms, all surcharges including port congestion surcharges, etc. levied by the shipping company, in addition to freight, shall be for the buyer's account.

The Buyer:
SUPERB AIM (HONG KONG) LTD.

The Seller
SHANGHAI TEXTILES IMP. & EXP. CORP.

图8.12 合同

000CT20　14:57:32　　LOGICAL TERMINAL POO5

MT:S700　ISSUE OF DOCUMENTARY CREDIT　PAGE 00001

FUNC SWPR3

UMR 00182387

APPLICATION HEADER　0700 1547 970225 SAIB H. K. JTC × × ×3846 992024 001015 1447
◆NANYANG COMMERCIAL BANK LTD.
◆HONG KONG

USER HEADER　SERVICE CODE 103:
BANK PRIORITY 113:
MSG USER REF 108:

INFO. FROMC1　115:

SEQUE NCE OF TOTAL　◆27: 1/2

FORM OF DOC. CREDIT　◆40: REVOCABLE

DOC, CREDIT NUMBER　◆20: L8959344

DATE OF ISSUE　◆31C: 001020

EXIPRY　◆31D: DATE 001231 AT NEGOTIATING BANK'S COUNTER

APPLICANT　◆50: SUPERB AIM (HONG KONG) LTD. HONG KONG

BENEFICIARY　◆59: SHANGHAI TEXTILES IMP& EXP CORPORATION

27 ZHONGSHAN ROAD E. 1

SHANGHAI, CHINA

AMOUNT　◆32B: CURRENCY USD AMOUNT 256,500.00

AVAILABLE WITH/BY　◆41D: NANYANG COMMERTIAL BANK, LTD. H. K.
BY NEGOTIATION

DRAFTS AT…　◆42C: DRAFTS AT 20 DAYS' SIGHT FOR FULL INVOICE VALUE

DRAWEE　◆42A: NANYANG COMMERCIAL BANK, LTD.

PARTIAL SHIPMENTS　◆43P: ALLOWED

TRANSHIPMENT　◆43T: PROHIBITED

LOADING IN CHARGE　◆44A: SHIPMENT FROM CHINESE PORT (S)

FOR TRANSPORT TO　◆44B: SINGAPORE/HONG KONG

LATEST DATE OF SHIP　◆44C: 001215

DESCRIPT. OF GOODS　◆45A: 80% COTTON 20% POLYESTER LADIES KNIT JACKET
AS PER S/C NO. GL0082

ART. NO.	QUANTITY	UNIT PRICE
49394(014428)	600 PIECES	USD14.25
49393(014428)	600 PIECES	USD14.25
55306(014429)	600 PIECES	USD14.25

PRICE TERM: CIF H. K.

DOCUMENTS REQUIRED　◆46A:

+3/3 SET OF ORIGINAL CLEAN ON BOARD OCEAN BILLS OF LADING MADE OUT TO ORDER OF SHIPPER AND BLANK ENDORSED AND MARKED "FREIGHT COLLECT" NOTIFY APPLICANT (WITH FULL NAME AND ADDRESS).

+ORIGINAL SIGNED COMMERCIAL INVOICE IN 5 FOLD INDICATION S/C NO.

+INSURANCE POLICY OR CERTIFICATE IN TWO FOLD ENDORSED IN BLANK, FOR 120 PCT OF THE INVOICE VALUE INCLUDING: THE INSTITUTE CARGO CLAUSES (A), THE INSTITUTE WAR CLAUSES, INSURANCE CLAIMS TO BE PAYABLE AT DESTINATION IN THE CURRENCY OF THE DRAFTS.

+CERTIFICATE OF ORIGIN GSP FORM A IN ONE ORIGINAL AND ONE COPY.

+PACKING LIST IN 3 FOLD.

+BENEFICIARY'S CERTIFICATE STATING THAT ALL DOCUMENTS HAVE BEEN SENT WITHIN 10 DAYS AFTER SHIPMENT.

ADDITIONAL COND.　◆47:

1. T. T. REIMBURSEMENT IS PROHIBITED.

2. THE GOODS TO BE PACKED IN EXPORT STRONG COLORED CARTONS.

3. INSPECTION IS TO BE EFFECTED BEFORE SHIPMENT AND RELEVANT CERTIFICATED/REPORTS ARE REQUIRED FROM THE INSPECTING AGENCY OR INSPECTOR DESIGNATED BY THE BUYER.

DETAILS OF CHARGES　◆71B:

ALL BANKING CHARGES OUTSIDE HONG KONG INCLUDING REIMBURSEMENT COMMISSION ARE FOR ACCOUNT OF BENEFICIARY.

PRESENTATION PERIOD　◆48:

DOCUMENTS TO BE PRESENTED WITHIN 15 DAYS AFTER THE DATE OF SHIPMENT, BUT WITHIN THE VALIDITY OF THE CREDIT.

CONFIRMATION　◆49: WITHOUT

INSTRUCTION　◆78:

THE NEGOTIATION BANK MUST FORWARD THE DRAFTS AND ALL DOCUMENTS BY REGISTERED AIRMAIL DIRECT TO US(NANYANG COMMERCIAL BANK, LTD. WESTERN DISTRICT BILLS CENTER 128 BONHAM STRAND E. HONG KONG) IN ONE LOTS, UPON RECEIPT OF THE DRAFTS AND DOCUMENTS IN ORDER, WE WILL REMIT THE PROCEEDS AS INSTRUCTED BY THE NEGOTIATING BANK.

TRAILER: ORDER IS <MAC:> <PAC:> <ENG:> <CHK:> <PDE:>

MAC: 3CDFF763

CHK: 8A1AA1203070

图 8.13　信用证

第 9 章 国际结算单据实务

9.1 提单制作

9.1.1 提单范本

空白提单范本如图 9.1 所示。

COMBINED TRANSPORT BILL OF LADING

<table>
<tr><td colspan="2" rowspan="2">1. Shipper</td><td>Booking No.</td><td>Bill of Lading No.</td></tr>
<tr><td colspan="2">Export References</td></tr>
<tr><td colspan="2" rowspan="2">2. Consignee</td><td colspan="2">Forwarding Agent and Reference</td></tr>
<tr><td colspan="2">Point and Country of Origin</td></tr>
<tr><td colspan="2">3. Notify Party</td><td colspan="2" rowspan="2">Also Notify Party routing & instructions</td></tr>
<tr><td>4. Pre-Carriage by</td><td>5. Place of Receipt</td></tr>
<tr><td>6. Ocean Vessel Voy. No.</td><td>7. Port of Loading</td><td>Service Contract No.</td><td>Commodity Code</td></tr>
<tr><td>8. Port of Discharge</td><td>9. Place of Delivery</td><td colspan="2">Type of Movement</td></tr>
</table>

<table>
<tr><td>Marks & Nos.
Container/Seal No.</td><td>No. of Container
or Packages</td><td>Description of Goods</td><td>Gross Weight</td><td>Measurement</td></tr>
<tr><td></td><td></td><td></td><td></td><td></td></tr>
<tr><td colspan="2">Declared Cargo Value US $</td><td colspan="3"></td></tr>
<tr><td colspan="5">10. Total Number of Containers and/or Packages (in words)</td></tr>
</table>

<table>
<tr><td>11. Freight & Charges</td><td>Revenue Tons</td><td>Rate</td><td>Per</td><td>Amount</td><td>Prepaid</td><td>Collect</td><td>Freight & Charges Payable at/by</td></tr>
<tr><td></td><td></td><td></td><td></td><td></td><td></td><td></td><td></td></tr>
</table>

<table>
<tr><td rowspan="2"></td><td>Date Loading on Board</td></tr>
<tr><td></td></tr>
<tr><td>Date of Issue</td><td>Place of Issue</td></tr>
</table>

图 9.1 空白提单

9.1.2　制单说明

(1) Shipper（托运人）：填写实际的委托运输的当事人，一般为出口商。该栏须注明出口商的名称及联系方式。

(2) Consignee（收货人）：该栏目不指定具体收货人，一般填写指示性抬头，如 to order of ABC。

(3) Notify Party（通知方）：填写需要通知的联系人，实际业务中一般为进口商。

(4) Pre-Carriage by（前程运输方式）：联运提单，第一程为海洋运输，一般不涉及前程运输方式，可免填。

(5) Place of Receipt（收货地）：在联运方式中，提单在收货后就签发，所以该栏目填写实际收货地的名称，一般为出口所在地。

(6) Ocean Vessel Voy. No.（海洋船舶及航次号）：填写货物运输船舶的名称和运输航次。

(7) Port of Loading（装运港）：填写货物实际装运的港口。

(8) Port of Discharge（卸货港）：填写货物实际卸货的港口，由于是联运提单，一般此项不是最终目的地。

(9) Place of Delivery（最终交货地）：填写该票货物最终的目的地。

(10) Booking No.（订舱号码）：填写订舱号。

(11) Bill of Lading No.（提单号码）：填写该份联运提单的号码。

(12) Export References（出口资料）：可免填。

(13) Forwarding Agent and Reference（货运代理资料）：有货代时填写。

(14) Point and Country of Origin（原产国或地区）：填写原产国家或地区信息。

(15) Also Notify Party routing & instructions（通知行说明）：通知行有特殊情况说明。

(16) Service Contract No.（服务合同标号）：根据实际需要填写。

(17) Commodity Code：（商品编码）：根据实际需要填写。

(18) Type of Movement（交接方式）：填写集装箱的交接方式。

(19) Marks & Nos. Container/Seal No.（唛头和集装箱号码）：填写该货物运输标志和集装箱号码。

(20) No. of Container or Packages（集装箱数量）：填写货物总数量。

(21) Description of Goods（货物描述）：填写货物的基本信息。

(22) Gross Weight（毛重）：填写货物的总毛重。

(23) Measurement（体积）：一般填写货物的总体积。

(24) Total Number of Containers and/or Packages (in words)（集装箱或包装数量大写）：填写集装箱数量或包装数量大写。

(25) Freight & Charges（运费支付）：根据贸易术语填写，卖方办运输填写 freight prepaid；卖方不办理运输填写 freight to collect。

(26) Date Loading on Board（装船日期）：填写货物的实际装船日期。

(27) Date of Issue（签发日期）：该份联运提单的签发日期。

(28) Place of Issue（签发地点）：一般填写装运地，特别注意在提单右下角须运输方或其代理人签署。

9.1.3 提单实例

提单实例如图9.2所示。

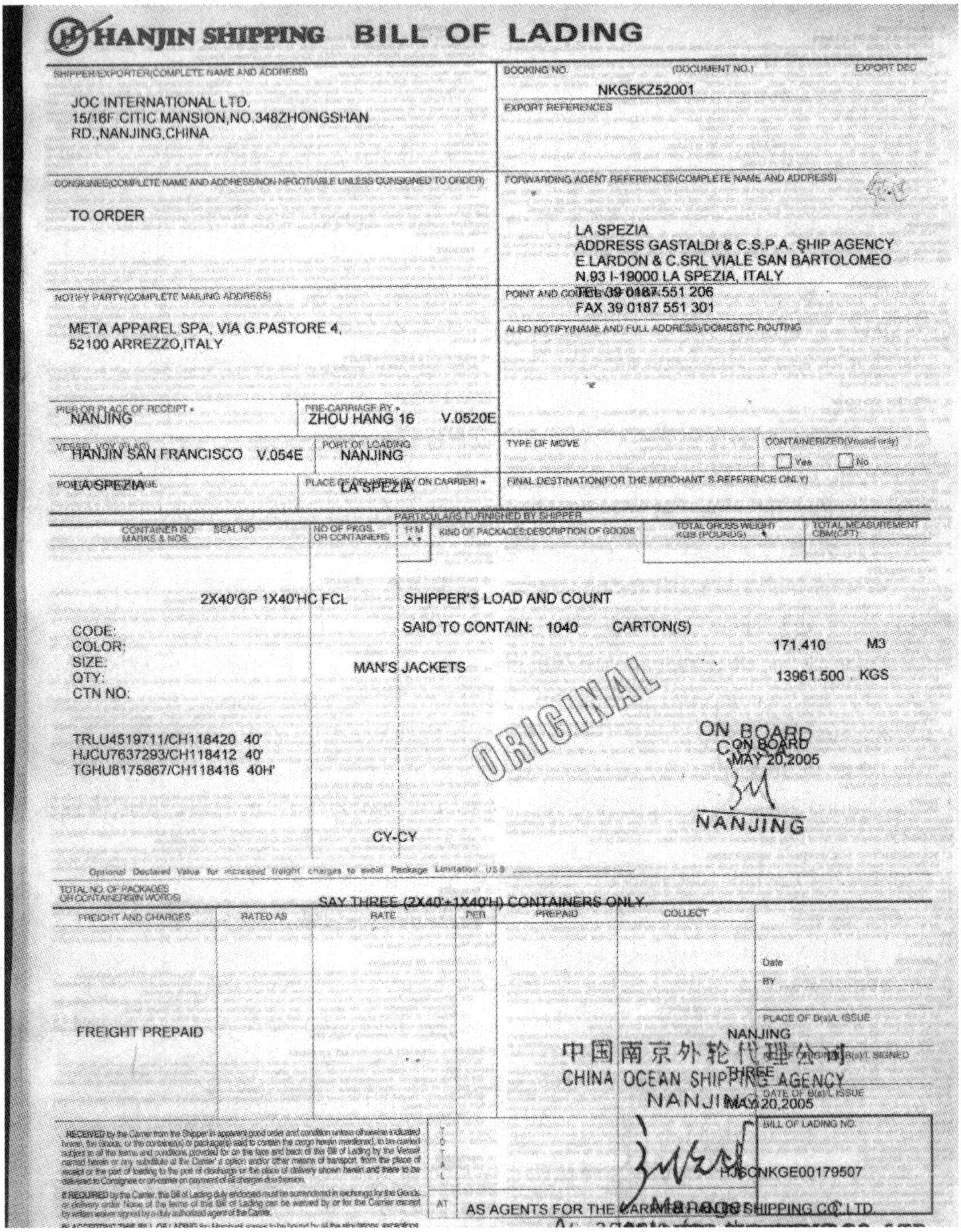

HANJIN SHIPPING BILL OF LADING

SHIPPER/EXPORTER(COMPLETE NAME AND ADDRESS)
JOC INTERNATIONAL LTD.
15/16F CITIC MANSION,NO.348ZHONGSHAN
RD.,NANJING,CHINA

BOOKING NO. (DOCUMENT NO.) EXPORT DEC
NKG5KZ52001

EXPORT REFERENCES

CONSIGNEE(COMPLETE NAME AND ADDRESS)NON NEGOTIABLE UNLESS CONSIGNED TO ORDER)
TO ORDER

FORWARDING AGENT REFERENCES(COMPLETE NAME AND ADDRESS)
LA SPEZIA
ADDRESS GASTALDI & C.S.P.A. SHIP AGENCY
E.LARDON & C.SRL VIALE SAN BARTOLOMEO
N.93 I-19000 LA SPEZIA, ITALY
TEL 39 0187 551 206
FAX 39 0187 551 301

NOTIFY PARTY(COMPLETE MAILING ADDRESS)
META APPAREL SPA, VIA G.PASTORE 4,
52100 ARREZZO,ITALY

POINT AND COUNTRY OF ORIGIN

ALSO NOTIFY(NAME AND FULL ADDRESS)/DOMESTIC ROUTING

PIER OR PLACE OF RECEIPT: NANJING
PRE-CARRIAGE BY: ZHOU HANG 16 V.0520E
VESSEL VOY (FLAG): HANJIN SAN FRANCISCO V.054E
PORT OF LOADING: NANJING
TYPE OF MOVE
CONTAINERIZED(Vessel only) Yes No
PORT OF DISCHARGE: LA SPEZIA
PLACE OF DELIVERY (BY ON CARRIER): LA SPEZIA
FINAL DESTINATION(FOR THE MERCHANT'S REFERENCE ONLY)

PARTICULARS FURNISHED BY SHIPPER

CONTAINER NO. SEAL NO. MARKS & NOS.	NO. OF PKGS. OR CONTAINERS	H M	KIND OF PACKAGES;DESCRIPTION OF GOODS	TOTAL GROSS WEIGHT KGS (POUNDS)	TOTAL MEASUREMENT CBM(CFT)
2X40'GP 1X40'HC FCL CODE: COLOR: SIZE: QTY: CTN NO: TRLU4519711/CH118420 40' HJCU7637293/CH118412 40' TGHU8175867/CH118416 40H'			SHIPPER'S LOAD AND COUNT SAID TO CONTAIN: 1040 CARTON(S) MAN'S JACKETS CY-CY	13961.500 KGS	171.410 M3

ORIGINAL

ON BOARD
MAY 20,2005
NANJING

Optional Declared Value for increased freight charges to avoid Package Limitation US$

TOTAL NO. OF PACKAGES OR CONTAINERS(IN WORDS)
SAY THREE (2X40'+1X40'H) CONTAINERS ONLY.

FREIGHT AND CHARGES	RATED AS	RATE	PER	PREPAID	COLLECT
FREIGHT PREPAID					

Date
BY
PLACE OF B(s)/L ISSUE: NANJING
NUMBER OF ORIGINAL B(s)/L SIGNED: THREE
DATE OF B(s)/L ISSUE: MAY.20,2005
BILL OF LADING NO.: HJSCNKGE00179507

中国南京外轮代理公司
CHINA OCEAN SHIPPING AGENCY
NANJING

RECEIVED by the Carrier from the Shipper in apparent good order and condition unless otherwise indicated herein, the Goods, or the container(s) or package(s) said to contain the cargo herein mentioned, to be carried subject to all the terms and conditions provided for on the face and back of this Bill of Lading by the Vessel named herein or any substitute at the Carrier's option and/or other means of transport, from the place of receipt or the port of loading to the port of discharge or the place of delivery shown herein and there to be delivered to Consignee or on-carrier on payment of all charges due thereon.

If REQUIRED by the Carrier, this Bill of Lading duly endorsed must be surrendered in exchange for the Goods or delivery order. None of the terms of this Bill of Lading can be waived by or for the Carrier except by written waiver signed by a duly authorized agent of the Carrier.

TOTAL

AT

AS AGENTS FOR THE CARRIER HANJIN SHIPPING CO.,LTD.

Manager

图9.2 提单实例

9.2 发票制作

发票实例如图 9.3 所示。

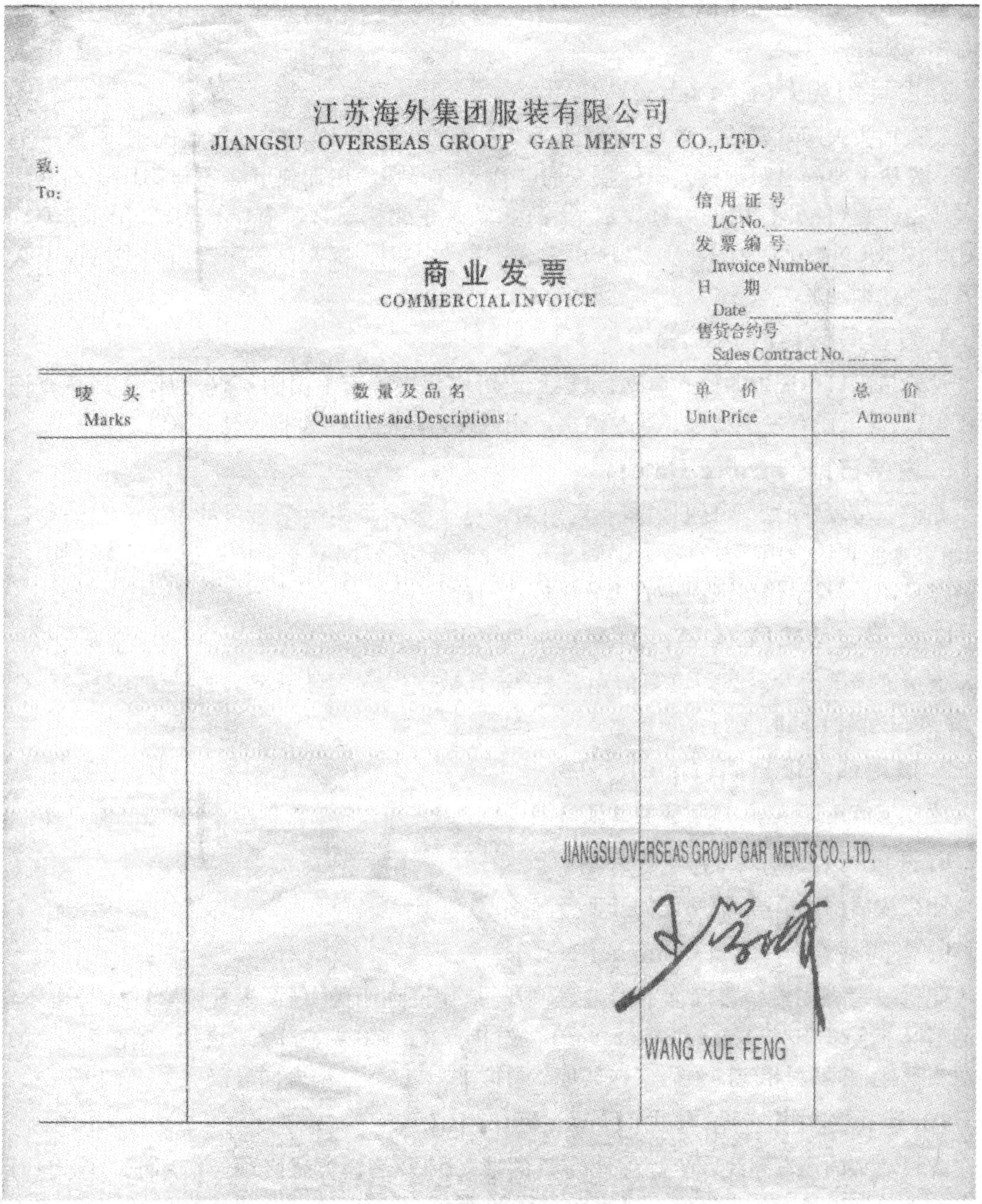

江苏海外集团服装有限公司
JIANGSU OVERSEAS GROUP GAR MENTS CO.,LTD.

致：
To:

信用证号
L/C No.
发票编号
Invoice Number
日　期
Date
售货合约号
Sales Contract No.

商业发票
COMMERCIAL INVOICE

唛　头 Marks	数量及品名 Quantities and Descriptions	单　价 Unit Price	总　价 Amount

JIANGSU OVERSEAS GROUP GAR MENTS CO.,LTD.

WANG XUE FENG

图 9.3　发票实例

1. 发票名称(Name of Invoice)

在明显位置上标明"INVOICE"(发票)或"COMMERCIAL INVOICE"(商业发票)字样。在信用证项下,发票名称应与信用证一致。

2. 出票人(Issuer)

填写出口企业的名称和详细地址。在信用证支付方式下,此栏必须与信用证中的受益人的名称和地址一致。

3. 发票抬头人(Consignee)

发票抬头人即发票的接受人,一般为买卖合同的买方或收货人,通常情况下,抬头人为进口商。发票上明确显示抬头人即付款人的名称、地址,在信用证项下必须与信用证的开证申请人严格一致(除非信用证另有规定)。商业发票在此栏通常印有"TO MESSRS"、"TO"或"FOR ACCOUNT AND RISK OF MESSRS"等字样,填制时只需在这些字样后分两行注明买方的名称和详细地址。

4. 发票号码(Invoice No.)

发票是出口单证中的核心单据,发票号码可以代表整套单据的号码,为便于信息查询和业务管理,应给所有发票编号。通常由出口企业按一定的规律和顺序统一编制。

5. 发票日期(Invoice Date)

此栏填写发票的出票日期。商业发票通常是全套单据中出票最早的单据。在信用证项下,出口企业收到信用证并审核无误后开立商业发票,其日期不早于信用证的开立日期,不迟于装运日期,不晚于信用证规定的交单议付日期。

6. 信用证号码(L/C No.)

信用证项下的发票必须填写信用证号码,其他支付方式可不填。如果信用证援引合同号,则须在发票上同时注明合同号。

7. 信用证开证日期(Date)

此栏按信用证填写,信用证的开证日期。

8. 开证行(Issued by)

此栏按信用证填写,信用证的开证行名称。

9. 合同或合约号码(Contract No.)

此栏填写合同或销售确认书的编号,应与信用证列明的一致,未规定合同编号可不填。有的情况下会以"S/C(Sales Confirmation)"或"P. O. (Purchase Order)"表示,应把对应栏的名称适当调整,并填写相应的号码。在其他支付方式下,必须注明合同号码。

10. 运输路线及运输方式(From. . . to…by)

此栏填写的运输路线、起运港(地)、目的港(地)及运输方式必须与信用证的规定一致,且与其他单据上显示的相一致。要写明具体的地名,不能用统称。如货物需经转运,应把转运港(地)的名称表示出来。

11. 单价及贸易术语(Unit Price and Trade Terms)

国际贸易中完整的单价包括计价货币、单位价格、计量单位和贸易术语四部分内容。单价应严格与合同或信用证一致。对于不同货物,应标明相应的单价,注意币种与信用证一致,数量单位与计价单位一致。如贸易术语变形或贸易术语有附加条件也应按信用证的规定在发票上注明。

12. 总值(Total Amount)

此栏填写发票总金额,即发票上列明的单价与数量的乘积,一般分别用大写和小写金额填写,大、小写金额应一致,不能超过信用证规定的总金额。(如信用证上有"约"、"大概"、"大约"或类似的词语用于描述信用证金额,发票的有关金额允许有不超过10%的增减幅度。)如合同单价含有佣金和折扣,发票上一般也会注明。此外,有时来证要求分别列明运费、保费和FOB价格,必须照办。

13. 唛头及件号(Marks & No.)

唛头是货物的识别标志,一般由收货人简称、合同号、目的港、件号等内容组成。其一般由出口企业自行设计,如果信用证规定了唛头,则须按规定缮制;唛头既要与实物货物相符,又要与信用证和提单一致。无唛头时,可填写"N/M"字样。如果是集装箱运输,应注明集装箱号及封号。

14. 货物描述(Descriptions of Goods)

此栏是发票的主要项目,一般印有"Name of commodity"或"Description of goods"的字样。该栏主要包括货物的名称、品质、规格、数量、重量、包装等内容,须与合同或信用证严格一致。为避免单证不符,可在货物描述处加上"All other details are as per Sales Contract No. . . . "。

根据UCP600的规定,当信用证在数量前用了约数的措辞"about"或"approximately"时,出运的货物可有10%的增减幅度。

15. 声明文句及其他内容(Declaration and Other Contents)

根据买方和信用证的要求,对一些特殊事项加以注明,如:加注参考号、进口许可证号、汇票出票条款等,证明发票内容的正确与真实、货物原产地、价值等。应当注意的是,发票在本栏证明了发票的内容真实、正确时,必须将发票末端所印就的"E&O. E. (有错当查)"划掉。因为它与上述证明文句相矛盾,必须去掉。

16. 出票人签章(Signature)

一般发票必须经出口商正式签字盖章才有效,即在发票右下角打上出口企业的名称,并由经办人签名或盖章,如信用证规定必须手签,则必须按规定办;如对墨西哥、阿根廷的出口,无论信用证是否规定,必须手签。应注意使用的图章和签字与其他单据的签章相一致。如果对方国家要求手签,要注意各国的习惯。

9.3 保险单制作

保险单实例如图9.4所示。

PICC 中国人民财产保险股份有限公司
PICC PROPERTY AND CASUALTY COMPANY LIMITED

总公司设于北京 Head Office Beijing　　一九四九年创立 Established in 1949

本保单限于2011年12月31日前填开使用有效

货物运输保险单
CARGO TRANSPORTATION INSURANCE POLICY

发票号(INVOICE NO.): 10BY187
合同号(CONTRACT NO.):
信用证号(L/C NO.):
被保险人: INSURED: HUZHOU BAIYE INDUSTRY CO.,LTD.

保单号次 POLICY NO.HW38Z/ PYIE201033058200001094

中国人民财产保险股份有限公司(以下简称本公司)根据被保险人的要求，由被保险人向本公司缴付约定的保险费，按照本保险单承保险别和背面所载条款与下列特款承保下述货物运输保险，特立本保险单。

THIS POLICY OF INSURANCE WITNESSES THAT PICC PROPERTY AND CASUALTY COMPANY LIMITED (HEREINAFTER CALLED "THE COMPANY") AT THE REQUEST OF THE INSURED AND IN CONSIDERATION OF THE AGREED PREMIUM PAID TO THE COMPANY BY THE INSURED, UNDERTAKES TO INSURE THE UNDERMENTIONED GOODS IN TRANSPORTATION SUBJECT TO THE CONDITIONS OF THIS POLICY AS PER THE CLAUSES PRINTED OVERLEAF AND OTHER SPECIAL CLAUSES ATTACHED HEREON.

标记 MARKS & NOS.	包装及数量 QUANTITY	保险货物项目 DESCRIPTION OF GOODS	保险金额 AMOUNT INSURED
AS PER INVOICE NO.10BY187	3115CTNS	FIRE FIGHTING EQUIPMENT PARTS	GBP54705.51

总保险金额: TOTAL AMOUNT INSURED: GBP FIFTY FOUR THOUSAND SEVEN HUNDRED AND FIVE AND CENTS FIFTY ONE ONLY

保费: PREMIUM: AS ARRANGED　启运日期: DATE OF COMMENCEMENT: AS PER B/L　装载运输工具: PER CONVEYANCE: PRAGUE EXPRESS 02W17

自 FROM: SHANGHAI　经 VIA:　至 TO: SOUTHAMPTON

承保险别: CONDITIONS:

COVERING TRANSPORT INSURANCE FROM PLACE
OF DISPATCH TO PLACE DESTINATION
INCLUDING
CARGO CLAUSES(A)
WAR CLAUSES(CARGO)
STRIKE CLAUSES(CARGO)

ORIGINAL

所保货物，如发生保险单项下可能引起索赔的损失或损坏，应立即通知本公司下述代理人查勘。如有索赔，应向本公司提交保单正本(本保险单共有 2 份正本)及有关文件。如一份正本已用于索赔，其余正本自动失效。

IN THE EVENT OF LOSS OR DAMAGE WHICH MAY RESULT IN A CLAIM UNDER THIS POLICY, IMMEDIATE NOTICE MUST BE GIVEN TO THE COMPANY'S AGENT AS MENTIONED HEREUNDER. CLAIMS, IF ANY, ONE OF THE ORIGINAL POLICY WHICH HAS BEEN ISSUED IN TWO ORIGINAL(S) TOGETHER WITH THE RELEVANT DOCUMENTS SHALL BE SURRENDERED TO THE COMPANY. IF ONE OF THE ORIGINAL POLICY HAS BEEN ACCOMPLISHED, THE OTHERS TO BE VOID.

SURVEY TO BE CARRIED OUT BY A LOCAL
COMPETENT SURVEYOR, CLAIM DOCUMENTS TO BE
MAILED TO THE UNDERWRITER, WE SHALL EFFECT
PAYMENT BY REMITTANCE TO THE CLAIMANT.

中国人民财产保险股份有限公司湖州市分公司
PICC Property and Casualty Company Limited Huzhou Branch

赔款偿付地点:

图 9.4　保险单实例

1. 发票号(INVOICE No.)

此栏填写发票号码。

2. 保单号次(POLICY No.)

此栏填写保险公司指定号码。

3. 被保险人(INSURED)

如信用证无特别规定,保险单的被保险人应是信用证的受益人。在 CIF 或 CIP 价格条件下,被保险人即为卖方(出口商),在信用证方式下指的是受益人,在托收方式下为委托人。但是实际发生货损时,索赔的权益属于买方(进口商),所以保险单以卖方为保险人时,卖方要在保险单的背面进行背书,以示将索赔的权益转让给保险单的持有人,同时受让人承担被保险人的义务。如信用证有特殊要求,所有单据以×××为抬头人,那么应在被保险人栏以×××为被保险人,这种保险单就不要背书了。

4. 保险货物项目(DESCRIPTION OF GOODS)

此栏填写货物名称,此栏允许填写货物总称。

5. 标记(MARKS & Nos.)

保险单的唛头应与发票、提单等一致,也可只填"AS PER INVOICE NO. ×××"。

6. 包装及数量(QUANTITY)

如以包装件数计价,则将最大包装的总件数填入;如以毛重或净重计价,可填件数及毛重或净重;如果是裸装货物,表示其件数即可;散装货物表示其重量,并在其后注明"IN BULK"字样。

7. 保险金额(AMOUNT INSURED)

一般按照发票总金额的110%投保。信用证项下的保险单必须按信用证的规定办理。此栏保险金额使用的货币应与信用证使用的货币相一致,大小写保持一致。

8. 总保险金额(TOTAL AMOUNT INSURED)

总保险金额即保险金额的大写数字,以英文表示,末尾应加"ONLY",以防涂改。

9. 保费(PREMIUM)

一般已由保险公司印就"AS ARRANGED"(如约定)字样。除非信用证另有规定,每笔保费及费率可以不具体表示。

10. 起运日期(DATE OF COMMENCEMENT)

一般填写提单的签发日期,也可填写提单签发日前后各五天之内任何一天的日期,或填"AS PER B/L DATE"。

11. 装载运输工具(PER CONVEYANCE)

填写装载船的船名。当运输由两程运输完成时,应分别填写一程船名和二程船名。如再转运到内陆加 OTHER CONVEYANCE。如空运,填"BY AIR"或"BY AEROPLANE";如陆运,填"BY TRAIN";如以邮包寄送,填"BY PARCEL POST";若采用海陆联运方式,填"BY S. S ×

×× AND THENCE BY OVERLAND TRANSPORTATION TO ×××”。

12. 起运地和目的地(FROM ... TO...)

此栏填写起运地和目的地名称。当货物经转船到达目的港时,可填写“FROM 装运港 TO 目的港 W/T AT 转运港(WITH TRANSHIPMENT AT ×××),也可填写“VIA 转运港 AND THENCE TO 投保最终目的地”。例如:货物由上海运达纽约港后,转运到芝加哥,提单可打成“FROM SHANHGAI TO NEW YORK AND THENCE TO CHICAGO”或“FROM SHANGHAI TO NEW YORK IN TRANSIT TO CHICAGO”。

13. 承保险别(CONDITIONS)

本栏系保险单的核心内容,填写时应注意保险险别及文句与信用证严格一致,即使信用证中有重复语句,为了避免混乱和误解,最好按信用证规定的顺序填写。如信用证没有规定具体险别,或只规定了“MARINE RISK”、“USUAL RISK”或“TRANSPORT RISK”等,可投保一切险(ALL RISKS)、水渍险(WA 或 WPA)、平安险(FPA)三种基本险中的任何一种。如信用证中规定使用《伦敦保险协会货物保险条款》,包括修订前或修订后的,可以按信用证的规定承保,保单应按要求填制。投保的险别除注明险别名称外,还应注明险别适用的文本及日期。

14. 货损检验及理赔代理人(SURVEYING AND CLAIM SETTLING AGENTS)

一般选择在目的港或目的港附近的有关机构为货损检验、理赔代理人,并详细注明代理人的地址。如果保险单上注明保险责任终止是在内地而非港口,则应填列内地代理人的名址。如当地无中国人民保险公司的代理机构,可以注明由当地法定检验机构代为检验。如果信用证自行指定买方选择的代理人,则不应接受。

15. 赔付地点(CLAIM PAYABLE AT)

此栏按合同或信用证的要求填制。如果信用证中并未列明,一般将目的港作为赔付地点。如买方指定理赔代理人,理赔代理人必须在货物到达目的港的所在国内,便于到货后检验,赔款货币一般为与投保额相同的货币。

16. 日期(DATE)

日期指保险单的签发日期。由于保险公司提供仓至仓(WAREHOUSE TO WAREHOUSE)服务,所以要求保险手续在货物离开出口方仓库前办理。保险单的日期也应是货物离开出口方仓库前的日期。

17. 投保地点(PLACE)

投保地点一般为装运港(地)的名称。

18. 签章(AUTHORIZED SIGNATURE)

由保险公司签字或盖章以示保险单正式生效。

19. 背书(ENDORSED)

1)空白背书(BLANK ENDORSED)

空白背书只注明被保险人的名称(包括出口商的名称和经办人的名字)。当来证没有规定使用哪一种背书时,也使用空白背书方式。

2)记名背书

若来证要求“DELIVERY TO(THE ORDER OF) × × × COMPANY(BANK)”或“ENDORSED IN THE NAME OF × × ×”,即规定使用记名方式背书。具体做法是:在保险单背面注明被保险人的名称和经办人的名字后,打上“DELIVERY TO × × × COMPANY(BANK)”或“IN THE NAME OF × × ×”的字样。记名背书在出口业务中较少使用。

3)记名指示背书

当来证保单条款规定“INSURANCE POLICY OR CERTIFICATE IN NEGOTIABLE FORM ISSUED TO THE ORDER OF × × ×”时,只要在保险单背面打上“TO ORDER OF × × ×”,然后签署被保险人的名称就行了。

9.4 装箱单制作

装箱单没有统一的格式和内容,制单时应根据信用证或合同的要求和货物的特点自行设计。缮制装箱单的主要依据是商业发票,其内容主要包括单据名称,编号,出单日期,货物描述,唛头,规格,件数,毛、净重,有的还涉及包装材料及包装方式等(图9.5)。具体来说,装箱单的栏内容及缮制方法如下。

1. 单据名称(Name of Document)

装箱单上应标明“Packing List”字样,且单据名称一般应与信用证或合同的要求一致。如信用证或合同中规定使用“Packing Note”或“Specifications List”等,应按要求填制单据名称。

2. 商业发票编号或号码(Invoice No.)

此栏应填写商业发票编号,便于业务管理,一般将商业发票编号作为装箱单编号。出口商也可自行编制装箱单编号。

3. 唛头及件数(Marks & No.)

此栏应与发票、提单的唛头内容一致。有时填写实际唛头,有时只注明“As per Invoice No. × × ×”。在单位包装货量或品种不固定的情况下,需详细列明每个包装件内的包装情况,因此,包装件应编号。在每个包装件内应列明有关包装的细节,如规格、型号、内装量等。

4. 品名和规格(Name of Commodity & Specification)

品名必须与发票和信用证一致。规格包括商品规格和包装规格,具体内容须按信用证的要求填列。

5. 出单日期(Date)

此栏可按发票日期填写。装箱单的制作一般在发票之后,不得早于发票日期,不能晚于提单日期。

6. 买方名称和地址(Buyer's Name and Address)

此栏填写抬头人名称,要求与信用证开证申请人或合同买方一致。

WUHAN RIGHT PAPER CONVERTER CO., LTD.

NO.13JIANGDA ROAD,JIANGHAN ECONOMIC

DEVELOPMENT ZONE, WUHAN,HUBEI,CHINA

PACKING LIST

TO: DELOS TRADING CO., LTD.
ROOM 830, WOOIN AKLIUM VILL 1, JANG HANG-DONG
ILSAN-GU,GOYANG-SI, GYEONGGI-DO KOREA
FROM: SHANGHAI PORT, CHINA TO:INCHON PORT,KOREA

INVOICE NO.: RT07001
DATE: JUNE.12,2007
CONTRACT NO: RT0703271
TERMS OF PAYMENT: T/T

C/No.	Commodity Description	Quantity	Net Weight	Gross Weight	Measurement
1-254	DIARY Item No.:ON 0449-52 Packing:20pcs/box, 3box/inner ctn, 4inner ctns/corrugating carton	@ 240PCS 60,960PCS	@ 33.00KGS 8,382.00KGS	@ 38.50KGS 9,779.00KGS	@ 0.089CBM 22.606CBM
TOTAL	254CTNS VVVVVVV	60,960PCS VVVVVVVV	8,382.00KGS VVVVVVVVV	9,779.00KGS VVVVVVVVVV	22.606CBM VVVVVVVV
	SAY TOTAL TWO HUNDRED AND FIFTY FOUR (254) CARTONS ONLY. ORIGIN: CHINA SHIPPING MARKS: N/M				

WUHAN RIGHT PAPER
CONVERTERCO.,LTD.

图 9.5 装箱单实例

7. 数量(Quantity)

此栏应注明每种货物的包装件数。如果每种规格的包装单位不同,应将不同规格的数量分别列示出来，累加出合计数并注明。若为裸装或散装货物，则应注明“IN BULK”或“IN NUDE”。

8. 毛重(Gross Weight 或 G. W.)

此栏应按照实际填写每件包装的毛重及总毛重，要与托运单的内容一致。如有几种规格，且每种规格的毛重不同，或来证要求列明货物的单件毛重，则应分别列出；如果是不定量包装货物，通常要逐件列出单件毛重。

9. 净重(Net Weight 或 N. W.)

此栏应按照实际填写每件包装的净重量以及总净重，要与托运单的内容一致。如一票货物中有几种规格，且每种规格的净重不同，或来证要求列明货物的单件净重，则应分别列出；如果是不定量包装货物，通常要逐件列出单件净重。

10. 体积或尺码(Meas./Measurement)

此栏按照货物的实际体积或尺码填写每个包装物件的长、宽、高以及总的体积，并与信用证的规定相符。

11. 包装种类及件数、货物描述(Number and Kind of Package, Description of Goods)

包装种类及件数、货物描述栏必须与发票和信用证一致，也可填写统称。

规格包括商品规格和包装规格，均要求按货物的实际情况和信用证的要求详细填列。

12. 签章(Signature)

此栏由出具本单据的单位和负责人签章，应与发票的签章一致。如果信用证要求中性包装或规定中性包装单，此栏应空白不签章。

9.5 原产地证明制作

9.5.1 一般原产地证明

一般原产地证明实例如图9.6所示。

1. 出口商(Exporter: Full Name, Address, Country)

此栏按实际填写，信用证项下为受益人。

2. 收货人(Consignee: Full Name, Address, Country)

此栏一般为进口商名称、地址及所在国。

3. 运输方式和路线(Means of transport and route)

按信用证或合同规定，填起运地、目的地及采用的运输方式。

4. 目的地国家或地区(Country/region of destination)

一般应与最终收货人或最终目的港国别一致，不能填中间商国家的名称。

ORIGINAL

1. Exporter	Certificate No. 031668035 CERTIFICATE OF ORIGIN OF THE PEOPLE' S REPUBLIC OF CHINA
2. Consignee	
3. Means of transport and route	5. For certifying authority use only
4. Country / region of destination	

6. Marks and numbers	7. Number and kind of packages;description of goods	8. H.S.Code	9. Quantity	10. Number and date of invoices

11. Declaration by the exporter The undersigned hereby declares that the above details and statements are correct, that all the goods were produced in China and that they comply with the Rules of Origin of the People's Republic of China. Place and date, signature and stamp of authorized signatory	12. Certification It is hereby certified that the declaration by the exporter is correct. Place and date, signature and stamp of certifying authority

图 9.6 一般原产地证明实例

5. 供出证方使用(For certifying authority use only)

由签证机构在签发后发证书、补发证书或加注其他声明时使用,一般留空不填。

6. 标记唛码(Marks and numbers)

应照发票上所列唛头填写完整,若没有唛头,则填“N/M”,不得留空不填。

7. 品名及包装种类和件数(Descripion of goods, number and kind of packages)

一般应按商业发票填写,品名要具体,不得概括;包装种类和件数要按具体单位填写总的包装件数,并在阿拉伯数字后加注英文表述,末行要打上表示结束的符号 * * * *,以防加添。若货物为散装,则在品名后加注“IN BULK”。

8. HS 编码(H. S. Code)

按规定填写,不得留空。

9. 数量或重量(Quantity or Weight)

填写出口货物和量值及商品计量单位,若无则填重量。

10. 发票号码及日期(Number and date of invoice)

按实际填写,如“INVOICE NO.:FHTO21T　INVOICE DATE:DEC 10, 2001”。

11. 出口商声明(Declaration by the exporter)

已事先印好,由出口公司填写签发地点、日期并盖公章和专人签字,且不得重合。

12. 证明(Certification)

由国际贸易促进委员会或商检局签发地点、日期、盖章和手签。

9.5.2　普惠制原产地证明书格式 A(FORM A)

普惠制原产地证明书实例如图 9.7 所示。

1. 证书号

普惠制原产地证明书标题栏(右上角)填上检验检疫机构编定的证书号。证书号编定规则:例如 ZC314 */070001(ZC314 * 代表公司注册号;07 代表 2007 年; 0001 代表企业流水号)。

2. 第 1 栏:出口商名称、地址、国家

此栏出口商名称应与注册时相同,必须打上国名、地址。例: SHENZHEN HUAYELONG IMPORTS & EXPORTS LTD. SHENZHEN,CHINA。

3. 第 2 栏:收货人名称、地址、国家

除欧盟 25 国、挪威外,此栏须填上给惠国最终收货人名称,不可填中间转口商的名称,此栏须打上国名。欧盟 25 国、挪威对此栏是非强制性要求。若第 2 栏进口商国家和第 12 栏最终目的国都是欧盟国家,则可以与第 12 栏国家不同,也可以不填详细地址,只填上“To Order”。

4. 第 3 栏:运输方式及路线

一般应填上装货、到货地点(始起运港、目的港)及运输方式(如海运、陆运、空运)。例:

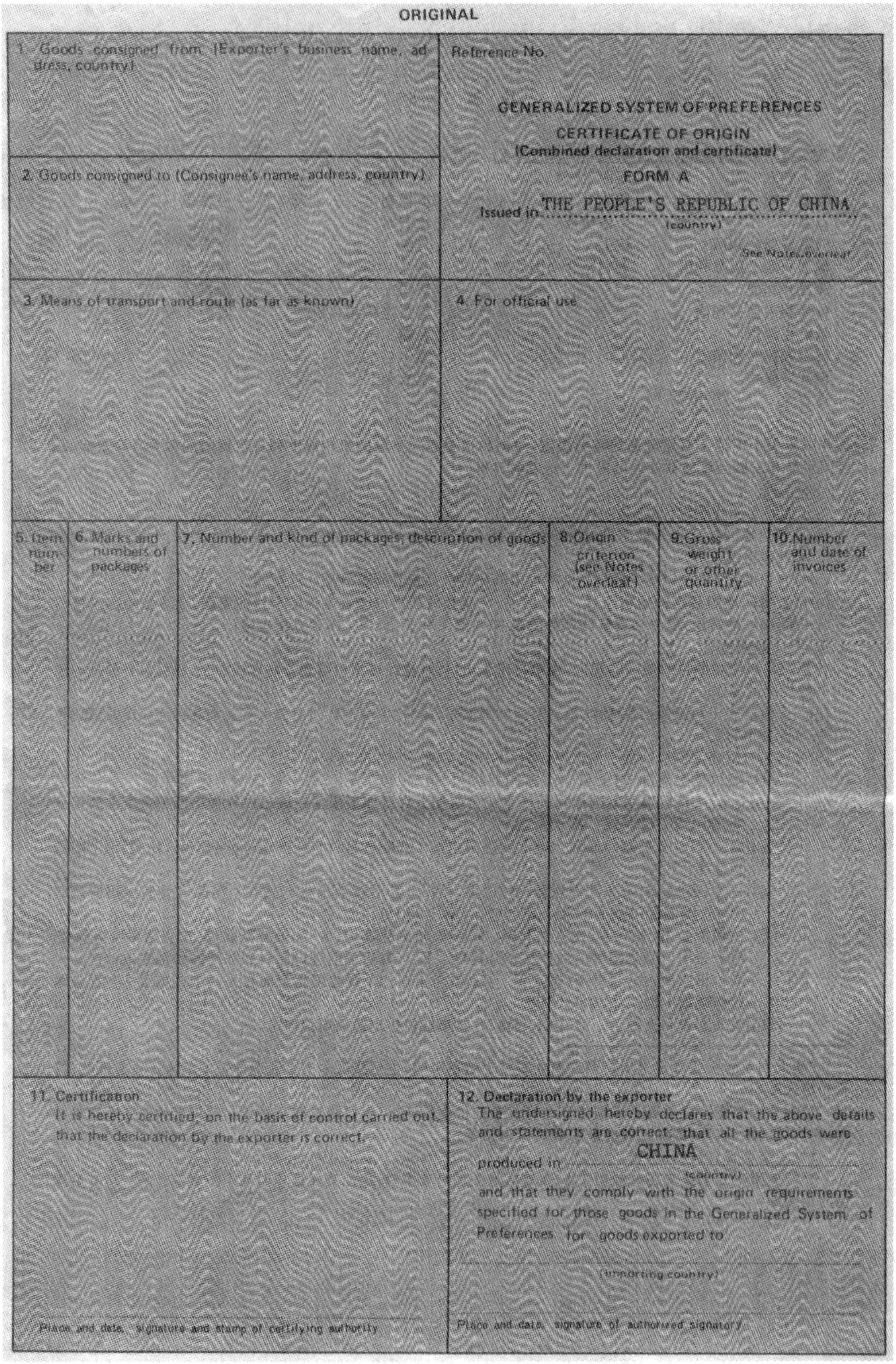

ORIGINAL

1. Goods consigned from (Exporter's business name, address, country)

Reference No.

GENERALIZED SYSTEM OF PREFERENCES
CERTIFICATE OF ORIGIN
(Combined declaration and certificate)
FORM A

Issued in THE PEOPLE'S REPUBLIC OF CHINA
(country)

See Notes overleaf

2. Goods consigned to (Consignee's name, address, country)

3. Means of transport and route (as far as known)

4. For official use

5. Item number	6. Marks and numbers of packages	7. Number and kind of packages; description of goods	8. Origin criterion (see Notes overleaf)	9. Gross weight or other quantity	10. Number and date of invoices

11. Certification
It is hereby certified, on the basis of control carried out, that the declaration by the exporter is correct.

Place and date, signature and stamp of certifying authority

12. Declaration by the exporter
The undersigned hereby declares that the above details and statements are correct; that all the goods were produced in CHINA
(country)
and that they comply with the origin requirements specified for those goods in the Generalized System of Preferences for goods exported to

(importing country)

Place and date, signature of authorized signatory

图 9.7　普惠制原产地证明书实例

FROM DONGGUAN TO SHENZHEN BY TRUCK, THENCE TRANSHIPPED TO HAMBURG BY SEA。

转运商品应加上转运港,例:FROM SHENZHEN TO HONG KONG BY TRUCK, THENCE TRANSHIPPED TO HAMBURG BY SEA。输往内陆给惠国,如瑞士、奥地利,由于这些国家没有海岸,因此如系海运,都须经第三国转运至该国,填证时应注明。例:BY VESSEL FROM SHENZHEN TO HAMBURG, IN TRANSIT TO SWITZERLAND。

5. 第4栏:供官方使用

此栏由签证当局填写,正常情况下此栏空白。特殊情况下,签证当局在此栏加注,例:①货物已出口,签证日期迟于出货日起,签发"后发"证书时,此栏盖上"ISSUED RETROSPECTIVELY"红色印章;②证书遗失、被盗或者损毁,签发"复本"证书时盖上"DUPLICATE"红色印章,并在此栏注明原证书的编号和签证日期,声明原发证书作废,其文字是"THIS CERTIFICATE IS IN REPLACEMENT OF CERTIFICATE OF ORIGIN NO. . . . DATED. . . WHICH IS CANCELLED"。

注意:在录入后发证书时,请在申请书备注栏注明"申请后发",否则计算机会退回。

6. 第5栏:商品顺序号

如同批出口货物有不同品种,则按不同品种分列"1"、"2"、"3",…,以此类推。单项商品此栏填"1"。

7. 第6栏:唛头及包装号

填写的唛头应与货物外包装上的唛头及发票的唛头一致,唛头不得出现中国以外的地区和国家制造的字样,也不能出现香港、澳门、台湾原产地字样(例如:MADE IN TAIWAN, IIONG KONG PRODUCTS 等)。如货物无唛头应填"N/M"。如唛头过多,此栏不够填则打上"SEE THE ATTACHMENT",用附页填打所有唛头(附页的纸张要与原证书一样大小),在右上角打上证书号,并由申请单位和签证当局授权签字人分别在附页末页的右下角和左下角手签、盖印。附页手签的笔迹、地点、日期均与证书第11、12栏相一致。

注意:有附页时,请在申请书备注栏注明"唛头见附页",否则计算机会退回。

8. 第7栏:包件数量及种类

商品的名称、包件数量必须由英文和阿拉伯数字同时表示,例如: ONE HUNDRED AND FIFTY (150) CARTONS OF WORKING GLOVES。注意如下方面。

(1)如果包件数量达到千以上,则千与百单位之间不能有连词"AND",否则计算机会退回。应填: TWO THOUSAND ONE HUNDRED AND FIFTY (2 150) CARTONS OF WORKING GLOVES。

(2)数量、品名要求在一页内打完,如果内容过长,可以合并包装箱数、品名。例: ONE HUNDRED AND FIFTY (150) CARTONS OF GLOVE, SCARF, TIE, CAP。

(3)包装必须打具体的包装种类(例:PP WOVEN BAG. DRUM, PALLET, WOODEN CASE 等),不能只填写"PACKAGE"。如果没有包装,应填写"NUDE CARGO"(裸装货),"IN BULK"(散装),"HANGING GARMENTS"(挂装)。

(4)商品名称必须具体填明(具体到能找到相对应的4位HS编码),不能笼统填"MA-

CHINE”(机器)、“GARMENT”(服装)等。例如:玩具电扇应注明“TOYS:ELECTRIC FANS”,不能只列“ELECTRIC FANS”(电扇)。

(5)商品的商标、品牌名(BRAND)及货号(ARTICLE NUMBER)一般可以不填。

商品名称等项列完后,应在下一行加上表示结束的符号,以防止加填伪造内容。国外信用证有时要求填写合同、信用证号码等,可加填在此栏空白处。

9. 第8栏:原产地标准

此栏是证书的核心。应注意如下方面。

(1)如果出口商品完全是中国原产的,不论出口至哪个给惠国,都填“P”。

(2)如果出口商品是含有进口成分的商品,则出口至欧盟、瑞士、挪威和日本,并符合有关给惠国的加工标准的,填“W”,并在“W”的下方加注商品的四位数字HS品目号。其条件为:①产品列入了上述给惠国的“加工清单”,符合其加工条件;②产品未列入“加工清单”,但产品生产过程中使用的非原产原材料和零部件经过充分的加工,产品的HS品目号不同于所用的原材料和零部件的HS品目号。出口至加拿大的含有进口成分的商品,进口成分的价值不超过该商品出厂价之40%的,填“F”。如果出口至澳大利亚和新西兰,此栏可留空。如果出口至俄罗斯、白俄罗斯、捷克、斯洛伐克、哈萨克斯坦和乌克兰,填“Y”,其下填明进口原料和部件的价值在出口产品离岸价格中所占百分数。在一个受惠国生产而在另一个或一个以上受惠国制作或加工的产品,填写“PK”。

10. 第9栏:毛重或其他数量

注意:此栏应以商品的正常计量单位填,例如“只”、“件”、“双”、“台”、“打”等。例如:3200 DOZ.或6270 KGS.。以重量计算的填毛重,只有净重的填净重亦可,但要标上N. W.(NET WEIGHT)。

11. 第10栏:发票号码及日期

注意:此栏不得留空。月份一律用英文(可用缩写)表示,例如:PHK50016 Apr. 6,2007。此栏的日期必须按照正式商业发票填写,发票日期不得迟于出货日期。

12. 第11栏:签证当局的证明

此栏填写签证机构的签证地点、日期,例如:SHENZHEN CHINA APR. 6,2007。质量监督检验检疫局签证人经审核后在此栏(正本)签名,盖签证印章。注意:此栏的日期不得早于发票日期(第10栏)和申报日期(第12栏),而且应早于货物的出运日期(第3栏)。

13. 第12栏:出口商的声明

进口国横线上填最终进口国,进口国必须与第3栏目的港的国别一致。另外,申请单位应授权专人在此栏手签,标上申报地点、日期,并加盖申请单位的中英文印章。手签人的笔迹必须在质量监督检验检疫局注册登记,并保持相对稳定。此栏日期不得早于发票日期(第10栏)(最早是同日)。盖章时应避免覆盖进口国名称和手签人姓名。本证书一律不得涂改,证书不得加盖校对章。

9.6 受益人证明制作

受益人证明范本如图 9.8 所示。

HUBEI TWIN HORSE TRADE CO. ,LTD. 1ST XUDONG ROAD, WUCHANG, 430077, WUHUAN, CHINA
BENEFICIARY'S CERTIFICATE
NO. HW003
MAY. 20TH, 2006
TO WHOM IT MAY CONCERN: RE: S/C NO. HW003 WE CERTIFY THAT ONE SET OF NON-NEGOTIABLE SHIPPING DOCU. HAS BEEN SET DIRECTLY TO HANWA CO. LTD. 24 HOURS AFTER THE SHIPMENT IS EFFECTED.
HUBEI TWIN HORSE TRADE CO. ,LTD. (**SIGNATURE**)

图 9.8　受益人证明

(1)单据名称。这种单据的名称因所证明事项不同而略异,可能是寄单证明,寄样证明(船样、样卡和码样等),取样证明,证明货物的产地、品质、唛头、包装和标签情况,电抄形式的装运通知,证明产品的生产过程,证明商品业已检验,环保人权方面的证明(非童工、非狱工制造)等。

(2)证明上通常会显示发票号、合同号或信用证号,以表明与其他单据的关系。

(3)证明的内容应严格与合同或信用证的规定相符。

(4)因属于证明性质,按有关规定证明人(受益人)必须签字。

(5)单据一般都应在规定的时间内做出。

9.7 装船通知制作

装船通知范本如图 9.9 所示。

(1)INVOICE No.:填写发票号。

(2)L/C No.:填写信用证编号。

(3)TO:填写进口商名称与地址,即信用证的开证申请人信息。

(4)FROM:填写出口商名称与地址,即信用证的受益人信息。

(5)COMMODITY:填写商品名称,注意符合信用证的内容。

(6)NUMBER OF PKGS:包装数量,与信用证一致。

(7)QUANTITY:填写商品数量,根据信用证的内容填写。

(8)TOTAL G. W. :填写商品的毛重。

(9)NET WEIGHT:填写商品的净重。

(10)B/L No. :填写提单号。

(11)SIGNATURE:公司负责人签名盖章。

SHIPPING ADVICE

INVOICE No. :__________

L/C No. :__________

S/C No. :__________

TO:__________

DEAR SIRS:

WE HEREBY INFORM YOU THAT THE GOODS UNDER THE ABOVE MENTIONED CREDIT HAVE BEEN SHIPPED. THE DETAILS OF THE SHIPMENT ARE STATED BELOW.

COMMODITY:__________

NUMBER OF PKGS:__________

TOTAL G. W:__________

OCEAN VESSEL:__________

DATE OF DEPARTURE:__________

B/L No. :__________

PORT OF LOADING:__________

DESTINATION:__________

SHIPPING MARKS:__________

图 9.9 装船通知

9.8 报检单制作

出境货物报检单范本如图 9.10 所示。

出境货物报检单所列各栏必须填写完整、准确、清晰，栏目内容确实无法填写的以“＊＊＊”表示，不得留空。

(1)报检单位:指向检验检疫机构申报检验、检疫、鉴定业务的单位;报检单应加盖公章。

(2)报检单位登记号:指在检验检疫机构的报检注册登记号。

(3)发货人:指本批货物的贸易合同中卖方的名称或信用证中受益人的名称，如需要出具英文证书，填写中英文。

(4)收货人:指本批出境货物的贸易合同中或信用证中买方的名称，如需要出具英文证书，填写中英文。

(5)货物名称:按贸易合同或发票所列货物名称所对应的国家检验检疫机构制定公布的《出入境检验检疫机构实施检验检疫的进出境商品目录》所列的货物名称填写。

(6)H. S. 编码:指货物对应的海关《商品名称及编码协调制度》中的代码，填写 8 位数或

报检单位（加盖公章）：　填写本单位的全称　　　　*编　号　检验检疫机构受理人填写

报检单位登记号：　　联系人：填报检员　电话：报检员电话　报检日期：实际受理日期

发货人 consignor	（中文）预检报检的，可填写生产单位，出口报检的，应与外贸合同中的卖方或信用证受益人一致
	（外文）
收货人 consignee	（中文）按外贸合同，信用证中所列买方名称填写
	（外文）

货物名称(中/外文) Description of goods	H.S.编码	产地	数/重量 Quantity weight	货物总值 declared	包装种类及数量 Number and type of packages
应与合同，信用证上所列名称及规格填写.	商品编码以当年海关公布为准	生产/加工的国家或地区	应与合同，发票或报关单一致，并注明数重量单位	总值及币种．应与合同，发票报关单一致	实际运输包装的种类及数量，应注明包装材质

运输工具名称号码	运输工具的名称和号码	贸易方式	进口的贸易方式	货物存放地点	存放的地点
合同号	对外贸易合同，订单或形式发票的号码	信用证号	本批货物对应的信用证编码	用途	记住11种用途
发货日期	出口装运日期	输往国家(地区)	按合同填写	许可证/审批号	有关的许可证号或审批号
启运地	启运口岸/城市名称	到达口岸	首次停靠的口岸	生产单位注册号	在检验检疫机构的编号
集装箱规格、数量及号码	货物若以集装箱运输应填写集装箱的规格，数量及号码				

合同、信用证订立的检验检疫条款或特殊要求	标 记 及 号 码	随附单据（画"✓"或补填）	
填写在合同中特别订立的有关质量，卫生等条款或报检单位对本批货物检验检疫的特别要求.	填写本批货物的标记号码，应与合同，发票等有关外贸单句保持一致．若没有标记号码则填"N/M".	□合同 □信用证 □发票 □换证凭单 □装箱单 □厂检单	□包装性能结果单 □许可/审批文件 □ □ □ □

需要证单名称（画"✓"或补填）		*检验检疫费	
□品质证书　_正_副 □重量证书　_正_副 □数量证书　_正_副 □兽医卫生证书　_正_副 □健康证书　_正_副 □卫生证书　_正_副 □动物卫生证书　_正_副	□植物检疫证书　_正_副 □熏蒸/消毒证书　_正_副 □出境货物换证凭单　_正_副 □ □ □ □	总金额（人民币元）	
		计费人	
		收费人	

报检人郑重声明：	领 取 证 单	
1. 本人被授权报检。 2. 上列填写内容正确属实，货物无伪造或冒用他人的厂名、标志、认证标志，并承担货物质量责任。 签名：报检人亲笔签名	日期	由报检人在领取证单时填写
	签名	由报检人在领取证单时填写

注：有"*"号栏由出入境检验检疫机关填写　　◆国家出入境检验检疫局制

图9.10　报检单

10位数。

(7)产地：指货物生产/加工的省(自治区、直辖市)以及地区(市)的名称。

(8)数/重量：填写报检货物的数/重量，重量一般以净重填写，如填写毛重，或以毛作净需注明。

(9)货物总值:按本批货物合同或发票上所列的总值填写(以美元计),如同一报检单报检多批货物,需列明每批货物的总值。(注:如申报货物总值与国内、国际市场价格有较大差异,检验检疫机构保留核价权力。)

(10)包装种类及数量:指本批货物运输包装的件数及种类。

(11)运输工具名称号码:填写货物实际装载的运输工具类别名称(如船、飞机、货柜车、火车等)及运输工具编号(船名、飞机航班号、车牌号码、火车车次)。报检时未能确定运输工具编号的,可只填写运输工具类别。

(12)贸易方式:①一般贸易,②三来一补,③边境贸易,④进料加工,⑤其他贸易。

(13)货物存放地点:指本批货物存放的地点位置。

(14)合同号:指贸易双方就本批货物出境而签订的贸易合同编号。

(15)信用证号:指本批货物所对应的信用证编号。

(16)用途:指本批货物的出境用途,如种用、食用、奶用、观赏或演艺、伴侣、实验、药用、饲用、加工等。

(17)发货日期:按本批货物的信用证或合同所列的出境日期填写。

(18)输往国家(地区):指贸易合同中买方(进口方)所在国家或地区。

(19)许可证/审批单号:对国家出入境检验检疫局已实施出口商品质量许可证制度的产品目录下的出口货物和其他已实行许可制度、审批制度管理的货物,报检时填写安全质量许可证编号或审批单编号。

(20)起运地:指装运本批货物离境的交通工具的起运口岸/地区城市名称。

(21)到达口岸:指装运本批货物的交通工具最终抵达目的地停靠的口岸名称。

(22)生产单位注册号:指生产/加工本批货物的单位在检验检疫机构的注册登记编号。

(23)集装箱规格、数量及号码:填写装载本批货物的集装箱规格(如40英尺、20英尺等)以及分别对应的数量和集装箱号码全称。若集装箱太多,可用附单形式填报。

(24)合同、信用证订立的检验检疫条款或特殊要求:指贸易合同或信用证中贸易双方对本批货物特别约定而订立的质量、卫生等条款和报检单位对本批出境货物的检验检疫的其他特别要求。

(25)标记及号码:按出境货物实际运输包装标填写,如没有标记,填写“N/M”,标记填写不下时可用附页填报。

(26)随附单据:按实际提供的单据在对应的窗口打“√”。

(27)需要证单名称:按需要检验检疫机构出具的证单在对应的窗口打“√”,并应注明所需证单的正副本的数量。

(28)报检人郑重声明:必须有报检人的亲笔签名。

图9.11为报检单实例。

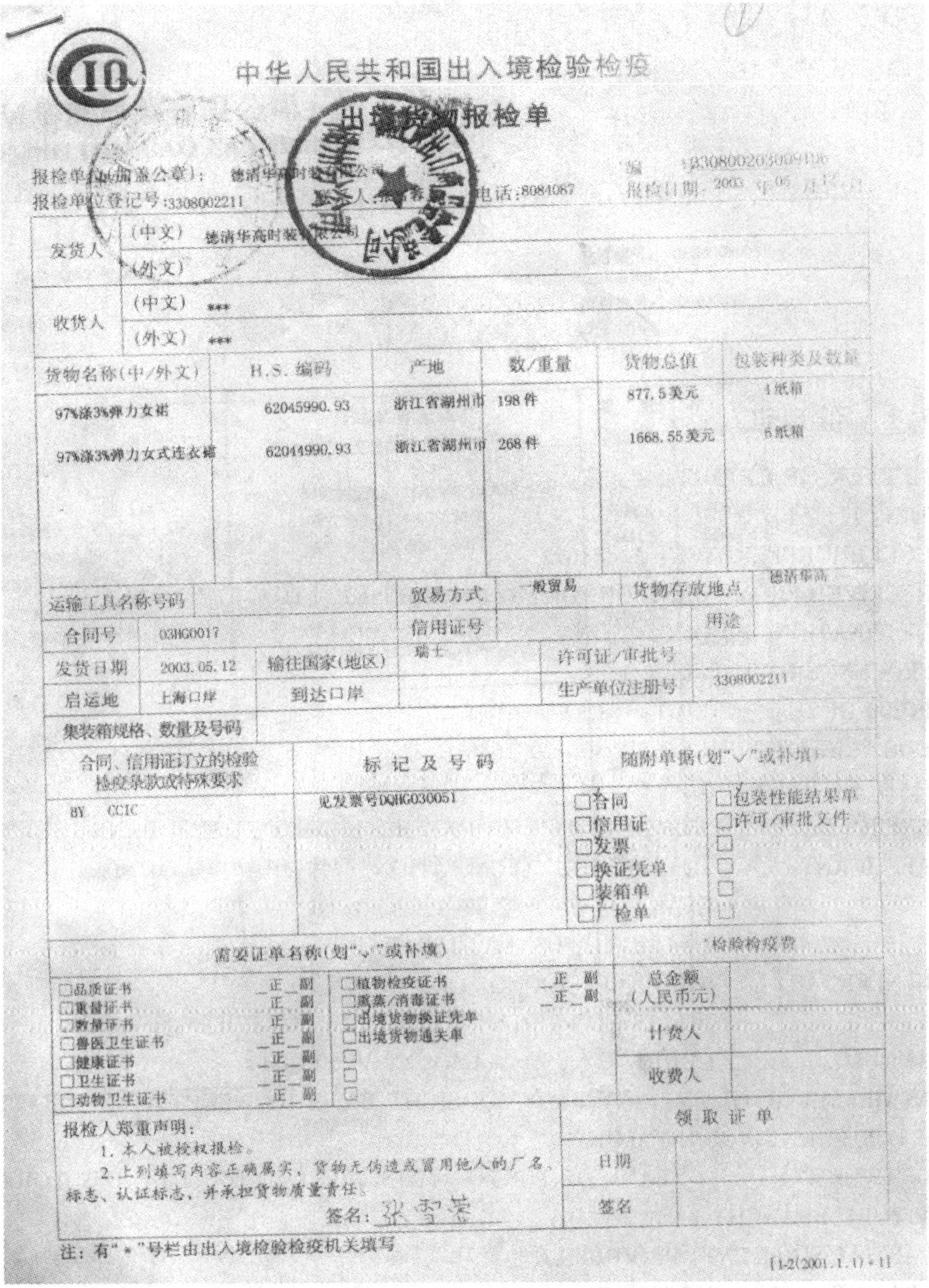

中华人民共和国出入境检验检疫

出境货物报检单

报检单位(加盖公章)：德清华高时装…　　　　*编　号 330800203009106

报检单位登记号：3308002211　联系人：张…　电话：8084087　报检日期：2003年05月12日

发货人	(中文)	德清华高时装有限公司
	(外文)	
收货人	(中文)	***
	(外文)	***

货物名称(中/外文)	H.S.编码	产地	数/重量	货物总值	包装种类及数量
97%涤3%弹力女裙	62045990.93	浙江省湖州市	198件	877.5美元	4纸箱
97%涤3%弹力女式连衣裙	62044990.93	浙江省湖州市	268件	1668.55美元	6纸箱

运输工具名称号码		贸易方式	一般贸易	货物存放地点	德清华高
合同号	03HG0017	信用证号		用途	
发货日期	2003.05.12	输往国家(地区)	瑞士	许可证/审批号	
启运地	上海口岸	到达口岸		生产单位注册号	3308002211
集装箱规格、数量及号码					

合同、信用证订立的检验检疫条款或特殊要求	标记及号码	随附单据(划"√"或补填)	
BY CCIC	见发票号DQHG030051	□合同	□包装性能结果单
		□信用证	□许可/审批文件
		□发票	□
		□换证凭单	□
		□装箱单	□
		□厂检单	□

需要证单名称(划"√"或补填)				*检验检疫费	
□品质证书	_正_副	□植物检疫证书	_正_副	总金额(人民币元)	
□重量证书	_正_副	□熏蒸/消毒证书	_正_副		
□数量证书	_正_副	□出境货物换证凭单		计费人	
□兽医卫生证书	_正_副	□出境货物通关单			
□健康证书	_正_副	□		收费人	
□卫生证书	_正_副	□			
□动物卫生证书	_正_副	□			

报检人郑重声明：	领取证单	
1. 本人被授权报检。	日期	
2. 上列填写内容正确属实，货物无伪造或冒用他人的厂名、标志、认证标志，并承担货物质量责任。		
签名：张雪莲	签名	

注：有"*"号栏由出入境检验检疫机关填写

[1-2(2001.1.1)*1]

图9.11 报检单实例

第 10 章 信用证下制单与审单(实例分析)

10.1 信用证分析

10.1.1 信用证

LETTER OF CREDIT

TRN: 1111510768

COURIER REFERENCE: A/888692

RECEIVED FROM: BANK OF TOKYO _ MITSUBISHI, LTD., THE OSAKA JAPAN

DESTINATION: BANK OF CHINA, NINGBO BRANCH

SEQUENCE OF TOTAL: 1/1

FORM OF DOC. CREDIT: IRREVOCABLE

DOC. CREDIT NUMBER: H486 - 2001689

DATE OF ISSUE: 070606

EXPIRY DATE: 070625 PLACE: COUNTERS OF NEGOTIATING BANK

APPLICANT: TOKO TRADE CORPORATION
OSAKA 2 - 6 - 7, KAWA RAMACHI,
1 - CHOME, OSAKA, JAPAN

BENEFICIARY: NINGBO HUADONG FOOD CO., LTD.
NO. 18 DONG SHAN ROAD, NINGBO, CHINA

AMOUNT: CURRENCY USD AMOUNT 30 600.00

AVAILABEL WITH/BY: ANY BANK ON SIGHT BASIS BY NEGOTIATION DRAFTS AT SIGHT FOR FULL INVOICE VALUE

DRAWEE: BANK OF TOKYO _ MITSUBISHI, LTD., THE NEW YORK, NY (NEW YORK BRANCH)

PARTIAL SHIPMENT: PROHIBITED

TRANSHIPMENT: PROHIBITED

LOADING IN CHARGE: CHINA

FOR TRANSPORT TO: OSAKA, JAPAN

LATEST DATE OF SHIP.: 070615

DESCRIPT. OF GOODS: 30 M/T FROZEN PEAPODS CIF OSAKA, JAPAN AS PER S/C

NO. JP070525

DOCUMENTS REQUIRED:

1. SIGNED COMMERCIAL INVOICE IN 3 ORIGINALS AND 3 COPIES
2. FULL SET OF CLEAN ON BOARD OCEAN BILLS OF LADING MADE OUT TO ORDER AND BLANK ENDORSED MARKED 'FREIGHT PREPAID' NOTIFY APPLICANT
3. PACKING LIST IN TRIPLICATE
4. BENEFICIARY'S CERTIFICATE STATING THAT 1 ORIGINAL INSPECTION CERTIFICATE OF QUALITY AND 1 ORIGINAL B/L ONE ORIGINAL INSURANCE POLICY HAVE BEEN SENT TO APPLICANT BY COURIER
5. INSURANCE POLICY IN DUPLICATE ENDORSED IN BLANK, COVERING ALL RISKS AND WAR RISK FOR 110% OF INVOICE VALUE. CLAIM PAYABLE AT OSAKA, JAPAN IN THE CURRENCY OF DRAFTS
6. INSPECTION CERTIFICATE ISSUED BY MANUFACTURERS

ADDITIONAL CONDITION:

DETAILS OF CHARGES: ALL BANKING CHARGES OUTSIDE JAPAN ARE FOR ACCOUNT OF BENEFICIARY

PRESENTATION PERIOD: DOCUMENTS MUST BE PRESENTED WITHIN 10 DAYS AFTER THE DATE OF SHIPMENT BUT WITHIN VALIDITY OF THE CREDIT

CONFIRMATION: WITHOUT

INSTRUCTIONS:

① REIMBURSEMENT BY TELECOMMUNICATION IS PROHIBITED.

②NEGOTIATING BANK MUST SEND ALL DOCUMENTS TO US, I. E. THE BANK OF TOKYO _ MITSUBISHI, LTD., 2 – 3, KITAHAMA 4 – CHOME, CHUO-KU, OSAKA 541 – 8535 AND/OR C. P. O. POX 388, OSAKA 530 – 8692 IN ONE LOT BY COURIER SERVICE AND REIMBURSE YOURSELVES FROM REIMBURSING BANK FOR EACH PRESENTATION OF DISCREPANT DOCUMENTS UNDER THIS CREDIT.

END OF L/C

THIS CREDIT IS ISSUED SUBJECT TO UNIFORM CUSTOMS AND PRACTICE FOR DOCUMNETARY CREDITS (1993 REVISION) ICC PUBL. 500.

10.1.2 有关资料

发票号码:07GESP3298	发票日期:2007 年 6 月 6 日
提单号码:CANE090318	提单日期:2007 年 6 月 12 日
船名:PRESIDENT V.006	运费:USD1600
保单号码:9076521	保险费:USD150.00
货物装箱情况:20KGS/CTN	H.S.编码:8712.1000
商品情况:30M/T FROZEN PEAPODS	净重:20KGS/CTN
毛重:21KGS/CTN	尺码:(50X40X60)CM/CTN

唛头:TOKO
MADE IN CHINA
NO. 1 - UP

生产单位:宁波华东食品有限公司(221089763214)

报检单位登记号:4478633213

集装箱号码:CGHU2332159(40')

封号:HD20071221

10.1.3 空白单证

请根据上述信用证与有关资料制单,空白单证如图 10.1 ~ 图 10.9 所示。

信用证分析结果单

序号	项目	内容
①	信用证的种类	
②	信用证号码	
③	开证日期	
④	信用证的到期日	
⑤	信用证的到期地点	
⑥	开证申请人	
⑦	受益人	
⑧	开证行名称	
⑨	信用证币制及金额	
⑩	分批装运	
⑪	转运	
⑫	装运港(地)	
⑬	目的港(地)	
⑭	最迟装运期	
⑮	货物描述	
⑯	价格术语	
⑰	交单期限	
⑱	信用证要求的单据	1.
		2.
		3.
		4.
		5.
		6.
⑲	特殊条款	

图 10.1 空白信用证分析结果单

Shipper Insert Name, Address and Phone

B/L No.

中远集装箱运输有限公司
COSCO CONTAINER LINES

TLX:　33057 COSCO CN
FAX:　+86(021) 6545 8984

ORIGINAL

Consignee Insert Name, Address and Phone

Notify Party Insert Name, Address and Phone
(It is agreed that no responsibility shall attach to the Carrier or his agents for failure to notify)

Port-to-Port or Combined Transport

BILL OF LADING

RECEIVED in external apparent good order and condition except as otherwise noted. The total number of packages or units stuffed in the container, the description of the goods and the weights shown in this Bill of Lading are furnished by the Merchants, and which the carrier has no reasonable means of checking and is not a part of this Bill of Lading contract. The carrier has issued the number of Bills of Lading stated below, all of this tenor and date, one of the original Bills of Lading must be surrendered and endorsed or signed against the delivery of the shipment and whereupon any other original Bills of Lading shall be void. The Merchants agree to be bound by the terms and conditions of this Bill o f Lading as if each had personally signed this Bill of Lading.
SEE clause 4 on the back of this Bill of Lading (Terms continued on the back hereof, please read carefully).
*Applicable Only When Document Used as a Combined Transport Bill of Lading.

Combined Transport * Pre-carriage by		Combined Transport* Place of Receipt	
Ocean Vessel Voy. No.		Port of Loading	
Port of Discharge		Combined Transport * Place of Delivery	

Container / Seal No.	Marks & Nos.	No. of Containers or Packages	Description of Goods	Gross Weight (Kgs)	Measurement(M^3)

Total Number of containers and/or packages (in words)

Freight & Charges	Revenue Tons	Rate	Per	Prepaid	Collect

Ex. Rate	Prepaid at	Payable at	Place and date of issue
	Total Prepaid	No. of Original B(s)/L	Signed for the Carrier, COSCO CONTAINER LINES

LADEN ON BOARD THE VESSEL

DATE		BY	

图 10.2　空白提单

NINGBO HUADONG FOOD CO., LTD.

NO. 18 DONG SHAN ROAD, NINGBO, CHINA

COMMERCIAL INVOICE

To:		Invoice No.:	
		Invoice Date:	
		S/C No.:	

From: To:

L/C No.: Issued by:

Marks & Nos.	Description of Goods	Quantity	Unit Price	Amount
TOTAL:				
SAY TOTAL:				

图 10.3 空白商业发票

NINGBO HUADONG FOOD CO., LTD.

NO. 18 DONG SHAN ROAD, NINGBO, CHINA

PACKING LIST

To:		Invoice No.:	
		Invoice Date:	

Marks & Nos.	Number and Kind of Packages Description of Goods	Weight(Kgs)		Measurement (M^3)
		Net	Gross	
TOTAL:				
SAY TOTAL:				

图 10.4 空白装箱单

中保财产保险有限公司

The People's Insurance (Property) Company of China Ltd.

Head Office: BEIJING	海洋货物运输保险单 MARINE CARGO TRANSPORTATION INSURANCE POLICY	Established in 1949
发票号码 Invoice No.		保险单号次 Policy No.

被保险人:
Insured:

中国人民保险公司(以下简称本公司)根据被保险人的要求及其所缴付的保险费,按照本保险单承保险别和背面所载条款与下列特别条款承保下述货物运输保险,特签发本保单。

This Policy of Insurance witnesses that The People's Insurance Company of China (hereinafter called "the Company") at the request of the "Insured" and in consideration of the agreed premium paid to the Company by the Insured undertakes to Insure the undermentioned goods in transportation subject to the conditions of this Policy as per the Clauses printed overleaf and other special clauses attached hereon.

标记及号码 Marks & Nos.	包装数量 Quantity	保险货物项目 Description of Goods	保险金额 Amount Insured

总保险金额
Total Amount Insured:

保费 Premium　　费率 Rate　　装载运输工具 Per conveyance S. S

开航日期 Slg. on or abt ____________　　起运港 From ____________　　目的港 To ____________

承保险别
Conditions

所保货物,如发生本保单项下可能引起索赔的损失或损坏,应立即通知本公司下述代理人勘察。如有索赔,应向本公司提交保险单正本(本保险单共有 份正本)及有关部门的文件。如一份正本已用于索赔,其余正本则自动失效。

In the event loss or damage which may result in a claim under this Policy, immediate notice applying for Survey must be given to the Company's Agent as mentioned hereunder. Claims, if any, one of the Original Policy which has been issued in 2 Original(s) together with other relevant documents shall be surrendered to the Company. If one of the Original Policy has been accomplished, the others to be void.

赔款偿付地点 Claim payable at	中保财产保险有限公司 THE PEOPLE'S INSURANCE(PROPERTY) COMPANY OF CHINA LTD
日期 Date	
地址 Address	

图 10.5 空白保险单

<table>
<tr><td rowspan="2"></td><td colspan="9">中华人民共和国出入境检验检疫</td></tr>
<tr><td colspan="9">出境货物报检单</td></tr>
<tr><td colspan="2">报检单位 (加盖公章):</td><td colspan="4"></td><td colspan="2">**编　号</td><td colspan="2"></td></tr>
<tr><td>报检单位登记号:</td><td></td><td>联系人:</td><td></td><td>电话:</td><td></td><td>报检日期:</td><td colspan="3">年　月　日</td></tr>
<tr><td rowspan="2">发货人</td><td>(中文)</td><td colspan="8"></td></tr>
<tr><td>(外文)</td><td colspan="8"></td></tr>
<tr><td rowspan="2">收货人</td><td>(中文)</td><td colspan="8"></td></tr>
<tr><td>(外文)</td><td colspan="8"></td></tr>
<tr><td>货物名称(中/外文)</td><td>H.S.编码</td><td>产地</td><td>数/重量</td><td>货物总值</td><td colspan="5">包装种类及数量</td></tr>
<tr><td></td><td></td><td></td><td></td><td></td><td colspan="5"></td></tr>
<tr><td>运输工具名称号码</td><td></td><td>贸易方式</td><td></td><td>货物存放地点</td><td colspan="5"></td></tr>
<tr><td>合同号</td><td></td><td>信用证号</td><td></td><td>用途</td><td colspan="5"></td></tr>
<tr><td>发货日期</td><td></td><td>输往国家(地区)</td><td></td><td>许可证 / 审批号</td><td colspan="5"></td></tr>
<tr><td>起运地</td><td></td><td>到达口岸</td><td></td><td>生产单位注册号</td><td colspan="5"></td></tr>
<tr><td>集装箱规格、数量及号码</td><td colspan="9"></td></tr>
<tr><td>合同、信用证订立的检验检疫条款或特殊要求</td><td colspan="3">标 记 及 号 码</td><td colspan="6">随附单据（划“✓”或补填）</td></tr>
<tr><td></td><td colspan="3"></td><td colspan="3">合同
□信用证
发票
□换证凭单
装箱单
□厂检单</td><td colspan="3">□包装性能结果单
□许可/审批文件
□
□
□</td></tr>
<tr><td colspan="4">需要证单名称（划“✓”或补填）</td><td colspan="6">*检验检疫费</td></tr>
<tr><td rowspan="3">品质证书
□重量证书
□数量证书
□兽医卫生证书
□健康证书
□卫生证书
□动物卫生证书</td><td rowspan="3">__正__副
__正__副
__正__副
__正__副
__正__副
__正__副
__正__副</td><td rowspan="3">□植物检疫证书
□熏蒸/消毒证书
□出境货物换证凭单
□
□
□
□</td><td rowspan="3">__正__副
__正__副
__正__副</td><td colspan="3">总金额
(人民币元)</td><td colspan="3"></td></tr>
<tr><td colspan="3">计费人</td><td colspan="3"></td></tr>
<tr><td colspan="3">收费人</td><td colspan="3"></td></tr>
<tr><td colspan="4" rowspan="3">报验人郑重声明:
1.本人被授权报检。
2.上列填写内容正确属实，货物无伪造或冒用他人的厂名、标志、认证标志，并承担货物质量责任。
签名: ___×××____</td><td colspan="6">领 取 证 单</td></tr>
<tr><td colspan="3">日期</td><td colspan="3"></td></tr>
<tr><td colspan="3">签名</td><td colspan="3"></td></tr>
<tr><td colspan="4">注：有“*”号栏由出入境检验检疫机关填写</td><td colspan="6">◆国家出入境检验检疫局制</td></tr>
<tr><td colspan="4"></td><td colspan="6">[1-2 (2000.1.1)]</td></tr>
</table>

图 10.6　空白报检单

NINGBO HUADONG FOOD CO., LTD.

NO. 18 DONG SHAN ROAD, NINGBO, CHINA

BENEFICIARY'S CERTIFICATE

INVOICE NO.:	L/C NO.:	DATE:

图 10.7　空白受益人证明书

BILL OF EXCHANGE												
凭 Drawn Under		不可撤销信用证 Irrevocable L/C No.										
日期 Dated		支 取 Payable With interest	@		%		按		息		付 款	
号码 No.		汇票金额 Exchange for										
	见票 At		日 后 (本 汇 票 之 副 本 未 付) 付 交 sight of this FIRST of Exchange (Second of Exchange Being unpaid)									
Pay to the order of												
金额 the sum of												
此致 To												

图 10.8　空白汇票

NINGBO HUADONG FOOD CO., LTD.

NO. 18 DONG SHAN ROAD, NINGBO, CHINA

SHIPPING ADVICE

TO:	NO.: DATE: VALUE: L/C NO.: INSURANCE COVER NOTE NO.:

PORT OF SHIPMENT:　　PORT OF DESTINATION:

DATE OF SHIPMENT:　　VESSEL'S NAME:

SHIPPING MARKS　DESCRIPTION OF GOODS　QUANTITY　WEIGHT　MEASUREMENT

图 10.9　空白装船通知

10.1.4 答案

缮制完成的单证如图 10.10 ~ 图 10.19 所示。

信用证分析结果单

序号	项目	内容
1	信用证的种类	SIGHT AND IRREVOCABLE L/C
2	信用证号码	H486 - 2001689
3	开证日期	JUN. 6, 2007
4	信用证的到期日	JUN. 25, 2007
5	信用证的到期地点	COUNTERS OF NEGOTIATING BANK
6	开证申请人	TOKO TRADE CORPORATION OSAKA 2 - 6 - 7, KAWA RAMACHI, 1 - CHOME, OSAKA, JAPAN
7	受益人	NINGBO HUADONG FOOD CO., LTD. NO. 18 DONG SHAN ROAD, NINGBO, CHINA
8	开证行名称	BANK OF TOKYO _ MITSUBISHI
9	信用证币制及金额	CURRENCY USD AMOUNT 30, 600. 00
10	分批装运	PROHIBITED
11	转运	PROHIBITED
12	装运港(地)	CHINA
13	目的港(地)	OSAKA, JAPAN
14	最迟装运期	JUN. 15, 2007
15	货物描述	FROZEN PEAPODS
16	价格术语	CIF OSAKA
17	交单期限	WITHIN 10 DAYS AFTER THE DATE OF SHIPMENT BUT WITHIN THE VALIDITY OF THE CREDIT
18	信用证要求的单据	1. COMMERCIAL INVOICE
		2. B/L
		3. PACKING LIST
		4. BENEFICIARY'S CERTIFICATE
		5. INSURANCE POLICY
		6. INSPECTION CERTIFICATE OF QUALITY
19	特殊条款	

图 10.10 信用证分析结果单

Shipper Insert Name, Address and Phone	B/L No.
NINGBO HUADONG FOOD CO., LTD. NO. 18 DONG SHAN ROAD, NINGBO, CHINA	CANE980318

中远集装箱运输有限公司
COSCO CONTAINER LINES

TLX: 33057 COSCO CN
FAX: +86(021) 6545 8984

ORIGINAL

Consignee Insert Name, Address and Phone

TO OREDER

Notify Party Insert Name, Address and Phone
(It is agreed that no responsibility shall attach to the Carrier or his agents for failure to notify)

TOKO TRADE CORPORATION
OSAKA 2-6-7, KAWA RAMACHI,
-CHOME, OSAKA, JAPAN.

Port-to-Port or Combined Transport

BILL OF LADING

RECEIVED in external apparent good order and condition except as otherwise noted. The total number of packages or units stuffed in the container, the description of the goods and the weights shown in this Bill of Lading are furnished by the Merchants, and which the carrier has no reasonable means of checking and is not a part of this Bill of Lading contract. The carrier has issued the number of Bills of Lading stated below, all of this tenor and date, one of the original Bills of Lading must be surrendered and endorsed or signed against the delivery of the shipment and whereupon any other original Bills of Lading shall be void. The Merchants agree to be bound by the terms and conditio ns of this Bill of Lading as if each had personally signed this Bill of Lading.
SEE clause 4 on the back of this Bill of Lading (Terms continued on the back hereof, please read carefully).
*Applicable Only When Document Used as a Combined Transport Billof Lading.

Combined Transport * Pre– carriage by	Combined Transport* Place of Receipt
Ocean Vessel Voy. No.	**Port of Loading**
PRESIDENT V.006	NINGBO,CHINA
Port of Discharge	**Combined Transport * Place of Delivery**
OSAKA,JAPAN	

Container / Seal No.	Marks & Nos.	No. of Containers or Packages	Description of Goods	Gross Weight (Kgs)	Measurement(M^3)
CN: CGHU2332159 SN: HD20071221	TOKO MADE IN CHINA NO.1-1500	1500CTNS	FROZEN PEAPODS	31500KCS	180CBMS

Total Number of containers and/or packages (in words)
SAY ONE THOUSAND FIVE HUNDRED CARTONS ONLY

Freight & Charges	Revenue Tons	Rate	Per	Prepaid	Collect
				FREIGHT PREPAID	

Ex. Rate	Prepaid at	Payable at	Place and date of issue
			NINGBO,CHINA JUN.12,2007
	Total Prepaid	No. of Original B(s)/L	Signed for the Carrier, COSCO CONTAINER LINES
		3	

LADEN ON BOARD THE VESSEL PRESIDENT V.006

DATE	JUN.12,2007	BY	COSCO CONTAINER LINES

图 10.11 提单

NINGBO HUADONG FOOD CO. , LTD.

NO. 18 DONG SHAN ROAD, NINGBO, CHINA

COMMERCIAL INVOICE

To:	TOKO TRADE CORPORATION OSAKA 2 - 6 - 7, KAWA RAMACHI, 1 - CHOME, OSAKA, JAPAN	Invoice No. :	07GESP3298
		Invoice Date:	JUN. 6,2007
		S/C No. :	JP070525

From: NINGBO,CHINA To: OSAKA, JAPAN

L/C No. : H486 - 2001689 Issued by: BANK OF TOKYO

Marks & Nos.	Description of Goods	Quantity	Unit Price	Amount
TOKO MADE IN CHINA NO. 1 - 1500	FROZEN PEAPODS	30 M/T	CIF OSAKA, JAPAN USD1020. 00 PER M/T	USD30 600. 00
TOTAL:				

SAY TOTAL: SAY U. S. DOLLARS THIRITY THOUSAND SIX HUNDRED ONLY

NINGBO HUADONG FOOD CO. , LTD.

图 10. 12 商业发票

NINGBO HUADONG FOOD CO. , LTD.

NO. 18 DONG SHAN ROAD, NINGBO, CHINA

PACKING LIST

To:	TOKO TRADE CORPORATION OSAKA 2 - 6 - 7, KAWA RAMACHI, 1 - CHOME, OSAKA, JAPAN	Invoice No. :	07GESP3298
		Invoice Date:	JUN. 6,2007

Marks & Nos.	Number and Kind of Packages Description of Goods	Weight(Kgs)		Measurement (M^3)
		Net	Gross	
TOKO MADE IN CHINA NO. 1 - 1500	FROZEN PEAPODS 20KGS/CTN 1500 CTNS	@20KGS /CTN 30000KGS	@21KGS /CTN 31500KGS	@ (50X40X60) CM/CTN 180CBMS
TOTAL:	1500 CTNS	30000KGS	31500KGS	180CBMS

SAY TOTAL: SAY ONE THOUSAND FIVE HUNDRED CARTONS ONLY

NINGBO HUADONG FOOD CO. , LTD.

图 10. 13 装箱单

中保财产保险有限公司

The People's Insurance (Property) Company of China Ltd.

<table>
<tr><td>Head Office: BEIJING</td><td rowspan="2">海洋货物运输保险单
MARINE CARGO TRANSPORTATION INSURANCE POLICY</td><td>Established in 1949</td></tr>
<tr><td>发票号码
Invoice No. 07GESP3298</td><td>保险单号次
Policy No. 9076521</td></tr>
</table>

被保险人:

Insured: NINGBO HUADONG FOOD CO., LTD.

中国人民保险公司(以下简称本公司)根据被保险人的要求及其所缴付的保险费,按照本保险单承保险别和背面所载条款与下列特别条款承保下述货物运输保险,特签发本保单。

This Policy of Insurance witnesses that The People's Insurance Company of China (hereinafter called "the Company") at the request of the "Insured" and in consideration of the agreed premium paid to the Company by the Insured undertakes to Insure the undermentioned goods in transportation subject to the conditions of this Policy as per the Clauses printed overleaf and other special clauses attached hereon.

标记及号码 Marks & Nos.	包装数量 Quantity	保险货物项目 Description of Goods	保险金额 Amount Insured
TOKO MADE IN CHINA NO. 1 - 1500	1500CTNS	FROZEN PEAPODS	USD33660.00

总保险金额

Total Amount Insured: SAY U.S. DOLLARS THIRTY THREE THOUSAND SIX HUNDRED AND SIXTY ONLY

保费 Premium AS ARRANGED　　费率 Rate AS ARRANGED　　装载运输工具 Per conveyance S.S. PRESIDENT V.006

开航日期 Slg. on or abt JUN. 12, 2007　　起运港 From NINGBO, CHINA　　目的港 To OSAKA, JAPAN

承保险别

Conditions COVERING ALL RISKS AND WAR RISK AS PER OMCC & OMWRC OF PICC DATED 1/1/1981 INCLUDING WARE HOUSE TO WARE HOUSE CLAUSE

所保货物,如发生本保单项下可能引起索赔的损失或损坏,应立即通知本公司下述代理人勘察。如有索赔,应向本公司提交保险单正本(本保险单共有　份正本)及有关部门的文件。如一份正本已用于索赔,其余正本则自动失效。

In the event loss or damage which may result in a claim under this Policy, immediate notice applying for Survey must be given to the Company's Agent as mentioned hereunder. Claims, if any, one of the Original Policy which has been issued in 2 Original(s) together with other relevant documents shall be surrendered to the Company. If one of the Original Policy has been accomplished, the others to be void.

<table>
<tr><td>赔款偿付地点
Claim payable at OSAKA, JAPAN</td><td rowspan="3">中保财产保险有限公司
THE PEOPLE'S INSURANCE (PROPERTY)
COMPANY OF CHINA LTD.</td></tr>
<tr><td>日期
Date JUN. 10, 2007</td></tr>
<tr><td>地址
Address</td></tr>
</table>

图10.14 保险单

中华人民共和国出入境检验检疫

出境货物报检单

报检单位（加盖公章）：	宁波华东食品有限公司			*编 号	
报检单位登记号：4478633213	联系人：		电话：		报检日期：2007年 6 月2 日

发货人	（中文）	宁波华东食品有限公司
	（外文）	NINGBO HUADONG FOOD CO., LTD.
收货人	（中文）	
	（外文）	TOKO TRADE CORPORATION

货物名称(中/外文)	H.S.编码	产地	数/重量	货物总值	包装种类及数量
冷冻豌豆 FROZEN PEAPODS	8 712.100 0	宁波	30公吨	30 600美元	1 500箱

运输工具名称号码	PRESIDENT V.006	贸易方式	一般贸易	货物存放地点	宁波
合同号	JP070525	信用证号	H486-2001689	用途	食用
发货日期	**2007. 6. 10**	输往国家(地区)	日本	许可证／审批号	
起运地	宁波海关	到达口岸	大阪	生产单位注册号	221089763214
集装箱规格、数量及号码	1×40'/ CGHU2332159				

合同、信用证订立的检验检疫条款或特殊要求	标 记 及 号 码	随附单据（划"✓"或补填）	
	TOKO **MADE IN CHINA** **NO.1-1500**	✓合同 □信用证 ✓发票 □换证凭单 ✓装箱单 □厂检单	□包装性能结果单 □许可/审批文件 □ □ □

需要证单名称（划"✓"或补填）				*检验检疫费	
✓品质证书	1正2副	□植物检疫证书	_正_副	总金额（人民币元）	
□ 重量证书	_正_副	□熏蒸/消毒证书	_正_副		
□ 数量证书	_正_副	□出境货物换证凭单	_正_副		
□ 兽医卫生证书	_正_副	□		计费人	
□ 健康证书	_正_副	□			
□ 卫生证书	_正_副	□		收费人	
□ 动物卫生证书	_正_副	□			

报验人郑重声明：	领 取 证 单	
1. 本人被授权报检。 2. 上列填写内容正确属实，货物无伪造或冒用他人的厂名、标志、认证标志，并承担货物质量责任。 签名：___×××____	日期	
	签名	

注：有"*"号栏由出入境检验检疫机关填写	◆国家出入境检验检疫局制
	[1-2 (2000.1.1)]

图 10.15 报检单

NINGBO HUADONG FOOD CO. , LTD.

NO. 18 DONG SHAN ROAD, NINGBO, CHINA

INSPECTION CERTIFICATE OF QUALITY

DATE:JUN. 5,2007

RE: INVOICE NO. :07GESP3298

DESCRIPTION OF GOODS:FROZEN PEAPODS

SHIPPING MARKS:TOKO

MADE IN CHINA

NO. 1 - 1500

TOTAL N. W. :30000KGS

TOTAL G. W. :31500KGS

THIS IS TO CERTIFY THAT WE HAVE INSPECTED THE CAPTIONED MERCHANDISES AND THE (CONTROL OF) QUALITY IS IN CONFORMITY WITH THE S/C NO. JP070525

CERTIFIED BY: NINGBO HUADONG FOOD CO. , LTD.

……

(INSPECTOR)

图 10.16　制造商检验证书

NINGBO HUADONG FOOD CO. , LTD. NO. 18 DONG SHAN ROAD, NINGBO, CHINA		
BENEFICIARY'S CERTIFICATE		
INVOICE NO. : 07GESP3298	L/C NO. : H486 - 2001689	DATE: JUN. 14,2007
WE HEREBY CERTIFY THAT 1 ORIGINAL INSPECTION CERTIFICATE OF QUALITY AND 1 ORIGINAL B/L ONE ORIGINAL INSURANCE POLICY HAVE BEEN SENT TO APPLICANT BY COURIER		

图 10.17　受益人证明书

BILL OF EXCHANGE

Drawn under BANK OF TOKYO, MITSUBISHI, LTD., THE OSAKA JAPAN 1)
信用证或购买证第 号
L/C or A/P No. H486-20001689 2)
日 期 年 月 日
Dated JUNE6,2007 3)
按 息 付 款
Payable with interest @ 4) % per annum
号码 汇票金额 中国，宁波 年 月 日
No. 07GESP3298 5) Exchange for USD 30600 6) NINGBO, China JUNE 20, 2007 7)
见票 日 后（本票之副本未付）付
At * * * * * 8) sight of this FIRST of Exchange (Second of exchange being unpaid)
pay to the order of BANK OF CHINA, NINGBO BRANCH 9) 或其指定人
金 额
the sum of SAY U.S.DOLLARS THIRTY THOUSAND AND SIX HUNDRED 10)
此致
To: BANKOFTOKYO,MITSUBISHI,LTD., NINGBO HUADONG FOOD CO., LTD.
THENEWYORKJAPAN 11) 12) 王飞

图 10.18

NINGBO HUADONG FOOD CO., LTD.
NO. 18 DONG SHAN ROAD, NINGBO, CHINA
SHIPPING ADVICE

TO: TOKO TRADE CORPORATION OSAKA 2-6-7, KAWA RAMACHI, 1-CHOME, OSAKA, JAPAN	NO.: 07GESP3298 DATE: JUN. 12, 2007 VALUE: USD30600.00 L/C NO.: H486-2001689 INSURANCE COVER NOTE NO.:

PORT OF SHIPMENT: NINGBO, CHINA　　PORT OF DESTINATION: OSAKA, JAPAN
DATE OF SHIPMENT: JUN. 12, 2007　　VESSEL'S NAME: PRESIDENT V. 006

SHIPPING MARKS	DESCRIPTION OF GOODS	QUANTITY	WEIGHT	MEASUREMENT
TOKO MADE IN CHINA NO. 1-1500	FROZEN PEAPODS	1500CTNS	31500KGS	180CBMS

NINGBO HUADONG FOOD CO., LTD.

图 10.19 装船通知

附录

国际结算相关规则与惯例

Appendix 1. International Commercial Terms-INCOTERMS 2000 or 2010

EX WORKS

(... named place)

"Ex works" means that the seller delivers when he places the goods at the disposal of the buyer at the seller's premises or another named place (i. e. works, factory, warehouse, etc.) not cleared for export and not loaded on any collecting vehicle.

This term thus represents the minimum obligation for the seller, and the buyer has to bear all costs and risks involved in taking the goods from the seller's premises.

However, if the parties wish the seller to be responsible for the loading of the goods on departure and to bear the risks and all the costs of such loading, this should be made clear by adding explicit wording to this effect in the contract of sale1. This term should not be used when the buyer cannot carry out the export formalities directly or indirectly. In such circumstances, the FCA term should be used, provided the seller agrees that he will load at his cost and risk.

注 1 Refer to Introduction Paragraph 11.

A THE SELLER'S OBLIGATIONS

B THE BUYER'S OBLIGATIONS

A1 Provision of goods in conformity with the contract

The seller must provide the goods and the commercial invoice, or its equivalent electronic message, in conformity with the contract of sale and any other evidence of conformity which may be required by the contract.

B1 Payment of the price

The buyer must pay the price as provided in the contract of sale.

A2 Licenses, authorizations and formalities

The seller must render the buyer, at the latter's request, risk and expense, every assistance in obtaining, where applicable2, any export licence or other official authorization necessary for the export of the goods.

B2 Licenses, authorizations and formalities

注 2 Refer to Introduction Paragraph 14.

The buyer must obtain at his own risk and expense any export and import licence or other official authorization and carry out, where applicable3, all customs formalities for the export of the goods.

注 3 Refer to Introduction Paragraph 14.

A3 Contracts of carriage and insurance

a) Contract of carriage

No obligation4.

注 4 Refer to Introduction Paragraph 10.

b) Contract of insurance

No obligation5.

注 5 Refer to Introduction Paragraph 10.

B3 Contracts of carriage and insurance

a) Contract of carriage

No obligation6.

注 6 Refer to Introduction Paragraph 10.

b) Contract of insurance

No obligation7.

注 7 Refer to Introduction Paragraph 10.

A4 Delivery

The seller must place the goods at the disposal of the buyer at the named place of delivery, not loaded on any collecting vehicle, on the date or within the period agreed or, if no such time is agreed, at the usual time for delivery of such goods. If no specific point has been agreed within the named place, and if there are several points available, the seller may select the point at the place of delivery which best suits his purpose.

B4 Taking delivery

The buyer must take delivery of the goods where they have been delivered in accordance with A4 and A7/B7.

A5 Transfer of risks

The seller must, subject to the provisions of B5, bear all risks of loss of or damage to the goods until such time as they have been delivered in accordance with A4.

B5 Transfer of risks

The buyer must bear all risks of loss of or damage to the goods

● from the time they have been delivered in accordance with A4; and

● from the agreed date or the expiry date of any period fixed for taking delivery which arise because he fails to give notice in accordance with B7, provided, however, that the goods have been duly appropriated to the contract, that is to say, clearly set aside or otherwise identified as the contract goods.

A6 Division of costs

The seller must, subject to the provisions of B6, pay all costs relating to the goods until such time as they have been delivered in accordance with A4.

B6 Division of costs

The buyer must pay

● all costs relating to the goods from the time they have been delivered in accordance with A4; and

● any additional costs incurred by failing either to take delivery of the goods when they have been placed at his disposal, or to give appropriate notice in accordance with B7 provided, however, that the goods have been duly appropriated to the contract, that is to say, clearly set aside or otherwise identified as the contract goods; and

● where applicable8, all duties, taxes and other charges as well as the costs of carrying out customs formalities payable upon export.

注 8 Refer to Introduction Paragraph 14.

The buyer must reimburse all costs and charges incurred by the seller in rendering assistance in accordance with A2.

A7 Notice to the buyer

The seller must give the buyer sufficient notice as to when and where the goods will be placed at his disposal.

B7 Notice to the seller

The buyer must, whenever he is entitled to determine the time within an agreed period and/or the place of taking delivery, give the seller sufficient notice thereof.

A8 Proof of delivery, transport document or equivalent electronic messages

No obligation9.

注 9 Refer to Introduction Paragraph 10.

B8 Proof of delivery, transport document or equivalent electronic messages.

The buyer must provide the seller with appropriate evidence of having taken delivery.

A9 Checking – packing – marking

The seller must pay the costs of those checking operations (such as checking quality, measuring, weighing, counting) which are necessary for the purpose of placing the goods at the buyer's disposal.

The seller must provide at his own expense packaging (unless it is usual for the particular trade to make the goods of the contract description available unpacked) which is required for the transport of the goods, to the extent that the circumstances relating to the transport (for example modalities, destination) are made known to the seller before the contract of sale is concluded. Packaging is to be marked appropriately.

B9 Inspection of goods

The buyer must pay the costs of any pre – shipment inspection, including inspection mandated by the authorities of the country of export.

A10 Other obligations

The seller must render the buyer at the latter's request, risk and expense, every assistance in obtaining any documents or equivalent electronic messages issued or transmitted in the country of delivery and/or of origin which the buyer may require for the export and/or import of the goods and, where necessary, for their transit through any country.

The seller must provide the buyer, upon request, with the necessary information for procuring insurance.

B10 Other obligations

The buyer must pay all costs and charges incurred in obtaining the documents or equivalent electronic messages mentioned in A10 and reimburse those incurred by the seller in rendering his assistance in accordance therewith.

FCA

FREE CARRIER

(... named place)

"Free Carrier" means that the seller delivers the goods, cleared for export, to the carrier nominated by the buyer at the named place. It should be noted that the chosen place of delivery has an impact on the obligations of loading and unloading the goods at that place. If delivery occurs at the seller's premises, the seller is responsible for loading. If delivery occurs at any other place, the seller is not responsible for unloading.

This term may be used irrespective of the mode of transport, including multimodal transport.

"Carrier" means any person who, in a contract of carriage, undertakes to perform or to procure the performance of transport by rail, road, air, sea, inland waterway or by a combination of such modes.

If the buyer nominates a person other than a carrier to receive the goods, the seller is deemed to have fulfilled his obligation to deliver the goods when they are delivered to that person.

A THE SELLER'S OBLIGATIONS

B THE BUYER'S OBLIGATIONS

A1 Provision of goods in conformity with the contract

The seller must provide the goods and the commercial invoice, or its equivalent electronic message, in conformity with the contract of sale and any other evidence of conformity which may be required by the contract.

B1 Payment of price

The buyer must pay the price as provided in the contract of sale.

A2 Licenses, authorizations and formalities

The seller must obtain at his own risk and expense any export licence or other official authorization and carry out, where applicable1, all customs formalities necessary for the export of the goods.

注 1 Refer to Introduction Paragraph 14.

B2 Licenses, authorizations and formalities

The buyer must obtain at his own risk and expense any import licence or other official authorization and carry out, where applicable2, all customs formalities for the import of the goods and for their transit through any country.

注 2 Refer to Introduction Paragraph 14.

A3 Contracts of carriage and insurance

a) Contract of carriage

No obligation3. However, if requested by the buyer or if it is commercial practice and the buyer does not give an instruction to the contrary in due time, the seller may contract for carriage on usual terms at the buyer's risk and expense. In either case, the seller may decline to make the contract and, if he does, shall promptly notify the buyer accordingly.

注 3 Refer to Introduction Paragraph 10.

b) Contract of insurance

No obligation4.

注 4 Refer to Introduction Paragraph 10.

B3 Contracts of carriage and insurance

a) Contract of carriage

The buyer must contract at his own expense for the carriage of the goods from the named place, except when the contract of carriage is made by the seller as provided for in A3 a).

b) Contract of insurance

No obligation5.

注 5 Refer to Introduction Paragraph 10.

A4 Delivery

The seller must deliver the goods to the carrier or another person nominated by the buyer, or chosen by the seller in accordance with A3 a), at the named place on the date or within the period agreed for delivery.

Delivery is completed,

a) If the named place is the seller's premises, when the goods have been loaded on the means of transport provided by the carrier nominated by the buyer or another person acting on his behalf.

b) If the named place is anywhere other than a), when the goods are placed at the disposal of the carrier or another person nominated by the buyer, or chosen by the seller in accordance with A3 a) on the seller's means of transport not unloaded.

If no specific point has been agreed within the named place, and if there are several points available, the seller may select the point at the place of delivery which best suits his purpose.

Failing precise instructions from the buyer, the seller may deliver the goods for carriage in such a manner as the transport mode and/or the quantity and/or nature of the goods may require.

B4 Taking delivery

The buyer must take delivery of the goods when they have been delivered in accordance with A4.

A5 Transfer of risks

The seller must, subject to the provisions of B5, bear all risks of loss of or damage to the goods until such time as they have been delivered in accordance with A4.

B5 Transfer of risks

The buyer must bear all risks of loss of or damage to the goods

● from the time they have been delivered in accordance with A4; and

● from the agreed date or the expiry date of any agreed period for delivery which arise either because he fails to nominate the carrier or another person in accordance with A4, or because the carrier or the party nominated by the buyer fails to take the goods into his charge at the agreed time, or because the buyer fails to give appropriate notice in accordance with B7, provided, however, that the goods have been duly appropriated to the contract, that is to say, clearly set aside or otherwise identified as the contract goods.

A6 Division of costs

The seller must, subject to the provisions of B6, pay

● all costs relating to the goods until such time as they have been delivered in accordance with A4; and

● where applicable6, the costs of customs formalities as well as all duties, taxes, and other charges payable upon export.

注 6 Refer to Introduction Paragraph 14.

B6 Division of costs

The buyer must pay

● all costs relating to the goods from the time they have been delivered in accordance with A4; and

● any additional costs incurred, either because he fails to nominate the carrier or another person in accordance with A4 or because the party nominated by the buyer fails to take the goods into his charge at the agreed time, or because he has failed to give appropriate notice in accordance with B7, provided, however, that the goods have been duly appropriated to the contract, that is to say, clearly set aside or otherwise identified as the contract goods; and

● where applicable7, all duties, taxes and other charges as well as the costs of carrying out customs formalities payable upon import of the goods and for their transit through any country.

注 7 Refer to Introduction Paragraph 14.

A7 Notice to the buyer

The seller must give the buyer sufficient notice that the goods have been delivered in accordance with A4. Should the carrier fail to take delivery in accordance with A4 at the time agreed, the seller must notify the buyer accordingly.

B7 Notice to the seller

The buyer must give the seller sufficient notice of the name of the party designated in A4 and, where necessary, specify the mode of transport, as well as the date or period for delivering the goods to him and, as the case may be, the point within the place where the goods should be delivered to that party.

A8 Proof of delivery, transport document or equivalent electronic message

The seller must provide the buyer at the seller's expense with the usual proof of delivery of the goods in accordance with A4.

Unless the document referred to in the preceding paragraph is the transport document, the seller must render the buyer at the latter's request, risk and expense, every assistance in obtaining a transport document for the contract of carriage (for example a negotiable bill of lading, a non negotiable sea waybill, an inland waterway document, an air waybill, a railway consignment note, a road consignment note, or a multimodal transport document).

When the seller and the buyer have agreed to communicate electronically, the document referred to in the preceding paragraph may be replaced by an equivalent electronic data interchange (EDI) message.

B8 Proof of delivery, transport document or equivalent electronic message

The buyer must accept the proof of delivery in accordance with A8.

A9 Checking - packaging - marking

The seller must pay the costs of those checking operations (such as checking quality, measuring, weighing, counting) which are necessary for the purpose of delivering the goods in accordance with A4.

The seller must provide at his own expense packaging (unless it is usual for the particular trade to send the goods of the contract description unpacked) which is required for the transport of the goods, to the extent that the circumstances relating to the transport (for example modalities, destination) are made known to the seller before the contract of sale is concluded. Packaging is to be marked appropriately.

B9 Inspection of goods

The buyer must pay the costs of any pre - shipment inspection except when such inspection is mandated by the authorities of the country of export.

A10 Other obligations

The seller must render the buyer at the latter's request, risk and expense, every assistance in obtaining any documents or equivalent electronic messages (other than those mentioned in A8) issued or transmitted in the country of delivery and/or of origin which the buyer may require for the import of the goods and, where necessary, for their transit through any country.

The seller must provide the buyer, upon request, with the necessary information for procuring insurance.

B10 Other obligations

The buyer must pay all costs and charges incurred in obtaining the documents or equivalent electronic messages mentioned in A10 and reimburse those incurred by the seller in rendering his assistance in accordance therewith and in contracting for carriage in accordance with A3 a).

The buyer must give the seller appropriate instructions whenever the seller's assistance in contracting for carriage is required in accordance with A3 a).

FAS

FREE ALONGSIDE SHIP

(... named port of shipment)

"Free Alongside Ship" means that the seller delivers when the goods are placed alongside the vessel at the named port of shipment. This means that the buyer has to bear all costs and risks of loss of or damage to the goods from that moment.

The FAS term requires the seller to clear the goods for export.

THIS IS A REVERSAL FROM PREVIOUS INCOTERMS VERSIONS WHICH REQUIRED THE BUYER TO ARRANGE FOR EXPORT CLEARANCE.

However, if the parties wish the buyer to clear the goods for export, this should be made clear by adding explicit wording to this effect in the contract of sale1.

注 1 Refer to Introduction Paragraph 11.

This term can be used only for sea or inland waterway transport.

A THE SELLER'S OBLIGATIONS

B THE BUYER'S OBLIGATIONS

A1 Provision of goods in conformity with the contract

The seller must provide the goods and the commercial invoice, or its equivalent electronic message, in conformity with the contract of sale and any other evidence of conformity which may be required by the contract.

B1 Payment of the price

The buyer must pay the price as provided in the contract of sale.

A2 Licenses, authorizations and formalities

The seller must obtain at his own risk and expense any export licence or other official authorization and carry out, where applicable2, all customs formalities necessary for the export of the goods.

注 2 Refer to Introduction Paragraph 14.

B2 Licenses, authorizations and formalities

The buyer must obtain at his own risk and expense any import licence or other official authorization and carry out, where applicable3, all customs formalities for the import of the goods and for their transit through any country.

注 3 Refer to Introduction Paragraph 14.

A3 Contracts of carriage and insurance

a) Contract of carriage

No obligation4.

注 4 Refer to Introduction Paragraph 10.

b) Contract of insurance

No obligation5.

注 5 Refer to Introduction Paragraph 10.

B3 Contracts of carriage and insurance

a) Contract of carriage

The buyer must contract at his own expense for the carriage of the goods from the named port of shipment.

b) Contract of insurance

No obligation6.

注 6 Refer to Introduction Paragraph 10.

A4 Delivery

The seller must place the goods alongside the vessel nominated by the buyer at the loading place named by the buyer at the named port of shipment on the date or within the agreed period and in the manner customary at the port.

B4 Taking delivery

The buyer must take delivery of the goods when they have been delivered in accordance with A4.

A5 Transfer of risks

The seller must, subject to the provisions of B5, bear all risks of loss of or damage to the goods until such time as they have been delivered in accordance with A4.

B5 Transfer of risks

The buyer must bear all risks of loss of or damage to the goods

● from the time they have been delivered in accordance with A4; and

● from the agreed date or the expiry date of the agreed period for delivery which arise because he fails to give notice in accordance with B7, or because the vessel nominated by him fails to arrive on time, or is unable to take the goods, or closes for cargo earlier than the time notified in accordance with B7, provided, however, that the goods have been duly appropriated to the contract, that is to say, clearly set aside or otherwise identified as the contract goods.

A6 Division of costs

The seller must, subject to the provisions of B6, pay

● all costs relating to the goods until such time as they have been delivered in accordance with A4; and

● where applicable7, the costs of customs formalities as well as all duties, taxes, and other charges payable upon export.

注 7 Refer to Introduction Paragraph 14.

B6 Division of costs

The buyer must pay

● all costs relating to the goods from the time they have been delivered in accordance with A4; and

● any additional costs incurred, either because the vessel nominated by him has failed to arrive on time, or is unable to take the goods, or closes for cargo earlier than the time notified in accordance with B7, or because the buyer has failed to give appropriate notice in accordance with B7 provided, however, that the goods have been duly appropriated to the contract, that is to say, clearly set aside or otherwise identified as the contract goods; and

- where applicable8, all duties, taxes and other charges as well as the costs of carrying out customs formalities payable upon import of the goods and for their transit through any country.

注 8 Refer to Introduction Paragraph 14.

A7 Notice to the buyer

The seller must give the buyer sufficient notice that the goods have been delivered alongside the nominated vessel.

B7 Notice to the seller

The buyer must give the seller sufficient notice of the vessel name, loading point and required delivery time.

A8 Proof of delivery, transport document or equivalent electronic message

The seller must provide the buyer at the seller's expense with the usual proof of delivery of the goods in accordance with A4.

Unless the document referred to in the preceding paragraph is the transport document, the seller must render the buyer at the latter's request, risk and expense, every assistance in obtaining a transport document (for example a negotiable bill of lading, a non – negotiable sea waybill, an inland waterway document).

When the seller and the buyer have agreed to communicate electronically, the document referred to in the preceding paragraphs may be replaced by an equivalent electronic data interchange (EDI) message.

B8 Proof of delivery, transport document or equivalent electronic message

The buyer must accept the proof of delivery in accordance with A8.

A9 Checking – packaging – marking

The seller must pay the costs of those checking operations (such as checking quality, measuring, weighing, counting) which are necessary for the purpose of delivering the goods in accordance with A4.

The seller must provide at his own expense packaging (unless it is usual for the particular trade to ship the goods of the contract description unpacked) which is required for the transport of the goods, to the extent that the circumstances relating to the transport (for example modalities, destination) are made known to the seller before the contract of sale is concluded. Packaging is to be marked appropriately.

B9 Inspection of goods

The buyer must pay the costs of any pre – shipment inspection, except when such inspection is mandated by the authorities of the country of export.

A10 Other obligations

The seller must Provide the buyer, at the latter's request, risk and expense, every assistance in obtaining any documents or equivalent electronic messages (other than those mentioned in A8) issued or transmitted in the country of shipment and/or of origin which the buyer may require for the import of the goods and, where necessary, for their transit through any country.

The seller must provide the buyer, upon request, with the necessary information for procuring insurance.

B10 Other obligations

The buyer must pay all costs and charges incurred in obtaining the documents or equivalent electronic messages mentioned in A10 and reimburse those incurred by the seller in rendering his assistance in accordance therewith.

FOB

FREE ON BOARD

(... named port of shipment)

"Free on Board" means that the seller delivers when the goods pass the ship's rail at the named port of shipment. This means that the buyer has to bear all costs and risks of loss of or damage to the goods from that point. The FOB term requires the seller to clear the goods for export. This term can be used only for sea or inland waterway transport. If the parties do not intend to deliver the goods across the ship's rail, the FCA term should be used.

A THE SELLER'S OBLIGATIONS

B THE BUYER'S OBLIGATIONS

A1 Provision of goods in conformity with the contract

The seller must provide the goods and the commercial invoice, or its equivalent electronic message, in conformity with the contract of sale and any other evidence of conformity which may be required by the contract.

B1 Payment of the price

The buyer must pay the price as provided in the contract of sale.

A2 Licenses, authorizations and formalities

The seller must obtain at his own risk and expense any export licence or other official authorization and carry out, where applicable1, all customs formalities necessary for the export of the goods.

注 1 Refer to Introduction Paragraph 14.

B2 Licenses, authorizations and formalities

The buyer must obtain at his own risk and expense any import licence or other official authorization and carry out, where applicable2, all customs formalities for the import of the goods and, where necessary, for their transit through any country.

注 2 Refer to Introduction Paragraph 14.

A3 Contracts of carriage and insurance

a) Contract of carriage

No obligation3.

注 3 Refer to Introduction Paragraph 10.

b) Contract of insurance

No obligation4.

注 4 Refer to Introduction Paragraph 10.

B3 Contracts of carriage and insurance

a) Contract of carriage

The buyer must contract at his own expense for the carriage of the goods from the named port of shipment.

b) Contract of insurance

No obligation5.

注 5 Refer to Introduction Paragraph 10.

A4 Delivery

The seller must deliver the goods on the date or within the agreed period at the named port of shipment and in the manner customary at the port on board the vessel nominated by the buyer.

B4 Taking delivery

The buyer must take delivery of the goods when they have been delivered in accordance with A4.

A5 Transfer of risks

The seller must, subject to the provisions of B5, bear all risks of loss of or damage to the goods until such time as they have passed the ship's rail at the named port of shipment.

B5 Transfer of risks

The buyer must bear all risks of loss of or damage to the goods

● from the time they have passed the ship's rail at the named port of shipment; and

● from the agreed date or the expiry date of the agreed period for delivery which arise because he fails to give notice in accordance with B7, or because the vessel nominated by him fails to arrive on time, or is unable to take the goods, or closes for cargo earlier than the time notified in accordance with B7, provided, however, that the goods have been duly appropriated to the contract, that is to say, clearly set aside or otherwise identified as the contract goods.

A6 Division of costs

The seller must, subject to the provisions of B6, pay

● all costs relating to the goods until such time as they have passed the ship's rail at the named port of shipment; and

● where applicable6, the costs of customs formalities necessary for export as well as all duties, taxes and other charges payable upon export.

注 6 Refer to Introduction Paragraph 14.

B6 Division of costs

The buyer must pay

● all costs relating to the goods from the time they have passed the ship's rail at the named port of shipment; and

● any additional costs incurred, either because the vessel nominated by him fails to arrive on time, or is unable to take the goods, or closes for cargo earlier than the time notified in accordance with B7, or because the buyer has failed to give appropriate notice in accordance with B7, provided, however, that the goods have been duly appropriated to the contract, that is to say, clearly set aside or otherwise identified as the contract goods; and

● where applicable7, all duties, taxes and other charges as well as the costs of carrying out customs formalities payable upon import of the goods and for their transit through any country.

注 7 Refer to Introduction paragraph 14.

A7　Notice to the buyer

The seller must give the buyer sufficient notice that the goods have been delivered in accordance with A4.

B7　Notice to the seller

The buyer must give the seller sufficient notice of the vessel name, loading point and required delivery time.

A8　Proof of delivery, transport document or equivalent electronic message

The seller must provide the buyer at the seller's expense with the usual proof of delivery in accordance with A4.

Unless the document referred to in the preceding paragraph is the transport document, the seller must render the buyer, at the latter's request, risk and expense, every assistance in obtaining a transport document for the contract of carriage (for example, a negotiable bill of lading, a non negotiable sea waybill, an inland waterway document, or a multimodal transport document).

Where the seller and the buyer have agreed to communicate electronically, the document referred to in the preceding paragraph may be replaced by an equivalent electronic data interchange (EDI) message.

B8　Proof of delivery, transport document or equivalent electronic message

The buyer must accept the proof of delivery in accordance with A8.

A9　Checking – packaging – marking

The seller must pay the costs of those checking operations (such as checking quality, measuring, weighing, counting) which are necessary for the purpose of delivering the goods in accordance with A4.

The seller must provide at his own expense packaging (unless it is usual for the particular trade to ship the goods of the contract description unpacked) which is required for the transport of the goods, to the extent that the circumstances relating to the transport (for example modalities, destination) are made known to the seller before the contract of sale is concluded. Packaging is to be marked appropriately.

B9　Inspection of goods

The buyer must pay the costs of any pre-shipment inspection except when such inspection is mandated by the authorities of the country of export.

A10 Other obligations

The seller must render the buyer at the latter's request, risk and expense, every assistance in obtaining any documents or equivalent electronic messages (other than those mentioned in A8) issued or transmitted in the country of shipment and/or of origin which the buyer may require for the import of the goods and, where necessary, for their transit through any country.

The seller must provide the buyer, upon request, with the necessary information for procuring insurance.

B10 Other obligations

The buyer must pay all costs and charges incurred in obtaining the documents or equivalent electronic messages mentioned in A10 and reimburse those incurred by the seller in rendering his assistance in accordance therewith.

CFR

COST AND FREIGHT

(... named port of destination)

"Cost and Freight" means that the seller delivers when the goods pass the ship's rail in the port of shipment.

The seller must pay the costs and freight necessary to bring the goods to the named port of destination BUT the risk of loss of or damage to the goods, as well as any additional costs due to events occurring after the time of delivery, are transferred from the seller to the buyer.

The CFR term requires the seller to clear the goods for export.

This term can be used only for sea and inland waterway transport. If the parties do not intend to deliver the goods across the ship's rail, the CPT term should be used.

A THE SELLER'S OBLIGATIONS

B THE BUYER'S OBLIGATIONS

A1 Provision of goods in conformity with the contract

The seller must provide the goods and the commercial invoice, or its equivalent electronic message, in conformity with the contract of sale and any other evidence of conformity which may be required by the contract.

B1 Payment of the price

The buyer must pay the price as provided in the contract of sale.

A2 Licenses, authorizations and formalities

The seller must obtain at his own risk and expense any export licence or other official authorization and carry out, where applicable1, all customs formalities necessary for the export of the goods.

注 1 Refer to Introduction Paragraph 14.

B2 Licenses, authorizations and formalities

The buyer must obtain at his own risk and expense any import licence or other official authorization and carry out, where applicable2, all customs formalities for the import of the goods and for their transit through any country.

注 2 Refer to Introduction Paragraph 14.

A3　Contracts of carriage and insurance

a) Contract of carriage

The seller must contract on usual terms at his own expense for the carriage of the goods to the named port of destination by the usual route in a seagoing vessel (or inland waterway vessel as the case may be) of the type normally used for the transport of goods of the contract description.

b) Contract of insurance

No obligation3.

注 3 Refer to Introduction Paragraph 10.

B3 Contracts of carriage and insurance

a) Contract of carriage

No obligation4.

注 4 Refer to Introduction Paragraph 10.

b) Contract of insurance

No obligation5.

注 5 Refer to Introduction Paragraph 10.

A4 Delivery

The seller must deliver the goods on board the vessel at the port of shipment on the date or within the agreed period.

B4 Taking delivery

The buyer must accept delivery of the goods when they have been delivered in accordance with A4 and receive them from the carrier at the named port of destination.

A5 Transfer of risks

The seller must, subject to the provisions of B5, bear all risks of loss of or damage to the goods until such time as they have passed the ship's rail at the port of shipment.

B5 Transfer of risks

The buyer must bear all risks of loss of or damage to the goods from the time they have passed the ship's rail at the port of shipment.

The buyer must, should he fail to give notice in accordance with B7, bear all risks of loss of or damage to the goods from the agreed date or the expiry date of the period fixed for shipment provided, however, that the goods have been duly appropriated to the contract, that is to say, clearly set aside or otherwise identified as the contract goods.

A6 Division of costs

The seller must, subject to the provisions of B6, pay

● all costs relating to the goods until such time as they have been delivered in accordance with A4; and

● the freight and all other costs resulting from A3 a), including the costs of loading the goods on board and any charges for unloading at the agreed port of discharge which were for the seller's account under the contract of carriage; and, where applicable6, the costs of customs formalities necessary for export as well as all duties, taxes and other charges payable upon export, and for their transit through any country if they were for the seller's account under the contract of carriage.

注 6 Refer to Introduction Paragraph 14.

B6 Division of costs

The buyer must, subject to the provisions of A3 a), pay

● all costs relating to the goods from the time they have been delivered in accordance with A4; and

● all costs and charges relating to the goods whilst in transit until their arrival at the port of destination, unless such costs and charges were for the seller's account under the contract of carriage; and

● unloading costs including lighterage and wharfage charges, unless such costs and charges were for the seller's account under the contract of carriage; and

● all additional costs incurred if he fails to give notice in accordance with B7, for the goods from the agreed date or the expiry date of the period fixed for shipment, provided, however, that the goods have been duly appropriated to the contract, that is to say, clearly set aside or otherwise identified as the contract goods; and

● where applicable7, all duties, taxes and other charges as well as the costs of carrying out customs formalities payable upon import of the goods and, where necessary, for their transit through any country unless included within the cost of the contract of carriage.

注 7 Refer to Introduction Paragraph 14.

A7 Notice to the buyer

The seller must give the buyer sufficient notice that the goods have been delivered in accordance with A4 as well as any other notice required in order to allow the buyer to take measures which are normally necessary to enable him to take the goods.

B7 Notice to the seller

The buyer must, whenever he is entitled to determine the time for shipping the goods and/or the port of destination, give the seller sufficient notice thereof.

A8 Proof of delivery, transport document or equivalent electronic message

The seller must at his own expense provide the buyer without delay with the usual transport document for the agreed port of destination.

This document (for example a negotiable bill of lading, a non-negotiable sea waybill or an inland waterway document) must cover the contract goods, be dated within the period agreed for shipment, enable the buyer to claim the goods from the carrier at the port of destination and, unless otherwise agreed, enable the buyer to sell the goods in transit by the transfer of the document to a subsequent buyer (the negotiable bill of lading) or by notification to the carrier.

When such a transport document is issued in several originals, a full set of originals must be presented to the buyer.

Where the seller and the buyer have agreed to communicate electronically, the document referred to in the preceding paragraphs may be replaced by an equivalent electronic data interchange (EDI) message.

B8 Proof of delivery, transport document or equivalent electronic message

The buyer must accept the transport document in accordance with A8 if it is in conformity with the contract.

A9 Checking - packaging - marking

The seller must pay the costs of those checking operations (such as checking quality, measuring, weighing, counting) which are necessary for the purpose of delivering the goods in accordance with A4.

The seller must provide at his own expense packaging (unless it is usual for the particular trade to ship the goods of the contract description unpacked) which is required for the transport of the goods arranged by him.

Packaging is to be marked appropriately.

B9 Inspection of goods

The buyer must pay the costs of any pre-shipment inspection except when such inspection is mandated by the authorities of the country of export.

A10 Other obligations

The seller must render the buyer at the latter's request, risk and expense, every assistance in obtaining any documents or equivalent electronic messages (other than those mentioned in A8) issued or transmitted in the country of shipment and/or of origin which the buyer may require for the import of the goods and, where necessary, for their transit through any country.

The seller must provide the buyer, upon request, with the necessary information for procuring insurance.

B10 Other obligations

The buyer must pay all costs and charges incurred in obtaining the documents or equivalent electronic messages mentioned in A10 and reimburse those incurred by the seller in rendering his assistance in accordance therewith.

CIF

COST, INSURANCE AND FREIGHT

(... named port of destination)

"Cost, Insurance and Freight" means that the seller delivers when the goods pass the ship's rail in the port of shipment.

The seller must pay the costs and freight necessary to bring the goods to the named port of destination BUT the risk of loss of or damage to the goods, as well as any additional costs due to events occurring after the time of delivery, are transferred from the seller to the buyer. However, in CIF the seller also has to procure marine insurance against the buyer's risk of loss of or damage to the goods during the carriage.

Consequently, the seller contracts for insurance and pays the insurance premium. The buyer should note that under the CIF term the seller is required to obtain insurance only on minimum cover1. Should the buyer wish to have the protection of greater cover, he would either need to agree as such expressly with the seller or to make his own extra insurance arrangements.

注 1 Refer to Introduction Paragraph 9. 3.

The CIF term requires the seller to clear the goods for export.

This term can be used only for sea and inland waterway transport. If the parties do not intend to deliver the goods across the ship's rail, the CIP term should be used.

A THE SELLER'S OBLIGATIONS

B THE BUYER'S OBLIGATIONS

A1 Provision of goods in conformity with the contract

The seller must provide the goods and the commercial invoice, or its equivalent electronic message, in conformity with the contract of sale and any other evidence of conformity which may be required by the contract.

B1 Payment of the price

The buyer must pay the price as provided in the contract of sale.

A2 Licenses, authorisation and formalities

The seller must obtain at his own risk and expense any export licence or other official authorization and carry out, where applicable2, all customs formalities necessary for the export of the goods.

注 2 Refer to Introduction Paragraph 14.

B2 Licenses, authorisation and formalities

The buyer must obtain at his own risk and expense any import licence or other official authorization and carry out, where applicable3, all customs formalities for the import of the goods and for their transit through any country.

注 3 Refer to Introduction Paragraph 14.

A3 Contracts of carriage and insurance

a) Contract of carriage

The seller must contract on usual terms at his own expense for the carriage of the goods to the named port of destination by the usual route in a seagoing vessel (or inland waterway vessel as the case may be) of the type normally used for the transport of goods of the contract description.

b) Contract of insurance

The seller must obtain at his own expense cargo insurance as agreed in the contract, such that the buyer, or any other person having an insurable interest in the goods, shall be entitled to claim directly from the insurer and provide the buyer with the insurance policy or other evidence of insurance cover.

The insurance shall be contracted with underwriters or an insurance company of good repute and, failing express agreement to the contrary, be in accordance with minimum cover of the Institute Cargo Clauses (Institute of London Underwriters) or any similar set of clauses. The duration of insurance cover shall be in accordance with B5 and B4. When required by the buyer, the seller shall provide at the buyer's expense war, strikes, riots and civil commotion risk insurance if procurable. The minimum insurance shall cover the price provided in the contract plus ten per cent (i. e. 110%) and shall be provided in the currency of the contract.

B3 Contracts of carriage and insurance

a) Contract of carriage

No obligation4.

注 4 Refer to Introduction Paragraph 10.

b) Contract of insurance

No obligation5.

注 5 Refer to Introduction Paragraph 10.

A4 Delivery

The seller must deliver the goods on board the vessel at the port of shipment on the date or within the agreed period.

B4 Taking delivery

The buyer must accept delivery of the goods when they have been delivered in accordance with A4 and receive them from the carrier at the named port of destination.

A5 Transfer of risks

The seller must, subject to the provisions of B5, bear all risks of loss of or damage to the goods until such time as they have passed the ship's rail at the port of shipment.

B5 Transfer of risks

The buyer must bear all risks of loss of or damage to the goods from the time they have passed the ship's rail at the port of shipment.

The buyer must, should he fail to give notice in accordance with B7, bear all risks of loss of or damage to the goods from the agreed date or the expiry date of the period fixed for shipment provided, however, that the goods have been duly appropriated to the contract, that is to say, clearly set aside or otherwise identified as the contract goods.

A6 Division of costs

The seller must, subject to the provisions of B6, pay

● all costs relating to the goods until such time as they have been delivered in accordance with A4; and

● the freight and all other costs resulting from A3 a), including the costs of loading the goods on board;

● and the costs of insurance resulting from A3 b); and

● any charges for unloading at the agreed port of discharge which were for the seller's account under the contract of carriage; and

● where applicable6, the costs of customs formalities necessary for export as well as all duties, taxes and other charges payable upon export, and for their transit through any country if they were for the seller's account under the contract of carriage.

注 6 Refer to Introduction Paragraph 14.

B6 Division of costs

The buyer must, subject to the provisions of A3, pay

● all costs relating to the goods from the time they have been delivered in accordance with A4; and

● all costs and charges relating to the goods whilst in transit until their arrival at the port of destination, unless such costs and charges were for the seller's account under the contract of carriage; and

● unloading costs including lighterage and wharfage charges, unless such costs and charges were for the seller's account under the contract of carriage; and

● all additional costs incurred if he fails to give notice in accordance with B7, for the goods from the agreed date or the expiry date of the period fixed for shipment, provided, however, that the goods have been duly appropriated to the contract, that is to say, clearly set aside or otherwise identified as the contract goods; and

● where applicable7, all duties, taxes and other charges as well as the costs of carrying out customs formalities payable upon import of the goods and, where necessary, for their transit through any country unless included within the cost of the contract of carriage.

注 7 Refer to Introduction Paragraph 14.

A7 Notice to the buyer

The seller must give the buyer sufficient notice that the goods have been delivered in accordance with A4 as well as any other notice required in order to allow the buyer to take measures which are normally necessary to enable him to take the goods.

B7 Notice to the seller

The buyer must, whenever he is entitled to determine the time for shipping the goods and/or the port of destination, give the seller sufficient notice thereof.

A8 Proof of delivery, transport document or equivalent electronic message

The seller must, at his own expense, provide the buyer without delay with the usual transport document for the agreed port of destination.

This document (for example a negotiable bill of lading, a non-negotiable sea waybill or an inland waterway document) must cover the contract goods, be dated within the period agreed for shipment, enable the buyer to claim the goods from the carrier at the port of destination and, unless otherwise agreed, enable the buyer to sell the goods in transit by the transfer of the document to a subsequent buyer (the negotiable bill of lading) or by notification to the carrier.

When such a transport document is issued in several originals, a full set of originals must be presented to the buyer.

Where the seller and the buyer have agreed to communicate electronically, the document referred to in the preceding paragraphs may be replaced by an equivalent electronic data interchange (EDI) message.

B8 Proof of delivery, transport document or equivalent electronic message

The buyer must accept the transport document in accordance with A8 if it is in conformity with the contract.

A9 Checking – packaging – marking

The seller must pay the costs of those checking operations (such as checking quality, measuring, weighing, counting) which are necessary for the purpose of delivering the goods in accordance with A4.

The seller must provide at his own expense packaging (unless it is usual for the particular trade to ship the goods of the contract description unpackaged) which is required for the transport of the goods arranged by him.

Packaging is to be marked appropriately.

B9 Inspection of goods

The buyer must pay the costs of any pre – shipment inspection except when such inspection is mandated by the authorities of the country of export.

A10 Other obligations

The seller must render the buyer at the latter's request, risk and expense, every assistance in obtaining any documents or equivalent electronic messages (other than those mentioned in A8) issued or transmitted in the country of shipment and/or of origin which the buyer may require for the import of the goods and, where necessary, for their transit through any country.

The seller must provide the buyer, upon request, with the necessary information for procuring any additional insurance.

B10 Other obligations

The buyer must pay all costs and charges incurred in obtaining the documents or equivalent electronic messages mentioned in A10 and reimburse those incurred by the seller in rendering his assistance in accordance therewith.

The buyer must provide the seller, upon request, with the necessary information for procuring insurance.

CPT

CARRIAGE PAID TO

(... named place of destination)

"Carriage paid to..." means that the seller delivers the goods to the carrier nominated by him, but the seller must in addition pay the cost of carriage necessary to bring the goods to the named destination. This means that the buyer bears all risks and any other costs occurring after the goods have been so delivered.

"Carrier" means any person who, in a contract of carriage, undertakes to perform or to procure the performance of transport, by rail, road, air, sea, inland waterway or by a combination of such modes. If subsequent carriers are used for the carriage to the agreed destination, the risk passes when the goods have been delivered to the first carrier. The CPT term requires the seller to clear the goods for export. This term may be used irrespective of the mode of transport including multimodal transport.

A THE SELLER'S OBLIGATIONS

B THE BUYER'S OBLIGATIONS

A1 Provision of goods in conformity with the contract

The seller must provide the goods and the commercial invoice, or its equivalent electronic message, in conformity with the contract of sale and any other evidence of conformity which may be required by the contract.

B1 Payment of the price

The buyer must pay the price as provided in the contract of sale.

A2 Licenses, authorizations and formalities

The seller must obtain at his own risk and expense any export licence or other official authorization and carry out, where applicable1, all customs formalities necessary for the export of the goods.

注 1 Refer to Introduction Paragraph 14.

B2 Licenses, authorizations and formalities

The buyer must obtain at his own risk and expense any import licence or other official authorization and carry out, where applicable2, all customs formalities for the import of the goods and for their transit through any country.

注 2 Refer to Introduction Paragraph 14.

A3 Contracts of carriage and insurance

a) Contract of carriage

The seller must contract on usual terms at his own expense for the carriage of the goods to the agreed point at the named place of destination by a usual route and in a customary manner. If a point is not agreed or is not determined by practice, the seller may select the point at the named place of destination which best suits his purpose.

b) Contract of insurance

No obligation3.

注 3 Refer to Introduction Paragraph 10.

B3 Contracts of carriage and insurance

a) Contract of carriage

No obligation4.

注 4 Refer to Introduction Paragraph 10.

b) Contract of insurance

No obligation5.

注 5 Refer to Introduction Paragraph 10.

A4 Delivery

The seller must deliver the goods to the carrier contracted in accordance with A3 or, if there are subsequent carriers to the first carrier, for transport to the agreed point at the named place on the date or within the agreed period.

B4 Taking delivery

The buyer must accept delivery of the goods when they have been delivered in accordance with A4 and receive them from the carrier at the named place.

A5 Transfer of risks

The seller must, subject to the provisions of B5, bear all risks of loss of or damage to the goods until such time as they have been delivered in accordance with A4.

B5 Transfer of risks

The buyer must bear all risks of loss of or damage to the goods from the time they have been delivered in accordance with A4.

The buyer must, should he fail to give notice in accordance with B7, bear all risks of the goods from the agreed date or the expiry date of the period fixed for delivery provided, however, that the goods have been duly appropriated to the contract, that is to say, clearly set aside or otherwise identified as the contract goods.

A6 Division of costs

The seller must, subject to the provisions of B6, pay

● all costs relating to the goods until such time as they have been delivered in accordance with A4 as well as the freight and all other costs resulting from A3 a), including the costs of loading the goods and any charges for unloading at the place of destination which were for the seller's account under the contract of carriage; and

● where applicable6, the costs of customs formalities necessary for export as well as all duties, taxes or other charges payable upon export, and for their transit through any country if they were for the seller's account under the contract of carriage.

注 6 Refer to Introduction Paragraph 14.

B6 Division of costs

The buyer must, subject to the provisions of A3 a), pay

● all costs relating to the goods from the time they have been delivered in accordance with A4; and

● all costs and charges relating to the goods whilst in transit until their arrival at the agreed place of destination, unless such costs and charges were for the seller's account under the contract of carriage; and

● unloading costs unless such costs and charges were for the seller's account under the contract of carriage; and

● all additional costs incurred if he fails to give notice in accordance with B7, for the goods from the agreed date or the expiry date of the period fixed for dispatch, provided, however, that the goods have been duly appropriated to the contract, that is to say, clearly set aside or otherwise identified as the contract goods; and

● where applicable7, all duties, taxes and other charges as well as the costs of carrying out customs formalities payable upon import of the goods and for their transit through any country unless included within the cost of the contract of carriage.

注 7 Refer to Introduction Paragraph 14.

A7 Notice to the buyer

The seller must give the buyer sufficient notice that the goods have been delivered in accordance with A4 as well as any other notice required in order to allow the buyer to take measures which are normally necessary to enable him to take the goods.

B7 Notice to the seller

The buyer must, whenever he is entitled to determine the time for dispatching the goods and/or the destination, give the seller sufficient notice thereof.

A8 Proof of delivery, transport document or equivalent electronic message

The seller must provide the buyer at the seller's expense, if customary, with the usual transport document or documents (for example a negotiable bill of lading, a non - negotiable sea waybill, an inland waterway document, an air waybill, a railway consignment note, a road consignment note, or a multimodal transport document) for the transport contracted in accordance with A3.

Where the seller and the buyer have agreed to communicate electronically, the document referred to in the preceding paragraph may be replaced by an equivalent electronic date interchange (EDI) message.

B8 Proof of delivery, transport document or equivalent electronic message

The buyer must accept the transport document in accordance with A8 if it is in conformity with the contract.

A9 Checking - packaging - marking

The seller must pay the costs of those checking operations (such as checking quality, measuring, weighing, counting) which are necessary for the purpose of delivering the goods in accordance with A4.

The seller must provide at his own expense packaging (unless it is usual for the particular trade to send the goods of the contract description unpacked) which is required for the transport of the goods arranged by him.

Packaging is to be marked appropriately.

B9 Inspection of goods

The buyer must pay the costs of any pre - shipment inspection except when such inspection is mandated by the authorities of the country of export.

A10 Other obligations

The seller must render the buyer at the latter's request, risk and expense, every assistance in obtaining any documents or equivalent electronic messages (other than those mentioned in A8) issued or transmitted in the country of dispatch and/or of origin which the buyer may require for the import of the goods and for their transit through any country.

The seller must provide the buyer, upon request, with the necessary information for procuring insurance.

B10 Other obligations

The buyer must pay all costs and charges incurred in obtaining the documents or equivalent electronic messages mentioned in A10 and reimburse those incurred by the seller in rendering his assistance in accordance therewith.

CIP

CARRIAGE AND INSURANCE PAID TO

(... named place of destination)

"Carriage and Insurance paid to..." means that the seller delivers the goods to the carrier nominated by him but the seller must in addition pay the cost of carriage necessary to bring the goods to the named destination.

This means that the buyer bears all risks and any additional costs occurring after the goods have been so delivered. However, in CIP the seller also has to procure insurance against the buyer's risk of loss of or damage to the goods during the carriage. Consequently, the seller contracts for insurance and pays the insurance premium.

The buyer should note that under the CIP term the seller is required to obtain insurance only on minimum cover1. Should the buyer wish to have the protection of greater cover, he would either need to agree as such expressly with the seller or to make his own extra insurance arrangements.

注 1 Refer to Introduction Paragraph 9. 3.

"Carrier" means any person who, in a contract of carriage, undertakes to perform or to procure the performance of transport, by rail, road, air, sea, inland waterway or by a combination of such modes. If subsequent carriers are used for the carriage to the agreed destination, the risk passes when the goods have been delivered to the first carrier. The CIP term requires the seller to clear the goods for export. This term may be used irrespective of the mode of transport including multimodal transport.

A THE SELLER'S OBLIGATIONS

B THE BUYER'S OBLIGATIONS

A1 Provision of goods in conformity with the contract

The seller must provide the goods and the commercial invoice, or its equivalent electronic message, in conformity with the contract of sale and any other evidence of conformity which may be required by the contract.

B1 Payment of the price

The buyer must pay the price as provided in the contract of sale.

A2 Licenses, authorizations and formalities

The seller must obtain at his own risk and expense any export licence or other official authorization and carry out, where applicable2, all customs formalities necessary for the export of the goods.

注 2 Refer to Introduction Paragraph 14.

B2 Licenses, authorizations and formalities

The buyer must obtain at his own risk and expense any import licence or other official authorization and carry out, where applicable3, all customs formalities for the import of the goods and for their transit through any country.

注 3 Refer to Introduction Paragraph 14.

A3 Contracts of carriage and insurance

a) Contract of carriage

The seller must contract on usual terms at his own expense for the carriage of the goods to the agreed point at the named place of destination by a usual route and in a customary manner. If a point is not agreed or is not determined by practice, the seller may select the point at the named place of destination which best suits his purpose.

b) Contract of insurance

The seller must obtain at his own expense cargo insurance as agreed in the contract, such that the buyer, or any other person having an insurable interest in the goods, shall be entitled to claim directly from the insurer and provide the buyer with the insurance policy or other evidence of insurance cover.

The insurance shall be contracted with underwriters or an insurance company of good repute and, failing express agreement to the contrary, be in accordance with minimum cover of the Institute Cargo Clauses (Institute of London Underwriters) or any similar set of clauses. The duration of insurance cover shall be in accordance with B5 and B4. When required by the buyer, the seller shall provide at the buyer's expense war, strikes, riots and civil commotion risk insurance if procurable. The minimum insurance shall cover the price provided in the contract plus ten per cent (i. e. 110%) and shall be provided in the currency of the contract.

B3 Contracts of carriage and insurance

a) Contract of carriage

No obligation4.

注 4 Refer to Introduction Paragraph 10.

b) Contract of insurance

No obligation5.

注 5 Refer to Introduction Paragraph 10.

A4 Delivery

The seller must deliver the goods to the carrier contracted in accordance with A3 or, if there are subsequent carriers to the first carrier, for transport to the agreed point at the named place on the date or within the agreed period.

B4 Taking delivery

The buyer must accept delivery of the goods when they have been delivered in accordance with A4 and receive them from the carrier at the named place.

A5 Transfer of risks

The seller must, subject to the provisions of B5, bear all risks of loss of or damage to the goods until such time as they have been delivered in accordance with A4.

B5 Transfer of risks

The buyer must bear all risks of loss of or damage to the goods from the time they have been delivered in accordance with A4.

The buyer must, should he fail to give notice in accordance with B7, bear all risks of the goods from the agreed date or the expiry date of the period fixed for delivery provided, however, that the goods have been duly appropriated to the contract, that is to say, clearly set aside or otherwise identified as the contract goods.

A6 Division of costs

The seller must, subject to the provisions of B6, pay

● all costs relating to the goods until such time as they have been delivered in accordance with A4 as well as the freight and all other costs resulting from A3 a), including the costs of loading the goods and any charges for unloading at the place of destination which were for the seller's account under the contract of carriage; and

● the costs of insurance resulting from A3 b); and

● where applicable6, the costs of customs formalities necessary for export as well as all duties, taxes or other charges payable upon export, and for their transit through any country if they were for the seller's account under the contract of carriage.

注 6 Refer to Introduction Paragraph 14.

B6 Division of costs

The buyer must, subject to the provisions of A3 a), pay

● all costs relating to the goods from the time they have been delivered in accordance with A4; and

● all costs and charges relating to the goods whilst in transit until their arrival at the agreed place of destination, unless such costs and charges were for the seller's account under the contract of carriage; and

● unloading costs unless such costs and charges were for the seller's account under the contract of carriage; and

● all additional costs incurred if he fails to give notice in accordance with B7, for the goods from the agreed date or the expiry date of the period fixed for dispatch, provided, however, that the goods have been duly appropriated to the contract, that is to say, clearly set aside or otherwise identified as the contract goods; and

● where applicable7, all duties, taxes and other charges as well as the costs of carrying out customs formalities payable upon import of the goods and for their transit through any country unless included within the cost of the contract of carriage.

注 7 Refer to Introduction Paragraph 14.

A7 Notice to the buyer

The seller must give the buyer sufficient notice that the goods have been delivered in accordance with A4 as well as any other notice required in order to allow the buyer to take measures which are normally necessary to enable him to take the goods.

B7 Notice to the seller

The buyer must, whenever he is entitled to determine the time for dispatching the goods and/or the destination, give the seller sufficient notice thereof.

A8 Proof of delivery, transport document or equivalent electronic message

The seller must provide the buyer at the seller's expense, if customary, with the usual transport document or documents (for example a negotiable bill of lading, a non-negotiable sea waybill, an inland waterway document, an air waybill, a railway consignment note, a road consignment note, or a multimodal transport document) for the transport contracted in accordance with A3.

Where the seller and the buyer have agreed to communicate electronically, the document referred to in the preceding paragraph may be replaced by an equivalent electronic data interchange (EDI) message.

B8 Proof of delivery, transport document or equivalent electronic message

The buyer must accept the transport document in accordance with A8 if it is in conformity with the contract.

A9 Checking - packaging - marking

The seller must pay the costs of those checking operations (such as checking quality, measuring, weighing, counting) which are necessary for the purpose of delivering the goods in accordance with A4.

The seller must provide at his own expense packaging (unless it is usual for the particular trade to send the goods of the contract description unpacked) which is required for the transport of the goods arranged by him.

Packaging is to be marked appropriately.

B9 Inspection of goods

The buyer must pay the costs of any pre-shipment inspection except when such inspection is mandated by the authorities of the country of export.

A10 Other obligations

The seller must render the buyer at the latter's request, risk and expense, every assistance in obtaining any documents or equivalent electronic messages (other than those mentioned in A8) issued or transmitted in the country of dispatch and/or of origin which the buyer may require for the import of the goods and for their transit through any country.

The seller must provide the buyer, upon request, with the necessary information for procuring any additional insurance.

B10 Other obligations

The buyer must pay all costs and charges incurred in obtaining the documents or equivalent electronic messages mentioned in A10 and reimburse those incurred by the seller in rendering his assistance in accordance therewith.

The buyer must provide the seller, upon request, with the necessary information for procuring insurance.

DAF

DELIVERED AT FRONTIER

(... named place)

"Delivered at Frontier" means that the seller delivers when the goods are placed at the disposal of the buyer on the arriving means of transport not unloaded, cleared for export, but not cleared for import at the named point and place at the frontier, but before the customs border of the adjoining country. The term "frontier" may be used for any frontier including that of the country of export. Therefore, it is of vital importance that the frontier in question be defined precisely by always naming the point and place in the term.

However, if the parties wish the seller to be responsible for the unloading of the goods from the arriving means of transport and to bear the risks and costs of unloading, this should be made clear by adding explicit wording to this effect in the contract of sale1.

注 1 Refer to Introduction Paragraph 11.

This term may be used irrespective of the mode of transport when goods are to be delivered at a land frontier. When delivery is to take place in the port of destination, on board a vessel or on the quay (wharf), the DES or DEQ terms should be used.

A THE SELLER'S OBLIGATIONS

B THE BUYER'S OBLIGATIONS

A1 Provision of goods in conformity with the contract

The seller must provide the goods and the commercial invoice, or its equivalent electronic message, in conformity with the contract of sale and any other evidence of conformity which may be required by the contract.

B1 Payment of the price

The buyer must pay the price as provided in the contract of sale.

A2 Licenses, authorizations and formalities

The seller must obtain at his own risk and expense any export licence or other official authorization or other document necessary for placing the goods at the buyer's disposal.

The seller must carry out, where applicable2, all customs formalities necessary for the export of the goods to the named place of delivery at the frontier and for their transit through any country.

注 2 Refer to Introduction Paragraph 14.

B2 Licenses, authorizations and formalities

The buyer must obtain at his own risk and expense any import licence or other official authorization or other documents and carry out, where applicable3, all customs formalities necessary for the import of the goods, and for their subsequent transport.

注 3 Refer to Introduction Paragraph 14.

A3 Contracts of carriage and insurance

a) Contract of carriage

i) The seller must contract at his own expense for the carriage of the goods to the named point, if any, at the place of delivery at the frontier. If a point at the named place of delivery at the frontier is not agreed or is not determined by practice, the seller may select the point at the named place of delivery which best suits his purpose.

ii) However, if requested by the buyer, the seller may agree to contract on usual terms at the buyer's risk and expense for the on – going carriage of the goods beyond the named place at the frontier to the final destination in the country of import named by the buyer. The seller may decline to make the contract and, if he does, shall promptly notify the buyer accordingly.

b) Contract of insurance

No obligation4.

注 4 Refer to Introduction Paragraph 10.

B3 Contracts of carriage and insurance

a) Contract of carriage

No obligation5.

注 5 Refer to Introduction Paragraph 10.

b) Contract of insurance

No obligation6.

注 6 Refer to Introduction Paragraph 10.

A4 Delivery

The seller must place the goods at the disposal of the buyer on the arriving means of transport not unloaded at the named place of delivery at the frontier on the date or within the agreed period.

B4 Taking delivery

The buyer must take delivery of the goods when they have been delivered in accordance with A4.

A5 Transfer of risks

The seller must, subject to the provisions of B5, bear all risks of loss of or damage to the goods until such time as they have been delivered in accordance with A4.

B5 Transfer of risks

The buyer must bear all risks of loss of or damage to the goods from the time they have been delivered in accordance with A4.

The buyer must, should he fail to give notice in accordance with B7, bear all risks of loss of or damage to the goods from the agreed date or the expiry date of the agreed period for delivery provided, however, that the goods have been duly appropriated to the contract, that is to say, clearly set aside or otherwise identified as the contract goods.

A6 Division of costs

The seller must, subject to the oivision of B6, pay

● in addition to the costs resulting from A3 a), all costs relating to the goods until such time as they have been delivered in accordance with A4; and

● where applicable7, the costs of customs formalities necessary for export as well as all duties, taxes or other charges payable upon export of the goods and for their transit through any country prior to delivery in accordance with A4.

注 7 Refer to Introduction Paragraph 14.

B6 Division of costs

The buyer must pay

● all costs relating to the goods from the time they have been delivered in accordance with A4 including the expenses of unloading necessary to take delivery of the goods from the arriving means of transport at the named place of delivery at the frontier; and

● all additional costs incurred if he fails to take delivery of the goods when they have been delivered in accordance with A4, or to give notice in accordance with B7, provided, however, that the goods have been appropriated to the contract, that is to say, clearly set aside or otherwise identified as the contract goods; and

● where applicable8, the cost of customs formalities as well as all duties, taxes and other charges payable upon import of the goods and for their subsequent transport.

注 8 Refer to Introduction Paragraph 14.

A7 Notice to the buyer

The seller must give the buyer sufficient notice of the dispatch of the goods to the named place at the frontier as well as any other notice required in order to allow the buyer to take measures which are normally necessary to enable him to take delivery of the goods.

B7 Notice to the seller

The buyer must, whenever he is entitled to determine the time within an agreed period and/or the point of taking delivery at the named place, give the seller sufficient notice thereof.

A8 Proof of delivery, transport document or equivalent electronic message

i) The seller must provide the buyer at the seller's expense with the usual document or other evidence of the delivery of the goods at the named place at the frontier in accordance with A3 a) i).

ii) The seller must, should the parties agree on – going carriage beyond the frontier in accordance with A3 a) ii), provide the buyer at the latter's request, risk and expense, with the through document of transport normally obtained in the country of dispatch covering on usual terms the transport of the goods from the point of dispatch in that country to the place of final destination in the country of import named by the buyer.

Where the seller and the buyer have agreed to communicate electronically, the document referred to in the preceding paragraph may be replaced by an equivalent electronic data interchange (EDI) message.

B8 Proof of delivery, transport document or equivalent electronic message

The buyer must accept the transport document and/or other evidence of delivery in accordance with A8.

A9 Checking - packaging - marking

The seller must pay the costs of those checking operations (such as checking quality, measuring, weighing, counting) which are necessary for the purpose of delivering the goods in accordance with A4.

The seller must provide at his own expense packaging (unless it is agreed or usual for the particular trade to deliver the goods of the contract description unpacked) which is required for the delivery of the goods at the frontier and for the subsequent transport to the extent that the circumstances (for example modalities, destination) are made known to the seller before the contract of sale is concluded. Packaging is to be marked appropriately.

B9 Inspection of goods

The buyer must pay the costs of any pre - shipment inspection except when such inspection is mandated by the authorities of the country of export.

A10 Other obligations

The seller must render the buyer at the latter's request, risk and expense, every assistance in obtaining any documents or equivalent electronic messages (other than those mentioned in A8) issued or transmitted in the country of dispatch and/or origin which the buyer may require for the import of the goods and, where necessary, for their transit through any country.

The seller must provide the buyer, upon request, with the necessary information for procuring insurance.

B10 Other obligations

The buyer must pay all costs and charges incurred in obtaining the documents or equivalent electronic messages mentioned in A10 and reimburse those incurred by the seller in rendering his assistance in accordance therewith.

If necessary, according to A3 a) ii), the buyer must provide the seller at his request and the buyer's risk and expense with the exchange control authorization, permits, other documents or certified copies thereof, or with the address of the final destination of the goods in the country of import for the purpose of obtaining the through document of transport or any other document contemplated in A8 ii).

DES

DELIVERED EX SHIP

(... named port of destination)

"Delivered Ex Ship" means that the seller delivers when the goods are placed at the disposal of the buyer on board the ship not cleared for import at the named port of destination. The seller has to bear all the costs and risks involved in bringing the goods to the named port of destination before discharging. If the parties wish the seller to bear the costs and risks of discharging the goods, then the DEQ term should be used.

This term can be used only when the goods are to be delivered by sea or inland waterway or multimodal transport on a vessel in the port of destination.

A THE SELLER'S OBLIGATIONS

B THE BUYER'S OBLIGATIONS

A1 Provision of goods in conformity with the contract

The seller must provide the goods and the commercial invoice, or its equivalent electronic message, in conformity with the contract of sale and any other evidence of conformity which may be required by the contract.

B1 Payment of the price

The buyer must pay the price as provided in the contract of sale.

A2 Licenses, authorizations and formalities

The seller must obtain at his own risk and expense any export licence or other official authorization or other documents and carry out, where applicable1, all customs formalities necessary for the export of the goods and for their transit through any country.

注 1 Refer to Introduction Paragraph 14.

B2 Licenses, authorizations and formalities

The buyer must obtain at his own risk and expense any import licence or other official authorization and carry out, where applicable2, all customs formalities necessary for the import of the goods.

注 2 Refer to Introduction Paragraph 14.

A3 Contracts of carriage and insurance

a) Contract of carriage

The seller must contract at his own expense for the carriage of the goods to the named point, if any, at the named port of destination. If a point is not agreed or is not determined by practice, the seller may select the point at the named port of destination which best suits his purpose.

b) Contract of insurance

No obligation3.

注 3 Refer to Introduction Paragraph 10.

B3 Contracts of carriage and insurance

a) Contract of carriage

No obligation4.

注 4 Refer to Introduction Paragraph 10.

b) Contract of insurance

No obligation5.

注 5 Refer to Introduction Paragraph 10.

A4 Delivery

The seller must place the goods at the disposal of the buyer on board the vessel at the unloading point referred to in A3 a), in the named port of destination on the date or within the agreed period, in such a way as to enable them to be removed from the vessel by unloading equipment appropriate to the nature of the goods.

B4 Taking delivery

The buyer must take delivery of the goods when they have been delivered in accordance with A4.

A5 Transfer of risks

The seller must, subject to the provisions of B5, bear all risks of loss of or damage to the goods until such time as they have been delivered in accordance with A4.

B5 Transfer of risks

The buyer must bear all risks of loss of or damage to the goods from the time they have been delivered in accordance with A4.

The buyer must, should he fail to give notice in accordance with B7, bear all risks of loss of or damage to the goods from the agreed date or the expiry date of the agreed period for delivery provided, however, that the goods have been duly appropriated to the contract, that is to say, clearly set aside or otherwise identified as the contract goods.

A6 Division of costs

The seller must, subject to the provisions of B6, pay

● in addition to costs resulting from A3 a), all costs relating to the goods until such time as they have been delivered in accordance with A4; and

● where applicable6, the costs of customs formalities necessary for export as well as all duties, taxes or other charges payable upon export of the goods and for their transit through any country prior to delivery in accordance with A4.

注 6 Refer to Introduction Paragraph 14.

B6 Division of costs

The buyer must pay

● all costs relating to the goods from the time they have been delivered in accordance with A4, including the expenses of discharge operations necessary to take delivery of the goods from the vessel; and

● all additional costs incurred if he fails to take delivery of the goods when they have been placed at his disposal in accordance with A4, or to give notice in accordance with B7, provided, however, that the goods have been appropriated to the contract, that is to say, clearly set aside or otherwise identified as the contract goods.

● where applicable7, the costs of customs formalities as well as all duties, taxes and other charges payable upon import of the goods.

注 7 Refer to Introduction Paragraph 14.

A7 Notice to the buyer

The seller must give the buyer sufficient notice of the estimated time of arrival of the nominated vessel in accordance with A4 as well as any other notice required in order to allow the buyer to take measures which are normally necessary to enable him to take delivery of the goods.

B7 Notice to the seller

The buyer must, whenever he is entitled to determine the time within an agreed period and/or the point of taking delivery in the named port of destination, give the seller sufficient notice thereof.

A8 Proof of delivery, transport document or equivalent electronic message

The seller must provide the buyer at the seller's expense with the delivery order and/or the usual transport document (for example a negotiable bill of lading, a non – negotiable sea waybill, an inland waterway document, or a multimodal transport document) to enable the buyer to claim the goods from the carrier at the port of destination.

Where the seller and the buyer have agreed to communicate electronically, the document referred to in the preceding paragraph may be replaced by an equivalent electronic data interchange (EDI) message.

B8 Proof of delivery, transport document or equivalent electronic message

The buyer must accept the delivery order or the transport document in accordance with A8.

A9 Checking – packaging – marking

The seller must pay the costs of those checking operations (such as checking quality, measuring, weighing, counting) which are necessary for the purpose of delivering the goods in accordance with A4.

The seller must provide at his own expense packaging (unless it is usual for the particular trade to deliver the goods of the contract description unpacked) which is required for the delivery of the goods. Packaging is to be marked appropriately.

B9 Inspection of goods

The buyer must pay the costs of any pre – shipment inspection except when such inspection is mandated by the authorities of the country of export.

A10 Other obligations

The seller must render the buyer at the latter's request, risk and expense, every assistance in obtaining any documents or equivalent electronic messages (other than those mentioned in A8) issued or transported in the country of dispatch and/or of origin which the buyer may require for the import of the goods.

The seller must provide the buyer, upon request, with the necessary information for procuring insurance.

B10 Other obligations

The buyer must pay all costs and charges incurred in obtaining the documents or equivalent electronic messages mentioned in A10 and reimburse those incurred by the seller in rendering his assistance in accordance therewith.

DEQ

DELIVERED EX QUAY

(... named port of destination)

"Delivered Ex Quay" means that the seller delivers when the goods are placed at the disposal of the buyer not cleared for import on the quay (wharf) at the named port of destination. The seller has to bear costs and risks involved in bringing the goods to the named port of destination and discharging the goods on the quay (wharf). The DEQ term requires the buyer to clear the goods for import and to pay for all formalities, duties, taxes and other charges upon import.

THIS IS A REVERSAL FROM PREVIOUS INCOTERMS VERSIONS WHICH REQUIRED THE SELLER TO ARRANGE FOR IMPORT CLEARANCE.

If the parties wish to include in the seller's obligations all or part of the costs payable upon import of the goods, this should be made clear by adding explicit wording to his effect in the contract of sale1.

注 1 Refer to Introduction Paragraph 11.

This term can be used only when the goods are to be delivered by sea or inland waterway or multimodal transport on discharging from a vessel onto the quay (wharf) in the port of destination. However if the parties wish to include in the seller's obligations the risks and costs of the handling of the goods from the quay to another place (warehouse, terminal, transport station, etc.) in or outside the port, the DDU or DDP terms should be used.

A THE SELLER'S OBLIGATIONS

B THE BUYER'S OBLIGATIONS

A1 Provision of goods in conformity with the contract

The seller must provide the goods and the commercial invoice, or its equivalent electronic message, in conformity with the contract of sale and any other evidence of conformity which may be required by the contract.

B1 Payment of the price

The buyer must pay the price as provided in the contract of sale.

A2 Licenses, authorizations and formalities

The seller must obtain at his own risk and expense any export licence or other official authorization or other documents and carry out, where applicable2, all customs formalities for the export of the goods, and for their transit through any country.

注 2 Refer to Introduction Paragraph 14.

B2 Licenses, authorizations and formalities

The buyer must obtain at his own risk and expense any import licence or official authorization or other documents and carry out, where applicable3, all customs formalities necessary for the import of the goods.

注 3 Refer to Introduction Paragraph 14.

A3 Contracts of carriage and insurance

a) Contract of carriage

The seller must contract at his own expense for the carriage of the goods to the named quay (wharf) at the named port of destination. If a specific quay (wharf) is not agreed or is not determined by practice, the seller may select the quay (wharf) at the named port of destination which best suits his purpose.

b) Contract of insurance

No obligation4.

注 4 Refer to Introduction Paragraph 10.

B3 Contracts of carriage and insurance

a) Contract of carriage

No obligation5.

注 5 Refer to Introduction Paragraph 10.

b) Contract of insurance

No obligation6.

注 6 Refer to Introduction Paragraph 10.

A4 Delivery

The seller must place the goods at the disposal of the buyer on the quay (wharf) referred to in A3 a), on the date or within the agreed period.

B4 Taking delivery

The buyer must take delivery of the goods when they have been delivered in accordance with A4.

A5 Transfer of risks

The seller must, subject to the provisions of B5, bear all risks of loss of or damage to the goods until such time as they have been delivered in accordance with A4.

B5 Transfer of risks

The buyer must bear all risks of loss of or damage to the goods from the time they have been delivered in accordance with A4.

The buyer must, should he fail to give notice in accordance with B7, bear all risks of loss of or damage to the goods from the agreed date or the expiry date of the agreed period for delivery provided, however, that the goods have been duly appropriated to the contract, that is to say, clearly set aside or otherwise identified as the contract goods.

A6 Division of costs

The seller must, subject to the provisions of B6, pay

- in addition to costs resulting from A3 a), all costs relating to the goods until such time as they are delivered on the quay (wharf) in accordance with A4; and
- where applicable7, the costs of customs formalities necessary for export as well as all duties, taxes and other charges payable upon export of the goods and for their transit through any

country prior to delivery.

注 7 Refer to Introduction Paragraph 14.

B6 Division of costs

The buyer must pay

● all costs relating to the goods from the time they have been delivered in accordance with A4, including any costs of handling the goods in the port for subsequent transport or storage in warehouse or terminal; and

● all additional costs incurred if he fails to take delivery of the goods when they have been placed at his disposal in accordance with A4, or to give notice in accordance with B7, provided, however, that the goods have been appropriated to the contract, that is to say, clearly set aside or otherwise identified as the contract goods; and

● where applicable8, the cost of customs formalities as well as all duties, taxes and other charges payable upon import of the goods and for their subsequent transport.

注 8 Refer to Introduction Paragraph 14.

A7 Notice to the buyer

The seller must give the buyer sufficient notice of the estimated time of arrival of the nominated vessel in accordance with A4, as well as any other notice required in order to allow the buyer to take measures which are normally necessary to enable him to take delivery of the goods.

B7 Notice to the seller

The buyer must, whenever he is entitled to determine the time within an agreed period and/or the point of taking delivery in the named port of destination, give the seller sufficient notice thereof.

A8 Transport document or equivalent electronic message

The seller must provide the buyer at the seller's expense with the delivery order and/or the usual transport document (for example a negotiable bill of lading, a non - negotiable sea waybill, an inland waterway document or a multimodal transport document) to enable him to take the goods and remove them from the quay (wharf).

Where the seller and the buyer have agreed to communicate electronically, the document referred to in the preceding paragraph may be replaced by an equivalent electronic data interchange (EDI) message.

B8 Proof of delivery, transport document or equivalent electronic message

The buyer must accept the delivery order or transport document in accordance with A8.

A9 Checking - packaging - marking

The seller must pay the costs of those checking operations (such as checking quality, measuring, weighing, counting) which are necessary for the purpose of delivering the goods in accordance with A4.

The seller must provide at his own expense packaging (unless it is usual for the particular trade to deliver the goods of the contract description unpacked) which is required for the delivery of the goods. Packaging is to be marked appropriately.

B9 Inspection of goods

The buyer must pay the costs of any pre – shipment inspection except when such inspection is mandated by the authorities of the country of export.

A10 Other obligations

The seller must render the buyer at the latter's request, risk and expense, every assistance in obtaining any documents or equivalent electronic messages (other than those mentioned in A8) issued or transmitted in the country of dispatch and/or origin which the buyer may require for the import of the goods.

The seller must provide the buyer, upon request, with the necessary information for procuring insurance.

B10 Other obligations

The buyer must pay all costs and charges incurred in obtaining the documents or equivalent electronic messages mentioned in A10 and reimburse those incurred by the seller in rendering his assistance in accordance therewith.

DDU

DELIVERED DUTY UNPAID

(... named place of destination)

"Delivered duty unpaid" means that the seller delivers the goods to the buyer, not cleared for import, and not unloaded from any arriving means of transport at the named place of destination. The seller has to bear the costs and risks involved in bringing the goods thereto, other than, where applicable1, any "duty" (which term includes the responsibility for and the risks of the carrying out of custom formalities, and the payment of formalities, customs duties, taxes and other charges) for import in the country of destination. Such "duty" has to be borne by the buyer as well as any costs and risks caused by his failure to clear the goods for import in time.

注 1 Refer to Introduction Paragraph 14.

However, if the parties wish the seller to carry out custom formalities and bear the costs and risks resulting therefrom as well as some of the costs payable upon import of the goods, this should be made clear by adding explicit wording to this effect in the contract of sale2.

注 2 Refer to Introduction Paragraph 11.

This term may be used irrespective of the mode of transport but when delivery is to take place in the port of destination on board the vessel or on the quay (wharf), the DES or DEQ term should be used.

A THE SELLER'S OBLIGATIONS

B THE BUYER'S OBLIGATIONS

A1 Provision of the goods in conformity with the contract

The seller must provide the goods and the commercial invoice, or its equivalent electronic message, in conformity with the contract of sale and any other evidence of conformity which may be required by the contract.

B1 Payment of the price

The buyer must pay the price as provided in the contract of sale.

A2 Licenses, authorizations and formalities

The seller must obtain at his own risk and expense any export licence and other official authorization or other documents and carry out, where applicable3, all customs formalities necessary for the export of the goods and for their transit through any country.

注 3 Refer to Introduction Paragraph 14.

B2 Licenses, authorizations and formalities

The buyer must obtain at his own risk and expense any import licence or other official authorization or other documents and carry out, where applicable4, all customs formalities necessary for the import of the goods.

注 4 Refer to Introduction Paragraph 14.

A3 Contracts of carriage and insurance

a) Contract of carriage

The seller must contract at his own expense for the carriage of the goods to the named place of destination. If a specific point is not agreed or is not determined by practice, the seller may select the point at the named place of destination which best suits his purpose.

b) Contract of insurance

No obligation5.

注 5 Refer to Introduction Paragraph 10.

B3 Contracts of carriage and insurance

a) Contract of carriage

No obligation6.

注 6 Refer to Introduction Paragraph 10.

b) Contract of insurance

No obligation7.

注 7 Refer to Introduction Paragraph 10.

A4 Delivery

The seller must place the goods at the disposal of the buyer, or at that of another person named by the buyer, on any arriving means of transport not unloaded, at the named place of destination on the date or within the period agreed for delivery.

B4 Taking delivery

The buyer must take delivery of the goods when they have been delivered in accordance with A4.

A5 Transfer of risks

The seller must, subject to the provisions of B5, bear all risks of loss of or damage to the goods until such time as they have been delivered in accordance with A4.

B5 Transfer of risks

The buyer must bear all risks of loss of or damage to the goods from the time they have been delivered in accordance with A4.

The buyer must, should he fail to fulfil his obligations in accordance with B2, bear all additional risks of loss of or damage to the goods incurred thereby.

The buyer must, should he fail to give notice in accordance with B7, bear all risks of loss of or damage to the goods from the agreed date or the expiry date of the agreed period for delivery provided, however, that the goods have been duly appropriated to the contract, that is to say, clearly set aside or otherwise identified as the contract goods.

A6 Division of costs

The seller must, subject to the provisions of B6, pay

● in addition to costs resulting from A3 a), all costs relating to the goods until such time as they have been delivered in accordance with A4; and

● where applicable8, the costs of customs formalities necessary for export as well as all duties, taxes and other charges payable upon export and for their transit through any country prior to delivery in accordance with A4.

注 8 Refer to Introduction Paragraph 14.

B6 Division of costs

The buyer must pay

● all costs relating to the goods from the time they have been delivered in accordance with A4; and

● all additional costs incurred if he fails to fulfil his obligations in accordance with B2, or to give notice in accordance with B7, provided, however, that the goods have been duly appropriated to the contract, that is to say, clearly set aside or otherwise identified as the contract goods; and

● where applicable9, the costs of customs formalities as well as all duties, taxes and other charges payable upon import of the goods.

注 9 Refer to Introduction Paragraph 14.

A7 Notice to the buyer

The seller must give the buyer sufficient notice of the dispatch of the goods as well as any other notice required in order to allow the buyer to take measures which are normally necessary to enable him to take delivery of the goods.

B7 Notice to the seller

The buyer must, whenever he is entitled to determine the time within an agreed period and/or the point of taking delivery at the named place, give the seller sufficient notice thereof.

A8 Proof of delivery, transport document or equivalent electronic message

The seller must provide the buyer at the seller's expense the delivery order and/or the usual transport document (for example a negotiable bill of lading, a non-negotiable sea waybill, an inland waterway document, an air waybill, a railway consignment note, a road consignment note, or a multimodal transport document) which the buyer may require to take delivery of the goods in accordance with A4/B4.

Where the seller and the buyer have agreed to communicate electronically, the document referred to in the preceding paragraph may be replaced by an equivalent electronic data interchange (EDI) message.

B8 Proof of delivery, transport document or equivalent electronic message

The buyer must accept the appropriate delivery order or transport document in accordance with A8.

A9 Checking - packaging - marking

The seller must pay the costs of those checking operations (such as checking quality, measuring, weighing, counting) which are necessary for the purpose of delivering the goods in accordance with A4.

The seller must provide at his own expense packaging (unless it is usual for the particular trade to deliver the goods of the contract description unpacked) which is required for the delivery of the goods. Packaging is to be marked appropriately.

B9 Inspection of goods

The buyer must pay the costs of any pre - shipment inspection except when such inspection is mandated by the authorities of the country of export.

A10 Other obligations

The seller must render the buyer at the latter's request, risk and expense, every assistance in obtaining any documents or equivalent electronic messages (other than those mentioned in A8) issued or transmitted in the country of dispatch and/or of origin which the buyer may require for the import of the goods.

The seller must provide the buyer, upon request, with the necessary information for procuring insurance.

B10 Other obligations

The buyer must pay all costs and charges incurred in obtaining the documents or equivalent electronic messages mentioned in A10 and reimburse those incurred by the seller in rendering his assistance in accordance therewith.

DDP

DELIVERED DUTY PAID

(... named place of destination)

"Delivered duty paid" means that the seller delivers the goods to the buyer, cleared for import, and not unloaded from any arriving means of transport at the named place of destination. The seller has to bear all the costs and risks involved in bringing the goods thereto including, where applicable1, any "duty" (which term includes the responsibility for and the risk of the carrying out of customs formalities and the payment of formalities, customs duties, taxes and other charges) for import in the country of destination.

注 1 Refer to Introduction Paragraph 14.

Whilst the EXW term represents the minimum obligation for the seller, DDP represents the maximum obligation. This term should not be used if the seller is unable directly or indirectly to obtain the import licence. However, if the parties wish to exclude from the seller's obligations some of the costs payable upon import of the goods (such as value - added tax : VAT), this should be made clear by adding explicit wording to this effect in the contract of sale2.

注 2 Refer to Introduction Paragraph 11.

If the parties wish the buyer to bear all risks and costs of the import, the DDU term should be used. This term may be used irrespective of the mode of transport but when delivery is to take place in the port of destination on board the vessel or on the quay (wharf), the DES or DEQ terms should be used.

A THE SELLER'S OBLIGATIONS

B THE BUYER'S OBLIGATIONS

A1 Provision of the goods in conformity with the contract

The seller must provide the goods and the commercial invoice, or its equivalent electronic message, in conformity with the contract of sale and any other evidence of conformity which may be required by the contract.

B1 Payment of the price

The buyer must pay the price as provided in the contract of sale.

A2 Licenses, authorizations and formalities

The seller must obtain at his own risk and expense any export and import licence and other official authorization or other documents and carry out, where applicable3, all customs formalities necessary for the export of the goods, for their transit through any country and for their import.

注 3 Refer to Introduction Paragraph 14.

B2 Licenses, authorizations and formalities

The buyer must render the seller at the latter's request, risk and expense, every assistance in obtaining, where applicable4, any import licence or other official authorization necessary for the import of the goods.

注 4 Refer to Introduction Paragraph 14.

A3 Contracts of carriage and insurance

a) Contract of carriage

The seller must contract at his own expense for the carriage of the goods to the named place of destination. If a specific point is not agreed or is not determined by practice, the seller may select the point at the named place of destination which best suits his purpose.

b) Contract of insurance

No obligation5.

注 5 Refer to Introduction Paragraph 10.

B3 Contracts of carriage and insurance

a) Contract of carriage

No obligation6.

注 6 Refer to Introduction Paragraph 10.

b) Contract of insurance

No obligation7.

注 7 Refer to Introduction Paragraph 10.

A4 Delivery

The seller must place the goods at the disposal of the buyer, or at that of another person named by the buyer, on any arriving means of transport not unloaded at the named place of destination on the date or within the period agreed for delivery.

B4 Taking delivery

The buyer must take delivery of the goods when they have been delivered in accordance with A4.

A5 Transfer of risks

The seller must, subject to the provisions of B5, bear all risks of loss of or damage to the goods until such time as they have been delivered in accordance with A4.

B5 Transfer of risks

The buyer must bear all risks of loss of or damage to the goods from the time they have been delivered in accordance with A4.

The buyer must, should he fail to fulfil his obligations in accordance with B2, bear all additional risks of loss of or damage to the goods incurred thereby.

The buyer must, should he fail to give notice in accordance with B7, bear all risks of loss of or damage to the goods from the agreed date or the expiry date of the agreed period for delivery provided, however, that the goods have been duly appropriated to the contract, that is to say, clearly set aside or otherwise identified as the contract goods.

A6 Division of costs

The seller must, subject to the provisions of B6, pay

● in addition to costs resulting from A3 a), all costs relating to the goods until such time as they have been delivered in accordance with A4; and

● where applicable8, the costs of customs formalities necessary for export and import as well as all duties, taxes and other charges payable upon export and import of the goods, and for their transit through any country prior to delivery in accordance with A4.

注 8 Refer to Introduction Paragraph 14.

B6 Division of costs

The buyer must pay

● all costs relating to the goods from the time they have been delivered in accordance with A4; and

● all additional costs incurred if he fails to fulfil his obligations in accordance with B2, or to give notice in accordance with B7, provided, however, that the goods have been duly appropriated to the contract, that is to say, clearly set aside or otherwise identified as the contract goods.

A7 Notice to the buyer

The seller must give the buyer sufficient notice of the dispatch of the goods as well as any other notice required in order to allow the buyer to take measures which are normally necessary to enable him to take delivery of the goods.

B7 Notice to the seller

The buyer must, when he is entitled to determine the time within an agreed period and/or the point of taking delivery at the named place, give the seller sufficient notice thereof.

A8 Proof of delivery, transport document or equivalent electronic message

The seller must provide the buyer at the seller's expense with the delivery order and/or the usual transport document (for example a negotiable bill of lading, a non – negotiable sea waybill, an inland waterway document, an air waybill, a railway consignment note, a road consignment note, or a multimodal transport document) which the buyer may require to take delivery of the goods in accordance with A4/B4.

Where the seller and the buyer have agreed to communicate electronically, the document referred to in the preceding paragraph may be replaced by an equivalent electronic data interchange (EDI) message.

B8 Proof of delivery, transport document or equivalent electronic message

The buyer must accept the appropriate delivery order or transport document in accordance with A8.

A9 Checking – packaging – marking

The seller must pay the costs of those checking operations (such as checking quality, measuring, weighing, counting) which are necessary for the purpose of delivering the goods in accordance with A4.

The seller must provide at his own expense packaging (unless it is usual for the particular trade to deliver the goods of the contract description unpacked) which is required for the delivery of the goods. Packaging is to be marked appropriately.

B9 Inspection of goods

The buyer must pay the costs of any pre – shipment inspection except when such inspection is mandated by the authorities of the country of export.

A10 Other obligations

The seller must pay all costs and charges incurred in obtaining the documents or equivalent electronic message mentioned in B10 and reimburse those incurred by the buyer in rendering his assistance herewith.

The seller must provide the buyer, upon request, with the necessary information for procuring insurance.

B10 Other obligations

The buyer must render the seller, at the latter's request, risk and expense, every assistance in obtaining any documents or equivalent electronic messages issued or transmitted in the country of import which the seller may require for the purpose of making the goods available to the buyer in accordance therewith.

Appendix 2. United Nations Convention for International Sale of Goods

UNITED NATIONS CONVENTION ON CONTRACTS FOR THE INTERNATIONAL SALE OF GOODS (1980)

PART Ⅰ

SPHERE OF APPLICATION AND GENERAL PROVISIONS

Chapter Ⅰ

SPHERE OF APPLICATION

Article 1

(1) This Convention applies to contracts of sale of goods between parties whose places of business are in different States:

(a) when the States are Contracting States; or

(b) when the rules of private international law lead to the application of the law of a Contracting State.

(2) The fact that the parties have their places of business in different States is to be disregarded whenever this fact does not appear either from the contract or from any dealings between, or from information disclosed by, the parties at any time before or at the conclusion of the contract.

(3) Neither the nationality of the parties nor the civil or commercial character of the parties or of the contract is to be taken into consideration in determining the application of this Convention.

Article 2

This Convention does not apply to sales:

(a) of goods bought for personal, family or household use, unless the seller, at any time before or at the conclusion of the contract, neither knew nor ought to have known that the goods were bought for any such use;

(b) by auction;

(c) on execution or otherwise by authority of law;

(d) of stocks, shares, investment securities, negotiable instruments or money;

(e) of ships, vessels, hovercraft or aircraft;

(f) of electricity.

Article 3

(1) Contracts for the supply of goods to be manufactured or produced are to be considered sales unless the party who orders the goods undertakes to supply a substantial part of the materials necessary for such manufacture or production.

(2) This Convention does not apply to contracts in which the preponderant part of the obligations of the party who furnishes the goods consists in the supply of labour or other services.

Article 4

This Convention governs only the formation of the contract of sale and the rights and obligations of the seller and the buyer arising from such a contract. In particular, except as otherwise expressly provided in this Convention, it is not concerned with:

(a) the validity of the contract or of any of its provisions or of any usage;

(b) the effect which the contract may have on the property in the goods sold.

Article 5

This Convention does not apply to the liability of the seller for death or personal injury caused by the goods to any person.

Article 6

The parties may exclude the application of this Convention or, subject to article 12, derogate from or vary the effect of any of its provisions.

Chapter Ⅱ

GENERAL PROVISIONS

Article 7

(1) In the interpretation of this Convention, regard is to be had to its international character and to the need to promote uniformity in its application and the observance of good faith in international trade.

(2) Questions concerning matters governed by this Convention which are not expressly settled in it are to be settled in conformity with the general principles on which it is based or, in the absence of such principles, in conformity with the law applicable by virtue of the rules of private international law.

Article 8

(1) For the purposes of this Convention statements made by and other conduct of a party are to be interpreted according to his intent where the other party knew or could not have been unaware what that intent was.

(2) If the preceding paragraph is not applicable, statements made by and other conduct of a party are to be interpreted according to the understanding that a reasonable person of the same kind as the other party would have had in the same circumstances.

(3) In determining the intent of a party or the understanding a reasonable person would have had, due consideration is to be given to all relevant circumstances of the case including the negotiations, any practices which the parties have established between themselves, usages and any subsequent conduct of the parties.

Article 9

(1) The parties are bound by any usage to which they have agreed and by any practices which they have established between themselves.

(2) The parties are considered, unless otherwise agreed, to have impliedly made applicable to their contract or its formation a usage of which the parties knew or ought to have known and which in international trade is widely known to, and regularly observed by, parties to contracts of the type involved in the particular trade concerned.

Article 10

For the purposes of this Convention:

(a) if a party has more than one place of business, the place of business is that which has the closest relationship to the contract and its performance, having regard to the circumstances known to or contemplated by the parties at any time before or at the conclusion of the contract;

(b) if a party does not have a place of business, reference is to be made to his habitual residence.

Article 11

A contract of sale need not be concluded in or evidenced by writing and is not subject to any other requirement as to form. It may be proved by any means, including witnesses.

Article 12

Any provision of article 11, article 29 or Part Ⅱ of this Convention that allows a contract of sale or its modification or termination by agreement or any offer, acceptance or other indication of intention to be made in any form other than in writing does not apply where any party has his place of business in a Contracting State which has made a declaration under article 96 of this Convention. The parties may not derogate from or vary the effect or this article.

Article 13

For the purposes of this Convention "writing" includes telegram and telex.

PART Ⅱ

FORMATION OF THE CONTRACT

Article 14

(1) A proposal for concluding a contract addressed to one or more specific persons constitutes an offer if it is sufficiently definite and indicates the intention of the offeror to be bound in case of acceptance. A proposal is sufficiently definite if it indicates the goods and expressly or implicitly fixes or makes provision for determining the quantity and the price.

(2) A proposal other than one addressed to one or more specific persons is to be considered merely as an invitation to make offers, unless the contrary is clearly indicated by the person making the proposal.

Article 15

(1) An offer becomes effective when it reaches the offeree.

(2) An offer, even if it is irrevocable, may be withdrawn if the withdrawal reaches the offeree before or at the same time as the offer.

Article 16

(1) Until a contract is concluded an offer may be revoked if the revocation reaches the offeree

before he has dispatched an acceptance.

(2) However, an offer cannot be revoked:

(a) if it indicates, whether by stating a fixed time for acceptance or otherwise, that it is irrevocable; or

(b) if it was reasonable for the offeree to rely on the offer as being irrevocable and the offeree has acted in reliance on the offer.

Article 17

An offer, even if it is irrevocable, is terminated when a rejection reaches the offeror.

Article 18

(1) A statement made by or other conduct of the offeree indicating assent to an offer is an acceptance. Silence or inactivity does not in itself amount to acceptance.

(2) An acceptance of an offer becomes effective at the moment the indication of assent reaches the offeror. An acceptance is not effective if the indication of assent does not reach the offeror within the time he has fixed or, if no time is fixed, within a reasonable time, due account being taken of the circumstances of the transaction, including the rapidity of the means of communication employed by the offeror. An oral offer must be accepted immediately unless the circumstances indicate otherwise.

(3) However, if, by virtue of the offer or as a result of practices which the parties have established between themselves or of usage, the offeree may indicate assent by performing an act, such as one relating to the dispatch of the goods or payment of the price, without notice to the offeror, the acceptance is effective at the moment the act is performed, provided that the act is performed within the period of time laid down in the preceding paragraph.

Article 19

(1) A reply to an offer which purports to be an acceptance but contains additions, limitations or other modifications is a rejection of the offer and constitutes a counter-offer.

(2) However, a reply to an offer which purports to be an acceptance but contains additional or different terms which do not materially alter the terms of the offer constitutes an acceptance, unless the offeror, without undue delay, objects orally to the discrepancy or dispatches a notice to that effect. If he does not so object, the terms of the contract are the terms of the offer with the modifications contained in the acceptance.

(3) Additional or different terms relating, among other things, to the price, payment, quality and quantity of the goods, place and time of delivery, extent of one party's liability to the other or the settlement of disputes are considered to alter the terms of the offer materially.

Article 20

(1) A period of time for acceptance fixed by the offeror in a telegram or a letter begins to run from the moment the telegram is handed in for dispatch or from the date shown on the letter or, if no such date is shown, from the date shown on the envelope. A period of time for acceptance fixed by the offeror by telephone, telex or other means of instantaneous communication, begins to run from

the moment that the offer reaches the offeree.

(2) Official holidays or non-business days occurring during the period for acceptance are included in calculating the period. However, if a notice of acceptance cannot be delivered at the address of the offeror on the last day of the period because that day falls on an official holiday or a non-business day at the place of business of the offeror, the period is extended until the first business day which follows.

Article 21

(1) A late acceptance is nevertheless effective as an acceptance if without delay the offeror orally so informs the offeree or dispatches a notice to that effect.

(2) If a letter or other writing containing a late acceptance shows that it has been sent in such circumstances that if its transmission had been normal it would have reached the offeror in due time, the late acceptance is effective as an acceptance unless, without delay, the offeror orally informs the offeree that he considers his offer as having lapsed or dispatches a notice to that effect.

Article 22

An acceptance may be withdrawn if the withdrawal reaches the offeror before or at the same time as the acceptance would have become effective.

Article 23

A contract is concluded at the moment when an acceptance of an offer becomes effective in accordance with the provisions of this Convention.

Article 24

For the purposes of this Part of the Convention, an offer, declaration of acceptance or any other indication of intention "reaches" the addressee when it is made orally to him or delivered by any other means to him personally, to his place of business or mailing address or, if he does not have a place of business or mailing address, to his habitual residence.

PART Ⅲ

SALE OF GOODS

Chapter Ⅰ

GENERAL PROVISIONS

Article 25

A breach of contract committed by one of the parties is fundamental if it results in such detriment to the other party as substantially to deprive him of what he is entitled to expect under the contract, unless the party in breach did not foresee and a reasonable person of the same kind in the same circumstances would not have foreseen such a result.

Article 26

A declaration of avoidance of the contract is effective only if made by notice to the other party.

Article 27

Unless otherwise expressly provided in this Part of the Convention, if any notice, request or other communication is given or made by a party in accordance with this Part and by means appropriate in the circumstances, a delay or error in the transmission of the communication or its failure to arrive does not deprive that party of the right to rely on the communication.

Article 28

If, in accordance with the provisions of this Convention, one party is entitled to require performance of any obligation by the other party, a court is not bound to enter a judgement for specific performance unless the court would do so under its own law in respect of similar contracts of sale not governed by this Convention.

Article 29

(1) A contract may be modified or terminated by the mere agreement of the parties.

(2) A contract in writing which contains a provision requiring any modification or termination by agreement to be in writing may not be otherwise modified or terminated by agreement. However, a party may be precluded by his conduct from asserting such a provision to the extent that the other party has relied on that conduct.

Chapter Ⅱ

OBLIGATIONS OF THE SELLER

Article 30

The seller must deliver the goods, hand over any documents relating to them and transfer the property in the goods, as required by the contract and this Convention.

Section Ⅰ. Delivery of the goods and handing over of documents

Article 31

If the seller is not bound to deliver the goods at any other particular place, his obligation to deliver consists:

(a) if the contract of sale involves carriage of the goods – in handing the goods over to the first carrier for transmission to the buyer;

(b) if, in cases not within the preceding subparagraph, the contract relates to specific goods, or unidentified goods to be drawn from a specific stock or to be manufactured or produced, and at the time of the conclusion of the contract the parties knew that the goods were at, or were to be manufactured or produced at, a particular place – in placing the goods at the buyer's disposal at that place;

(c) in other cases – in placing the goods at the buyer's disposal at the place where the seller had his place of business at the time of the conclusion of the contract.

Article 32

(1) If the seller, in accordance with the contract or this Convention, hands the goods over to a carrier and if the goods are not clearly identified to the contract by markings on the goods, by shipping documents or otherwise, the seller must give the buyer notice of the consignment specifying the goods.

(2) If the seller is bound to arrange for carriage of the goods, he must make such contracts as are necessary for carriage to the place fixed by means of transportation appropriate in the circum-

stances and according to the usual terms for such transportation.

(3) If the seller is not bound to effect insurance in respect of the carriage of the goods, he must, at the buyer's request, provide him with all available information necessary to enable him to effect such insurance.

Article 33

The seller must deliver the goods:

(a) if a date is fixed by or determinable from the contract, on that date;

(b) if a period of time is fixed by or determinable from the contract, at any time within that period unless circumstances indicate that the buyer is to choose a date; or

(c) in any other case, within a reasonable time after the conclusion of the contract.

Article 34

If the seller is bound to hand over documents relating to the goods, he must hand them over at the time and place and in the form required by the contract. If the seller has handed over documents before that time, he may, up to that time, cure any lack of conformity in the documents, if the exercise of this right does not cause the buyer unreasonable inconvenience or unreasonable expense. However, the buyer retains any right to claim damages as provided for in this Convention.

Section Ⅱ. Conformity of the goods and third party claims

Article 35

(1) The seller must deliver goods which are of the quantity, quality and description required by the contract and which are contained or packaged in the manner required by the contract.

(2) Except where the parties have agreed otherwise, the goods do not conform with the contract unless they:

(a) are fit for the purposes for which goods of the same description would ordinarily be used;

(b) are fit for any particular purpose expressly or impliedly made known to the seller at the time of the conclusion of the contract, except where the circumstances show that the buyer did not rely, or that it was unreasonable for him to rely, on the seller's skill and judgement;

(c) possess the qualities of goods which the seller has held out to the buyer as a sample or model;

(d) are contained or packaged in the manner usual for such goods or, where there is no such manner, in a manner adequate to preserve and protect the goods.

(3) The seller is not liable under subparagraphs (a) to (d) of the preceding paragraph for any lack of conformity of the goods if at the time of the conclusion of the contract the buyer knew or could not have been unaware of such lack of conformity.

Article 36

(1) The seller is liable in accordance with the contract and this Convention for any lack of conformity which exists at the time when the risk passes to the buyer, even though the lack of conformity becomes apparent only after that time.

(2) The seller is also liable for any lack of conformity which occurs after the time indicated in

the preceding paragraph and which is due to a breach of any of his obligations, including a breach of any guarantee that for a period of time the goods will remain fit for their ordinary purpose or for some particular purpose or will retain specified qualities or characteristics.

Article 37

If the seller has delivered goods before the date for delivery, he may, up to that date, deliver any missing part or make up any deficiency in the quantity of the goods delivered, or deliver goods in replacement of any non-conforming goods delivered or remedy any lack of conformity in the goods delivered, provided that the exercise of this right does not cause the buyer unreasonable inconvenience or unreasonable expense. However, the buyer retains any right to claim damages as provided for in this Convention.

Article 38

(1) The buyer must examine the goods, or cause them to be examined, within as short a period as is practicable in the circumstances.

(2) If the contract involves carriage of the goods, examination may be deferred until after the goods have arrived at their destination.

(3) If the goods are redirected in transit or redispatched by the buyer without a reasonable opportunity for examination by him and at the time of the conclusion of the contract the seller knew or ought to have known of the possibility of such redirection or redispatch, examination may be deferred until after the goods have arrived at the new destination.

Article 39

(1) The buyer loses the right to rely on a lack of conformity of the goods if he does not give notice to the seller specifying the nature of the lack of conformity within a reasonable time after he has discovered it or ought to have discovered it.

(2) In any event, the buyer loses the right to rely on a lack of conformity of the goods if he does not give the seller notice thereof at the latest within a period of two years from the date on which the goods were actually handed over to the buyer, unless this time-limit is inconsistent with a contractual period of guarantee.

Article 40

The seller is not entitled to rely on the provisions of articles 38 and 39 if the lack of conformity relates to facts of which he knew or could not have been unaware and which he did not disclose to the buyer.

Article 41

The seller must deliver goods which are free from any right or claim of a third party, unless the buyer agreed to take the goods subject to that right or claim. However, if such right or claim is based on industrial property or other intellectual property, the seller's obligation is governed by article 42.

Article 42

(1) The seller must deliver goods which are free from any right or claim of a third party based

on industrial property or other intellectual property, of which at the time of the conclusion of the contract the seller knew or could not have been unaware, provided that the right or claim is based on industrial property or other intellectual property:

(a) under the law of the State where the goods will be resold or otherwise used, if it was contemplated by the parties at the time of the conclusion of the contract that the goods would be resold or otherwise used in that State; or

(b) in any other case, under the law of the State where the buyer has his place of business.

(2) The obligation of the seller under the preceding paragraph does not extend to cases where:

(a) at the time of the conclusion of the contract the buyer knew or could not have been unaware of the right or claim; or

(b) the right or claim results from the seller's compliance with technical drawings, designs, formulae or other such specifications furnished by the buyer.

Article 43

(1) The buyer loses the right to rely on the provisions of article 41 or article 42 if he does not give notice to the seller specifying the nature of the right or claim of the third party within a reasonable time after he has become aware or ought to have become aware of the right or claim.

(2) The seller is not entitled to rely on the provisions of the preceding paragraph if he knew of the right or claim of the third party and the nature of it.

Article 44

Notwithstanding the provisions of paragraph (1) of article 39 and paragraph (1) of article 43, the buyer may reduce the price in accordance with article 50 or claim damages, except for loss of profit, if he has a reasonable excuse for his failure to give the required notice.

Section Ⅲ. Remedies for breach of contract by the seller

Article 45

(1) If the seller fails to perform any of his obligations under the contract or this Convention, the buyer may:

(a) exercise the rights provided in articles 46 to 52;

(b) claim damages as provided in articles 74 to 77.

(2) The buyer is not deprived of any right he may have to claim damages by exercising his right to other remedies.

(3) No period of grace may be granted to the seller by a court or arbitral tribunal when the buyer resorts to a remedy for breach of contract.

Article 46

(1) The buyer may require performance by the seller of his obligations unless the buyer has resorted to a remedy which is inconsistent with this requirement.

(2) If the goods do not conform with the contract, the buyer may require delivery of substitute goods only if the lack of conformity constitutes a fundamental breach of contract and a request for substitute goods is made either in conjunction with notice given under article 39 or within a reasona-

ble time thereafter.

(3) If the goods do not conform with the contract, the buyer may require the seller to remedy the lack of conformity by repair, unless this is unreasonable having regard to all the circumstances. A request for repair must be made either in conjunction with notice given under article 39 or within a reasonable time thereafter.

Article 47

(1) The buyer may fix an additional period of time of reasonable length for performance by the seller of his obligations.

(2) Unless the buyer has received notice from the seller that he will not perform within the period so fixed, the buyer may not, during that period, resort to any remedy for breach of contract. However, the buyer is not deprived thereby of any right he may have to claim damages for delay in performance.

Article 48

(1) Subject to article 49, the seller may, even after the date for delivery, remedy at his own expense any failure to perform his obligations, if he can do so without unreasonable delay and without causing the buyer unreasonable inconvenience or uncertainty of reimbursement by the seller of expenses advanced by the buyer. However, the buyer retains any right to claim damages as provided for in this Convention.

(2) If the seller requests the buyer to make known whether he will accept performance and the buyer does not comply with the request within a reasonable time, the seller may perform within the time indicated in his request. The buyer may not, during that period of time, resort to any remedy which is inconsistent with performance by the seller.

(3) A notice by the seller that he will perform within a specified period of time is assumed to include a request, under the preceding paragraph, that the buyer make known his decision.

(4) A request or notice by the seller under paragraph (2) or (3) of this article is not effective unless received by the buyer.

Article 49

(1) The buyer may declare the contract avoided:

(a) if the failure by the seller to perform any of his obligations under the contract or this Convention amounts to a fundamental breach of contract; or

(b) in case of non-delivery, if the seller does not deliver the goods within the additional period of time fixed by the buyer in accordance with paragraph (1) of article 47 or declares that he will not deliver within the period so fixed.

(2) However, in cases where the seller has delivered the goods, the buyer loses the right to declare the contract avoided unless he does so:

(a) in respect of late delivery, within a reasonable time after he has become aware that delivery has been made;

(b) in respect of any breach other than late delivery, within a reasonable time:

(i) after he knew or ought to have known of the breach;

(ii) after the expiration of any additional period of time fixed by the buyer in accordance with paragraph (1) of article 47, or after the seller has declared that he will not perform his obligations within such an additional period; or

(iii) after the expiration of any additional period of time indicated by the seller in accordance with paragraph (2) of article 48, or after the buyer has declared that he will not accept performance.

Article 50

If the goods do not conform with the contract and whether or not the price has already been paid, the buyer may reduce the price in the same proportion as the value that the goods actually delivered had at the time of the delivery bears to the value that conforming goods would have had at that time. However, if the seller remedies any failure to perform his obligations in accordance with article 37 or article 48 or if the buyer refuses to accept performance by the seller in accordance with those articles, the buyer may not reduce the price.

Article 51

(1) If the seller delivers only a part of the goods or if only a part of the goods delivered is in conformity with the contract, articles 46 to 50 apply in respect of the part which is missing or which does not conform.

(2) The buyer may declare the contract avoided in its entirety only if the failure to make delivery completely or in conformity with the contract amounts to a fundamental breach of the contract.

Article 52

(1) If the seller delivers the goods before the date fixed, the buyer may take delivery or refuse to take delivery.

(2) If the seller delivers a quantity of goods greater than that provided for in the contract, the buyer may take delivery or refuse to take delivery of the excess quantity. If the buyer takes delivery of all or part of the excess quantity, he must pay for it at the contract rate.

Chapter Ⅲ

OBLIGATIONS OF THE BUYER

Article 53

The buyer must pay the price for the goods and take delivery of them as required by the contract and this Convention.

Section Ⅰ. Payment of the price

Article 54

The buyer's obligation to pay the price includes taking such steps and complying with such formalities as may be required under the contract or any laws and regulations to enable payment to be made.

Article 55

Where a contract has been validly concluded but does not expressly or implicitly fix or make provision for determining the price, the parties are considered, in the absence of any indication to the contrary, to have impliedly made reference to the price generally charged at the time of the conclusion of the contract for such goods sold under comparable circumstances in the trade concerned.

Article 56

If the price is fixed according to the weight of the goods, in case of doubt it is to be determined by the net weight.

Article 57

(1) If the buyer is not bound to pay the price at any other particular place, he must pay it to the seller:

(a) at the seller's place of business; or

(b) if the payment is to be made against the handing over of the goods or of documents, at the place where the handing over takes place.

(2) The seller must bear any increases in the expenses incidental to payment which is caused by a change in his place of business subsequent to the conclusion of the contract.

Article 58

(1) If the buyer is not bound to pay the price at any other specific time, he must pay it when the seller places either the goods or documents controlling their disposition at the buyer's disposal in accordance with the contract and this Convention. The seller may make such payment a condition for handing over the goods or documents.

(2) If the contract involves carriage of the goods, the seller may dispatch the goods on terms whereby the goods, or documents controlling their disposition, will not be handed over to the buyer except against payment of the price.

(3) The buyer is not bound to pay the price until he has had an opportunity to examine the goods, unless the procedures for delivery or payment agreed upon by the parties are inconsistent with his having such an opportunity.

Article 59

The buyer must pay the price on the date fixed by or determinable from the contract and this Convention without the need for any request or compliance with any formality on the part of the seller.

Section Ⅱ. Taking delivery

Article 60

The buyer's obligation to take delivery consists:

(a) in doing all the acts which could reasonably be expected of him in order to enable the seller to make delivery; and

(b) in taking over the goods.

Section Ⅲ. Remedies for breach of contract by the buyer

Article 61

(1) If the buyer fails to perform any of his obligations under the contract or this Convention,

the seller may:

(a) exercise the rights provided in articles 62 to 65;

(b) claim damages as provided in articles 74 to 77.

(2) The seller is not deprived of any right he may have to claim damages by exercising his right to other remedies.

(3) No period of grace may be granted to the buyer by a court or arbitral tribunal when the seller resorts to a remedy for breach of contract.

Article 62

The seller may require the buyer to pay the price, take delivery or perform his other obligations, unless the seller has resorted to a remedy which is inconsistent with this requirement.

Article 63

(1) The seller may fix an additional period of time of reasonable length for performance by the buyer of his obligations.

(2) Unless the seller has received notice from the buyer that he will not perform within the period so fixed, the seller may not, during that period, resort to any remedy for breach of contract. However, the seller is not deprived thereby of any right he may have to claim damages for delay in performance.

Article 64

(1) The seller may declare the contract avoided:

(a) if the failure by the buyer to perform any of his obligations under the contract or this Convention amounts to a fundamental breach of contract; or

(b) if the buyer does not, within the additional period of time fixed by the seller in accordance with paragraph (1) of article 63, perform his obligation to pay the price or take delivery of the goods, or if he declares that he will not do so within the period so fixed.

(2) However, in cases where the buyer has paid the price, the seller loses the right to declare the contract avoided unless he does so:

(a) in respect of late performance by the buyer, before the seller has become aware that performance has been rendered; or

(b) in respect of any breach other than late performance by the buyer, within a reasonable time:

(i) after the seller knew or ought to have known of the breach; or

(ii) after the expiration of any additional period of time fixed by the seller in accordance with paragraph (1) of article 63, or after the buyer has declared that he will not perform his obligations within such an additional period.

Article 65

(1) If under the contract the buyer is to specify the form, measurement or other features of the goods and he fails to make such specification either on the date agreed upon or within a reasonable time after receipt of a request from the seller, the seller may, without prejudice to any other rights

he may have, make the specification himself in accordance with the requirements of the buyer that may be known to him.

(2) If the seller makes the specification himself, he must inform the buyer of the details thereof and must fix a reasonable time within which the buyer may make a different specification. If, after receipt of such a communication, the buyer fails to do so within the time so fixed, the specification made by the seller is binding.

Chapter Ⅳ

PASSING OF RISK

Article 66

Loss of or damage to the goods after the risk has passed to the buyer does not discharge him from his obligation to pay the price, unless the loss or damage is due to an act or omission of the seller.

Article 67

(1) If the contract of sale involves carriage of the goods and the seller is not bound to hand them over at a particular place, the risk passes to the buyer when the goods are handed over to the first carrier for transmission to the buyer in accordance with the contract of sale. If the seller is bound to hand the goods over to a carrier at a particular place, the risk does not pass to the buyer until the goods are handed over to the carrier at that place. The fact that the seller is authorized to retain documents controlling the disposition of the goods does not affect the passage of the risk.

(2) Nevertheless, the risk does not pass to the buyer until the goods are clearly identified to the contract, whether by markings on the goods, by shipping documents, by notice given to the buyer or otherwise.

Article 68

The risk in respect of goods sold in transit passes to the buyer from the time of the conclusion of the contract. However, if the circumstances so indicate, the risk is assumed by the buyer from the time the goods were handed over to the carrier who issued the documents embodying the contract of carriage. Nevertheless, if at the time of the conclusion of the contract of sale the seller knew or ought to have known that the goods had been lost or damaged and did not disclose this to the buyer, the loss or damage is at the risk of the seller.

Article 69

(1) In cases not within articles 67 and 68, the risk passes to the buyer when he takes over the goods or, if he does not do so in due time, from the time when the goods are placed at his disposal and he commits a breach of contract by failing to take delivery.

(2) However, if the buyer is bound to take over the goods at a place other than a place of business of the seller, the risk passes when delivery is due and the buyer is aware of the fact that the goods are placed at his disposal at that place.

(3) If the contract relates to goods not then identified, the goods are considered not to be placed at the disposal of the buyer until they are clearly identified to the contract.

Article 70

If the seller has committed a fundamental breach of contract, articles 67, 68 and 69 do not impair the remedies available to the buyer on account of the breach.

Chapter Ⅴ

PROVISIONS COMMON TO THE OBLIGATIONS OF THE SELLER AND OF THE BUYER

Section Ⅰ. Anticipatory breach and instalment contracts

Article 71

(1) A party may suspend the performance of his obligations if, after the conclusion of the contract, it becomes apparent that the other party will not perform a substantial part of his obligations as a result of:

(a) a serious deficiency in his ability to perform or in his creditworthiness; or

(b) his conduct in preparing to perform or in performing the contract.

(2) If the seller has already dispatched the goods before the grounds described in the preceding paragraph become evident, he may prevent the handing over of the goods to the buyer even though the buyer holds a document which entitles him to obtain them. The present paragraph relates only to the rights in the goods as between the buyer and the seller.

(3) A party suspending performance, whether before or after dispatch of the goods, must immediately give notice of the suspension to the other party and must continue with performance if the other party provides adequate assurance of his performance.

Article 72

(1) If prior to the date for performance of the contract it is clear that one of the parties will commit a fundamental breach of contract, the other party may declare the contract avoided.

(2) If time allows, the party intending to declare the contract avoided must give reasonable notice to the other party in order to permit him to provide adequate assurance of his performance.

(3) The requirements of the preceding paragraph do not apply if the other party has declared that he will not perform his obligations.

Article 73

(1) In the case of a contract for delivery of goods by instalments, if the failure of one party to perform any of his obligations in respect of any instalment constitutes a fundamental breach of contract with respect to that instalment, the other party may declare the contract avoided with respect to that instalment.

(2) If one party's failure to perform any of his obligations in respect of any instalment gives the other party good grounds to conclude that a fundamental breach of contract will occur with respect to future instalments, he may declare the contract avoided for the future, provided that he does so within a reasonable time.

(3) A buyer who declares the contract avoided in respect of any delivery may, at the same time, declare it avoided in respect of deliveries already made or of future deliveries if, by reason of

their interdependence, those deliveries could not be used for the purpose contemplated by the parties at the time of the conclusion of the contract.

Section Ⅱ. Damages

Article 74

Damages for breach of contract by one party consist of a sum equal to the loss, including loss of profit, suffered by the other party as a consequence of the breach. Such damages may not exceed the loss which the party in breach foresaw or ought to have foreseen at the time of the conclusion of the contract, in the light of the facts and matters of which he then knew or ought to have known, as a possible consequence of the breach of contract.

Article 75

If the contract is avoided and if, in a reasonable manner and within a reasonable time after avoidance, the buyer has bought goods in replacement or the seller has resold the goods, the party claiming damages may recover the difference between the contract price and the price in the substitute transaction as well as any further damages recoverable under article 74.

Article 76

(1) If the contract is avoided and there is a current price for the goods, the party claiming damages may, if he has not made a purchase or resale under article 75, recover the difference between the price fixed by the contract and the current price at the time of avoidance as well as any further damages recoverable under article 74. If, however, the party claiming damages has avoided the contract after taking over the goods, the current price at the time of such taking over shall be applied instead of the current price at the time of avoidance.

(2) For the purposes of the preceding paragraph, the current price is the price prevailing at the place where delivery of the goods should have been made or, if there is no current price at that place, the price at such other place as serves as a reasonable substitute, making due allowance for differences in the cost of transporting the goods.

Article 77

A party who relies on a breach of contract must take such measures as are reasonable in the circumstances to mitigate the loss, including loss of profit, resulting from the breach. If he fails to take such measures, the party in breach may claim a reduction in the damages in the amount by which the loss should have been mitigated.

Section Ⅲ. Interest

Article 78

If a party fails to pay the price or any other sum that is in arrears, the other party is entitled to interest on it, without prejudice to any claim for damages recoverable under article 74.

Section Ⅳ. Exemptions

Article 79

(1) A party is not liable for a failure to perform any of his obligations if he proves that the failure was due to an impediment beyond his control and that he could not reasonably be expected to

have taken the impediment into account at the time of the conclusion of the contract or to have avoided or overcome it or its consequences.

(2) If the party's failure is due to the failure by a third person whom he has engaged to perform the whole or a part of the contract, that party is exempt from liability only if:

(a) he is exempt under the preceding paragraph; and

(b) the person whom he has so engaged would be so exempt if the provisions of that paragraph were applied to him.

(3) The exemption provided by this article has effect for the period during which the impediment exists.

(4) The party who fails to perform must give notice to the other party of the impediment and its effect on his ability to perform. If the notice is not received by the other party within a reasonable time after the party who fails to perform knew or ought to have known of the impediment, he is liable for damages resulting from such non-receipt.

(5) Nothing in this article prevents either party from exercising any right other than to claim damages under this Convention.

Article 80

A party may not rely on a failure of the other party to perform, to the extent that such failure was caused by the first party's act or omission.

Section Ⅴ. Effects of avoidance

Article 81

(1) Avoidance of the contract releases both parties from their obligations under it, subject to any damages which may be due. Avoidance does not affect any provision of the contract for the settlement of disputes or any other provision of the contract governing the rights and obligations of the parties consequent upon the avoidance of the contract.

(2) A party who has performed the contract either wholly or in part may claim restitution from the other party of whatever the first party has supplied or paid under the contract. If both parties are bound to make restitution, they must do so concurrently.

Article 82

(1) The buyer loses the right to declare the contract avoided or to require the seller to deliver substitute goods if it is impossible for him to make restitution of the goods substantially in the condition in which he received them.

(2) The preceding paragraph does not apply:

(a) if the impossibility of making restitution of the goods or of making restitution of the goods substantially in the condition in which the buyer received them is not due to his act or omission;

(b) if the goods or part of the goods have perished or deteriorated as a result of the examination provided for in article 38; or

(c) if the goods or part of the goods have been sold in the normal course of business or have been consumed or transformed by the buyer in the course of normal use before he discovered or ought to have discovered the lack of conformity.

Article 83

A buyer who has lost the right to declare the contract avoided or to require the seller to deliver substitute goods in accordance with article 82 retains all other remedies under the contract and this Convention.

Article 84

(1) If the seller is bound to refund the price, he must also pay interest on it, from the date on which the price was paid.

(2) The buyer must account to the seller for all benefits which he has derived from the goods or part of them:

(a) if he must make restitution of the goods or part of them; or

(b) if it is impossible for him to make restitution of all or part of the goods or to make restitution of all or part of the goods substantially in the condition in which he received them, but he has nevertheless declared the contract avoided or required the seller to deliver substitute goods.

Section Ⅵ. Preservation of the goods

Article 85

If the buyer is in delay in taking delivery of the goods or, where payment of the price and delivery of the goods are to be made concurrently, if he fails to pay the price, and the seller is either in possession of the goods or otherwise able to control their disposition, the seller must take such steps as are reasonable in the circumstances to preserve them. He is entitled to retain them until he has been reimbursed his reasonable expenses by the buyer.

Article 86

(1) If the buyer has received the goods and intends to exercise any right under the contract or this Convention to reject them, he must take such steps to preserve them as are reasonable in the circumstances. He is entitled to retain them until he has been reimbursed his reasonable expenses by the seller.

(2) If goods dispatched to the buyer have been placed at his disposal at their destination and he exercises the right to reject them, he must take possession of them on behalf of the seller, provided that this can be done without payment of the price and without unreasonable inconvenience or unreasonable expense. This provision does not apply if the seller or a person authorized to take charge of the goods on his behalf is present at the destination. If the buyer takes possession of the goods under this paragraph, his rights and obligations are governed by the preceding paragraph.

Article 87

A party who is bound to take steps to preserve the goods may deposit them in a warehouse of a third person at the expense of the other party provided that the expense incurred is not unreasonable.

Article 88

(1) A party who is bound to preserve the goods in accordance with article 85 or 86 may sell

them by any appropriate means if there has been an unreasonable delay by the other party in taking possession of the goods or in taking them back or in paying the price or the cost of preservation, provided that reasonable notice of the intention to sell has been given to the other party.

(2) If the goods are subject to rapid deterioration or their preservation would involve unreasonable expense, a party who is bound to preserve the goods in accordance with article 85 or 86 must take reasonable measures to sell them. To the extent possible he must give notice to the other party of his intention to sell.

(3) A party selling the goods has the right to retain out of the proceeds of sale an amount equal to the reasonable expenses of preserving the goods and of selling them. He must account to the other party for the balance.

PART Ⅳ

FINAL PROVISIONS

Article 89

The Secretary-General of the United Nations is hereby designated as the depositary for this Convention.

Article 90

This Convention does not prevail over any international agreement which has already been or may be entered into and which contains provisions concerning the matters governed by this Convention, provided that the parties have their places of business in States parties to such agreement.

Article 91

(1) This Convention is open for signature at the concluding meeting of the United Nations Conference on Contracts for the International Sale of Goods and will remain open for signature by all States at the Headquarters of the United Nations, New York until 30 September 1981.

(2) This Convention is subject to ratification, acceptance or approval by the signatory States.

(3) This Convention is open for accession by all States which are not signatory States as from the date it is open for signature.

(4) Instruments of ratification, acceptance, approval and accession are to be deposited with the Secretary-General of the United Nations.

Article 92

(1) A Contracting State may declare at the time of signature, ratification, acceptance, approval or accession that it will not be bound by Part Ⅱ of this Convention or that it will not be bound by Part Ⅲ of this Convention.

(2) A Contracting State which makes a declaration in accordance with the preceding paragraph in respect of Part Ⅱ or Part Ⅲ of this Convention is not to be considered a Contracting State within paragraph (1) of article 1 of this Convention in respect of matters governed by the Part to which the declaration applies.

Article 93

(1) If a Contracting State has two or more territorial units in which, according to its constitu-

tion, different systems of law are applicable in relation to the matters dealt with in this Convention, it may, at the time of signature, ratification, acceptance, approval or accession, declare that this Convention is to extend to all its territorial units or only to one or more of them, and may amend its declaration by submitting another declaration at any time.

(2) These declarations are to be notified to the depositary and are to state expressly the territorial units to which the Convention extends.

(3) If, by virtue of a declaration under this article, this Convention extends to one or more but not all of the territorial units of a Contracting State, and if the place of business of a party is located in that State, this place of business, for the purposes of this Convention, is considered not to be in a Contracting State, unless it is in a territorial unit to which the Convention extends.

(4) If a Contracting State makes no declaration under paragraph (1) of this article, the Convention is to extend to all territorial units of that State.

Article 94

(1) Two or more Contracting States which have the same or closely related legal rules on matters governed by this Convention may at any time declare that the Convention is not to apply to contracts of sale or to their formation where the parties have their places of business in those States. Such declarations may be made jointly or by reciprocal unilateral declarations.

(2) A Contracting State which has the same or closely related legal rules on matters governed by this Convention as one or more non-Contracting States may at any time declare that the Convention is not to apply to contracts of sale or to their formation where the parties have their places of business in those States.

(3) If a State which is the object of a declaration under the preceding paragraph subsequently becomes a Contracting State, the declaration made will, as from the date on which the Convention enters into force in respect of the new Contracting State, have the effect of a declaration made under paragraph (1), provided that the new Contracting State joins in such declaration or makes a reciprocal unilateral declaration.

Article 95

Any State may declare at the time of the deposit of its instrument of ratification, acceptance, approval or accession that it will not be bound by subparagraph (1)(b) of article 1 of this Convention.

Article 96

A Contracting State whose legislation requires contracts of sale to be concluded in or evidenced by writing may at any time make a declaration in accordance with article 12 that any provision of article 11, article 29, or Part Ⅱ of this Convention, that allows a contract of sale or its modification or termination by agreement or any offer, acceptance, or other indication of intention to be made in any form other than in writing, does not apply where any party has his place of business in that State.

Article 97

(1) Declarations made under this Convention at the time of signature are subject to confirma-

tion upon ratification, acceptance or approval.

(2) Declarations and confirmations of declarations are to be in writing and be formally notified to the depositary.

(3) A declaration takes effect simultaneously with the entry into force of this Convention in respect of the State concerned. However, a declaration of which the depositary receives formal notification after such entry into force takes effect on the first day of the month following the expiration of six months after the date of its receipt by the depositary. Reciprocal unilateral declarations under article 94 take effect on the first day of the month following the expiration of six months after the receipt of the latest declaration by the depositary.

(4) Any State which makes a declaration under this Convention may withdraw it at any time by a formal notification in writing addressed to the depositary. Such withdrawal is to take effect on the first day of the month following the expiration of six months after the date of the receipt of the notification by the depositary.

(5) A withdrawal of a declaration made under article 94 renders inoperative, as from the date on which the withdrawal takes effect, any reciprocal declaration made by another State under that article.

Article 98

No reservations are permitted except those expressly authorized in this Convention.

Article 99

(1) This Convention enters into force, subject to the provisions of paragraph (6) of this article, on the first day of the month following the expiration of twelve months after the date of deposit of the tenth instrument of ratification, acceptance, approval or accession, including an instrument which contains a declaration made under article 92.

(2) When a State ratifies, accepts, approves or accedes to this Convention after the deposit of the tenth instrument of ratification, acceptance, approval or accession, this Convention, with the exception of the Part excluded, enters into force in respect of that State, subject to the provisions of paragraph (6) of this article, on the first day of the month following the expiration of twelve months after the date of the deposit of its instrument of ratification, acceptance, approval or accession.

(3) A State which ratifies, accepts, approves or accedes to this Convention and is a party to either or both the Convention relating to a Uniform Law on the Formation of Contracts for the International Sale of Goods done at the Hague on 1 July 1964 (1964 Hague Formation Convention) and the Convention relating to a Uniform Law on the International Sale of Goods done at the Hague on 1 July 1964 (1964 Hague Sales Convention) shall at the same time denounce, as the case may be, either or both the 1964 Hague Sales Convention and the 1964 Hague Formation Convention by notifying the Government of the Netherlands to that effect.

(4) A State party to the 1964 Hague Sales Convention which ratifies, accepts, approves or accedes to the present Convention and declares or has declared under article 52 that it will not be bound by Part Ⅱ of this Convention shall at the time of ratification, acceptance, approval or acces-

sion denounce the 1964 Hague Sales Convention by notifying the Government of the Netherlands to that effect.

(5) A State party to the 1964 Hague Formation Convention which ratifies, accepts, approves or accedes to the present Convention and declares or has declared under article 92 that it will not be bound by Part Ⅲ of this Convention shall at the time of ratification, acceptance, approval or accession denounce the 1964 Hague Formation Convention by notifying the Government of the Netherlands to that effect.

(6) For the purpose of this article, ratifications, acceptances, approvals and accessions in respect of this Convention by States parties to the 1964 Hague Formation Convention or to the 1964 Hague Sales Convention shall not be effective until such denunciations as may be required on the part of those States in respect of the latter two Conventions have themselves become effective. The depositary of this Convention shall consult with the Government of the Netherlands, as the depositary of the 1964 Conventions, so as to ensure necessary co-ordination in this respect.

Article 100

(1) This Convention applies to the formation of a contract only when the proposal for concluding the contract is made on or after the date when the Convention enters into force in respect of the Contracting States referred to in subparagraph (1)(a) or the Contracting State referred to in subparagraph (1)(b) of article 1.

(2) This Convention applies only to contracts concluded on or after the date when the Convention enters into force in respect of the Contracting States referred to in subparagraph (1)(a) or the Contracting State referred to in subparagraph (1)(b) of article 1.

Article 101

(1) A Contracting State may denounce this Convention, or Part Ⅱ or Part Ⅲ of the Convention, by a formal notification in writing addressed to the depositary.

(2) The denunciation takes effect on the first day of the month following the expiration of twelve months after the notification is received by the depositary. Where a longer period for the denunciation to take effect is specified in the notification, the denunciation takes effect upon the expiration of such longer period after the notification is received by the depositary.

DONE at Vienna, this day of eleventh day of April, one thousand nine hundred and eighty, in a single original, of which the Arabic, Chinese, English, French, Russian and Spanish texts are equally authentic.

IN WITNESS WHEREOF the undersigned plenipotentiaries, being duly authorized by their respective Governments, have signed this Convention.

Appendix 3. Uniform Rules for Collections, ICC Publication No. 522

ICC Uniform Rules for Collections

ICC Publication No. 522

1995 Revision in force as of January 1, 1996

CONTENTs

A. General Provisions and Definitions

Article 1

Application of URC 522

a. The Uniform Rules for Collections, 1995 Revision, ICC Publication No. 522, shall apply to all collections as defined in Article 2 where such rules are incorporated into the text of the "collection instruction" referred to in Article 4 and are binding on all parties thereto unless otherwise expressly agreed or contrary to the provisions of a national, state or local law and/or regulation which cannot be departed from.

b. Banks shall have no obligation to handle either a collection or any collection instruction or subsequent related instructions.

c. If a bank elects, for any reason, not to handle a collection or any related instructions received by it, it must advise the party from whom it received the collection or the instructions by telecommunication or, if that is not possible, by other expeditious means, without delay.

Article 2

Definition of Collection

For the purposes of these Articles:

a. "Collection" means the handling by banks of documents as defined in sub-Article 2 (b), in accordance with instructions received, in order to:

i. obtain payment and/or acceptance, or

ii. deliver documents against payment and/or against acceptance, or

iii. deliver documents on other terms and conditions.

b. "Documents" means financial documents and/or commercial documents:

i. "Financial documents" means bills of exchange, promissory notes, cheques, or other similar instruments used for obtaining the payment of money;

ii. "Commercial documents" means invoice, transport documents, documents of title or other similar documents, or any other documents whatsoever, not being financial documents.

c. "Clean collection" means collection of financial documents not accompanied by commercial documents.

d. "Documentary collection" means collection of:

i. Financial documents accompanied by commercial documents;

ii. Commercial documents not accompanied by financial documents.

Article 3

Parties to a collection

a. For the purposes of these Articles the "parties thereto" are:

i. the "principal" who is the party entrusting the handling of a collection to a bank;

ii. the "remitting bank" which is the bank to which the principal has entrusted the handling of a collection;

iii. "collecting bank" which is any bank, other than the remitting bank, involved in processing the collection;

iv. the "presenting bank" which is the collecting bank making presentation to the drawee.

b. The "drawee" is the one to whom presentation is to be made in accordance with the collection instruction.

B. Form and Structure of Collections

Article 4

Collection Instruction

a. i. All documents sent for collection must be accompanied by a collection instruction indicating that the collection is subject to URC 522 and giving complete and precise instructions. Banks are only permitted to act upon the instructions given in such collection instruction, and in accordance with these Rules.

ii. Banks will not examine documents in order to obtain instructions.

iii. Unless otherwise authorized in the collection instruction, banks will disregard any instructions from any party/bank other than the party/bank from whom they received the collections.

b. A collection instruction should contain the following items of information, as appropriate.

i. Details of the bank from which the collection was received including full name, postal and SWIFT addresses, telex, telephone, facsimile numbers and reference.

ii. Details of the principal including full name, postal address, and if applicable telex, telephone and facsimile numbers.

iii. Details of the drawee including full name, postal address, or the domicile at which presentation is to be made and if applicable telex, telephone and facsimile numbers.

iv. Details of the presenting bank, if any, including full name, postal address, and if applicable telex, telephone and facsimile numbers.

v. Amount(s) and currency(ies) to be collected.

vi. List of documents enclosed and the numerical count of each document.

vii. a) Terms and conditions upon which payment and/or acceptance is to be obtained.

b) Terms of delivery of documents against:

1) payment and/or acceptance

2) other terms and conditions

It is the responsibility of the party preparing the collection instruction to ensure that the terms for the delivery of documents are clearly and unambiguously stated, otherwise banks will not be responsible for any consequences arising therefrom.

viii. Charges to be collected, indicating whether they may be waived or not.

ix. Interest to be collected, if applicable, indicating whether it may be waived or not, including:

a) rate of interest;

b) interest period;

c) basis of calculation (for example 360 or 365 days in year) as applicable.

x. Method of payment and form of payment advice.

xi. Instructions in case of non-payment, non-acceptance and/or non-compliance with other instructions.

c. i. Collection instructions should bear the complete address of the drawee or of the domicile at which the presentation is to be made. If the address is incomplete or incorrect, the collecting bank may, without any liability and responsibility on its part, endeavour to ascertain the proper address.

ii. The collecting bank will not be liable or responsible for any ensuing delay as a result of an incomplete/incorrect address being provided.

C. Form of Presentation

Article 5

Presentation

a. For the purposes of these Articles, presentation is the procedure whereby the presenting bank makes the documents available to the drawee as instructed.

b. The collection instruction should state the exact period of time within which any action is to be taken by the drawee.

Expressions such as "first", "prompt", "immediate", and the like should not be used in connection with presentation or with reference to any period of time within which documents have to be taken up or for any other action that is to be taken by the drawee. If such terms are used banks will disregard them.

c. Documents are to be presented to the drawee in the form in which they are received, except that banks are authorized to affix any necessary stamps, at the expense of the party from whom they received the collection unless otherwise instructed, and to make any necessary endorsements or place any rubber stamps or other identifying marks or symbols customary to or required for the collection operation.

d. For the purpose of giving effect to the instructions of the principal, the remitting bank will utilize the bank nominated by the principal as the collecting bank. In the absence of such nomination, the remitting bank will utilize any bank of its own, or another bank's choice in the country of payment or acceptance or in the country where other terms and conditions have to be complied with.

e. The documents and collection instruction may be sent directly by the remitting bank to the collecting bank or through another bank as intermediary.

f. If the remitting bank does not nominate a specific presenting bank, the collecting bank may utilize a presenting bank of its choice.

Article 6

Sight/Acceptance

In the case of documents payable at sight the presenting bank must make presentation for payment without delay.

In the case of documents payable at a tenor other than sight the presenting bank must, where acceptance is called for, make presentation for acceptance without delay, and where payment is called for, make presentation for payment not later than the appropriate maturity date.

Article 7

Release of Commercial Documents

Documents against Acceptance (D/A) vs. Documents against Payment (D/P)

a. Collections should not contain bills of exchange payable at a future date with instruction that commercial documents are to be delivered against payment.

b. If a collection contains a bill of exchange payable at a future date, the collection instruction should state whether the commercial documents are to be released to the drawee against acceptance (D/A) or against payment (D/P).

In the absence of such statement commercial documents will be released only against payment and the collecting bank will not be responsible for any consequences arising out of any delay in the delivery of documents.

c. If a collection contains a bill of exchange payable at a future date and the collection instruction indicates that commercial documents are to be released against payment, documents will be released only against such payment and the collecting bank will not be responsible for any consequences arising out of any delay in the delivery of documents.

Article 8

Creation of Documents

Where the remitting bank instructs that either the collecting bank or the drawee is to create documents (bills of exchange, promissory notes, trust receipts, letters of undertaking or other documents) that were not included in the collection, the form and wording of such documents shall be provided by the remitting bank, otherwise the collecting bank shall not be liable or responsible for the form and wording of any such document provided by the collecting bank and/or the drawee.

D. Liabilities and Responsibilities

Good Faith and Reasonable Care

Banks will act in good faith and exercise reasonable care.

Article 10

Documents vs. Goods/Services/Performances

a. Goods should not be dispatched directly to the address of a bank or consigned to or to the order of a bank without prior agreement on the part of that bank.

Nevertheless, in the event that goods are dispatched directly to the address of a bank or consigned to or to the order of a bank for release to a drawee against payment or acceptance or upon other terms and conditions without prior agreement on the part of that bank, such bank shall have no obligation to take delivery of the goods, which remain at the risk and responsibility of the party dispatching the goods.

b. Banks have no obligation to take any action in respect of the goods to which a documentary collection relates, including storage and insurance of the goods even when specific instructions are given to do so. Banks will only take such action if, when, and to the extent that they agree to do so in each case, notwithstanding the provisions of sub-Article 1 (c), this rule applies even in the absence of any specific advice to this effect by the collecting bank.

c. Nevertheless, in the case that banks take action for the protection of the goods, whether instructed or not, they assume no liability or responsibility with regard to the fate and/or condition of the goods and/or for any acts and/or omissions on the part of any third parties entrusted with the custody and/or protection of the goods. However, the collecting bank must advise without delay the bank from which the collection instruction was received of any such action taken.

d. Any charges and/or expenses incurred by banks in connection with any action taken to protect the goods will be for the account of the party from whom they received the collection.

e. i. Notwithstanding the provisions of sub-Article 10 (a), where the goods are consigned to or the order of the collecting bank and the drawee has honoured the collection by payment, acceptance or other terms and conditions, and the collecting bank arranges for the release of the goods, the remitting bank shall be deemed to have authorized the collecting bank to do so.

ii. Where a collecting bank on the instructions of the remitting bank or in terms of sub-Article 10 (e) i, arranges for the release of the goods, the remitting bank shall indemnify such collecting bank for all damages and expenses incurred.

Article 11

Disclaimer for Acts of an Instructed Party

a. Banks utilizing the services of another bank or other banks for the purpose of giving effect to the instructions of the principal, do so for the account and at the risk of such principal.

b. Banks assume no liability or responsibility should the instructions they transmit not be carried out, even if they have themselves taken the initiative in the choice of such other bank(s).

c. A party instructing another party to perform services shall be bound by and liable to indemnify the instructed party against all obligations and responsibilities imposed by foreign laws and usages.

Article 12

Disclaimer on Documents Received

a. Banks must determine that the documents received appear to be as listed in the collection instruction and must advise by telecom munication or, if that is not possible, by other expeditious means, without delay, the party from whom the collection instruction was received of any documents missing, or found to be other than listed.

Banks have no further obligation in this respect.

b. If the documents do not appear to be listed, the remitting bank shall be precluded from disputing the type and number of documents received by the collecting bank.

c. Subject to sub-Article 5 (c) and sub-Article 12 (a) and 12 (b) above, banks will present documents as received without further examination.

Article 13

Disclaimer on Effectiveness of Documents

Banks assume no liability or responsibility for the form, sufficiency, accuracy, genuineness, falsification or legal effect of any document (s), or for the general and/or particular conditions stipulated in the document(s) or superimposed thereon; nor do they assume any liability or responsibility for the description, quantity, weight, quality, condition, packing, delivery, value or existence of the goods represented by any document (s), or for the good faith or acts and/or omission, solvency, performance or standing of the consignors, the carriers, the forwarders, the consignees or the insurers of the goods, or any other person whomsoever.

Article 14

Disclaimer on Delays, Loss in Transit and Translation

a. Banks assume no liability or responsibility for the consequences arising out of delay and/or loss in transit of any message (s), letter(s) or document(s), or for delay, mutilation or other error(s) arising in transmission of any telecommunication or for error(s) in translation and/or interpretation of technical terms.

b. Banks will not be liable or responsible for any delays resulting from the need to obtain clarification of any instructions received.

Article 15

Force Majeure

Banks assume no liability or responsibility for consequences arising out of the interruption of their business by Acts of God, riots, civil commotions, insurrections, wars, or any other causes beyond their control or by strikes or lockouts.

E. Payment

Article 16

Payment Without Delay

a. Amounts collected (less charges and/or disbursements and/or expenses where applicable) must be made available without delay to the party from whom the collection instruction was received in accordance with the terms and conditions of the collection instruction.

b. Notwithstanding the provisions of sub-Article 1 (c) and unless otherwise agreed, the collecting bank will effect payment of the amount collected in favour of the remitting bank only.

Article 17

Payment in Local Currency

In the case of documents payable in the currency of the country of payment (local currency), the presenting bank must, unless otherwise instructed in the collection instruction, release the documents to the drawee against payment in local currency only if such currency is immediately available for disposal in the manner specified in the collection instruction.

Article 18

Payment in Foreign Currency

In the case of documents payable in a currency other than of the country of payment (foreign currency), the presenting bank must, unless otherwise instructed in the collection instruction, release the documents to the drawee against payment in the designated foreign currency only if such foreign currency can immediately be remitted in accordance with the instructions given in the collection instruction.

Article 19

Partial Payments

a. In respect of clean collections, partial payments may be accepted if and to the extent to which and on the conditions on which partial payments are authorized by the law in force in the place of payment. The financial document(s) will be released to the drawee only when full payment thereof has been received.

b. In respect of documentary collections, partial payments will only be accepted if specifically authorized in the collection instruction. However, unless otherwise instructed, the presenting bank will release the documents to the drawee only after full payment has been received, and the presenting bank will not be responsible for any consequences arising out of any delay in the delivery of documents.

c. In all cases partial payments will be accepted only subject to compliance with the provisions of either Article 17 or Article 18 as appropriate. Partial payment, if accepted, will be dealt with in accordance with the provisions of Article 16.

F. Interest, Charges and Expenses

Article 20

Interest

a. If the collection instruction specifies that interest is to be collected and the drawee refuses to pay such interest, the presenting bank may deliver the document (s) against payment of acceptance or on other terms and conditions as the case may be, without collecting such interest, unless sub-Article 20 (c) applies.

b. Where such interest is to be collected, the collection instruction must specify the rate of interest, interest period and basis of calculation.

c. Where the collection instruction expressly states that interest may not be waived and the drawee refuses to pay such interest the presenting bank will not deliver documents and will not be responsible for any consequences arising out of any delay in the delivery of document(s). When payment of interest has been refused, the presenting bank must inform by telecommunication or, if that is not possible, by other expeditious means without delay the bank from which the collection instruction was received.

Article 21

Charges and Expenses

a. If the collection instruction specifies that collection charges and/or expenses are to be for account of the drawee and the drawee refuses to pay them, the presenting bank may deliver the document(s) against payment or acceptance or on other terms and conditions as the case may be, without collecting charges and/or expenses, unless sub-Article 21 (b) applies.

Whenever collection charges and/or expenses are so waived they will be for the account of the party from whom the collection was received and may be deducted from the proceeds.

b. Where the collection instruction expressly states that charges and/or expenses may not be waived and the drawee refuses to pay such charges and/or expenses, the presenting bank will not deliver documents and will not be responsible for any consequences arising out of any delay in the delivery of the document(s). When payment of collection charges and/or expenses has been refused the presenting bank must inform by telecommunication or, if that is not possible, by other expeditious means without delay the bank from which the collection instruction was received.

c. In all cases where in the express terms of a collection instruction or under these Rules, disbursements and/or expenses and/or collection charges are to be borne by the principal, the collecting bank(s) shall be entitled to recover promptly outlays in respect of disbursements, a expenses and charges from the bank form which the collection instruction was received, and the remitting bank shall be entitled to recover promptly from the principal any amount so paid out by it, together with its own disbursements, expenses and charges, regardless of the fate of the collection.

d. Banks reserve the right to demand payment of charges and/or expenses in advance from the party from whom the collection instruction was received, to cover costs in attempting to carry out any instructions, and pending receipt of such payment, also reserve the right not to carry out such instructions.

G. Other Provisions

Article 22

Acceptance

The presenting bank is responsible for seeing that the form of the acceptance of a bill of exchange appears to be complete and correct, but is not responsible for the genuineness of any signature or for the authority of any signatory to sign the acceptance.

Article 23

Promissory Notes and Other Instruments

The presenting bank is not responsible fo the genuineness of any signature or for the authority of any signatory to sign a promissory note, receipt, or other instruments.

Article 24

Protest

The collection instruction should give specific instructions regarding protest (or other legal process in lieu thereof), in the event of non-payment or non-acceptance.

In the absence of such specific instructions, the banks concerned with the collection have no obligation to have the document(s) protested (or subjected to other legal process in lieu thereof) for non-payment or non-acceptance.

Any charges and/or expenses incurred by banks in connection with such protest, or other legal process, will be for the account of the party from whom the collection instruction was received.

Article 25

Case-of-Need

If the principal nominates a representative to act as case-of-need in the event of non-payment and/or non-acceptance the collection instruction should clearly and fully indicate the powers of such case-of-need. In the absence of such indication banks will not accept any instructions from the case-of-need.

Article 26

Advices

Collecting banks are to advise fate in accordance with the following rules:

a. Form of Advice

All advices or information from the collecting bank to the bank from which the collection instruction was received? must bear appropriate details including, in all cases, the latter bank's reference as stated in the collection instruction.

b. Method of Advice

It shall be the responsibility of the remitting bank to instruct the collecting bank regarding the method by which the advices detailed in sub – Articles (c) i, (c) ii and (c) iii are to be given. In the absence of such instructions, the collecting bank will send the relative advices by the method of its choice at the expense of the bank from which the collection instruction was received.

c. i. Advice of Payment

The collecting bank must send without delay advice of payment to the bank from which the collection instruction was received, detailing the amount or amounts collected, charges and/or disbursements and/or expenses deducted, where appropriate, and method of disposal of the funds.

ii. Advice of Acceptance

The collecting bank must send without delay advice of acceptance to the bank from which the collection instruction was received.

iii. Advice of Non-payment and/or Non-acceptance

The presenting bank should endeavour to ascertain the reasons for non-payment and/or non-acceptance and advise accordingly, without delay, the bank from which it received the collection instruction.

The presenting bank must send without delay advice of non-payment and/or advice of non-acceptance to the bank from which it received the collection instruction.

On receipt of such advice the remitting bank must give appropriate instructions as to the further handling of the documents. If such instructions are not received by the presenting bank within 60 days after its advice of non-payment and/or non-acceptance, the documents may be returned to the bank from which the collection instruction was received without any further responsibility on the part of the presenting bank.

Appendix 4. Uniform Customs and Practice for Documentary Credits, ICC Publication No. 600

FOREWORD

This revision of the Uniform Customs and Practice for Documentary Credits (commonly called "UCP") is the sixth revision of the rules since they were first promulgated in 1933. It is the fruit of more than three years of work by the International Chamber of Commerce's (ICC) Commission on Banking Technique and Practice.

ICC, which was established in 1919, had as its primary objective facilitating the flow of international trade at a time when nationalism and protectionism posed serious threats to the world trading system. It was in that spirit that the UCP were first introduced – to alleviate the confusion caused by individual countries' promoting their own national rules on letter of credit practice. The objective, since attained, was to create a set of contractual rules that would establish uniformity in that practice, so that practitioners would not have to cope with a plethora of often conflicting national regulations. The universal acceptance of the UCP by practitioners in countries with widely divergent economic and judicial systems is a testament to the rules' success.

It is important to recall that the UCP represent the work of a private international organization, not a governmental body. Since its inception, ICC has insisted on the central role of self-regulation in business practice. These rules, formulated entirely by experts in the private sector, have validated that approach. The UCP remain the most successful set of private rules for trade ever developed.

A range of individuals and groups contributed to the current revision, which is entitled UCP 600. These include the UCP Drafting Group, which sifted through more than 5000 individual comments before arriving at this consensus text; the UCP Consulting Group, consisting of members from more than 25 countries, which served as the advisory body reacting to and proposing changes to the various drafts; the more than 400 members of the ICC Commission on Banking Technique and Practice who made pertinent suggestions for changes in the text; and ICC national committees worldwide which took an active role in consolidating comments from their members. ICC also expresses its gratitude to practitioners in the transport and insurance industries, whose perceptive suggestions honed the final draft.

Guy Sebban

Secretary General

International Chamber of Commerce

INTRODUCTION

In May 2003, the International Chamber of Commerce authorized the ICC Commission on Banking Technique and Practice (Banking Commission) to begin a revision of the Uniform Customs and Practice for Documentary Credits, ICC Publication 500.

As with other revisions, the general objective was to address developments in the banking, transport and insurance industries. Additionally, there was a need to look at the language and style used in the UCP to remove wording that could lead to inconsistent application and interpretation.

When work on the revision started, a number of global surveys indicated that, because of discrepancies, approximately 70% of documents presented under letters of credit were being rejected on first presentation. This obviously had, and continues to have, a negative effect on the letter of credit being seen as a means of payment and, if unchecked, could have serious implications for maintaining or increasing its market share as a recognized means of settlement in international trade. The introduction by banks of a discrepancy fee has highlighted the importance of this issue, especially when the underlying discrepancies have been found to be dubious or unsound. Whilst the number of cases involving litigation has not grown during the lifetime of UCP 500, the introduction of the ICC's Documentary Credit Dispute Resolution Expertise Rules (DOCDEX) in October 1997 (subsequently revised in March 2002) has resulted in more than 60 cases being decided.

To address these and other concerns, the Banking Commission established a Drafting Group to revise UCP 500. It was also decided to create a second group, known as the Consulting Group, to review and advise on early drafts submitted by the Drafting Group. The Consulting Group, made up of over 40 individuals from 26 countries, consisted of banking and transport industry experts. Ably co-chaired by John Turnbull, Deputy General Manager, Sumitomo Mitsui Banking Corporation Europe Ltd., London and Carlo Di Ninni, Adviser, Italian Bankers Association, Rome, the Consulting Group provided valuable input to the Drafting Group prior to release of draft texts to ICC national committees. The Drafting Group began the review process by analyzing the content of the official Opinions issued by the Banking Commission under UCP 500. Some 500 Opinions were reviewed to assess whether the issues involved warranted a change in, an addition to or a deletion of any UCP article. In addition, consideration was given to the content of the four Position Papers issued by the Commission in September 1994, the two Decisions issued by the Commission (concerning the introduction of the euro and the determination of what constituted an original document under UCP 500 sub-article 20(b) and the decisions issued in DOCDEX cases. During the revision process, notice was taken of the considerable work that had been completed in creating the *International Standard Banking Practice for the Examination of Documents under Documentary Credits* (ISBP), ICC Publication 645. This publication has evolved into a necessary companion to the UCP for determining compliance of documents with the terms of letters of credit. It is the expectation of the Drafting Group and the Banking Commission that the application of the principles contained in the ISBP, including subsequent revisions thereof, will continue during the time UCP 600 is in force. At the time UCP 600 is implemented, there will be an updated version of the ISBP to bring its contents in line with the substance and style of the new rules. The four Position Papers issued in September 1994 were issued subject to their application under UCP 500; therefore, they will not be applicable under UCP 600. The essence of the Decision covering the determination of an original document has been incorporated into the text of UCP 600. The outcome of the DOCDEX cases were invariably based on existing ICC Banking Commission Opinions and therefore contained no specific issues that required addressing in these rules. One of the structural changes to the UCP is the introduction of articles covering definitions (article 2) and interpretations (article 3). In providing definitions of roles played by banks and the meaning of specific terms and events, UCP 600 avoids the necessity of repetitive text to explain their interpretation and application. Similarly, the article covering interpretations aims to take the ambiguity out of vague or unclear language that appears in letters of credit and to provide a definitive elucidation of other characteristics of the UCP or the credit. During the course of the last three years, ICC national committees were canvassed on a range of issues to determine their preferences on alternative texts submitted by the Drafting Group. The results of this exercise and the considerable input from national committees on individual items in the text is reflected in the content of UCP 600. The Drafting Group considered, not only the current practice relative to the documentary credit, but also tried to envisage the future evolution of that practice. This revision of the UCP represents the culmination of over three years of extensive analysis, review, debate and compromise amongst the various members of the Drafting Group, the members of the Banking Commission and the respective ICC national committees. Valuable comment has also been received from the ICC Commission on Transport and Logistics, the Commission on Commercial Law and Practice and the Committee on Insurance. It is not appropriate for this publication to provide an explanation as to why an article has been worded in such a way or what is intended by its incorporation into the rules. For those interested in understanding the rationale and interpretation of the articles of UCP 600, this information will be found in the Commentary to the rules, ICC Publication 601, which represents the Drafting Group's views. On behalf of the Drafting Group I would like to extend our deep appreciation to the members of the Consulting Group, ICC national committees and members of the Banking Commission for their professional comments and their constructive participation in this process. Special thanks are due to the members of the Drafting Group and their institutions, who are listed below in alphabetical order. Nicole Keller – Vice President, Service International Products, Dresdner Bank AG, Frankfurt, Germany; Representative to the ICC Commission on Banking Technique and Practice; Laurence Kooy – Legal Adviser, BNP Paribas, Paris, France; Representative to the ICC Commission on Banking Technique and Practice.

Katja Lehr – Business Manager, Trade Services Standards, SWIFT, La Hulpe, Belgium, then Vice President, Membership Representation, International Financial Services Association, New Jersey, USA; Representative to the ICC Commission on Banking Technique and Practice;

Ole Malmqvist – Vice President, Danske Bank, Copenhagen, Denmark; Representative to the ICC Commission on Banking Technique and Practice;

Paul Miserez – Head of Trade Finance Standards, SWIFT, La Hulpe, Belgium; Representative to the ICC Commission on Banking Technique and Practice; René Mueller – Director, Credit Suisse, Zurich, Switzerland; Representative to the ICC Commission on Banking Technique and Practice;

Chee Seng Soh – Consultant, Association of Banks in Singapore, Singapore;

Representative to the ICC Commission on Banking Technique and Practice;

Dan Taylor – President and CEO, International Financial Services Association, New Jersey USA; Vice Chairman, ICC Commission on Banking Technique and Practice; Alexander Zelenov – Director, Vnesheconombank, Moscow, Russia; Vice Chairman, ICC Commission on Banking Technique and Practice; Ron Katz – Policy Manager, ICC Commission on Banking Technique and Practice, International Chamber of Commerce, Paris, France. The undersigned had the pleasure of chairing the Drafting Group. It was through the generous giving of their knowledge, time and energy that this revision was accomplished so successfully. As Chair of the Drafting Group, I would like to extend to them and to their institutions my gratitude for their contribution, for a job well done and for their friendship. I would also like to extend my sincere thanks to the management of ABN AMRO Bank N. V. , for their understanding, patience and support during the course of this revision process. Gary Collyer Corporate Director, ABN AMRO Bank N. V. , London, England and Technical Adviser to the ICC Commission on Banking Technique and Practice.

November 2006

Article 1 Application of UCP

The Uniform Customs and Practice for Documentary Credits, 2007 Revision, ICC Publication no. 600 ("UCP") are rules that apply to any documentary credit ("credit") (including, to the extent to which they may be applicable, any standby letter of credit) when the text of the credit expressly indicates that it is subject to these rules. They are binding on all parties thereto unless expressly modified or excluded by the credit.

Article 2 Definitions

For the purpose of these rules:

Advising bank means the bank that advises the credit at the request of the issuing bank.

Applicant means the party on whose request the credit is issued.

Banking day means a day on which a bank is regularly open at the place at which an act subject to these rules is to be performed.

Beneficiary means the party in whose favour a credit is issued.

Complying presentation means a presentation that is in accordance with the terms and conditions of the credit, the applicable provisions of these rules and international standard banking practice.

Confirmation means a definite undertaking of the confirming bank, in addition to that of the issuing bank, to honour or negotiate a complying presentation.

Confirming bank means the bank that adds its confirmation to a credit upon the issuing bank's authorization or request.

Credit means any arrangement, however named or described, that is irrevocable and thereby constitutes a definite undertaking of the issuing bank to honour a complying presentation.

Honour means:

a. to pay at sight if the credit is available by sight payment.

b. to incur a deferred payment undertaking and pay at maturity if the credit is available by deferred payment.

c. to accept a bill of exchange ("draft") drawn by the beneficiary and pay at maturity if the credit is available by acceptance.

Issuing bank means the bank that issues a credit at the request of an applicant or on its own behalf.

Negotiation means the purchase by the nominated bank of drafts (drawn on a bank other than the nominated bank) and/or documents under a complying presentation, by advancing or agreeing to advance funds to the beneficiary on or before the banking day on which reimbursement is due to the nominated bank.

Nominated bank means the bank with which the credit is available or any bank in the case of a credit available with any bank.

Presentation means either the delivery of documents under a credit to the issuing bank or nominated bank or the documents so delivered.

Presenter means a beneficiary, bank or other party that makes a presentation.

Article 3 Interpretations

For the purpose of these rules:

Where applicable, words in the singular include the plural and in the plural include the singular.

A credit is irrevocable even if there is no indication to that effect.

A document may be signed by handwriting, facsimile signature, perforated signature, stamp, symbol or any other mechanical or electronic method of authentication.

A requirement for a document to be legalized, visaed, certified or similar will be satisfied by any signature, mark, stamp or label on the document which appears to satisfy that requirement.

Branches of a bank in different countries are considered to be separate banks.

Terms such as "first class", "well known", "qualified", "independent", "official", "competent" or "local" used to describe the issuer of a document allow any issuer except the beneficiary to issue that document.

Unless required to be used in a document, words such as "prompt", "immediately" or "as soon as possible" will be disregarded.

The expression "on or about" or similar will be interpreted as a stipulation that an event is to occur during a period of five calendar days before until five calendar days after the specified date, both start and end dates included.

The words "to", "until", "till", "from" and "between" when used to determine a period of shipment include the date or dates mentioned, and the words "before" and "after" exclude the date mentioned.

The words "from" and "after" when used to determine a maturity date exclude the date mentioned.

The terms "first half" and "second half" of a month shall be construed respectively as the 1st to the 15th and the 16th to the last day of the month, all dates inclusive.

The terms "beginning", "middle" and "end" of a month shall be construed respectively as the 1st to the 10th, the 11th to the 20th and the 21st to the last day of the month, all dates inclusive.

Article 4 Credits v. Contracts

a. A credit by its nature is a separate transaction from the sale or other contract on which it may be based. Banks are in no way concerned with or bound by such contract, even if any reference whatsoever to it is included in the credit. Consequently, the undertaking of a bank to honour, to negotiate or to fulfil any other obligation under the credit is not subject to claims or defences by the applicant resulting from its relationships with the issuing bank or the beneficiary. A beneficiary can in no case avail itself of the contractual relationships existing between banks or between the applicant and the issuing bank.

b. An issuing bank should discourage any attempt by the applicant to include, as an integral part of the credit, copies of the underlying contract, proforma invoice and the like.

Article 5 Documents v. Goods, Services or Performance

Banks deal with documents and not with goods, services or performance to which the documents may relate.

Article 6 Availability, Expiry Date and Place for Presentation

a. A credit must state the bank with which it is available or whether it is available with any bank. A credit available with a nominated bank is also available with the issuing bank.

b. A credit must state whether it is available by sight payment, deferred payment, acceptance or negotiation.

c. A credit must not be issued available by a draft drawn on the applicant.

d. i. A credit must state an expiry date for presentation. An expiry date stated for honour or negotiation will be deemed to be an expiry date for presentation.

ii. The place of the bank with which the credit is available is the place for presentation. The place for presentation under a credit available with any bank is that of any bank. A place for presentation other than that of the issuing bank is in addition to the place of the issuing bank.

e. Except as provided in sub-article 29 (a), a presentation by or on behalf of the beneficiary must be made on or before the expiry date.

Article 7 Issuing Bank Undertaking

a. Provided that the stipulated documents are presented to the nominated bank or to the issuing bank and that they constitute a complying presentation, the issuing bank must honour if the credit is available by:

i. sight payment, deferred payment or acceptance with the issuing bank;

ii. sight payment with a nominated bank and that nominated bank does not pay;

iii. deferred payment with a nominated bank and that nominated bank does not incur its deferred payment undertaking or, having incurred its deferred payment undertaking, does not pay at maturity;

iv. acceptance with a nominated bank and that nominated bank does not accept a draft drawn on it or, having accepted a draft drawn on it, does not pay at maturity;

v. negotiation with a nominated bank and that nominated bank does not negotiate.

b. An issuing bank is irrevocably bound to honour as of the time it issues the credit.

c. An issuing bank undertakes to reimburse a nominated bank that has honoured or negotiated a complying presentation and forwarded the documents to the issuing bank. Reimbursement for the amount of a complying presentation under a credit available by acceptance or deferred payment is due at maturity, whether or not the nominated bank prepaid or purchased before maturity. An issuing bank's undertaking to reimburse a nominated bank is independent of the issuing bank's undertaking to the beneficiary.

Article 8 Confirming Bank Undertaking

a. Provided that the stipulated documents are presented to the confirming bank or to any other nominated bank and that they constitute a complying presentation, the confirming bank must:

i. honour, if the credit is available by

a. sight payment, deferred payment or acceptance with the confirming bank;

b. sight payment with another nominated bank and that nominated bank does not pay;

c. deferred payment with another nominated bank and that nominated bank does not incur its deferred payment undertaking or, having incurred its deferred payment undertaking, does not pay at maturity;

d. acceptance with another nominated bank and that nominated bank does not accept a draft drawn on it or, having accepted a draft drawn on it, does not pay at maturity;

e. negotiation with another nominated bank and that nominated bank does not negotiate.

ii. negotiate, without recourse, if the credit is available by negotiation with the confirming bank.

b. A confirming bank is irrevocably bound to honour or negotiate as of the time it adds its confirmation to the credit.

c. A confirming bank undertakes to reimburse another nominated bank that has honoured or negotiated a complying presentation and forwarded the documents to the confirming bank. Reimbursement for the amount of a complying presentation under a credit available by acceptance or deferred payment is due at maturity, whether or not another nominated bank prepaid or purchased before maturity. A confirming bank's undertaking to reimburse another nominated bank is independent of the confirming bank's undertaking to the beneficiary.

d. If a bank is authorized or requested by the issuing bank to confirm a credit but is not prepared to do so, it must inform the issuing bank without delay and may advise the credit without confirmation.

Article 9 Advising of Credits and Amendments

a. A credit and any amendment may be advised to a beneficiary through an advising bank. An advising bank that is not a confirming bank advises the credit and any amendment without any undertaking to honour or negotiate.

b. By advising the credit or amendment, the advising bank signifies that it has satisfied itself as to the apparent authenticity of the credit or amendment and that the advice accurately reflects the terms and conditions of the credit or amendment received.

c. An advising bank may utilize the services of another bank ("second advising bank") to advise the credit and any amendment to the beneficiary. By advising the credit or amendment, the second advising bank signifies that it has satisfied itself as to the apparent authenticity of the advice it has received and that the advice accurately reflects the terms and conditions of the credit or amendment received.

d. A bank utilizing the services of an advising bank or second advising bank to advise a credit must use the same bank to advise any amendment thereto.

e. If a bank is requested to advise a credit or amendment but elects not to do so, it must so inform, without delay, the bank from which the credit, amendment or advice has been received.

f. If a bank is requested to advise a credit or amendment but cannot satisfy itself as to the apparent authenticity of the credit, the amendment or the advice, it must so inform, without delay, the bank from which the instructions appear to have been received. If the advising bank or second advising bank elects nonetheless to advise the credit or amendment, it must inform the beneficiary or second advising bank that it has not been able to satisfy itself as to the apparent authenticity of the credit, the amendment or the advice.

Article 10 Amendments

a. Except as otherwise provided by article 38, a credit can neither be amended nor cancelled without the agreement of the issuing bank, the confirming bank, if any, and the beneficiary.

b. An issuing bank is irrevocably bound by an amendment as of the time it issues the amendment. A confirming bank may extend its confirmation to an amendment and will be irrevocably bound as of the time it advises the amendment. A confirming bank may, however, choose to advise an amendment without extending its confirmation and, if so, it must inform the issuing bank without delay and inform the beneficiary in its advice.

c. The terms and conditions of the original credit (or a credit incorporating previously accepted amendments) will remain in force for the beneficiary until the beneficiary communicates its acceptance of the amendment to the bank that advised such amendment. The beneficiary should give notification of acceptance or rejection of an amendment. If the beneficiary fails to give such notification, a presentation that complies with the credit and to any not yet accepted amendment will be deemed to be notification of acceptance by the beneficiary of such amendment. As of that moment the credit will be amended.

d. A bank that advises an amendment should inform the bank from which it received the amendment of any notification of acceptance or rejection.

e. Partial acceptance of an amendment is not allowed and will be deemed to be notification of rejection of the amendment.

f. A provision in an amendment to the effect that the amendment shall enter into force unless rejected by the beneficiary within a certain time shall be disregarded.

Article 11 Teletransmitted and Pre-Advised Credits and Amendments

a. An authenticated teletransmission of a credit or amendment will be deemed to be the operative credit or amendment, and any subsequent mail confirmation shall be disregarded. If a teletransmission states "full details to follow" (or words of similar effect), or states that the mail confirmation is to be the operative credit or amendment, then the teletransmission will not be deemed to be the operative credit or amendment. The issuing bank must then issue the operative credit or amendment withoutd elay in terms not inconsistent with the teletransmission.

b. A preliminary advice of the issuance of a credit or amendment ("pre-advice") shall only be sent if the issuing bank is prepared to issue the operative credit or amendment. An issuing bank that sends a pre-advice is irrevocably committed to issue the operative credit or amendment, without delay, in terms not inconsistent with the pre-advice.

Article 12 Nomination

a. Unless a nominated bank is the confirming bank, an authorization to honour or negotiate does not impose any obligation on that nominated bank to honour or negotiate, except when expressly agreed to by that nominated bank and so communicated to the beneficiary.

b. By nominating a bank to accept a draft or incur a deferred payment undertaking, an issuing bank authorizes that nominated bank to prepay or purchase a draft accepted or a deferred payment undertaking incurred by that nominated bank.

c. Receipt or examination and forwarding of documents by a nominated bank that is not a confirming bank does not make that nominated bank liable to honour or negotiate, nor does it constitute honour or negotiation.

Article 13 Bank-to-Bank Reimbursement Arrangements

a. If a credit states that reimbursement is to be obtained by a nominated bank ("claiming bank") claiming on another party ("reimbursing bank"), the credit must state if the reimbursement is subject to the ICC rules for bank-to-bank reimbursements in effect on the date of issuance of the credit.

b. If a credit does not state that reimbursement is subject to the ICC rules for bank-to-bank reimbursements, the following apply:

i. An issuing bank must provide a reimbursing bank with a reimbursement authorization that conforms with the availability stated in the credit. The reimbursement authorization should not be subject to an expiry date.

ii. A claiming bank shall not be required to supply a reimbursing bank with a certificate of compliance with the terms and conditions of the credit.

iii. An issuing bank will be responsible for any loss of interest, together with any expenses incurred, if reimbursement is not provided on first demand by a reimbursing bank in accordance with the terms and conditions of the credit.

iv. A reimbursing bank's charges are for the account of the issuing bank. However, if the charges are for the account of the beneficiary, it is the responsibility of an issuing bank to so indicate in the credit and in the reimbursement authorization. If a reimbursing bank's charges are for the account of the beneficiary, they shall be deducted from the amount due to a claiming bank when reimbursement is made. If no reimbursement is made, the reimbursing bank's charges remain the obligation of the issuing bank.

c. An issuing bank is not relieved of any of its obligations to provide reimbursement if reimbursement is not made by a reimbursing bank on first demand.

Article 14 Standard for Examination of Documents

a. A nominated bank acting on its nomination, a confirming bank, if any, and the issuing bank must examine a presentation to determine, on the basis of the documents alone, whether or not the documents appear on their face to constitute a complying presentation.

b. A nominated bank acting on its nomination, a confirming bank, if any, and the issuing bank shall each have a maximum of five banking days following the day of presentation to determine if a presentation is complying. This period is not curtailed or otherwise affected by the occurrence on or after the date of presentation of any expiry date or last day for presentation.

c. A presentation including one or more original transport documents subject to articles 19, 20, 21, 22, 23, 24 or 25 must be made by or on behalf of the beneficiary not later than 21 calendar days after the date of shipment as described in these rules, but in any event not later than the expiry date of the credit.

d. Data in a document, when read in context with the credit, the document itself and international standard banking practice, need not be identical to, but must not conflict with, data in that document, any other stipulated document or the credit.

e. In documents other than the commercial invoice, the description of the goods, services or performance, if stated, may be in general terms not conflicting with their description in the credit.

f. If a credit requires presentation of a document other than a transport document, insurance document or commercial invoice, without stipulating by whom the document is to be issued or its data content, banks will accept the document as presented if its content appears to fulfil the function of the required document and otherwise complies with sub-article 14 (d).

g. A document presented but not required by the credit will be disregarded and may be returned to the presenter.

h. If a credit contains a condition without stipulating the document to indicate compliance with the condition, banks will deem such condition as not stated and will disregard it.

i. A document may be dated prior to the issuance date of the credit, but must not be dated later than its date of presentation.

j. When the addresses of the beneficiary and the applicant appear in any stipulated document, they need not be the same as those stated in the credit or in any other stipulated document, but must be within the same country as the respective addresses mentioned in the credit. Contact details (telefax, telephone, email and the like) stated as part of the beneficiary's and the applicant's address will be disregarded. However, when the address and contact details of the applicant appear as part of the consignee or notify party details on a transport document subject to articles 19, 20, 21, 22, 23, 24 or 25, they must be as stated in the credit.

k. The shipper or consignor of the goods indicated on any document need not be the beneficiary of the credit.

l. A transport document may be issued by any party other than a carrier, owner, master or charterer provided that the transport document meets the requirements of articles 19, 20, 21, 22, 23 or 24 of these rules.

Article 15 Complying Presentation

a. When an issuing bank determines that a presentation is complying, it must honour.

b. When a confirming bank determines that a presentation is complying, it must honour or negotiate and forward the documents to the issuing bank.

c. When a nominated bank determines that a presentation is complying and honours or negotiates, it must forward the documents to the confirming bank or issuing bank.

Article 16 Discrepant Documents, Waiver and Notice

a. When a nominated bank acting on its nomination, a confirming bank, if any, or the issuing bank determines that a presentation does not comply, it may refuse to honour or negotiate.

b. When an issuing bank determines that a presentation does not comply, it may in its sole judgement approach the applicant for a waiver of the discrepancies. This does not, however, extend the period mentioned in sub-article 14 (b).

c. When a nominated bank acting on its nomination, a confirming bank, if any, or the issuing bank decides to refuse to honour or negotiate, it must give a single notice to that effect to the presenter.

The notice must state:

i. that the bank is refusing to honour or negotiate; and

ii. each discrepancy in respect of which the bank refuses to honour or negotiate; and

iii. a) that the bank is holding the documents pending further instructions from the presenter; or

b) that the issuing bank is holding the documents until it receives a waiver from the applicant and agrees to accept it, or receives further instructions from the presenter prior to agreeing to accept a waiver; or

c) that the bank is returning the documents; or

d) that the bank is acting in accordance with instructions previously received from the presenter.

d. The notice required in sub-article 16 (c) must be given by telecommunication or, if that is not possible, by other expeditious means no later than the close of the fifth banking day following the day of presentation.

e. A nominated bank acting on its nomination, a confirming bank, if any, or the issuing bank may, after providing notice required by sub-article 16 (c) (iii) (a) or (b), return the documents to the presenter at any time.

f. If an issuing bank or a confirming bank fails to act in accordance with the provisions of this article, it shall be precluded from claiming that the documents do not constitute a complying presentation.

g. When an issuing bank refuses to honour or a confirming bank refuses to honour or negotiate and has given notice to that effect in accordance with this article, it shall then be entitled to claim a refund, with interest, of any reimbursement made.

Article 17 Original Documents and Copies

a. At least one original of each document stipulated in the credit must be presented.

b. A bank shall treat as an original any document bearing an apparently original signature, mark, stamp, or label of the issuer of the document, unless the document itself indicates that it is not an original.

c. Unless a document indicates otherwise, a bank will also accept a document as original if it:

i. appears to be written, typed, perforated or stamped by the document issuer's hand; or

ii. appears to be on the document issuer's original stationery; or

iii. states that it is original, unless the statement appears not to apply to the document presented.

d. If a credit requires presentation of copies of documents, presentation of either originals or copies is permitted.

e. If a credit requires presentation of multiple documents by using terms such as "in duplicate", "in two fold" or "in two copies", this will be satisfied by the presentation of at least one original and the remaining number in copies, except when the document itself indicates otherwise.

Article 18 Commercial Invoice

a. A commercial invoice:

i. must appear to have been issued by the beneficiary (except as provided in article 38);

ii. must be made out in the name of the applicant (except as provided in subarticle 38 (g));

iii. must be made out in the same currency as the credit; and

iv. need not be signed.

b. A nominated bank acting on its nomination, a confirming bank, if any, or the issuing bank may accept a commercial invoice issued for an amount in excess of the amount permitted by the credit, and its decision will be binding upon all parties, provided the bank in question has not honoured or negotiated for an amount in excess of that permitted by the credit.

c. The description of the goods, services or performance in a commercial invoice must correspond with that appearing in the credit.

Article 19 Transport Document Covering at Least Two Different Modes of Transport

a. A transport document covering at least two different modes of transport (multimodal or combined transport document), however named, must appear to:

i. indicate the name of the carrier and be signed by:

the carrier or a named agent for or on behalf of the carrier, or

the master or a named agent for or on behalf of the master.

Any signature by the carrier, master or agent must be identified as that of the carrier, master or agent.

Any signature by an agent must indicate whether the agent has signed for or on behalf of the carrier or for or on behalf of the master.

ii. indicate that the goods have been dispatched, taken in charge or shipped on board at the place stated in the credit, by:

pre-printed wording, or a stamp or notation indicating the date on which the goods have been dispatched, taken in charge or shipped on board. The date of issuance of the transport document will be deemed to be the date of dispatch, taking in charge or shipped on board, and the date of shipment. However, if the transport document indicates, by stamp or notation, a date of dispatch, taking in charge or shipped on board, this date will be deemed to be the date of shipment.

iii. indicate the place of dispatch, taking in charge or shipment and the place of final destination stated in the credit, even if:

a. the transport document states, in addition, a different place of dispatch, taking in charge or shipment or place of final destination, or

b. the transport document contains the indication "intended" or similar qualification in relation to the vessel, port of loading or port of discharge.

iv. be the sole original transport document or, if issued in more than one original, be the full set as indicated on the transport document.

v. contain terms and conditions of carriage or make reference to another source containing the terms and conditions of carriage (short form or blank back transport document). Contents of terms and conditions of carriage will not be examined.

vi. contain no indication that it is subject to a charter party.

b. For the purpose of this article, transhipment means unloading from one means of conveyance and reloading to another means of conveyance (whether or not in different modes of transport) during the carriage from the place of dispatch, taking in charge or shipment to the place of final destination stated in the credit.

c. i. A transport document may indicate that the goods will or may be transhipped provided that the entire carriage is covered by one and the same transport document.

ii. A transport document indicating that transhipment will or may take place is acceptable, even if the credit prohibits transhipment.

Article 20 Bill of Lading

a. A bill of lading, however named, must appear to:

i. indicate the name of the carrier and be signed by:

the carrier or a named agent for or on behalf of the carrier, or

the master or a named agent for or on behalf of the master.

Any signature by the carrier, master or agent must be identified as that of the carrier, master or agent.

Any signature by an agent must indicate whether the agent has signed for or on behalf of the carrier or for or on behalf of the master.

ii. indicate that the goods have been shipped on board a named vessel at the port of loading stated in the credit by:

pre-printed wording, or

an on board notation indicating the date on which the goods have been shipped on board.

The date of issuance of the bill of lading will be deemed to be the date of shipment unless the bill of lading contains an on board notation indicating the date of shipment, in which case the date stated in the on board notation will be deemed to be the date of shipment. If the bill of lading contains the indication "intended vessel" or similar qualification in relation to the name of the vessel, an on board notation indicating the date of shipment and the name of the actual vessel is required.

iii. indicate shipment from the port of loading to the port of discharge stated in the credit.

If the bill of lading does not indicate the port of loading stated in the credit as the port of loading, or if it contains the indication "intended" or similar qualification in relation to the port of loading, an on board notation indicating the port of loading as stated in the credit, the date of shipment and the name of the vessel is required. This provision applies even when loading on board or shipment on a named vessel is indicated by preprinted wording on the bill of lading.

iv. be the sole original bill of lading or, if issued in more than one original, be the full set as indicated on the bill of lading.

v. contain terms and conditions of carriage or make reference to another source containing the terms and conditions of carriage (short form or blank back bill of lading). Contents of terms and conditions of carriage will not be examined.

vi. contain no indication that it is subject to a charter party.

b. For the purpose of this article, transhipment means unloading from one vessel and reloading to another vessel during the carriage from the port of loading to the port of discharge stated in the credit.

c. i. A bill of lading may indicate that the goods will or may be transhipped provided that the entire carriage is covered by one and the same bill of lading.

ii. A bill of lading indicating that transhipment will or may take place is acceptable, even if the credit prohibits transhipment, if the goods have been shipped in a container, trailer or LASH barge as evidenced by the bill of lading.

d. Clauses in a bill of lading stating that the carrier reserves the right to transhipment will be disregarded.

Article 21 Non-Negotiable Sea Waybill

a. A non-negotiable sea waybill, however named, must appear to:

i. indicate the name of the carrier and be signed by:

the carrier or a named agent for or on behalf of the carrier, or

the master or a named agent for or on behalf of the master.

Any signature by the carrier, master or agent must be identified as that of the carrier, master or agent.

Any signature by an agent must indicate whether the agent has signed for or on behalf of the carrier or for or on behalf of the master.

ii. indicate that the goods have been shipped on board a named vessel at the port of loading stated in the credit by:

pre-printed wording, or

an on board notation indicating the date on which the goods have been shipped on board.

The date of issuance of the non-negotiable sea waybill will be deemed to be the date of shipment unless the non-negotiable sea waybill contains an on board notation indicating the date of shipment, in which case the date stated in the on board notation will be deemed to be the date of shipment.

If the non-negotiable sea waybill contains the indication "intended vessel" or similar qualification in relation to the name of the vessel, an on board notation indicating the date of shipment and the name of the actual vessel is required.

iii. indicate shipment from the port of loading to the port of discharge stated in the credit.

If the non-negotiable sea waybill does not indicate the port of loading stated in the credit as the port of loading, or if it contains the indication "intended" or similar qualification in relation to the port of loading, an on board notation indicating the port of loading as stated in the credit, the date of shipment and the name of the vessel is required. This provision applies even when loading on board or shipment on a named vessel is indicated by pre-printed wording on the non-negotiable sea waybill.

iv. be the sole original non-negotiable sea waybill or, if issued in more than one original, be the full set as indicated on the non-negotiable sea waybill.

v. contain terms and conditions of carriage or make reference to another source containing the terms and conditions of carriage (short form or blank back non-negotiable sea waybill). Contents of terms and conditions of carriage will not be examined.

vi. contain no indication that it is subject to a charter party.

b. For the purpose of this article, transhipment means unloading from one vessel and reloading to another vessel during the carriage from the port of loading to the port of discharge stated in the credit.

c. i. A non-negotiable sea waybill may indicate that the goods will or may be transhipped provided that the entire carriage is covered by one and the same non-negotiable sea waybill.

ii. A non-negotiable sea waybill indicating that transhipment will or may take place is acceptable, even if the credit prohibits transhipment, if the goods have been shipped in a container, trailer or LASH barge as evidenced by the non-negotiable sea waybill.

d. Clauses in a non-negotiable sea waybill stating that the carrier reserves the right to tranship will be disregarded.

Article 22 Charter Party Bill of Lading

a. A bill of lading, however named, containing an indication that it is subject to a charter party (charter party bill of lading), must appear to:

i. be signed by:

the master or a named agent for or on behalf of the master, or

the owner or a named agent for or on behalf of the owner, or

the charterer or a named agent for or on behalf of the charterer.

Any signature by the master, owner, charterer or agent must be identified as that of the master, owner, charterer or agent.

Any signature by an agent must indicate whether the agent has signed for or on behalf of the master, owner or charterer.

An agent signing for or on behalf of the owner or charterer must indicate the name of the owner or charterer.

ii. indicate that the goods have been shipped on board a named vessel at the port of loading stated in the credit by:

pre-printed wording, or

an on board notation indicating the date on which the goods have been shipped on board.

The date of issuance of the charter party bill of lading will be deemed to be the date of shipment unless the charter party bill of lading contains an on board notation indicating the date of shipment, in which case the date stated in the on board notation will be deemed to be the date of shipment.

iii. indicate shipment from the port of loading to the port of discharge stated in the credit. The port of discharge may also be shown as a range of ports or a geographical area, as stated in the credit.

iv. be the sole original charter party bill of lading or, if issued in more than one original, be the full set as indicated on the charter party bill of lading.

b. A bank will not examine charter party contracts, even if they are required to be presented by the terms of the credit.

Article 23 Air Transport Document

a. An air transport document, however named, must appear to:

i. indicate the name of the carrier and be signed by:

the carrier, or a named agent for or on behalf of the carrier.

Any signature by the carrier or agent must be identified as that of the carrier or agent.

Any signature by an agent must indicate that the agent has signed for or on behalf of the carrier.

ii. indicate that the goods have been accepted for carriage.

iii. indicate the date of issuance. This date will be deemed to be the date of shipment unless the air transport document contains a specific notation of the actual date of shipment, in which case the date stated in the notation will be deemed to be the date of shipment.

Any other information appearing on the air transport document relative to the flight number and date will not be considered in determining the date of shipment.

iv. indicate the airport of departure and the airport of destination stated in the credit.

v. be the original for consignor or shipper, even if the credit stipulates a full set of originals.

vi. contain terms and conditions of carriage or make reference to another source containing the terms and conditions of carriage. Contents of terms and conditions of carriage will not be examined.

b. For the purpose of this article, transhipment means unloading from one aircraft and reloading to another aircraft during the carriage from the airport of departure to the airport of destination stated in the credit.

c. i. An air transport document may indicate that the goods will or may be transhipped, provided that the entire carriage is covered by one and the same air transport document.

ii. An air transport document indicating that transhipment will or may take place is acceptable, even if the credit prohibits transhipment.

Article 24 Road, Rail or Inland Waterway Transport Documents

a. A road, rail or inland waterway transport document, however named, must appear to:

i. indicate the name of the carrier and: be signed by the carrier or a named agent for or on behalf of the carrier, or indicate receipt of the goods by signature, stamp or notation by the carrier or a named agent for or on behalf of the carrier.

Any signature, stamp or notation of receipt of the goods by the carrier or agent must be identified as that of the carrier or agent.

Any signature, stamp or notation of receipt of the goods by the agent must indicate that the agent has signed or acted for or on behalf of the carrier.

If a rail transport document does not identify the carrier, any signature or stamp of the railway company will be accepted as evidence of the document being signed by the carrier.

ii. indicate the date of shipment or the date the goods have been received for shipment, dispatch or carriage at the place stated in the credit. Unless the transport document contains a dated reception stamp, an indication of the date of receipt or a date of shipment, the date of issuance of the transport document will be deemed to be the date of shipment.

iii. indicate the place of shipment and the place of destination stated in the credit.

b. i. A road transport document must appear to be the original for consignor or shipper or bear no marking indicating for whom the document has been prepared.

ii. A rail transport document marked "duplicate" will be accepted as an original.

iii. A rail or inland waterway transport document will be accepted as an original whether marked as an original or not.

c. In the absence of an indication on the transport document as to the number of originals issued, the number presented will be deemed to constitute a full set.

d. For the purpose of this article, transhipment means unloading from one means of conveyance and reloading to another means of conveyance, within the same mode of transport, during the carriage from the place of shipment, dispatch or carriage to the place of destination stated in the credit.

e. i. A road, rail or inland waterway transport document may indicate that the goods will or may be transhipped provided that the entire carriage is covered by one and the same transport document.

ii. A road, rail or inland waterway transport document indicating that transhipment will or may take place is acceptable, even if the credit prohibits transhipment.

Article 25 Courier Receipt, Post Receipt or Certificate of Posting

a. A courier receipt, however named, evidencing receipt of goods for transport, must appear to:

i. indicate the name of the courier service and be stamped or signed by the named courier service at the place from which the credit states the goods are to be shipped; and

ii. indicate a date of pick-up or of receipt or wording to this effect. This date will be deemed to be the date of shipment.

b. A requirement that courier charges are to be paid or prepaid may be satisfied by a transport document issued by a courier service evidencing that courier charges are for the account of a party other than the consignee.

c. A post receipt or certificate of posting, however named, evidencing receipt of goods for transport, must appear to be stamped or signed and dated at the place from which the credit states the goods are to be shipped. This date will be deemed to be the date of shipment.

Article 26 "On Deck", "Shipper's Load and Count", "Said by Shipper to Contain" and Charges Additional to Freight

a. A transport document must not indicate that the goods are or will be loaded on deck. A clause on a transport document stating that the goods may be loaded on deck is acceptable.

b. A transport document bearing a clause such as "shipper's load and count" and "said by shipper to contain" is acceptable.

c. A transport document may bear a reference, by stamp or otherwise, to charges additional to the freight.

Article 27 Clean Transport Document

A bank will only accept a clean transport document. A clean transport document is one bearing no clause or notation expressly declaring a defective condition of the goods or their packaging. The word "clean" need not appear on a transport document, even if a credit has a requirement for that transport document to be "clean on board".

Article 28 Insurance Document and Coverage

a. An insurance document, such as an insurance policy, an insurance certificate or a declaration under an open cover, must appear to be issued and signed by an insurance company, an underwriter or their agents or their proxies.

Any signature by an agent or proxy must indicate whether the agent or proxy has signed for or on behalf of the insurance company or underwriter.

b. When the insurance document indicates that it has been issued in more than one original, all originals must be presented.

c. Cover notes will not be accepted.

d. An insurance policy is acceptable in lieu of an insurance certificate or a declaration under an open cover.

e. The date of the insurance document must be no later than the date of shipment, unless it appears from the insurance document that the cover is effective from a date not later than the date of shipment.

f. i. The insurance document must indicate the amount of insurance coverage and be in the same currency as the credit.

ii. A requirement in the credit for insurance coverage to be for a percentage of the value of the goods, of the invoice value or similar is deemed to be the minimum amount of coverage required.

If there is no indication in the credit of the insurance coverage required, the amount of insurance coverage must be at least 110% of the CIF or CIP value of the goods. When the CIF or CIP value cannot be determined from the documents, the amount of insurance coverage must be calculated on the basis of the amount for which honour or negotiation is requested or the gross value of the goods as shown on the invoice, whichever is greater.

iii. The insurance document must indicate that risks are covered at least between the place of taking in charge or shipment and the place of discharge or final destination as stated in the credit.

g. A credit should state the type of insurance required and, if any, the additional risks to be covered. An insurance document will be accepted without regard to any risks that are not covered if the credit uses imprecise terms such as "usual risks" or "customary risks".

h. When a credit requires insurance against "all risks" and an insurance document is presented containing any "all risks" notation or clause, whether or not bearing the heading "all risks", the insurance document will be accepted without regard to any risks stated to be excluded.

i. An insurance document may contain reference to any exclusion clause.

j. An insurance document may indicate that the cover is subject to a franchise or excess (deductible).

Article 29 Extension of Expiry Date or Last Day for Presentation

a. If the expiry date of a credit or the last day for presentation falls on a day when the bank to which presentation is to be made is closed for reasons other than those referred to in article 36, the expiry date or the last day for presentation, as the case may be, will be extended to the first following banking day.

b. If presentation is made on the first following banking day, a nominated bank must provide the issuing bank or confirming bank with a statement on its covering schedule that the presentation was made within the time limits extended in accordance with sub-article 29 (a).

c. The latest date for shipment will not be extended as a result of sub-article 29 (a).

Article 30 Tolerance in Credit Amount, Quantity and Unit Prices

a. The words "about" or "approximately" used in connection with the amount of the credit or the quantity or the unit price stated in the credit are to be construed as allowing a tolerance not to exceed 10% more or 10% less than the amount, the quantity or the unit price to which they refer.

b. A tolerance not to exceed 5% more or 5% less than the quantity of the goods is allowed, provided the credit does not state the quantity in terms of a stipulated number of packing units or individual items and the total amount of the drawings does not exceed the amount of the credit.

c. Even when partial shipments are not allowed, a tolerance not to exceed 5% less than the amount of the credit is allowed, provided that the quantity of the goods, if stated in the credit, is shipped in full and a unit price, if stated in the credit, is not reduced or that sub-article 30 (b) is not applicable. This tolerance does not apply when the credit stipulates a specific tolerance or uses the expressions referred to in sub-article 30 (a).

Article 31 Partial Drawings or Shipments

a. Partial drawings or shipments are allowed.

b. A presentation consisting of more than one set of transport documents evidencing shipment commencing on the same means of conveyance and for the same journey, provided they indicate the same destination, will not be regarded as covering a partial shipment, even if they indicate different dates of shipment or different ports of loading, places of taking in charge or dispatch. If the presentation consists of more than one set of transport documents, the latest date of shipment as evidenced on any of the sets of transport documents will be regarded as the date of shipment.

A presentation consisting of one or more sets of transport documents evidencing shipment on more than one means of conveyance within the same mode of transport will be regarded as covering a partial shipment, even if the means of conveyance leave on the same day for the same destination.

c. A presentation consisting of more than one courier receipt, post receipt or certificate of posting will not be regarded as a partial shipment if the courier receipts, post receipts or certificates of posting appear to have been stamped or signed by the same courier or postal service at the same place and date and for the same destination.

Article 32 Instalment Drawings or Shipments

If a drawing or shipment by instalments within given periods is stipulated in the credit and any instalment is not drawn or shipped within the period allowed for that instalment, the credit ceases to be available for that and any subsequent instalment.

Article 33 Hours of Presentation

A bank has no obligation to accept a presentation outside of its banking hours.

Article 34 Disclaimer on Effectiveness of Documents

A bank assumes no liability or responsibility for the form, sufficiency, accuracy, genuineness, falsification or legal effect of any document, or for the general or particular conditions stipulated in a document or superimposed thereon; nor does it assume any liability or responsibility for the description, quantity, weight, quality, condition, packing, delivery, value or existence of the goods, services or other performance represented by any document, or for the good faith or acts or omissions, solvency, performance or standing of the consignor, the carrier, the forwarder, the consignee or the insurer of the goods or any other person.

Article 35 Disclaimer on Transmission and Translation

A bank assumes no liability or responsibility for the consequences arising out of delay, loss in transit, mutilation or other errors arising in the transmission of any messages or delivery of letters or documents, when such messages, letters or documents are transmitted or sent according to the requirements stated in the credit, or when the bank may have taken the initiative in the choice of the delivery service in the absence of such instructions in the credit.

If a nominated bank determines that a presentation is complying and forwards the documents to the issuing bank or confirming bank, whether or not the nominated bank has honoured or negotiated, an issuing bank or confirming bank must honour or negotiate, or reimburse that nominated bank, even when the documents have been lost in transit between the nominated bank and the issuing bank or confirming bank, or between the confirming bank and the issuing bank.

A bank assumes no liability or responsibility for errors in translation or interpretation of technical terms and may transmit credit terms without translating them.

Article 36 Force Majeure

A bank assumes no liability or responsibility for the consequences arising out of the interruption of its business by Acts of God, riots, civil commotions, insurrections, wars, acts of terrorism, or by any strikes or lockouts or any other causes beyond its control.

A bank will not, upon resumption of its business, honour or negotiate under a credit that expired during such interruption of its business.

Article 37 Disclaimer for Acts of an Instructed Party

a. A bank utilizing the services of another bank for the purpose of giving effect to the instructions of the applicant does so for the account and at the risk of the applicant.

b. An issuing bank or advising bank assumes no liability or responsibility should the instructions it transmits to another bank not be carried out, even if it has taken the initiative in the choice of that other bank.

c. A bank instructing another bank to perform services is liable for any commissions, fees, costs or expenses ("charges") incurred by that bank in connection with its instructions.

If a credit states that charges are for the account of the beneficiary and charges cannot be collected or deducted from proceeds, the issuing bank remains liable for payment of charges.

A credit or amendment should not stipulate that the advising to a beneficiary is conditional upon the receipt by the advising bank or second advising bank of its charges.

d. The applicant shall be bound by and liable to indemnify a bank against all obligations and responsibilities imposed by foreign laws and usages.

Article 38 Transferable Credits

a. A bank is under no obligation to transfer a credit except to the extent and in the manner expressly consented to by that bank.

b. For the purpose of this article:

Transferable credit means a credit that specifically states it is "transferable". A transferable credit may be made available in whole or in part to another beneficiary ("second beneficiary") at the request of the beneficiary ("first beneficiary").

Transferring bank means a nominated bank that transfers the credit or, in a credit available with any bank, a bank that is specifically authorized by the issuing bank to transfer and that transfers the credit. An issuing bank may be a transferring bank.

Transferred credit means a credit that has been made available by the transferring bank to a second beneficiary.

c. Unless otherwise agreed at the time of transfer, all charges (such as commissions, fees, costs or expenses) incurred in respect of a transfer must be paid by the first beneficiary.

d. A credit may be transferred in part to more than one second beneficiary provided partial drawings or shipments are allowed.

A transferred credit cannot be transferred at the request of a second beneficiary to any subsequent beneficiary. The first beneficiary is not considered to be a subsequent beneficiary.

e. Any request for transfer must indicate if and under what conditions amendments may be advised to the second beneficiary. The transferred credit must clearly indicate those conditions.

f. If a credit is transferred to more than one second beneficiary, rejection of an amendment by one or more second beneficiary does not invalidate the acceptance by any other second beneficiary, with respect to which the transferred credit will be amended accordingly. For any second beneficiary that rejected the amendment, the transferred credit will remain unamended.

g. The transferred credit must accurately reflect the terms and conditions of the credit, including confirmation, if any, with the exception of:

the amount of the credit,

any unit price stated therein,

the expiry date,

the period for presentation, or

the latest shipment date or given period for shipment,

any or all of which may be reduced or curtailed.

The percentage for which insurance cover must be effected may be increased to provide the amount of cover stipulated in the credit or these articles.

The name of the first beneficiary may be substituted for that of the applicant in the credit.

If the name of the applicant is specifically required by the credit to appear in any document other than the invoice, such requirement must be reflected in the transferred credit.

h. The first beneficiary has the right to substitute its own invoice and draft, if any, for those of a second beneficiary for an amount not in excess of that stipulated in the credit, and upon such substitution the first beneficiary can draw under the credit for the difference, if any, between its invoice and the invoice of a second beneficiary.

i. If the first beneficiary is to present its own invoice and draft, if any, but fails to do so on first demand, or if the invoices presented by the first beneficiary create discrepancies that did not exist in the presentation made by the second beneficiary and the first beneficiary fails to correct them on first demand, the transferring bank has the right to present the documents as received from the second beneficiary to the issuing bank, without further responsibility to the first beneficiary.

j. The first beneficiary may, in its request for transfer, indicate that honour or negotiation is to be effected to a second beneficiary at the place to which the credit has been transferred, up to and including the expiry date of the credit. This is without prejudice to the right of the first beneficiary in accordance with subarticle 38 (h).

k. Presentation of documents by or on behalf of a second beneficiary must be made to the transferring bank.

Article 39 Assignment of Proceeds

The fact that a credit is not stated to be transferable shall not affect the right of the beneficiary to assign any proceeds to which it may be or may become entitled under the credit, in accordance with the provisions of applicable law. This article relates only to the assignment of proceeds and not to the assignment of the right to perform under the credit.

Appendix 5. The International Standby Practices—ISP98 1998

Foreword

PROLOGUE

by Dr. Gerold Herrmann, Secretary, United Nations Commission on International Trade Law (UNCITRAL)

It was an extremely interesting and enriching experience for me to assist in drafting ISP98. This participation allowed me to witness (and now bear witness to) the very thorough and pragmatic drafting process in a superbly selected group, with representatives of all interested sectors actively involved in standby letter of credit practice such as: bankers, especially those responsible for letter of credit operations and global trade transactions, bank counsel, attorneys, academics, regulators, government officials, corporate treasurers, and likely influential beneficiaries. The treasure trove of experience and expertise and the diversity of interests and perspectives proved invaluable in determining – as was continuously done by examining concrete practical examples – whether on a given issue an operational rule would be desirable and useful and, if so, which solution would work best and reflect good practice.

Continued participation in the preparatory work has also convinced me – as, I am sure, it would have anyone else – of the special characteristics of standbys at the operational level of practical detail and usage. Their special features, in my view, not only justify but also necessitate special contractual rules designed for standbys. As the constant comparison with the UCP clearly revealed, quite a few UCP Articles are inappropriate for standbys and quite a few issues of paramount importance in standby practice are not addressed at all in the UCP. While a similar disparity in practice exists between the standby and the independent guarantee (the bank or demand guarantee European style), this seems particularly, if not exclusively, true for those types of actual use (e. g. financial standby, direct-pay standby) hitherto found only extremely rarely in guarantee practice. For this and other reasons, including firmness of the undertaking, I would not be surprised to see not only standbys but also some demand guarantees issued subject to ISP98.

For a professional unifier of law, participation in the preparatory work was particularly satisfying because of its interconnection with other harmonisation and reform efforts. In addition to the concordance with revised Article 5 UCC (the letter-of-credit law of the homeland of the standby) and the similarly close contact (and personal overlap) with the 1993 UCP revision task force, I am referring in particular to UNCITRAL's work which culminated in the adoption in 1995 by the General Assembly of the "United Nations Convention on Independent Guarantees and Stand-by Letters of Credit". The idea of preparing special operational rules for standbys was born during the extensive debates comparing national laws as well as the two instruments to be married by that Convention. Since bride and groom were presented there in all facets and critically scrutinized by their future in-laws, UNCITRAL's travaux preparatories make for highly informative reading (as will future abstracts of court decisions to be published in UNCITRAL's case collection system called CLOUT; homepage: www. un. or. at/uncitral). It was gratifying to see the group preparing ISP98 refer continuously to the UNCITRAL Convention in order to ensure complete consistency. I must admit to special gratification by overhearing one of the world's leading letter of credit expert's remark to his banking colleague: "The more I look at this UN Convention, the more I really like it."

The above coordination or cooperation in the universal harmonisation and modernization efforts is welcome and in fact crucial because of the (often neglected or ignored) interdependence between the two very different levels of legal norms: the contractual level, where such sets of rules like ISP98, UCP 500, or URDG become effective by agreement of the individual parties, and the statutory level, where internationally elaborated law like the UN Convention or domestic law (e. g. Art. 5 UCC) recognise and give full effect to the exercise of that party autonomy and regulate certain issues that can effectively be settled only at that level (e. g. standards of fraud exception, injunctive relief and other court matters). Therefore, ISP98 and the Convention supplement each other in an ideal manner and together lay the necessary basis for a smooth functioning of standby practice worldwide.

Preface

The International Standby Practices (ISP98) reflects generally accepted practice, custom, and usage of standby letters of credit. It provides separate rules for standby letters of credit in the same sense that the Uniform Customs and Practice for Documentary Credits (UCP) and the Uniform Rules for Demand Guarantees (URDG) do for commercial letters of credit and independent bank guarantees.

The formulation of standby letter of credit practices in separate rules evidences the maturity and importance of this financial product. The amounts outstanding of standbys greatly exceed the outstanding amounts of commercial letters of credit. While the standby is associated with the United States where it originated and where it is most widely used, it is truly an international product. Non-U. S. bank outstandings have exceeded those of U. S. banks in the United States alone. Moreover, the standby is used increasingly throughout the world.

For convenience, standbys are commonly classified descriptively (and without operative significance in the application of these Rules) based on their function in the underlying transaction or other factors not necessarily related to the terms and conditions of the standby itself. For example:

A "Performance Standby" supports an obligation to perform other than to pay money including for the purpose of covering losses arising from a default of the applicant in completion of the underlying transactions.

An "Advance Payment Standby" supports an obligation to account for an advance payment made by the beneficiary to the applicant.

A "Bid Bond/Tender Bond Standby" supports an obligation of the applicant to execute a contract if the applicant is awarded a bid.

A "Counter Standby" supports the issuance of a separate standby or other undertaking by the beneficiary of the counter standby.

A "Financial Standby" supports an obligation to pay money, including any instrument evidencing an obligation to repay borrowed money.

A "Direct Pay Standby" supports payment when due of an underlying payment obligation typically in connection with a financial standby without regard to a default.

An "Insurance Standby" supports an insurance or reinsurance obligation of the applicant.

A "Commercial Standby" supports the obligations of an applicant to pay for goods or services in the event of non-payment by other methods.

In the past, many standbys have been issued subject to the UCP even though it was intended for commercial letters of credit. The UCP reinforced the independence and documentary character of the standby. It also provided standards for examination and notice of dishonor and a basis to resist market pressures to embrace troublesome practices such as the issuance of standbys without expiration dates.

Despite these important contributions, it has long been apparent that the UCP was not fully applicable nor appropriate for standbys, as is recognized in UCP 500 Article 1 which provides that it applies to the extent to which they may be applicable. Even the least complex standbys (those calling for presentation of a draft only) pose problems not addressed by the UCP. More complex standbys (those involving longer terms or automatic extensions, transfer on demand, requests that the beneficiary issue its own undertaking to another, and the like) require more specialized rules of practice. The ISP fills these needs.

The ISP differs from the UCP in style and approach because it must receive acceptance not only from bankers and merchants, but also from a broader range of those actively involved in standby law and practice corporate treasurers and credit managers, rating agencies, government agencies and regulators, and indenture trustees as well as their counsel. Because standbys are often intended to be available in the event of disputes or applicant insolvency, their texts are subject to a degree of scrutiny not encountered in the commercial letter of credit context. As a result, the ISP is also written to provide guidance to lawyers and judges in the interpretation of standby practice.

Differences in substance result either from different practices, different problems, or the need for more precision. In addition, the ISP proposes basic definitions should the standby permit or require presentation of documents by electronic means. Since standbys infrequently require presentation of negotiable documents, standby practice is currently more conducive to electronic presentations, and the ISP provides definitions and rules encouraging such presentations. The development of S. W. I. F. T. message types for the ISP is anticipated.

The ISP, like the UCP for commercial letters of credit, simplifies, standardizes, and streamlines the drafting of standbys, and provides clear and widely accepted answers to common problems. There are basic similarities with the UCP because standby and commercial practices are fundamentally the same. Even where the rules overlap, however, the ISP is more precise, stating the intent implied in the UCP rule, in order to make the standby more dependable when a drawing or honor is questioned.

Like the UCP and the URDG, the ISP will apply to any independent undertaking issued subject to it. This approach avoids the impractical and often impossible task of identifying and distinguishing standbys from independent guarantees and, in many cases, commercial letters of credit. The choice of which set of rules to select is, therefore, left to the parties as it should be. One may well choose to use the ISP for certain types of standbys, the UCP for others, and the URDG for still others. While the ISP is not intended to be used for dependent undertakings such as accessory guarantees and insurance contracts, it may be useful in some situations in indicating that a particular undertaking which might otherwise be treated as dependent under local law is intended to be independent.

For the ISP to apply to a standby, an undertaking should be made subject to these Rules by including language such as (but not limited to):

This undertaking is issued subject to the International Standby Practices 1998.

or

Subject to ISP98.

Although the ISP can be varied by the text of a standby, it provides neutral rules acceptable in the majority of situations and a useful starting point for negotiations in other situations. It will save parties (including banks that issue, confirm, or are beneficiaries of standbys) considerable time and expense in negotiating and drafting standby terms.

The ISP is designed to be compatible with the United Nations Convention on Independent Guarantees and Stand-by Letters of Credit (which represents a useful and practical formulation of basic standby and independent guarantee law) and also with local law, whether statutory or judicial, and to embody standby letter of credit practice under that law. If these rules conflict with mandatory law on issues such as assignment of proceeds or transfer by operation of law, applicable law will, of course, control. Nonetheless, most of these issues are rarely addressed by local law and progressive commercial law will often look to the practice as recorded in the ISP for guidance in such situations, especially with respect to cross border under takings. As a result, it is expected that the ISP will complement local law rather than conflict with it.

The ISP is intended to be used also in arbitration as well as judicial proceedings (such as the expert based letter of credit arbitration system developed by the International Center for Letter of Credit Arbitration (ICLOCA) Rules or general commercial ICC arbitration) or with alternative methods of dispute resolution. Such a choice should be made expressly and with appropriate detail. At a minimum, it can be made in connection with the clause relating to ISP98 – e.g. This undertaking is issued subject to ISP98, and all disputes arising out of it or related to it are subject to arbitration under ICLOCA Rules (1996).

Although translations of the ISP into other languages are envisioned and will be monitored for integrity, the English text is the official text of the ISP in the event of disputes.

The ISP is the product of the work of the ISP Working Group under the auspices of the Institute of International Banking Law and Practice, Inc. which interacted with hundreds of persons over a five year period, and has benefited from comments received from individuals, banks, and national and international associations. In particular, the participation of the International Financial Services Association (formerly the USCIB) and the Ad Hoc Working Group under the chairmanship of Gary Collyer (which led to its endorsement by the ICC Banking Commission) is gratefully recognized. In addition, the sponsorship and support of Citibank N. A., The Chase Manhattan Bank, ABN-AMRO, Baker and McKenzie, and the National Law Center for Inter-American Free Trade is acknowledged. Perhaps the greatest significance of the ISP is that its creation marks a new chapter in the collaboration between the international banking operations community and the legal community at an international level. In this respect, the active role played in this process by the Secretariat of the United Nations Commission on International Trade Law has been invaluable.

The ISP is drafted as a set of rules intended for use in daily practice. It is not intended to provide introductory information on standbys and their uses. While it is recognized that specific rules would benefit from explanatory comments, such comments are not appended to the ISP because the resulting work would be too cumbersome for daily use. Instead, introductory materials and Official Comments are available in the Official Commentary on the International Standby Practices (ISP98). For further information on support materials and developments on the ISP and to pose queries, consult the ISP98 website: www.ISP98.com.

Professor James E. Byrne

Director, Institute of International Banking Law and Practice, Inc.; Chair and Reporter, P. Working Group

James G. Barnes

Baker and McKenzie; Vice Chair, ISP Working Group

Gary W. Collyer

Vice President, Citibank, N. A; Chair, ICC Ad Hoc Working Group and Technical Adviser to the ICC Banking Commission

1. GENERAL PROVISIONS

Scope, Application, Definitions, and Interpretation of These Rules

1.01 Scope and Application

a. These Rules are intended to be applied to standby letters of credit (including performance, financial, and direct pay standby letter of credit).

b. A standby letter of credit or other similar undertaking, however named or described, whether for domestic or international use, may be made subject to these Rules by express reference to them.

c. An undertaking subject to these Rules may expressly modify or exclude their application.

d. An undertaking subject to these Rules is hereinafter referred to as a "standby".

1.02 Relationship to Law and Other Rules

a. These Rules supplement the applicable law to the extent not prohibited by that law.

b. These Rules supersede conflicting provisions in any other rules of practice to which a standby letter of credit is also made subject.

1.03 Interpretative Principles

These Rules shall be interpreted as mercantile usage with regard for:

a. integrity of standbys as reliable and efficient undertakings to pay

b. practice and terminology of banks and businesses in day-to-day transactions

c. consistency within the worldwide system of banking operations and commerce; and

d. worldwide uniformity in their interpretation and application.

1.04 Effect of the Rules

Unless the context otherwise requires, or unless expressly modified or excluded, these Rules apply as terms and conditions incorporated into a standby, confirmation, advice, nomination, amendment, transfer, request for issuance, or other agreement of:

i. the issuer;

ii. the beneficiary to the extent it uses the standby;

iii. any advisor;

iv. any confirmer;

v. any person nominated in the standby who acts or agrees to act; and

vi. the applicant who authorizes issuance of the standby or otherwise agrees to the application of these Rules

1.05 Exclusion of Matters Related to Due Issuance and Fraudulent or Abusive Drawing

These Rules do not define or otherwise provide for

a. power or authority to issue a standby;

b. formal requirements for execution of a standby (e.g. a signed writing); or

c. defense to honour based on fraud, abuse, or similar matters.

These matters are left to applicable law.

General Principles

1.06 Nature of Standbys

a. A standby is an irrevocable, independent, documentary, and binding undertaking when issued and need not so sate.

b. Because a standby is irrevocable, an issuer's obligations under a standby cannot be amended or cancelled by the issuer except as provided in the standby or as consented to by the person against whom the amendment or cancellation is asserted.

c. Because a standby is independent, the enforceability of an issuer's obligations under a standby does not depend on:

i. the issuer's right or ability to obtain reimbursement from the applicant

ii. the beneficiary's right or ability to obtain payment from the applicant

iii. a reference in the standby to any reimbursement agreement or underlying transaction; or

iv. the issuer's knowledge of performance or breach of any reimbursement agreement or underlying transaction.

d. Because a standby is documentary, an issuer's obligations depend on the presentation of documents and an examination of required documents on their face.

e. Because a standby or amendment is binding when issued, it is enforceable against an issuer whether or not the applicant authorised its issuance, the issuer received a fee, or the beneficiary received or relied on the standby or the amendment.

1.07 Independence of the Issuer-Beneficiary Relationship

An issuer's obligations toward the beneficiary are not affected by the issuer's rights and obligations toward the applicant under any applicable agreement, practice, or law.

1.08 Limits to Responsibilities

An issuer is not responsible for:

a. performance or breach of any underlying transaction.

b. accuracy, genuineness, or effect of any document presented under the standby;

c. action or omission of others even if the other person is chosen by the issuer or nominated person, or

d. observance of law or practice other than that chosen in the standby or applicable at the place of issuance.

Terminology

1.09 Defined Terms

In addition to the meanings given in standard banking practice and applicable law, the following terms have or include the meanings indicated below:

a. Definitions

"Applicant" is a person who applies for issuance of a standby or for whose account it is issued, and include (i) a person applying in its own name but for the account of another person or (ii) an issue acting for its own account.

"Beneficiary" is named person who is entitled to draw under a standby. See Rule 1.11(c)(ii).

"Business Day" means a day on which the place of business at which the relevant act is to be performed is regularly open; and

"Banking day" means a day on which the relevant bank is regularly open at the place at which the relevant act is to be performed.

"Confirmer" is a person who, upon an issuer's nomination to do so, adds to the issuer's undertaking its own undertaking to honour a standby. See Rule 1.11(c)(i).

"Document" means a draft, demand, document of title, investment security, invoice, certificate of default, or any other representation of fact, law, right, or opinion, that upon presentation (whether in a paper or electronic medium), is capable of being examined for compliance with the terms and conditions of a standby.

"Drawing" means, depending on the context, either a demand presented or a demand honoured.

"Expiration Date" means the latest day for a complying presentation provided in a standby.

"Person" includes a natural person, partnership, corporation, limited liability company, government agency, bank, trustee, and any other legal or commercial association or entity.

"Presentation" means, depending on the context, either the act of delivering documents for examination under a standby or the documents so delivered.

"Presenter" is a person who makes a presentation as or on behalf of a beneficiary or nominated person.

"Signature" includes any symbol executed or adopted by person with a present intent to authenticate a document.

b. Cross References

"Amendment" – Rule 2.06

"Advice" – Rule 2.05

"Approximately" ("About" or "Circa") – Rule 3.08

"Assignment of Proceeds" – Rule 6.06

"Automatic Amendment" – Rule 2.06(a)

"Copy" – Rule 4.15(d)

"Cover Instructions" – Rule 5.08

"Honour" – Rule 2.01

"Issuer" – Rule 2.01

"Multiple Presentations" – Rule 3.08(b)

"Nominated Person" – Rule 2.04

"Non-documentary Conditions" – Rule 4.11

"Original" – Rule 4. 15(b) & (c)

"Partial Drawing" – Rule 3. 08(a)

"Standby" – Rule 1. 01(d)

"Transfer" – Rule 6. 01

"Transferee Beneficiary" – Rule 1. 11(c)(ii)

"Transfer by Operation of Law" – Rule 6. 11

c. Electronic Presentations

The following terms in a standby providing for or permitting electronic presentation shall have the following meanings unless the context otherwise requires:

"Electronic Record" means:

i. a record (information that is inscribed on a tangible medium or that is stored in an electronic or other medium and is retrievable in perceivable form)

ii. communicated by electronic means to a system for receiving, storing, re-transmitting, or otherwise processing information (data, text, images, sounds, code, computer programs, software, databases, and the like); and

iii. capable of being authenticated and then examined for compliance with the terms and conditions of the standby.

"Authenticate" means to verify an electronic record by generally accepted procedure or methodology in commercial practice:

i. the identity of a sender or source, and

ii. the integrity of or errors in the transmission of information content.

The criteria for assessing the integrity of information in an electronic record is whether the information has remained complete and unaltered, apart from the addition of any endorsement and any change which arises in the normal course of communication, storage, and display.

"Electronic signature" means letters, characters, numbers, or other symbols in electronic form, attached to or logically associated with an electronic record that are executed or adopted by a party with present intent to authenticate an electronic record.

"Receipt" occurs when:

i. an electronic record enters in a form capable of being processed by the information system designated in the standby, or

ii. an issuer retrieves an electronic record sent to an information system other than that designated by the issuer.

1. 10 Redundant or Otherwise Undesirable Terms

a. A standby should not or need not state that it is:

i. unconditional or abstract (if it does, it signifies merely that payment under it is conditioned solely on presentation of specified documents);

ii. absolute (if it does, it signifies merely that it is irrevocable);

iii. primary (if it does, it signifies merely that it is the independent obligation of the issuer);

iv. payable from the issuer's own funds (if it does, it signifies merely that payment under it does not depend on the availability of applicant funds and is made to satisfy the issuer's own independent obligation)

v. clean or payable on demand (if it does, it signifies merely that it is payable upon presentation of a written demand or other documents specified in the standby).

b. A standby should not use the term "and/or" (if it does it means either or both).

c. The following terms have no single accepted meaning:

i. and shall be disregarded:

"callable",

"divisible",

"fractionable",

"indivisible", and

"revolving".

ii. and shall be disregarded unless their context gives them meaning:

"assignable",

"evergreen",

"reinstate", and

"revolving".

1.11 Interpretation of These Rules

a. These Rules are to be interpreted in the context of applicable standby practice.

b. In these Rule, "standby letter of credit" refers to the type of independent undertaking for which these Rules were intended, whereas "standby" refers to an undertaking subject to these Rules.

c. Unless the context otherwise requires:

i. "Issue" includes a "confirmer" as if the confirmer were a separate issuer and its confirmation were a separate standby issued for the account of the issuer.

ii. "Beneficiary" includes a person to whom the named beneficiary has effectively transferred drawing rights ("transferee beneficiary");

iii. "Including" means "including but not limited to";

iv. "A or B" means "A or B or both"; "either A or B" means "A or B, but not both"; and "A and B" means "both A or B";

v. Words in the singular number include the plural, and in the plural include the singular; and

vi. Words of the neuter gender include any gender.

d. i. Use of the phrase "unless a standby otherwise states" or the like in a rule emphasizes that the text of the standby controls over the rule;

ii. Absence of such a phrase in other rules does not imply that other rules have priority over the text of the standby;

iii. Addition of the term "expressly" or "clearly" to the phrase "unless a standby otherwise states" or the like emphasizes that the rule should be excluded or modified only by wording in the standby that is specific and unambiguous; and

iv. While the effect of all of these Rules may be varied by the text of the standby, variations of the effect of some of these Rules may disqualify the standby as an independent undertaking under applicable law.

e. The phrase "stated in the standby" or the like refers to the actual text of a standby (whether as issued or effectively amended) whereas the phrase "provided in the standby" or the like refers to both the text of the standby and these Rules as incorporated.

2. OBLIGATIONS

2.01 Undertaking to Honour by Issuer Any Confirmer to Beneficiary

a. An issuer undertakes to the beneficiary to honour a presentation that appears on its face to comply with the terms and conditions of the standby in accordance with these Rules supplemented by standard standby practice.

b. An issuer honours a complying presentation made to it by paying the amount demanded of it at sight, unless the standby provides for honour:

i. by acceptance of a draft drawn by the beneficiary on the issuer, in which case the issuer honours by:

(a) timely accepting the draft; and

(b) thereafter paying the holder of the draft on presentation of the accepted draft on or after its maturity.

ii. by deferred payment of a demand made by the beneficiary on the issue, in which case the issuer honours by:

(a) timely incurring a deferred payment obligation; and

(b) thereafter paying at maturity.

iii. by negotiation, in which case the issuer honours by paying the amount demanded at sight without recourse.

c. An issuer acts in a timely manner if it pays at sight, accepts a draft, or undertakes a deferred payment obligation (or if it gives notice of dishonour) within the time permitted for examining the presentation and giving notice of dishonour.

d. i. A confirmer undertakes to honour a complying presentation made to it by paying the amount demanded of it at sight or, if the standby so states, by another method of honour consistent with the issuer's a undertaking.

ii. If the confirmation permits presentation to the issuer, then the confirmation undertakes also to honour upon the issuer's wrongful dishonour by performing as if the presentation had been made to the confirmer.

iii. If the standby permits presentation to the confirmer, then the issuer undertakes also to honour upon the confirmer's wrongful dishonour by performing as if the presentation had been made to the issuer.

e. An issuer honors by paying in immediately available funds in the currency designated in the standby unless the standby states it is payable by:

i. payment of a monetary unit of account, in which case the undertaking is to pay in that unit of account; or

ii. delivery of other items of value, in which case the undertaking is to deliver those items.

2.02 Obligation of Different Branches, Agencies, or Other Offices

For the purposes of these Rules, an issuer's branch, agency, or other office acting or undertaking to act under a standby in a capacity other than as issuer is obligated in that capacity only and shall be treated as a different person.

2.03 Conditions to Issuance

A standby is issued when it leaves an issuer's control unless it clearly specifies that it is not then "issued" or "enforceable". Statements that a standby is not "available", "operative", "effective", or the like do not affect its irrevocable and binding nature at the time it leaves the issuer's control.

2.04 Nomination

a. A standby may nominate a person to advise, receive a presentation, effect a transfer, confirm, pay, negotiate, incur a deferred payment obligation, or accept a draft.

b. Nomination does not obligate the nominated person to act except to the extent that the nominated person undertakes to act.

c. A nominated person is not authorised to bind the person making the nomination.

2.05 Advice of Standby or Amendment

a. Unless an advice states otherwise, it signifies that:

i. the advisor has checked the apparent authenticity of the advised message in accordance with standard letter of credit practice; and

ii. the advice accurately reflects what has been received.

b. A person who is requested to advise a standby and decides not to do so should notify the requesting party.

2.06 When an Amendment is Authorised and Binding

a. If a standby expressly states that it is subject to "automatic amendment" by an increase or decrease in the amount available, an extension of the expiration date, or the like, the amendment is effective automatically without any further notification or consent beyond that expressly provided for in the standby. (Such an amendment may also be referred to as becoming effective "without amendment").

b. If there is no provision for automatic amendment:

i. the issuer when it leaves the issuer's control; and;

ii. the confirmer when it leaves the issuer's control, unless the confirmer indicates that it does not confirm the amendment.

c. If there is no provision for automatic amendment:

i. the beneficiary must consent to the amendment for it to be binding

ii. the beneficiary's consent must be made by an express communication to the person advising the amendment unless the beneficiary presents documents which comply with the standby as amended and which would not comply with the standby prior to such amendment; and

iii. an amendment does not require the applicant's consent to be binding on the issuer, the confirmer, or the beneficiary.

d. Consent to only part of an amendment is a rejection of the entire amendment.

2.07 Routing of Amendments

a. An issue using another person to advise a standby must advise all amendments to that person.

b. An amendment or cancellation of a standby does not affect the issuer's obligation to a nominated person that has acted within the scope of its nomination before receipt of notice of the amendment or cancellation.

c. Non-extension of an automatically extendable (renewable) standby does not affect an issuer's obligation to a nominated person who has acted within the scope of its nomination before receipt of a notice of non-extension.

3. PRESENTATION

3.01 Complying Presentation Under a Standby

A standby should indicate the time, place and location within that place, person to whom, and medium in which presentation should be made. If so, presentation must be so made in order to comply. To the extent that a standby does not so indicate, presentation must be made in accordance with these Rules in order to be complying.

3.02 What Constitutes a Presentation

The receipt of document required by and presented under a standby constitutes a presentation requiring examination for compliance with the terms and conditions of the standby even if not all of the required documents have been presented.

3.03 Identification of Standby

a. A presentation must identify the standby under which the presentation is made.

b. A presentation may identify the standby by stating the complete reference number of the standby and the name and location of the issuer or by attaching the original or a copy of the standby.

c. If the issuer cannot determine from the face of a document received that it should be processed under a standby or cannot identify the standby to which it relates, presentation is deemed to have been made on the date of identification.

3.04 Where and to Whom Complying Presentation Made

a. To comply, a presentation must be made at the place and any location at that place indicated in the standby or provided in these Rules.

b. If no place of presentation to the issuer is indicated in the standby, presentation to the issuer must be made at the place of business from which the standby was issued.

c. If a standby is confirmed, but no place for presentation is indicated in the confirmation, presentation for the purpose of obligating the confirmer (and the issuer) must be made at the place of business of the confirmer from which the confirmation was issued or to the issuer.

d. If no location at a place of presentation is indicated (such as department, floor, room, station, mail stop, post office box, or other location), presentation may be made to:

i. the general postal address indicated in the standby;

ii. any location at the place designated to receive deliveries of mail or documents; or

iii. any person at the place of presentation actually or apparently authorised to receive it.

3.05 When Timely Presentation Made

a. A presentation is timely if made at any time after issuance and before expiry on the expiration date.

b. A presentation made after the close of business at the place of presentation is deemed to have been made on the next business day.

3.06 Complying Medium of Presentation

a. To comply, a document must be presented in the medium indicated in the standby.

b. Where no medium is indicated, to comply a document must be presented as a paper document, unless only a demand is required in which case:

i. a demand that is presented via S. W. I. F. T., tested telex, or other similar authenticated means by a beneficiary that is a S. W. I. F. T. participant or a bank complies; otherwise

ii. a demand that is not presented as a paper document does not comply unless the issuer permits, in its sole discretion, the use of that medium.

c. A document is not presented as a paper document if it is communicated by electronic means even if the issuer or nominated person receiving it generates a paper document from it.

d. Where presentation in an electronic medium is indicated, to comply a document must be presented as an electronic record capable of being authenticated by the issuer or nominated person to whom it is presented.

3.07 Separateness of Each Presentation

a. Making a non-complying presentation, withdrawing a presentation, or failing to make any one of a number of scheduled or permitted presentations does not waive or otherwise prejudice the right to make another timely presentation or a timely re-presentation whether or not the standby prohibits partial or multiple drawings or presentations.

b. Wrongful dishonour of a complying presentation does not constitute dishonour of any other presentation under a standby or repudiation of the standby.

c. Honour of a non-complying presentation, with or without notice of its non-compliance, does not waive requirements of a standby for other presentations.

3.08 Partial Drawing and Multiple Presentation; Amount of Drawings

a. A presentation may be made for less than the full amount available ("partial drawing").

b. More than one presentation ("multiple presentation") may be made.

c. The statement "partial drawing prohibited" or similar expression means that a presentation must be for the full amount available.

d. The statement "multiple drawing prohibited" or a similar expression means that only one presentation may be made and honoured but that it may be for less than the full amount available.

e. If a demand exceeds the amount available under the standby, the drawing is discrepant. Any document other than the demand stating an amount in excess of the amount demanded is not discrepant for that reason.

f. Use of "approximately", "about", "circa", or a similar word permits a tolerance not to exceed 10% more or 10% less of the amount to which such word refers.

3.09 Extend or Pay

A beneficiary's request to extend the expiration date of the standby or, alternatively, to pay the amount available under it;

a. is a presentation demanding payment under the standby, to be examined as such in accordance with these Rules; and

b. implies that the beneficiary:

i. consents to the amendment to extend the expiry date to the date requested.

ii. requests the issuer to exercise its discretion to seek the approval of the applicant and to issue that amendment;

iii. upon issuance of that amendment, retracts its demand for payment; and

iv. consents to the maximum time available under these Rules for examination and notice of dishonour.

3.10 No Notice of Receipt of Presentation

An issuer is not required to notify the applicant of receipt of a presentation under the standby.

3.11 Issuer Waiver and Applicant Consent to Waive of Presentation Rules

In addition to other discretionary provision in a standby or these Rules, an issuer may, in its sole discretion, without notice to or consent of the applicant and without effect on the applicant's obligations to the issuer, waive.

a. the following Rules and any similar terms stated in the standby which are primarily for the issuer's benefit or operational convenience:

i. treatment of documents received, at the request of the presenter, as having been presented at a later date (Rule 3.02)

ii. identification of a presentation to the standby under which it is presented (Rule 3.03(a));

iii. where and to whom presentation to the standby under which it is presented (Rule 3.04 (b), (c), and(d)), except the country of presentation stated in the standby; or

iv. treatment of a presentation made after the close of business as if it were made on the next business day (Rule 3.05(b)).

b. the following Rule but not similar terms stated in the standby:

i. a required document dated after the date of its stated presentation(Rule 4.06); or

ii. the requirement that a document issued by the beneficiary be in the language of the standby (Rule 4.04).

c. the following Rule relating to the operational integrity of the standby only in so far as the bank is in fact clearing with the true beneficiary: acceptance of a demand in an electronic medium (Rule 3.06(b)).

Waiver by the confirmer requires the consent of the issuer with respect to paragraphs (b) and (c) of this Rule.

3.12 Original Standby Lost, Stolen, Mutilated, or Destroyed

a. If an original standby is lost, stolen, mutilated, or destroyed, the issuer need not replace it or waive any requirement that the original be presented under the standby.

b. If the issuer agrees to replace an original standby or to waive a requirement for its presentation, it may provide a replacement or copy to the beneficiary without affecting the applicant's obligations to the issuer to reimburse, but, if it does so, the issuer must mark the replacement or copy as such. The issuer may, in its sole discretion, require indemnities satisfactory to it from the beneficiary and assurances from nominated persons that no payment has been made.

Closure on Expiry Date

3.13 Expiry Date on a Non-Business Day

a. If the last day for presentation stated in a standby (whether stated to be the expiration date or the date by which documents must be received) is not a business day of the issuer or nominated person where presentation is to be made, then presentation made there on the first following business day shall be deemed timely.

b. A nominated person to whom such a presentation is made must so notify the issuer.

3.14 Closure on a Business Day and Authorization of Another Reasonable Place for Presentation

a. If on the last business day for presentation stated in standby is for any reason closed and presentation is not timely made because of the closure, then the last day for presentation is automatically extended to the day occurring thirty calendar days after the place for presentation re-opens for business, unless the standby otherwise provide.

b. Upon or in anticipation of closure of the place of presentation, an issuer may authorise another reasonable place for presentation in the standby or in a communication received by the beneficiary. If it does so, then

i. presentation must be made at that reasonable place; and

ii. if the communication is received fewer than thirty calendar days before the last day for presentation and for that reason presentation is not timely made, the last day for presentation is automatically extended to the day occurring thirty calendar days after the last day for presentation.

4. EXAMINATION

4.01 Examination for Compliance

a. Demands for honour of a standby must comply with the terms and conditions of the standby.

b. Whether a presentation appears to comply is determined by examining the presentation on its face against the terms and conditions stated in the standby as interpreted and supplemented by these Rules which are to be read in the context of standard standby practice.

4.02 Non-Examination of Extraneous Documents

Documents presented which are not required by the standby need not be examined and, in any event, shall be disregarded for purposes of determining compliance of the presentation. They may without responsibility be returned to the presenter or passed on with other documents presented.

4.03 Examination for Inconsistency

An issuer or nominated person is required to examine documents for inconsistency with each other only to the extent provided in the standby.

4.04 Language of Documents

The language of all documents issued by the beneficiary is to be that of that standby.

4.05 Issuer of Documents

Any required document must be issued by the beneficiary unless the standby indicates that the document is to be issued by a third person or the document is of type that standard standby practice requires to be issued by a third person.

4.06 Date of Documents

The issuance date of a required document may be earlier but not later than the date of its presentation.

4.07 Required Signature on a Document

a. A required document need not be signed unless the standby indicates that the document must be signed or the document is of a type that standard standby practice requires be signed.

b. A required signature may be made in any manner that corresponds to the medium in which the signed document is presented.

c. Unless a standby specifies:

i. the name of a person who must sign a document, any signature authentication will be regarded as a complying signature.

ii. the status of a person who must sign, no indication of status in necessary.

d. If a standby specifies that a signature must be made by:

i. a named natural person without requiring that the signer's status be identified, a signature complies that appears to be that of the named person;

ii. a named legal person or government agency without identifying who is to sign on its behalf or its status, any signature complies that appears to have been made on behalf of the named legal person or government agency; or

iii. a named natural person , legal person , government agency requiring the status of the signer be indicated, a signature complies which appears to be that of the named natural person, legal person, or government agency and indicates its status.

4.08 Demand Document Implied

If a standby does not specify any required document, it will still be deemed to require a documentary demand for payment.

4.09 Identical Wording and Quotation Marks

If a standby requires:

a. a statement without specifying precise wording, then the wording in the wording in the document presented must appear to convey the same meaning as that required by the standby.

b. Specified wording by the use of quotation marks, blocked wording, or an attached exhibit or form, then typographical errors in spelling, punctuation, spacing, or the like that are apparent when read in context are not required to be duplicated and blank lines or spaces for data may be completed in any manner not inconsistent with the standby, or

c. Specified wording by the use of quotation marks, blocked wording, or an attached exhibit or form, and also provides that the specified wording be "exact" or "identical", then the wording in the documents presented, including typographical errors in spelling, punctuation, spacing and the like, as well as blank lines and spaces for data, must be exactly reproduced.

4.10 Applicant Approval

A standby should not specify that a required document be issued, signed, or counter-signed by the applicant. However, if the standby includes such a requirement, the issuer may not waive the requirement and is not responsible for the applicant's withholding of the document or signature.

4.11 Non-Documentary Terms or Conditions

a. A standby term or condition which is non-documentary must be disregarded whether or not it affects the issuer's obligation to treat a presentation as complying or to treat the standby as issued, amended, or terminated.

b. Terms or conditions are non-documentary if the standby does not require presentation of a document in which they are to be evidenced and if their fulfillment cannot be determined by the issuer from the issuer's own records or within the issuer's normal operations.

c. Determinations from the issuer's own records or within the issuer's normal operations include determinations from the issuer's own records or within the issuer's normal operations include determinations of:

i. when, where, and how documents are presented or otherwise delivered to the issuer;

ii. when, where, and how communication affecting the standby are sent or received by the issuer, beneficiary, or any nominated person;

iii. amounts transferred into or out of accounts with the issuer; and

iv. amounts determinable from a published index (e.g., if a standby provides for determining amounts of interest accruing according to published interest rates).

d. An issuer need not re-compute a beneficiary's computations under a formula stated or referenced in a standby except to the extent that the standby so provides.

4. 12 Formality of Statements in Documents

a. A required statement need not be accompanied by a solemnity, officialization, or any other formality.

b. If a standby provides for the addition of a formality to a required statement by the person making it without specifying form or content, the statement complies if it indicates that it was declared, averred, warranted, attested, sworn under oath, affirmed, certified, or the like.

c. If a standby provides for a statement to be witnessed by an other person other than the beneficiary with an indication that the person is acting as a witness.

d. If a standby provides for a statement to be counter-signed, legalized, visaed, or the like by a person other than the beneficiary acting in a governmental, judicial, corporate, or other representative capacity without specifying form or content, the statement complies if it contains the signature of a person other than the beneficiary and includes an indication of that person's representative capacity and the organization on whose behalf the person has acted.

4. 13 No Responsibility to Identify Beneficiary

Except to the extent that a standby requires presentation of an electronic record:

a. a person honouring a presentation has no obligation to the applicant to ascertain the identity of any person making a presentation or any assignee of proceeds.

b. payment to a named beneficiary, transferee, an acknowledged assignee, successor by operation of law, to an account or account number stated in the standby or in a cover instruction from the beneficiary or nominated person fulfills the obligation under the standby to effect payment.

4. 14 Name of Acquired or Merged Issuer or Confirmer

If the issuer or confirmer is reorganized, merged, or changes its name, any required reference by name to the issuer or confirmer in the documents presented be to it or its successor.

4. 15 Original, Copy, and Multiple Documents

a. A presented document must be an original.

b. Presentation of an electronic record, where an electronic presentation is permitted or required is deemed to be an "original".

c. i. A presented document is deemed to be an "original" unless it appears on its face to have been reproduced from an original.

ii. A document which appears to have been reproduced from an original is deemed to be an original if the signature or authentication appears to be original.

d. A standby that requires presentation of a "copy" permits presentation of either an or copy unless the standby states that only a copy be presented or otherwise addresses the disposition of all originals.

e. If multiples of the same document are requested, only one must be an original unless:

i. "duplicate originals" or "multiple originals" are requested in which case all must be originals; or

ii. "two copies", "two-fold", or the like are requested in which case either originals or copies may be presented.

Standby Document Types

4.16 Demand for Payment

a. A demand for payment need not be separate from the beneficiary's statement or other required document.

b. If a separate demand is required, it must contain:

i. a demand for payment from the beneficiary directed to the issuer or nominated person;

ii. a date indicating when the demand was issued;

iii. the amount demanded; and

iv. the beneficiary's signature.

c. A demand may be in the form of a draft or other instruction, order, or request to pay. If a standby requires presentation of a "draft" or "bill of exchange", that draft or bill of exchange need not be in negotiable form unless the standby so states.

4.17 Statement of Default or Other Drawing Event

If a standby requires a statement, certificate, or other recital content, the document complies if it contains:

a. a presentation to the effect that payment is due because a drawing event described in the standby has occurred;

b. a date indicating when it was issued; and

c. the beneficiary's signature.

4.18 Negotiable Documents

If a standby requires presentation of a document that is transferable by endorsement and delivery without stating whether, how, or to whom endorsement must be made, then the document may be presented without endorsement, or, if endorsed, the endorsement may be in blank and, in any event, the document may be issued or negotiated with or without recourse.

4.19 Legal or Judicial Documents

If a standby requires presentation of a government-issued document, a court order, an arbitration award, or the like, a document or a copy is deemed to comply if appears to be:

i. issued by a government agency, court, tribunal, or the like;

ii. suitably titled or named;

iii. signed;

iv. dated; and

v. originally certified or authenticated by an official of a government agency, court, tribunal, or the like.

4.20 Other Documents

a. If a standby requires a document other than one whose content is specified in these Rules without specifying the issuer, data content, or wording, a document complies if it appears to be appropriately titled or to serve the function of that type of document under standard standby practice.

b. A document presented under a standby is to be examined in the context of standby practice under these Rules even if the document is of a type (such as a commercial invoice, transport documents, insurance documents or the like) for which the Uniform Customs and Practice for Documentary Credits contains detailed rules.

4.21 Request to Issue Separate Undertaking

If a standby requests that the beneficiary of the standby issue its own separate undertaking to another (whether or not the standby recites the text of that undertaking):

a. the beneficiary receives no rights other than its rights to draw under the standby even if the issuer pays a fee to the beneficiary for issuing the separate undertaking;

b. neither the separate undertaking nor any documents presented under it are received by the issuer although not required to be presented as a condition to honour of the standby:

i. the issuer need not examine, and in any event, shall disregard their compliance or consistency with the standby, with the beneficiary's demand under the standby, or with the beneficiary's separate undertaking; and

ii. the issuer may without responsibility return them to the presenter or forward them to the applicant with the presentation.

5. NOTICE, PRECLUSION, AND DISPOSITION OF DOCUMENTS

5.01 Timely Notice of Dishonour

a. Notice of dishonour must be given within a time after presentation of documents which is not unreasonable.

i. Notice given within three business days is deemed to be not unreasonable and beyond seven business days is deemed to be unreasonable.

ii. Whether the time within which notice is given is unreasonable does not depend upon an imminent deadline for presentation.

iii. The time for calculating when notice of dishonour must be given begins on the business day following the business day of presentation.

iv. Unless a standby otherwise expressly states a shortened time within which notice of dishonour must be given, the issuer has no obligation to accelerate its examination of a presentation.

b. i. The means by which a notice of dishonour is to be given is by telecommunication, if available, and, if not, by another available means which allows for prompt notice.

ii. If notice of dishonour is received within the time permitted for giving the notice, then it is deemed to have been given by prompt means.

c. Notice of dishonour must be given to the person from whom the documents were received (whether the beneficiary, nominated person, or person other than a delivery person) except as otherwise requested by the presenter.

5.02 Statement of Grounds for Dishonour

A notice of dishonour shall state all discrepancies upon which dishonour is based.

5. 03 Failure to Give Timely Notice of Dishonour

a. Failure to give notice of a discrepancy in a notice of dishonour within the time and by the means specified in the standby or these rules precludes assertion of that discrepancy in any document containing the discrepancy that is retained or represented, but does not preclude assertion of that discrepancy in any different presentation under the same or a separate standby.

b. Failure to give notice of dishonour or acceptance or acknowledgment that a deferred payment undertaking has been incurred obligates the issuer to pay at maturity.

5. 04 Notice of Expiry

Failure to given notice that a presentation was made after the expiration date does not preclude dishonour for that reason.

5. 05 Issuer Request for Applicant Waiver without Request by Presenter

If the issuer decides that a presentation does not comply and if presenter does not otherwise instruct, the issuer may, in its sole discretion, request the applicant to waive noncompliance or other wise to authorise honour within the time available for giving notice of dishonour but without extending it. Obtaining the applicant's waiver does not obligate the issuer to waive non-compliance.

5. 06 Issuer Request for Applicant Waiver upon Request of Presenter

If, after receipt of notice of dishonor, a presenter requests that the presented documents be forwarded to the issuer or that the issuer seek the applicant's waiver:

a. no person is obligated to forward the discrepant documents or seek the applicant's waiver;

b. the presentation to the issuer remains subject to these Rules unless departure from them is expressly consented to by the presenter, and

c. if the document are forwarded or if a waiver is sought:

i. the presenter is precluded from objecting to the discrepancies notified to it by the issuer;

ii. the issuer is not relieved from examining the presentation under these Rules;

iii. the issuer is not obligated to waive the discrepancy even if the applicant waives it; and

iv. the issuer must hold the documents until it receives a response from the applicant or is requested by the presenter to return the documents, and if the issuer receives no such response or request within ten business days of its notice of dishonour, it may return the documents to the presenter.

5. 07 Disposition of Documents

Dishonoured documents must be returned, held, or disposed of as reasonably instructed by the presenter. Failure to give notice of the disposition of documents in the notice of dishonour does not preclude the issuer from asserting any defense otherwise available to it against honour.

5. 08 Cover Instructions/Transmittal Letter

a. Instructions accompanying a presentation made under a standby may be relied on to the extent that they are not contrary to the terms or conditions of the standby, the demand, or these Rules.

b. Representations made by a nominated person accompanying a presentation may be relied upon to the extent that they are not contrary to the terms or conditions of a standby or these Rules.

c. Notwithstanding receipt of instructions, an issuer or nominated person may pay, give notice, return the documents or otherwise deal directly with the presenter.

d. A statement in the cover letter that the documents are discrepant does not relieve the issuer from examining the presentation for compliance.

5.09 Applicant Notice of Objection

a. An applicant must timely object to an issuer's honour of a non-complying presentation by giving timely notice by prompt means.

b. An applicant acts timely if it objects to discrepancies by sending a notice to the issuer stating the discrepancies on which the objection is based within a time after the applicant's receipt of the documents which is not unreasonable.

c. Failure to give a timely notice of objection by prompt means precludes assertion by the applicant against the face of the documents received by the applicant, but does not preclude assertion of that objection to any different presentation under the same or a different standby.

6. TRANSFER, ASSIGNMENT, AND TRANSFER BY OPERATION OF LAW

Transfer of Drawing Rights

6.01 Request to Transfer Drawing Rights

Where a beneficiary requests that an issuer or nominated person honour a drawing from another person as if that person were the beneficiary, these Rules on transfer of drawing rights ("transfer") apply.

6.02 When Drawing Rights are Transferable

a. A standby is not transferable unless it so states.

b. A standby that states that is transferable without further provision means that drawing rights:

i. may be transferred in their entirety more than once;

ii. may not be partially transferred; and

iii. may not be transferred unless the issuer (including the confirmer) or another person specifically nominated in the standby agrees to and effects the transfer requested by the beneficiary.

6.03 Conditions to Transfer

An issuer of a transferable standby or a nominated person need not effect a transfer unless:

a. it is satisfied as to the existence and authenticity of the original standby; and

b. the beneficiary submits or fulfills:

i. a request in a form acceptable to the issuer or nominated person including the effective date of the transfer and the name and address of the transferee;

ii. the original standby;

iii. verification of the signature of the person signing for the beneficiary;

iv. verification of the authority of the person signing for the beneficiary;

v. payment of the transfer fee; and

vi. any other reasonable requirement.

6.04 Effect of Transfer on Required Documents

Where there has been a transfer of drawing rights in their entirety:

a. a draft of the transferee beneficiary may be used in place of the name of the transferor beneficiary in any other required document.

b. the name of the transferee beneficiary may be used in place of the name of the transferor beneficiary in any other required document.

6.05 Reimbursement for Payment Based on Transfer

An issuer or nominated person paying under a transfer pursuant to Rule 6.03(a), (b)(i), and (b)(ii) is entitled to reimbursement as if it had made payment to the beneficiary.

Acknowledgment of Assignment of Proceeds

6.06 Assignment of Proceeds

Where an issuer or nominated person is asked acknowledge a beneficiary's drawing under the standby, these Rules on acknowledgment of an assignment of proceeds apply except where applicable law otherwise requires.

6.07 Request for Acknowledgment

a. Unless applicable law otherwise requires, an issuer or nominated person

i. is not obligated to give effect to an assignment of proceeds which it has not acknowledged; and

ii. is not obligated to assignment the assignment.

b. If an assignment is acknowledged:

i. the acknowledgment confers no rights with respect to the standby to the assignee who is only entitled to the proceeds assigned, if any, and whose rights may be affected by amendment or cancellation; and

ii. the rights of the assignee are subject to:

(a) the existence of any net proceeds payable to the beneficiary by the person making the acknowledgment;

(b) rights of nominated persons and transferee beneficiaries;

(c) rights of other acknowledged assignees; and

(d) any other rights or interests that may have priority under applicable law.

6.08 Conditions to Acknowledgment of Assignment of Proceeds

An issuer or nominated person may condition its acknowledgment on receipt of:

a. the original standby for examination or notation;

b. verification of signature of the person signing for the beneficiary;

c. verification of the authority of the person signing for the beneficiary;

d. an irrevocable request signed by the beneficiary for acknowledgment of assignment that includes statements, covenants, indemnities, and other provisions which may be contained in the issuer's or nominated person's required form requesting acknowledgment of assignment, such as:

i. the identity of the affected drawings if the standby permits multiple drawings;

ii. the full name, legal form, location, and mailing address of the beneficiary and the assignee;

iii. details of any request affecting the method of payment or delivery of the standby proceeds;

iv. limitation on partial assignments and prohibition of successive assignments;

v. statements regarding the legality and relative priority of the assignment; or

vi. right of recovery by the issuer or nominated person of any proceeds received by the assignee that are recoverable from the beneficiary;

e. payment of a fee for the acknowledgment; and

f. fulfillment of other reasonable requirements.

6.09 Conflicting Claims to Proceeds

If there are conflicting claims to proceeds, then payment to an acknowledged assignee may be suspended pending resolution of the conflict.

6.10 Reimbursement for Payment Based on an Assignment

An issuer or nominated person paying under an acknowledged assignment pursuant to Rule 6.08(a) and (b) is entitled to reimbursement as if it had made payment to the beneficiary. If the beneficiary is a bank, the acknowledgment may be based solely upon an authenticated communication.

Transfer by Operation of Law

6.11 Transfer by Operation of Law

Where an heir, personal representative, liquidator, trustee, receive, successor corporation, or similar person who claims to be designated by law to succeed to the interests of a beneficiary presents documents in its own name as if it were the authorised transferee of the beneficiary, these Rules on transfer by operation of law apply.

6.12 Additional Document in Event of Drawing in Successor's Name

A claimed successor may be treated as if it were an authorise transferee of a beneficiary's drawing rights in their entirety if it presents an additional document or documents which appear to be issued by a public official or representative (including a judicial officer) and indicate:

a. that the claimed successor is the survivor of a merger, consolidation, or similar action of a corporation, limited liability company, or other similar organization;

b. that the claimed successor is authorised or appointed to act on behalf of the named beneficiary or its estate because of an insolvency proceeding;

c. that the claimed successor is authorised or appointed to act on behalf of the named beneficiary because of death or incapability; or

d. that the name of the named beneficiary has been changed to that of the claimed successor.

6.13 Suspension of Obligations upon Presentation by Successor

a. may request in a manner satisfactory as to form and substance;

i. a legal opinion;

ii. an additional document referred to in Rule 6.12 (Additional Document in Event of Drawing in Successor's Name) from a public official;

iii. statement, covenants, and indemnities regarding the status of the claimed successor as successor by operation of law;

iv. payment of fees reasonably related to these determinations; and

v. anything which may be required for a transfer under Rule 6.03 (Conditions to Transfer) or an acknowledgment of assignment of proceeds under Rule 6.08 (Conditions to Acknowledgment of Assignment of Proceeds); but such documentation shall not constitute a required document for purposes of expiry of the standby.

b. Until the issuer or nominated person receives the requested documentation, its obligation to honour or give notices of dishonour is suspended, but any deadline for presentation of required documents is not thereby extended.

6.14 Reimbursement for Payment Based on a Transfer by Operation of Law

An issuer or nominated person paying under a transfer by operation of law pursuant to Rule 6.12 (Additional Document in Event of Drawing in Successor's Name) is entitled to reimbursement as if it had made payment to the beneficiary.

7. CANCELLATION

7.01 When an Irrevocable Standby is Cancelled or Terminated

A beneficiary's rights under a standby may not be cancelled without its consent. Consent may be evidenced in writing or by an action such as return of the original standby in a manner which implies that the beneficiary consents to cancellation. A beneficiary's consent to cancellation is irrevocable when communicated to the issuer.

7.02 Issuer's Discretion Regarding a Decision to Cancel

Before acceding to a beneficiary's authorization to cancel and treating the standby as cancelled for all purposes, an issuer may require in a manner satisfactory as to form and substance:

a. the original standby;

b. verification of the signature of the person signing for the beneficiary;

c. verification of authorization of the person signing for the authorization;

d. a legal opinion;

e. an irrevocable authority signed by the authorization for cancellation that includes statements, covenants, indemnities, and similar provisions contained in a required form;

f. satisfaction that the obligation of any confirmer has been cancelled;

g. satisfaction that there has not been a transfer or payment by any nominated person; and

h. any other reasonable measure.

8. REIMBURSEMENT OBLIGATIONS

8.01 Right to Reimbursement

a. Where payment is made against a complying presentation in accordance with these Rules, reimbursement must be made by:

i. an applicant to an issuer requested to issue a standby;

ii. an issuer to a person nominated to honour or otherwise give value.

b. An applicant must indemnify the issuer against all claims, obligations, and responsibilities (including attorney's fees) arising out of:

i. the imposition of law or practice other than that chosen in the standby or applicable at the place of issuance;

ii. the fraud, forgery, or illegal action of others; or

iii. the issuer's performance of the obligations of a confirmer that wrongfully dishonours a confirmation.

8.02 Charges for Fees and Costs

a. An applicant must pay the issuer's charges and reimburse the issuer for any charges that the issuer is obligated to pay to persons nominated with the applicant's consent to advise, confirm, honour, negotiate, transfer, or to issue a separate undertaking.

b. An issuer is obligated to pay the charges of other persons:

i. if they are payable in accordance with the terms of the standby; or

ii. if they are the reasonable and customary fees and expenses of a person requested by the issuer to advise, honour, negotiate, transfer, or to issue a separate undertaking and they are unrecovered and unrecoverable from the beneficiary or other presenter because no demand is made under the standby.

8.03 Refund of Reimbursement

A nominated person that obtains reimbursement before the issuer timely dishonours the presentation must refund the reimbursement with interest if the issuer dishonours. The refund does not preclude the nominated person's wrongful dishonour claims.

8.04 Bank-to-Bank Reimbursement

Any instruction or authorization to obtain reimbursement from another bank is subject to the International Chamber of Commerce standard rules for bank-to-bank reimbursements.

9. TIMING

9.01 Duration of Standby

A standby must:

a. contain an expiry date; or

b. permit the issuer to terminate the standby upon reasonable prior notice payment.

9.02 Effect of Expiration on Nominated Person

The rights of a nominated person that acts within the scope of its nomination are not affected by the subsequent expiry of the standby.

9.03 Calculation of Time

a. A period of time within which an action must be taken under these Rules begins to run on the first business day following the business day when the action could have been undertaken at the place where the action should have been undertaken.

b. An extension period starts on the calendar day following the stated expiry date even if either day falls on a day when the issuer is closed.

9.04 Time of Day of Expiration

If no time of day is stated for expiration, it occurs at the close of business at the place of presentation.

9.05 Retention of Standby

Retention of the original standby does not preserve any rights under the standby after the right to demand payment ceases.

10. SYNDICATION/PARTICIPATION

10.01 Syndication

If a standby with more than one issuer does not state to whom presentation may be made, presentation may be made to any issuer with binding effect on all issuers.

10.02 Participation

a. Unless otherwise agreed between an applicant and an issuer, the issuer may sell participations in the issuer's rights against the applicant and any presenter and may disclose relevant applicant information in confidential to potential participants.

b. An issuer's sale of participation participations does not affect the obligations of the issuer under the standby or create any rights or obligations between the beneficiary and any participant.

Appendix 6. International Standard Banking Practice for the Examination of Documents under Documentary Credits subject to UCP 600

Originals and copies
Shipping marks
Signatures
Title of documents and combined documents
DRAFTS AND CALCULATION OF MATURITY DATE
Tenor
Maturity date
Banking days, grace days, delays in remittance
Endorsement
Amounts
How the draft is drawn
Drafts on the applicant
Corrections and alterations
INVOICES
Definition of invoice
Description of the goods and other general issues related to invoices
TRANSPORT DOCUMENT COVERING AT LEAST TWO DIFFERENT MODES OF TRANSPORT
Application of UCP 600 article 19
Full set of originals
Signing of multimodal transport documents
On board notations
Place of taking in charge, dispatch, loading on board and destination
Consignee, order party, shipper and endorsement, notify party
Transhipment and partial shipment
Clean multimodal transport documents
Goods description
Corrections and alterations
Freight and additional costs
Goods covered by more than one multimodal transport document
BILL OF LADING
Application of UCP 600 article 20
Full set of originals
Signing of bills of lading
On board notations
Ports of loading and ports of discharge
Consignee, order party, shipper and endorsement, notify party
Transhipment and partial shipment

Clean bills of lading
Goods description
Corrections and alterations
Freight and additional costs
Goods covered by more than one bill of lading
CHARTER PARTY BILL OF LADING
Application of UCP 600 article 22
Full set of originals
Signing of charter party bills of lading
On board notations
Ports of loading and ports of discharge
Consignee, order party, shipper and endorsement, notify party
Partial shipment
Clean charter party bills of lading
Goods description
Corrections and alterations
Freight and additional costs
AIR TRANSPORT DOCUMENT
Application of UCP 600 article 23
Original air transport documents
Signing of air transport documents
Goods accepted for carriage, date of shipment, and requirement for an actual date of dispatch
Airports of departure and destination
Consignee, order party and notify party
Transhipment and partial shipment
Clean air transport documents
Goods description
Corrections and alterations
Freight and additional costs
ROAD, RAIL OR INLAND WATERWAY TRANSPORT DOCUMENTS
Application of UCP 600 article 24
Original and duplicate of road, rail or inland waterway transport documents
Carrier and signing of road, rail or inland waterway transport documents
Order party and notify party
Partial shipment
Goods description
Corrections and alterations
Freight and additional costs

INSURANCE DOCUMENT AND COVERAGE

Application of UCP 600 article 28

Issuers of insurance documents

Risks to be covered

Dates

Currency and amount

Insured party and endorsement

CERTIFICATES OF ORIGIN

Basic requirements

Issuers of certificates of origin

Contents of certificates of origin

INTRODUCTION

Since the approval of International Standard Banking Practice (ISBP) by the ICC Banking Commission in 2002, ICC Publication 645 has become an invaluable aid to banks, corporates, logistics specialists and insurance companies alike, on a global basis. Participants in ICC seminars and workshops have indicated that rejection rates have dropped due to the application of the 200 practices that are detailed in ISBP.

However, there have also been comments that although the ISBP Publication 645 was approved by the Banking Commission its application had no relationship with UCP 500. With the approval of UCP 600 in October 2006, it has become necessary to provide an updated version of the ISBP. It is emphasized that this is an updated version as opposed to a revision of ICC Publication 645. Where it was felt appropriate, paragraphs that appeared in Publication 645 and that have now been covered in effectively the same text in UCP 600 have been removed from this updated version of ISBP.

As a means of creating a relationship between the UCP and ISBP, the introduction to UCP 600, states: "During the revision process, notice was taken of the considerable work that had been completed in creating the International Standard Banking Practice for the Examination of Documents under Documentary Credits (ISBP), ICC Publication 645. This publication has evolved into a necessary companion to the UCP for determining compliance of documents with the terms of letters of credit. It is the expectation of the Drafting Group and the Banking Commission that the application of the principles contained in the ISBP, including subsequent revisions thereof, will continue during the time UCP 600 is in force. At the time UCP 600 is implemented, there will be an updated version of the ISBP to bring its contents in line with the substance and style of the new rules."

The international standard banking practices documented in this publication are consistent with UCP 600 and the Opinions and Decisions of the ICC Banking Commission. This document does not amend UCP 600. It explains how the practices articulated in UCP 600 are applied by documentary practitioners. This publication and the UCP should be read in their entirety and not in isolation. It is, of course, recognized that the law in some countries may compel a different practice than those stated here.

No single publication can anticipate all the terms or the documents that may be used in connection with documentary credits or their interpretation under UCP 600 and the standard practice it reflects. However, the Task Force that prepared Publication 645 endeavoured to cover terms commonly seen on a day-to-day basis and the documents most often presented under documentary credits. The Drafting Group have reviewed and updated this publication to conform with UCP 600.

It should be noted that any term in a documentary credit which modifies or excludes the applicability of a provision of UCP 600 may also have an impact on international standard banking practice. Therefore, in considering the practices described in this publication, parties must take into account any term in a documentary credit that expressly modifies or excludes a rule contained in UCP 600. This principle is implicit throughout this publication. Where examples are given, these are solely for the purpose of illustration and are not exhaustive.

This publication reflects international standard banking practice for all parties to a documentary credit. Since applicants' obligations, rights and remedies depend upon their undertaking with the issuing bank, the performance of the underlying transaction and the timeliness of any objection under applicable law and practice, applicants should not assume that they may rely on these provisions in order to excuse their obligations to reimburse the issuing bank. The incorporation of this publication into the terms of a documentary credit should be discouraged, as the requirement to follow agreed practices is implicit in UCP 600.

PRELIMINARY CONSIDERATIONS

The application and issuance of the credit

1) The terms of a credit are independent of the underlying transaction even if a credit expressly refers to that transaction. To avoid unnecessary costs, delays, and disputes in the examination of documents, however, the applicant and beneficiary should carefully consider which documents should be required, by whom they should be produced and the time frame for presentation.

2) The applicant bears the risk of any ambiguity in its instructions to issue or amend a credit. Unless expressly stated otherwise, a request to issue or amend a credit authorizes an issuing bank to supplement or develop the terms in a manner necessary or desirable to permit the use of the credit.

3) The applicant should be aware that UCP 600 contains articles such as 3, 14, 19, 20, 21, 23, 24, 28(i), 30 and 31 that define terms in a manner that may produce unexpected results unless the applicant fully acquaints itself with these provisions. For example, a credit requiring presentation of a bill of lading and containing a prohibition against transhipment will, in most cases, have to exclude UCP 600 sub-article 20(c) to make the prohibition against transhipment effective.

4) A credit should not require presentation of documents that are to be issued or countersigned by the applicant. If a credit is issued including such terms, the beneficiary must either seek amendment or comply with them and bear the risk of failure to do so.

5) Many of the problems that arise at the examination stage could be avoided or resolved by careful attention to detail in the underlying transaction, the credit application, and issuance of the credit as discussed.

GENERAL PRINCIPLES

Abbreviations

6) The use of generally accepted abbreviations, for example "Ltd." instead of "Limited", "Int'l" instead of "International", "Co." instead of "Company", "kgs" or "kos." instead of "kilos", "Ind" instead of "Industry", "mfr" instead of "manufacturer" or "mt" instead of "metric tons" – or vice versa – does not make a document discrepant.

7) Virgules (slash marks "/") may have different meanings, and unless apparent in the context used, should not be used as a substitute for a word.

Certifications and declarations

8) A certification, declaration or the like may either be a separate document or contained within another document as required by the credit. If the certification or declaration appears in another document which is signed and dated, any certification or declaration appearing on that document does not require a separate signature or date if the certification or declaration appears to have been given by the same entity that issued and signed the document.

Corrections and alterations

9) Corrections and alterations of information or data in documents, other than documents created by the beneficiary, must appear to be authenticated by the party who issued the document or by a party authorized by the issuer to do so. Corrections and alterations in documents which have been legalized, visaed, certified or similar, must appear to be authenticated by the party who legalized, visaed, certified etc., the document. The authentication must show by whom the authentication has been made and include the signature or initials of that party. If the authentication appears to have been made by a party other than the issuer of the document, the authentication must clearly show in which capacity that party has authenticated the correction or alteration.

10) Corrections and alterations in documents issued by the beneficiary itself, except drafts, which have not been legalized, visaed, certified or similar, need not be authenticated.

See also "Drafts and calculation of maturity date".

11) The use of multiple type styles or font sizes or handwriting in the same document does not, by itself, signify a correction or alteration.

12) Where a document contains more than one correction or alteration, either each correction must be authenticated separately or one authentication must be linked to all corrections in an appropriate way. For example, if the document shows three corrections numbered 1, 2 and 3, one statement such as "Correction numbers 1, 2 and 3 above authorized by XXX" or similar, will satisfy the requirement for authentication.

Dates

13) Drafts, transport documents and insurance documents must be dated even if a credit does not expressly so require. A requirement that a document, other than those mentioned above, be dated, may be satisfied by reference in the document to the date of another document forming part of the same presentation (e.g., where a shipping certificate is issued which states "date as per bill of

lading number xxx" or similar terms). Although it is expected that a required certificate or declaration in a separate document be dated, its compliance will depend on the type of certification or declaration that has been requested, its required wording and the wording that appears within it. Whether other documents require dating will depend on the nature and content of the document in question.

14) Any document, including a certificate of analysis, inspection certificate and pre-shipment inspection certificate, may be dated after the date of shipment. However, if a credit requires a document evidencing a pre-shipment event (e. g., pre-shipment inspection certificate), the document must, either by its title or content, indicate that the event (e. g., inspection) took place prior to or on the date of shipment. A requirement for an "inspection certificate" does not constitute a requirement to evidence a pre-shipment event. Documents must not indicate that they were issued after the date they are presented.

15) A document indicating a date of preparation and a later date of signing is deemed to be issued on the date of signing.

16) Phrases often used to signify time on either side of a date or event:

a) "within 2 days after" indicates a period from the date of the event until 2 days after the event.

b) "not later than 2 days after" does not indicate a period, only a latest date. If an advice must not be dated prior to a specific date, the credit must so state.

c) "at least 2 days before" indicates that something must take place not later than 2 days before an event. There is no limit as to how early it may take place.

d) "within 2 days of" indicates a period 2 days prior to the event until 2 days after the event.

17) The term "within" when used in connection with a date excludes that date in the calculation of the period.

18) Dates may be expressed in different formats, e. g., the 12th of November 2007 could be expressed as 12 Nov 07, 12Nov07, 12. 11. 2007, 12. 11. 07, 2007. 11. 12, 11. 12. 07, 121107, etc. Provided that the date intended can be determined from the document or from other documents included in the presentation, any of these formats are acceptable.

To avoid confusion it is recommended that the name of the month should be used instead of the number.

Documents for which the UCP 600 transport articles do not apply

19) Some documents commonly used in relation to the transportation of goods, e. g., Delivery Order, Forwarder's Certificate of Receipt, Forwarder's Certificate of Shipment, Forwarder's Certificate of Transport, Forwarder's Cargo Receipt and Mate's Receipt do not reflect a contract of carriage and are not transport documents as defined in UCP 600 articles 19 - 25. As such, UCP 600 sub-article 14(c) would not apply to these documents. Therefore, these documents will be examined in the same manner as other documents for which there are no specific provisions in UCP 600, i. e., under sub-article 14(f). In any event, documents must be presented not later than the

expiry date for presentation as stated in the credit.

20) Copies of transport documents are not transport documents for the purpose of UCP 600 articles 19 – 25 and sub-article 14(c). The UCP 600 transport articles apply where there are original transport documents presented. Where a credit allows for the presentation of a copy transport document rather than an original, the credit must explicitly state the details to be shown. Where copies (non-negotiable) are presented, they need not evidence signature, dates, etc.

Expressions not defined in UCP 600

21) Expressions such as "shipping documents", "stale documents acceptable", "third party documents acceptable", and "exporting country" should not be used as they are not defined in UCP 600. If used in a credit, their meaning should be made apparent. If not, they have the following meaning under international standard banking practice:

a) "shipping documents" – all documents (not only transport documents), except drafts, required by the credit.

b) "stale documents acceptable" – documents presented later than 21 calendar days after the date of shipment are acceptable as long as they are presented no later than the expiry date for presentation as stated in the credit.

c) "third party documents acceptable" – all documents, excluding drafts but including invoices, may be issued by a party other than the beneficiary. If it is the intention of the issuing bank that the transport or other documents may show a shipper other than the beneficiary, the clause is not necessary because it is already permitted by sub-article 14(k).

d) "exporting country" – the country where the beneficiary is domiciled, or the country of origin of the goods, or the country of receipt by the carrier or the country from which shipment or dispatch is made.

Issuer of documents

22) If a credit indicates that a document is to be issued by a named person or entity, this condition is satisfied if the document appears to be issued by the named person or entity. It may appear to be issued by a named person or entity by use of its letterhead, or, if there is no letterhead, the document appears to have been completed or signed by, or on behalf of, the named person or entity.

Language

23) Under international standard banking practice, it is expected that documents issued by the beneficiary will be in the language of the credit. When a credit states that documents in two or more languages are acceptable, a nominated bank may, in its advice of the credit, limit the number of acceptable languages as a condition of its engagement in the credit.

Mathematical calculations

24) Detailed mathematical calculations in documents will not be checked by banks. Banks are only obliged to check total values against the credit and other required documents.

Misspellings or typing errors

25) A misspelling or typing error that does not affect the meaning of a word or the sentence in which it occurs, does not make a document discrepant. For example, a description of the merchandise as "mashine" instead of "machine", "fountan pen" instead of "fountain pen" or "modle" instead of "model" would not make the document discrepant. However, a description as "model 123" instead of "model 321" would not be regarded as a typing error and would constitute a discrepancy.

Multiple pages and attachments or riders

26) Unless the credit or a document provides otherwise, pages which are physically bound together, sequentially numbered or contain internal cross references, however named or entitled, are to be examined as one document, even if some of the pages are regarded as an attachment. Where a document consists of more than one page, it must be possible to determine that the pages are part of the same document.

27) If a signature or endorsement is required to be on a document consisting of more than one page, the signature is normally placed on the first or last page of the document, but unless the credit or the document itself indicates where a signature or endorsement is to appear, the signature or endorsement may appear anywhere on the document.

Originals and copies

28) Documents issued in more than one original may be marked "Original", "Duplicate", "Triplicate", "First Original", "Second Original", etc. None of these markings will disqualify a document as an original.

29) The number of originals to be presented must be at least the number required by the credit, the UCP 600, or, where the document itself states how many originals have been issued, the number stated on the document.

30) It can sometimes be difficult to determine from the wording of a credit whether it requires an original or a copy, and to determine whether that requirement is satisfied by an original or a copy.

For example, where the credit requires:

a) "Invoice", "One Invoice" or "Invoice in 1 copy", it will be understood to be a requirement for an original invoice.

b) "Invoice in 4 copies", it will be satisfied by the presentation of at least one original and the remaining number as copies of an invoice.

c) "One copy of Invoice", it will be satisfied by presentation of either a copy or an original of an invoice.

31) Where an original would not be accepted in lieu of a copy, the credit must prohibit an original, e. g., "photocopy of invoice – original document not acceptable in lieu of photocopy", or the like. Where a credit calls for a copy of a transport document and indicates the disposal instructions for the original of that transport document, an original transport document will not be acceptable.

32) Copies of documents need not be signed.

33) In addition to UCP 600 article 17, the ICC Banking Commission Policy Statement, document 470/871(Rev), titled "The determination of an "Original" document in the context of UCP 500 sub-Article 20(b)" is recommended for further guidance on originals and copies and remains valid under UCP 600. The content of the Policy Statement appears in the Appendix of this publication, for reference purposes.

Shipping marks

34) The purpose of a shipping mark is to enable identification of a box, bag or package. If a credit specifies the details of a shipping mark, the documents mentioning the marks must show these details, but additional information is acceptable provided it is not in conflict with the credit terms.

35) Shipping marks contained in some documents often include information in excess of what would normally be considered "shipping marks", and could include information such as the type of goods, warnings as to the handling of fragile goods, net and/or gross weight of the goods, etc. The fact that some documents show such additional information, while others do not, is not a discrepancy.

36) Transport documents covering containerized goods will sometimes only show a container number under the heading "Shipping marks". Other documents that show a detailed marking will not be considered to be in conflict for that reason.

Signatures

37) Even if not stated in the credit, drafts, certificates and declarations by their nature require a signature. Transport documents and insurance documents must be signed in accordance with the provisions of UCP 600.

38) The fact that a document has a box or space for a signature does not necessarily mean that such box or space must be completed with a signature. For example, banks do not require a signature in the area titled "Signature of shipper or their agent" or similar phrases, commonly found on transport documents such as air waybills or road transport documents. If the content of a document indicates that it requires a signature to establish its validity (e.g., "This document is not valid unless signed" or similar terms), it must be signed.

39) A signature need not be handwritten. Facsimile signatures, perforated signatures, stamps, symbols (such as chops) or any electronic or mechanical means of authentication are sufficient. However, a photocopy of a signed document does not qualify as a signed original document, nor does a signed document transmitted through a fax machine, absent an original signature. A requirement for a document to be "signed and stamped", or a similar requirement, is also fulfilled by a signature and the name of the party typed, or stamped, or handwritten, etc.

40) A signature on a company letterhead paper will be taken to be the signature of that company, unless otherwise stated. The company name need not be repeated next to the signature.

Title of documents and combined documents

41) Documents may be titled as called for in the credit, bear a similar title, or be untitled.

For example, a credit requirement for a "Packing List" may also be satisfied by a document containing packing details whether titled "Packing Note", "Packing and Weight List", etc., or an untitled document. The content of a document must appear to fulfill the function of the required document.

42) Documents listed in a credit should be presented as separate documents. If a credit requires a packing list and a weight list, such requirement will be satisfied by presentation of two separate documents, or by presentation of two original copies of a combined packing and weight list, provided such document states both packing and weight details.

DRAFTS AND CALCULATION OF MATURITY DATE

Tenor

43) The tenor must be in accordance with the terms of the credit.

a) If a draft is drawn at a tenor other than sight, or other than a certain period after sight, it must be possible to establish the maturity date from the data in the draft itself.

b) As an example of where it is possible to establish a maturity date from the data in the draft, if a credit calls for drafts at a tenor 60 days after the bill of lading date, where the date of the bill of lading is 12 July 2007, the tenor could be indicated on the draft in one of the following ways:

i. "60 days after bill of lading date 12 July 2007", or

ii. "60 days after 12 July 2007", or

iii. "60 days after bill of lading date" and elsewhere on the face of the draft state "bill of lading date 12 July 2007", or

iv. "60 days date" on a draft dated the same day as the date of the bill of lading, or

v. "10 September 2007", i. e. 60 days after the bill of lading date.

c) If the tenor refers to xxx days after the bill of lading date, the on board date is deemed to be the bill of lading date even if the on board date is prior to or later than the date of issuance of the bill of lading.

d) UCP 600 article 3 provides guidance that where the words "from" and "after" are used to determine maturity dates of drafts, the calculation of the maturity commences the day following the date of the document, shipment, or other event, i. e., 10 days after or from March 1 is March 11.

e) If a bill of lading showing more than one on board notation is presented under a credit which requires drafts to be drawn, for example, at 60 days after or from bill of lading date, and the goods according to both or all on board notations were shipped from ports within a permitted geographical area or region, the earliest of these on board dates will be used for calculation of the maturity date. Example: the credit requires shipment from European port, and the bill of lading evidences on board vessel "A" from Dublin August 16 and on board vessel "B" from Rotterdam August 18. The draft should reflect 60 days from the earliest on board date in a European port, i. e., August 16.

f) If a credit requires drafts to be drawn, for example, at 60 days after or from bill of lading date, and more than one set of bills of lading is presented under one draft, the date of the last bill of lading will be used for the calculation of the maturity date.

44) While the examples refer to bill of lading dates, the same principles apply to all transport documents.

Maturity date

45) If a draft states a maturity date by using an actual date, the date must have been calculated in accordance with the requirements of the credit.

46) For drafts drawn "at XXX days sight", the maturity date is established as follows:

a) in the case of complying documents, or in the case of non-complying documents where the drawee bank has not provided a notice of refusal, the maturity date will be XXX days after the date of receipt of documents by the drawee bank.

b) in the case of non-complying documents where the drawee bank has provided a notice of refusal and subsequent approval, at the latest XXX days after the date of acceptance of the draft by the drawee bank. The date of acceptance of the draft must be no later than the date the issuing bank accepts the waiver of the applicant.

47) In all cases the drawee bank must advise the maturity date to the presenter. The calculation of tenor and maturity dates, as shown above, would also apply to credits designated as being available by deferred payment, i. e. , where there is no requirement for a draft to be presented by the beneficiary.

Banking days, grace days, delays in remittance

48) Payment must be available in immediately available funds on the due date at the place where the draft or documents are payable, provided such due date is a banking day in that place. If the due date is a non-banking day, payment will be due on the first banking day following the due date. Delays in the remittance of funds, such as grace days, the time it takes to remit funds, etc. , must not be in addition to the stated or agreed due date as defined by the draft or documents.

Endorsement

49) The draft must be endorsed, if necessary.

Amounts

50) The amount in words must accurately reflect the amount in figures if both are shown, and indicate the currency, as stated in the credit.

51) The amount must agree with that of the invoice, unless as a result of UCP 600 sub-article 18(b).

How the draft is drawn

52) The draft must be drawn on the party stated in the credit.

53) The draft must be drawn by the beneficiary.

Drafts on the applicant

54) A credit may be issued requiring a draft drawn on the applicant as one of the required documents, but must not be issued available by drafts drawn on the applicant.

Corrections and alterations

55) Corrections and alterations on a draft, if any, must appear to have been authenticated by the drawer.

56) In some countries a draft showing corrections or alterations will not be acceptable even

with the drawer's authentication. Issuing banks in such countries should make a statement in the credit to the effect that no correction or alteration must appear in the draft.

INVOICES

Definition of invoice

57) A credit requiring an "invoice" without further definition will be satisfied by any type of invoice presented (commercial invoice, customs invoice, tax invoice, final invoice, consular invoice, etc.). However, invoices identified as "provisional", "pro-forma" or the like are not acceptable. When a credit requires presentation of a commercial invoice, a document titled "invoice" will be acceptable.

Description of the goods, services or performance and other general issues related to invoices

58) The description of the goods, services or performance in the invoice must correspond with the description in the credit. There is no requirement for a mirror image. For example, details of the goods may be stated in a number of areas within the invoice which, when collated together, represents a description of the goods corresponding to that in the credit.

59) The description of goods, services or performance in an invoice must reflect what has actually been shipped or provided. For example, where there are two types of goods shown in the credit, such as 10 trucks and 5 tractors, an invoice that reflects only shipment of 4 trucks would be acceptable provided the credit does not prohibit partial shipment. An invoice showing the entire goods description as stated in the credit, then stating what has actually been shipped is also acceptable.

60) An invoice must evidence the value of the goods shipped or services or performance provided. Unit price(s), if any, and currency shown in the invoice must agree with that shown in the credit. The invoice must show any discounts or deductions required in the credit. The invoice may also show a deduction covering advance payment, discount, etc., not stated in the credit.

61) If a trade term is part of the goods description in the credit, or stated in connection with the amount, the invoice must state the trade term specified, and if the description provides the source of the trade term, the same source must be identified (e.g., a credit term "CIF Singapore Incoterms 2000" would not be satisfied by "CIF Singapore Incoterms"). Charges and costs must be included within the value shown against the stated trade term in the credit and invoice. Any charges and costs shown beyond this value are not allowed.

62) Unless required by the credit, an invoice need not be signed or dated.

63) The quantity of merchandise, weights and measurements shown on the invoice must not conflict with the same quantities appearing on other documents.

64) An invoice must not show:

a) over-shipment (except as provided in UCP 600 sub-article 30(b)), or

b) merchandise not called for in the credit (including samples, advertising materials, etc.) even if stated to be free of charge.

65) The quantity of the goods required in the credit may vary within a tolerance of +/- 5%.

This does not apply if a credit states that the quantity must not be exceeded or reduced, or if a credit states the quantity in terms of a stipulated number of packing units or individual items. A variance of up to +5% in the goods quantity does not allow the amount of the drawing to exceed the amount of the credit.

66) Even when partial shipments are prohibited, a tolerance of 5% less in the credit amount is acceptable, provided that the quantity is shipped in full and that any unit price, if stated in the credit, has not been reduced. If no quantity is stated in the credit, the invoice will be considered to cover the full quantity.

67) If a credit calls for instalment shipments, each shipment must be in accordance with the instalment schedule. TRANSPORT DOCUMENT COVERING AT LEAST TWO DIFFERENT MODES OF TRANSPORT

Application of UCP 600 article 19

68) If a credit requires presentation of a transport document covering transportation utilizing at least two modes of transport (multimodal or combined transport document), and if the transport document clearly shows that it covers a shipment from the place of taking in charge or port, airport or place of loading to the place of final destination mentioned in the credit, UCP 600 article 19 is applicable. In such circumstances, the transport document must not indicate that shipment or dispatch has been effected by only one mode of transport, but it may be silent regarding the modes of transport utilized.

69) In all places where the term "multimodal transport document" is used within this document, it also includes the term combined transport document. A document need not be titled "Multimodal transport document" or "Combined transport document" to be acceptable under UCP 600 article 19, even if such expressions are used in the credit.

Full set of originals

70) A UCP 600 article 19 transport document must indicate the number of originals that have been issued. Transport documents marked "First Original", "Second Original", "Third Original", "Original", "Duplicate", "Triplicate", etc., or similar expressions are all originals. Multimodal transport documents need not be marked "original" to be acceptable under a credit. In addition to UCP 600 article 17, the ICC Banking Commission Policy Statement, document 470/871(Rev), titled "The determination of an 'Original' document in the context of UCP 500 sub-Article 20(b)" is recommended for further guidance on originals and copies and remains valid under UCP 600. The content of the Policy Statement appears in the Appendix of this publication, for reference purposes.

Signing of multimodal transport documents

71) Original multimodal transport documents must be signed in the form described in UCP 600 sub-article 19(a)(i) and indicate the name of the carrier, identified as the carrier.

a. If an agent signs a multimodal transport document on behalf of the carrier, the agent must be identified as agent, and must identify on whose behalf it is signing, unless the carrier has been identified elsewhere on the multimodal transport document.

b. If the master (captain) signs the multimodal transport document, the signature of the master (captain) must be identified as "master" ("captain"). In this event, the name of the master (captain) need not be stated.

c. If an agent signs the multimodal transport document on behalf of the master (captain), the agent must be identified as agent. In this event, the name of the master (captain) need not be stated.

72) If a credit states "Freight Forwarder's Multimodal transport document is acceptable" or uses a similar phrase, then the multimodal transport document may be signed by a freight forwarder in the capacity of a freight forwarder, without the need to identify itself as carrier or agent for the named carrier. In this event, it is not necessary to show the name of the carrier.

On board notations

73) The issuance date of a multimodal transport document will be deemed to be the date of dispatch, taking in charge or shipped on board unless it bears a separate dated notation evidencing dispatch, taking in charge or shipped on board from the location required by the credit, in which event the date of the notation will be deemed to be the date of shipment whether or not the date is before or after the issuance date of the document.

74) "Shipped in apparent good order", "Laden on board", "clean on board" or other phrases incorporating words such as "shipped" or "on board" have the same effect as "Shipped on board".

Place of taking in charge, dispatch, loading on board and destination

75) If a credit gives a geographical range for the place of taking in charge, dispatch, loading on board and destination (e. g., "Any European Port"), the multimodal transport document must indicate the actual place of taking in charge, dispatch, shipped on board and destination, which must be within the geographical area or range stated in the credit.

Consignee, order party, shipper and endorsement, notify party

76) If a credit requires a multimodal transport document to show that the goods are consigned to a named party, e. g., "consigned to Bank X" (a "straight" consignment), rather than "to order" or "to order of Bank X", the multimodal transport document must not contain words such as "to order" or "to order of" that precede the name of that named party, whether typed or pre-printed. Likewise, if a credit requires the goods to be consigned "to order" or "to order of" a named party, the multimodal transport document must not show that the goods are consigned straight to the named party.

77) If a multimodal transport document is issued to order or to order of the shipper, it must be endorsed by the shipper. An endorsement indicating that it is made for or on behalf of the shipper is acceptable.

78) If a credit does not stipulate a notify party, the respective field on the multimodal transport document may be left blank or completed in any manner.

Transhipment and partial shipment

79) In a multimodal transport, transhipment will occur, i. e., unloading from one means of conveyance and reloading to another means of conveyance (whether or not in different modes of

transport) during the carriage from the place of dispatch, taking in charge or shipment to the place of final destination stated in the credit.

80) If a credit prohibits partial shipments and more than one set of original multimodal transport documents are presented covering shipment, dispatch or taking in charge from one or more points of origin (as specifically allowed, or within the geographical area or range stated in the credit), such documents are acceptable, provided that they cover the movement of goods on the same means of conveyance and same journey and are destined for the same destination. In the event that more than one set of multimodal transport documents are presented and if they incorporate different dates of shipment, dispatch or taking in charge, the latest of these dates will be taken for the calculation of any presentation period and such date must fall on or before any latest date of shipment, dispatch or taking in charge specified in the credit.

81) Shipment on more than one means of conveyance (more than one truck (lorry), vessel, aircraft, etc.) is a partial shipment, even if such means of conveyance leave on the same day for the same destination.

Clean multimodal transport documents

82) Clauses or notations on multimodal transport documents that expressly declare a defective condition of the goods or packaging are not acceptable. Clauses or notations that do not expressly declare a defective condition of the goods or packaging (e. g., "packaging may not be sufficient for the journey") do not constitute a discrepancy. A statement that the packaging "is not sufficient for the journey" would not be acceptable.

83) If the word "clean" appears on a multimodal transport document and has been deleted, the multimodal transport document will not be deemed to be claused or unclean unless it specifically bears a clause or notation declaring that the goods or packaging are defective.

Goods description

84) A goods description in the multimodal transport document may be shown in general terms not in conflict with that stated in the credit.

Corrections and alterations

85) Corrections and alterations on a multimodal transport document must be authenticated. Such authentication must appear to have been made by the carrier or master (captain) or any one of their agents who may be different from the agent that may have issued or signed it, provided they are identified as an agent of the carrier or master (captain).

86) Non-negotiable copies of multimodal transport documents do not need to include any signature on, or authentication of, any alterations or corrections that may have been made on the original.

Freight and additional costs

87) If a credit requires that a multimodal transport document show that freight has been paid or is payable at destination, the multimodal transport document must be marked accordingly.

88) Applicants and issuing banks should be specific in stating the requirements of documents

to show whether freight is to be prepaid or collected.

89) If a credit states that costs additional to freight are not acceptable, a multimodal transport document must not indicate that costs additional to the freight have been or will be incurred. Such indication may be by express reference to additional costs or by the use of shipment terms which refer to costs associated with the loading or unloading of goods, such as Free In (FI), Free Out (FO), Free In and Out (FIO) and Free In and Out Stowed (FIOS). A reference in the transport document to costs which may be levied as a result of a delay in unloading the goods or after the goods have been unloaded e. g. , costs covering the late return of containers, is not considered to be an indication of additional costs in this context. Goods covered by more than one multimodal transport document

90) If a multimodal transport document states that the goods in a container are covered by that multimodal transport document plus one or more other multimodal transport documents, and the document states that all multimodal transport documents must be surrendered or words of similar effect, this means that all multimodal transport documents related to that container must be presented in order for the container to be released. Such a multimodal transport document is not acceptable unless all the multimodal transport documents form part of the same presentation under the same credit.

BILL OF LADING

Application of UCP 600 Article 20

91) If a credit requires presentation of a bill of lading ("marine", "ocean" or "port-to-port" or similar) covering sea shipment only, UCP 600 article 20 is applicable.

92) To comply with UCP 600 article 20, a bill of lading must appear to cover a port-to-port shipment but need not be titled "marine bill of lading", "ocean bill of lading", "port-to-port bill of lading" or similar.

Full set of originals

93) A UCP 600 article 20 transport document must indicate the number of originals that have been issued. Transport documents marked "First Original", "Second Original", "Third Original", "Original", "Duplicate", "Triplicate", etc. , or similar expressions are all originals. Bills of lading need not be marked "original" to be acceptable as an original bill of lading. In addition to UCP 600 article 17, the ICC Banking Commission Policy Statement, document 470/871 (Rev), titled "The determination of an 'Original' document in the context of UCP 500 sub-Article 20(b)" is recommended for further guidance on originals and copies and remains valid under UCP 600. The content of the Policy Statement appears in the Appendix of this publication, for reference purposes.

Signing of bills of lading

94) Original bills of lading must be signed in the form described in UCP 600 sub-article 20 (a)(i) and indicate the name of the carrier, identified as the carrier.

d. If an agent signs a bill of lading on behalf of the carrier, the agent must be identified as agent and must identify on whose behalf it is signing, unless the carrier has been identified elsewhere on the bill of lading.

e. If the master (captain) signs the bill of lading, the signature of the master (captain) must be identified as "master" ("captain"). In this event, the name of the master (captain) need not be stated.

f. If an agent signs the bill of lading on behalf of the master (captain), the agent must be identified as agent. In this event, the name of the master (captain) need not be stated.

95) If a credit states "Freight Forwarder's Bill of Lading is acceptable" or uses a similar phrase, then the bill of lading may be signed by a freight forwarder in the capacity of a freight forwarder, without the need to identify itself as carrier or agent for the named carrier. In this event, it is not necessary to show the name of the carrier.

On board notations

96) If a pre-printed "Shipped on board" bill of lading is presented, its issuance date will be deemed to be the date of shipment unless it bears a separate dated on board notation, in which event the date of the on board notation will be deemed to be the date of shipment whether or not the on board date is before or after the issuance date of the bill of lading.

97) "Shipped in apparent good order", "Laden on board", "clean on board" or other phrases incorporating words such as "shipped" or "on board" have the same effect as "Shipped on board".

Ports of loading and ports of discharge

98) While the named port of loading, as required by the credit, should appear in the port of loading field within the bill of lading, it may instead be stated in the field headed "Place of receipt" or the like, if it is clear that the goods were transported from that place of receipt by vessel, and provided there is an on board notation evidencing that the goods were loaded on that vessel at the port stated under "Place of receipt" or like term.

99) While the named port of discharge, as required by the credit, should appear in the port of discharge field within the bill of lading, it may be stated in the field headed "Place of final destination" or the like if it is clear that the goods were to be transported to that place of final destination by vessel, and provided there is a notation evidencing that the port of discharge is that stated under "Place of final destination" or like term.

100) If a credit gives a geographical area or range of ports of loading or discharge (e. g., "Any European Port"), the bill of lading must indicate the actual port of loading or discharge, which must be within the geographical area or range stated in the credit.

Consignee, order party, shipper and endorsement, notify party

101) If a credit requires a bill of lading to show that the goods are consigned to a named party, e. g., "consigned to Bank X" (a "straight" bill of lading), rather than "to order" or "to order of Bank X", the bill of lading must not contain words such as "to order" or "to order of" that precede the name of that named party, whether typed or pre-printed.

Likewise, if a credit requires the goods to be consigned "to order" or "to order of" a named party, the bill of lading must not show that the goods are consigned straight to the named party.

102) If a bill of lading is issued to order or to order of the shipper, it must be endorsed by the shipper. An endorsement indicating that it is made for or on behalf of the shipper is acceptable.

103) If a credit does not state a notify party, the respective field on the bill of lading may be left blank or completed in any manner.

Transhipment and partial shipment

104) Transhipment is the unloading from one vessel and reloading to another vessel during the carriage from the port of loading to the port of discharge stated in the credit. If it does not occur between these two ports, unloading and reloading is not considered to be transhipment.

105) If a credit prohibits partial shipments and more than one set of original bills of lading are presented covering shipment from one or more ports of loading (as specifically allowed, or within the geographical area or range stated in the credit), such documents are acceptable provided that they cover the shipment of goods on the same vessel and same journey and are destined for the same port of discharge. In the event that more than one set of bills of lading are presented and incorporate different dates of shipment, the latest of these dates of shipment will be taken for the calculation of any presentation period and must fall on or before the latest shipment date specified in the credit. Shipment on more than one vessel is a partial shipment, even if the vessels leave on the same day for the same destination.

Clean bills of lading

106) Clauses or notations on bills of lading which expressly declare a defective condition of the goods or packaging are not acceptable. Clauses or notations which do not expressly declare a defective condition of the goods or packaging (e. g., "packaging may not be sufficient for the sea journey") do not constitute a discrepancy. A statement that the packaging "is not sufficient for the sea journey" would not be acceptable.

107) If the word "clean" appears on a bill of lading and has been deleted, the bill of lading will not be deemed to be claused or unclean unless it specifically bears a clause or notation declaring that the goods or packaging are defective.

Goods description

108) A goods description in the bill of lading may be shown in general terms not in conflict with that stated in the credit.

Corrections and alterations

109) Corrections and alterations on a bill of lading must be authenticated. Such authentication must appear to have been made by the carrier, master (captain) or any of their agents (who may be different from the agent that may have issued or signed it), provided they are identified as an agent of the carrier or the master (captain).

110) Non-negotiable copies of bills of lading do not need to include any signature on, or authentication of, any alterations or corrections that may have been made on the original.

Freight and additional costs

111) If a credit requires that a bill of lading show that freight has been paid or is payable at destination, the bill of lading must be marked accordingly.

112) Applicants and issuing banks should be specific in stating the requirements of documents to show whether freight is to be prepaid or collected.

113) If a credit states that costs additional to freight are not acceptable, a bill of lading must not indicate that costs additional to the freight have been or will be incurred. Such indication may be by express reference to additional costs or by the use of shipment terms which refer to costs associated with the loading or unloading of goods, such as Free In (FI), Free Out (FO), Free In and Out (FIO) and Free In and Out Stowed (FIOS).

A reference in the transport document to costs which may be levied as a result of a delay in unloading the goods or after the goods have been unloaded, e. g., costs covering the late return of containers, is not considered to be an indication of additional costs in this context.

Goods covered by more than one bill of lading

114) If a bill of lading states that the goods in a container are covered by that bill of lading plus one or more other bills of lading, and the bill of lading states that all bills of lading must be surrendered, or words of similar effect, this means that all bills of lading related to that container must be presented in order for the container to be released. Such a bill of lading is not acceptable unless all the bills of lading form part of the same presentation under the same credit.

CHARTER PARTY BILL OF LADING

Application of UCP 600 article 22

115) If a credit requires presentation of a charter party bill of lading or if a credit allows presentation of a charter party bill of lading and a charter party bill of lading is presented UCP 600 article 22 is applicable.

116) A transport document containing any indication that it is subject to a charter party is a charter party bill of lading under UCP 600 article 22.

Full set of originals

117) A UCP 600 article 22 transport document must indicate the number of originals that have been issued. Transport documents marked "First Original", "Second Original", "Third Original", "Original", "Duplicate", "Triplicate", etc. or similar expressions are all originals. Charter party bills of lading need not be marked "original" to be acceptable under a credit. In addition to UCP 600 article 17, the ICC Banking Commission Policy Statement, document 470/871 (Rev), titled "The determination of an 'Original' document in the context of UCP 500 sub-Article 20(b)" is recommended for further guidance on originals and copies and remains valid under UCP 600. The content of the Policy Statement appears in the Appendix of this publication, for reference purposes.

Signing of charter party bills of lading

118) Original charter party bills of lading must be signed in the form described in UCP 600 sub-article 22(a)(i).

a. If the master (captain), charterer or owner signs the charter party bill of lading, the signature of the master (captain), charterer or owner must be identified as "master" ("captain"), charterer or "owner".

b. If an agent signs the charter party bill of lading on behalf of the master (captain), charterer or owner, the agent must be identified as agent of the master (captain), charterer or owner. In this event, the name of the master (captain) need not be stated, but the name of the charterer or owner must appear.

On board notations

119) If a pre-printed "Shipped on board" charter party bill of lading is presented, its issuance date will be deemed to be the date of shipment unless it bears an on board notation, in which event the date of the on board notation will be deemed to be the date of shipment whether or not the on board date is before or after the issuance date of the document.

120) "Shipped in apparent good order", "Laden on board", "clean on board" or other phrases incorporating words such as "shipped" or "on board" have the same effect as "shipped on board".

Ports of loading and ports of discharge

121) If a credit gives a geographical area or range of ports of loading or discharge (e. g., "Any European Port"), the charter party bill of lading must indicate the actual port or ports of loading, which must be within the geographical area or range stated in the credit but may show the geographical area or range of ports as the port of discharge.

Consignee, order party, shipper and endorsement, notify party

122) If a credit requires a charter party bill of lading to show that the goods are consigned to a named party, e. g., "consigned to Bank X" (a "straight" bill of lading), rather than "to order" or "to order of Bank X", the charter party bill of lading must not contain words such as "to order" or "to order of" that precede the name of that named party, whether typed or pre-printed. Likewise, if a credit requires the goods to be consigned "to order" or "to order of" a named party, the charter party bill of lading must not show that the goods are consigned straight to the named party.

123) If a charter party bill of lading is issued to order or to order of the shipper, it must be endorsed by the shipper. An endorsement indicating that it is made for or on behalf of the shipper is acceptable.

124) If a credit does not state a notify party, the respective field on the charter party bill of lading may be left blank or completed in any manner.

Partial shipment

125) If a credit prohibits partial shipments, and more than one set of original charter party bills of lading are presented covering shipment from one or more ports of loading (as specifically allowed, or within the geographical area or range stated in the credit), such documents are acceptable, provided that they cover the shipment of goods on the same vessel and same journey and are destined for the same port of discharge, range of ports or geographical area. In the event that more than one set of charter party bills of lading are presented and incorporate different dates of ship-

ment, the latest of these dates of shipment will be taken for the calculation of any presentation period and must fall on or before the latest shipment date specified in the credit. Shipment on more than one vessel is a partial shipment, even if the vessels leave on the same day for the same destination.

Clean charter party bills of lading

126) Clauses or notations on charter party bills of lading which expressly declare a defective condition of the goods or packaging are not acceptable. Clauses or notations that do not expressly declare a defective condition of the goods or packaging (e. g. , "packaging may not be sufficient for the sea journey") do not constitute a discrepancy. A statement that the packaging "is not sufficient for the sea journey" would not be acceptable.

127) If the word "clean" appears on a charter party bill of lading and has been deleted, the charter party bill of lading will not be deemed to be claused or unclean unless it specifically bears a clause or notation declaring that the goods or packaging are defective.

Goods description

128) A goods description in charter party bills of lading may be shown in general terms not in conflict with that stated in the credit.

Corrections and alterations

129) Corrections and alterations on charter party bills of lading must be authenticated. Such authentication must appear to have been made by the owner, charterer, master (captain) or any of their agents (who may be different from the agent that may have issued or signed it), provided they are identified as an agent of the owner, charterer or the master (captain).

130) Non-negotiable copies of charter party bills of lading do not need to include any signature on, or authentication of, any alterations or corrections that may have been made on the original.

Freight and additional costs

131) If a credit requires that a charter party bill of lading show that freight has been paid or is payable at destination, the charter party bill of lading must be marked accordingly.

132) Applicants and issuing banks should be specific in stating the requirements of documents to show whether freight is to be prepaid or collected.

133) If a credit states that costs additional to freight are not acceptable, a charter party bill of lading must not indicate that costs additional to the freight have been or will be incurred. Such indication may be by express reference to additional costs or by the use of shipment terms which refer to costs associated with the loading or unloading of goods, such as Free In (FI), Free Out (FO), Free In and Out (FIO) and Free In and Out Stowed (FIOS). A reference in the transport document to costs which may be levied as a result of a delay in unloading the goods, or after the goods have been unloaded, is not considered to be an indication of additional costs in this context.

AIR TRANSPORT DOCUMENT

Application of UCP 600 article 23

134) If a credit requires presentation of an air transport document covering an airport-to-airport shipment, UCP 600 article 23 is applicable.

135) If a credit requires presentation of an "air waybill", "air consignment note" or similar, UCP 600 article 23 applies. To comply with UCP 600 article 23, an air transport document must appear to cover an airport-to-airport shipment but need not be titled "air waybill", "air consignment note" or similar.

Original air transport document

136) The air transport document must appear to be the original for consignor or shipper. A requirement for a full set of originals is satisfied by the presentation of a document indicating that it is the original for consignor or shipper.

Signing of air transport documents

137) An original air transport document must be signed in the form described in UCP 600 sub-article 23(a)(i) and indicate the name of the carrier, identified as carrier. If an agent signs an air transport document on behalf of a carrier, the agent must be identified as agent and must identify on whose behalf it is signing, unless the carrier has been identified elsewhere on the air transport document.

138) If a credit states "House air waybill is acceptable" or "Freight Forwarder's air waybill is acceptable" or uses a similar phrase, then the air transport document may be signed by a freight forwarder in the capacity of a freight forwarder without the need to identify itself as a carrier or agent for a named carrier. In this event, it is not necessary to show the name of the carrier.

Goods accepted for carriage, date of shipment, and requirement for an actual date of dispatch

139) An air transport document must indicate that the goods have been accepted for carriage.

140) The date of issuance of an air transport document is deemed to be the date of shipment unless the document shows a separate notation of the flight date, in which case this will be deemed to be the date of shipment. Any other information appearing on the air transport document relative to the flight number and date will not be considered in determining the date of shipment.

Airports of departure and destination

141) An air transport document must indicate the airport of departure and airport of destination as stated in the credit. The identification of airports by the use of IATA codes instead of writing out the name in full (e.g., LHR instead of London Heathrow) is not a discrepancy.

142) If a credit gives a geographical area or range of airports of departure or destination (e.g., "Any European Airport"), the air transport document must indicate the actual airport of departure or destination, which must be within the geographical area or range stated in the credit.

Consignee, order party and notify party

143) An air transport document should not be issued "to order" or "to order of" a named party, because it is not a document of title. Even if a credit calls for an air transport document made out "to order" or "to order of" a named party, a document presented showing goods consigned to that party, without mention of "to order" or "to order of", is acceptable.

144) If a credit does not state a notify party, the respective field on the air transport document may be left blank or completed in any manner.

Transhipment and partial shipment

145) Transhipment is the unloading from one aircraft and reloading to another aircraft during the carriage from the airport of departure to the airport of destination stated in the credit. If it does not occur between these two airports, unloading and reloading is not considered to be transhipment.

146) If a credit prohibits partial shipments and more than one air transport document is presented covering dispatch from one or more airports of departure (as specifically allowed, or within the geographical area or range stated in the credit), such documents are acceptable, provided that they cover the dispatch of goods on the same aircraft and same flight and are destined for the same airport of destination. In the event that more than one air transport document is presented incorporating different dates of shipment, the latest of these dates of shipment will be taken for the calculation of any presentation period and must fall on or before the latest shipment date specified in the credit.

147) Shipment on more than one aircraft is a partial shipment, even if the aircraft leave on the same day for the same destination.

Clean air transport documents

148) Clauses or notations on an air transport document which expressly declare a defective condition of the goods or packaging are not acceptable. Clauses or notations on the air transport document which do not expressly declare a defective condition of the goods or packaging (e. g., "packaging may not be sufficient for the air journey") do not constitute a discrepancy. A statement that the packaging "is not sufficient for the air journey" would not be acceptable.

149) If the word "clean" appears on an air transport document and has been deleted, the air transport document will not be deemed to be claused or unclean unless it specifically bears a clause or notation declaring that the goods or packaging are defective.

Goods description

150) A goods description in an air transport document may be shown in general terms not in conflict with that stated in the credit.

Corrections and alterations

151) Corrections and alterations on air transport documents must be authenticated. Such authentication must appear to have been made by the carrier or any of its agents (who may be different from the agent that may have issued or signed it), provided it is identified as an agent of the carrier.

152) Copies of air transport documents do not need to include any signature of the carrier or agent (or shipper, even if required by the credit to appear on the original air transport document), nor any authentication of any alterations or corrections that may have been made on the original.

Freight and additional costs

153) If a credit requires that an air transport document show that freight has been paid or is payable at destination, the air transport document must be marked accordingly.

154) Applicants and issuing banks should be specific in stating the requirements of documents to show whether freight is to be prepaid or collected.

155) If a credit states that costs additional to freight are not acceptable, an air transport docu-

ment must not indicate that costs additional to the freight have been or will be incurred. Such indication may be by express reference to additional costs or by the use of shipment terms that refer to costs associated with the loading or unloading of goods.

A reference in the transport document to costs which may be levied as a result of a delay in unloading the goods or after the goods have been unloaded is not considered an indication of additional costs in this context.

156) Air transport documents often have separate boxes which, by their pre-printed headings, indicate that they are for freight charges "prepaid" and for freight charges "to collect", respectively. A requirement in a credit for an air transport document to show that freight has been prepaid will be fulfilled by a statement of the freight charges under the heading "Freight Prepaid" or a similar expression or indication, and a requirement that an air transport document show that freight has to be collected will be fulfilled by a statement of the freight charges under the heading "Freight to Collect" or a similar expression or indication.

ROAD, RAIL OR INLAND WATERWAY TRANSPORT DOCUMENTS

Application of UCP 600 article 24

157) If a credit requires presentation of a transport document covering movement by road, rail or inland waterway, UCP 600 article 24 is applicable.

Original and duplicate of road, rail or inland waterway transport documents

158) If a credit requires a rail or inland waterway transport document, the transport document presented will be accepted as an original whether or not it is marked as an original. A road transport document must appear to be the original for consignor or shipper or bear no marking indicating for whom the document has been prepared. With respect to rail waybills, the practice of many railway companies is to provide the shipper or consignor with only a duplicate (often a carbon copy) duly authenticated by the railway company's stamp. Such a duplicate will be accepted as an original.

Carrier and signing of road, rail or inland waterway transport documents

159) The term "carrier" need not appear at the signature line provided the transport document appears to be signed by the carrier or an agent on behalf of the carrier, if the carrier is otherwise identified as the "carrier" on the transport document. International standard banking practice is to accept a railway bill evidencing date stamp by the railway company or railway station of departure without showing the name of the carrier or a named agent signing for or on behalf of the carrier.

160) The term "carrier" used in UCP 600 article 24 includes terms in transport documents such as "issuing carrier", "actual carrier", "succeeding carrier" and "contracting carrier".

161) Any signature, stamp or notation of receipt on the transport document must appear to be made either by:

a. the carrier, identified as the carrier or

b. a named agent acting or signing for or on behalf of the carrier and indicating the name and capacity of the carrier on whose behalf that agent is acting or signing.

Order party and notify party

162) Transport documents which are not documents of title should not be issued "to order" or "to order of" a named party. Even if a credit calls for a transport document which is not a document of title to be made out "to order" or "to order of" a named party, such a document, showing goods consigned to that party, without mention of "to order" or "to order of", is acceptable.

163) If a credit does not stipulate a notify party, the respective field on the transport document may be left blank or completed in any manner.

Partial shipment

164) Shipment on more than one means of conveyance (more than one truck (lorry), train, vessel, etc.) is a partial shipment, even if such means of conveyance leave on the same day for the same destination.

Goods description

165) A goods description in the transport document may be shown in general terms not in conflict with that stated in the credit.

Corrections and alterations

166) Corrections and alterations on a UCP 600 article 24 transport document must be authenticated. Such authentication must appear to have been made by the carrier or any one of their named agents, who may be different from the agent that may have issued or signed it, provided they are identified as an agent of the carrier.

167) Copies of UCP 600 article 24 transport documents do not need to include any signature on, or authentication of, any alterations or corrections that may have been made on the original.

Freight and additional costs

168) If a credit requires that a UCP 600 article 24 transport document show that freight has been paid or is payable at destination, the transport document must be marked accordingly.

169) Applicants and issuing banks should be specific in stating the requirements of documents to show whether freight is to be prepaid or collected.

INSURANCE DOCUMENT AND COVERAGE

Application of UCP 600 article 28

170) If a credit requires presentation of an insurance document such as an insurance policy, insurance certificate or declaration under an open cover, UCP 600 article 28 is applicable.

Issuers of insurance documents

171) Insurance documents must appear to have been issued and signed by insurance companies or underwriters or their agents or proxies. If required by the insurance document or in accordance with the credit terms, all originals must appear to have been countersigned.

172) An insurance document is acceptable if issued on an insurance broker's stationery, provided the insurance document has been signed by an insurance company or its agent or proxy, or by an underwriter or its agent or proxy. A broker may sign as agent for the named insurance company or named underwriter.

Risks to be covered

173) An insurance document must cover the risks defined in the credit. Even though a credit may be explicit with regard to risks to be covered, there may be reference to exclusion clauses in the document. If a credit requires "all risks" coverage, this is satisfied by the presentation of an insurance document evidencing any "all risks" clause or notation, even if it is stated that certain risks are excluded. An insurance document indicating that it covers Institute Cargo Clauses (A) satisfies a condition in a credit calling for an "all risks" clause or notation.

174) Insurance covering the same risk for the same shipment must be covered under one document unless the insurance documents for partial cover each clearly reflect, by percentage or otherwise, the value of each insurer's cover and that each insurer will bear its share of the liability severally and without pre-conditions relating to any other insurance cover that may have been effected for that shipment.

Dates

175) An insurance document that incorporates an expiry date must clearly indicate that such expiry date relates to the latest date that loading on board or dispatch or taking in charge of the goods (as applicable) is to occur, as opposed to an expiry date for the presentation of any claims thereunder.

Percentage and amount

176) An insurance document must be issued in the currency of and, as a minimum, for the amount required by the credit. The UCP does not provide for any maximum percentage of insurance coverage.

177) If a credit requires the insurance cover to be irrespective of percentage, the insurance document must not contain a clause stating that the insurance cover is subject to a franchise or an excess deductible.

178) If it is apparent from the credit or from the documents that the final invoice amount only represents a certain part of the gross value of the goods (e. g. , due to discounts, pre-payments or the like, or because part of the value of the goods is to be paid at a later date), the calculation of insurance cover must be based on the full gross value of the goods.

Insured party and endorsement

179) An insurance document must be in the form as required by the credit and, where necessary, be endorsed by the party to whose order claims are payable. A document issued to bearer is acceptable where the credit requires an insurance document endorsed in blank and vice versa.

180) If a credit is silent as to the insured party, an insurance document evidencing that claims are payable to the order of the shipper or beneficiary would not be acceptable unless endorsed. An insurance document should be issued or endorsed so that the right to receive payment under it passes upon, or prior to, the release of the documents.

CERTIFICATES OF ORIGIN

Basic requirement

181) A requirement for a certificate of origin will be satisfied by the presentation of a signed,

dated document that certifies to the origin of the goods.

Issuers of certificates of origin

182) A certificate of origin must be issued by the party stated in the credit. However, if a credit requires a certificate of origin to be issued by the beneficiary, the exporter or the manufacturer, a document issued by a chamber of commerce will be deemed acceptable, provided it clearly identifies the beneficiary, the exporter or the manufacturer as the case may be. If a credit does not state who is to issue the certificate, then a document issued by any party, including the beneficiary, is acceptable.

Contents of certificates of origin

183) The certificate of origin must appear to relate to the invoiced goods. The goods description in the certificate of origin may be shown in general terms not in conflict with that stated in the credit or by any other reference indicating a relation to the goods in a required document.

184) Consignee information, if shown, must not be in conflict with the consignee information in the transport document. However, if a credit requires a transport document to be issued "to order", "to the order of shipper", "to order of the issuing bank" or "consigned to the issuing bank", the certificate of origin may show the applicant of the credit, or another party named therein, as consignee. If a credit has been transferred, the name of the first beneficiary as consignee would also be acceptable.

185) The certificate of origin may show the consignor or exporter as a party other than the beneficiary of the credit or the shipper on the transport document.

参考文献

[1] 肖美香,刘茹,柳国华. 国际结算[M]. 北京：对外经济贸易大学出版社，2010.

[2] EDWARD G HINKELMAN. A short course in international payments. 4th ed. Petaluma：Word Trade Press，2010.

[3] 史恩义,彭泰. 外贸单证与国际结算[M]. 北京：中国传媒大学出版社，2011.

[4] 刘昊虹. 国际结算实验[M]. 北京：经济科学出版社，2010.

[5] 王益平,莫再树 国际支付与结算[M]. 北京：清华大学出版社，北京交通大学出版社，2009.